Race Struggles

Race
Struggles

Edited by
THEODORE KODITSCHEK,
SUNDIATA KEITA CHA-JUA,
AND HELEN A. NEVILLE

UNIVERSITY OF ILLINOIS PRESS

Urbana and Chicago

Library of Congress Cataloging-in-Publication Data
Race struggles / edited by Theodore Koditschek,
Sundiata Keita Cha-Jua, and Helen A. Neville.
p.   cm.
Includes bibliographical references and index.
ISBN 978-0-252-03449-7 (cloth : acid-free paper)
ISBN 978-0-252-07648-0 (pbk. : acid-free paper)
1. Race—Study and teaching.
2. Race relations—Study and teaching.
I. Koditschek, Theodore.
II. Cha-Jua, Sundiata Keita, 1953–
III. Neville, Helen A.
HT1506.R335   2009
305.80071—dc22   2009015037

Contents

Introduction

    This book is intended as a contribution to the ongoing examination of race and its relation to class and gender in capitalist society. Most recent discussions of all three categories have been heavily influenced by postmodernism, and have tended to treat them largely as discursive concepts. The capitalist social and economic context has faded into the background, and class, race, and gender have been reconsidered almost entirely in cultural terms. Constantly constructed and reconstructed in the play of disputation, these categories are generally treated as contingent, almost accidental, identities. Our understanding of race has been further fragmented by the proliferation of work in a series of disjunct, noncommensurate disciplines—history, sociology, anthropology, economics, psychology, and ethnic studies—each with its own distinctive methodologies, problems, paradigms, and professional communities.

    The authors of the essays in this volume are a group of interdisciplinary scholars who are striving for a more actively integrative approach. While we agree that race (like class and gender) is socially constructed, we also believe that this social construction cannot be separated from the capitalist context in which it occurs. Racial ideologies, identities, resistances, and struggle have all played out within the framework of structures, which have profoundly influenced (and continue to influence) their character and shape. Race, in other words, is a historical category that develops in dialectical relation to class and gender, and to the material conditions in which all three are forged. Like class and gender it is dual-sided: at once objectively experienced as a power of oppression, but also then subjectively enacted as an expression of struggle, resistance, and subaltern agency.

    These assumptions underlie the organization of our volume, which is divided accordingly into three parts: "Racial Structures," "Racial Ideology and Identity," and "Struggle." Although this tripartite organization reflects our underlying framework for understanding how race relations unfold, we reject any rigidly deterministic line of explanation from structure to ideology and then to struggle. On the contrary, as many of the individual essays demonstrate, both racial ideologies and the engagements of racial struggle feed back on one another, and on racial structures, in a dialectical way. For this reason, each section problematizes the structure-ideology-struggle interface in a slightly different manner.

Our book is further informed by a tension between history and the social sciences. Although many of our authors are historians and others are social scientists, we are convinced that the present state of race relations is best understood in historical context. Conversely, we believe that the history of race can be interrogated only by questions that are necessarily interdisciplinary, and rooted in the conditions of our time. We are deeply conscious that in the current epoch of rapid globalization, the character of capitalism is fundamentally changing, and the very meaning of the category "race"—as well as its relation to class and gender—cannot fail to be correspondingly transformed. Our book is best seen as a preliminary effort to take the measure of these impending transformations by exploring the trajectories that have brought us to our present point. We write in a time when classical paradigms of radical social transformation have exploded, but no new ones have yet arisen to take their place. We are thoroughly mindful of the limitations of this initial exploratory venture, and we make no claims to comprehensiveness either in theoretical sweep or in empirical scope.

We do not propose a new theory, nor do we attempt to cover all subjects. Our essays are focused primarily on race relations in U.S. history, although we also include an essay on the nineteenth-century British Empire and another on twenty-first-century Africa, to extend our coverage. Some problems, particularly those having to do with the interface of race and gender, are largely absent from our volume. We hope, however, that our return to structural and materialist analysis will encourage other scholars to press this approach in other directions so as to illuminate those issues that we have left unaddressed. In our own structural-materialist examinations of the class-race interface we have found ourselves facing a curious paradox: On the one hand, there exists a weighty and venerable body of classic literature upon which we can build, and with which we must reengage. On the other hand, over the past two decades, postmodernism has so far deconstructed this classic literature that we now scarcely know how to apply it to the problems of our day.

This state of affairs has been dramatically and tragically illustrated by the recent catastrophe in New Orleans and the Mississippi Delta. Given the enormity of what happened, news reports could not help but note the inescapable fact that the overwhelming majority of the people displaced or destroyed by this disaster were black or poor or both. Yet the mainstream media have shown themselves completely devoid of the intellectual resources that would enable them to make sense of this fact. Indeed, no sense can be made of this calamity without some understanding of the "invisible hand" of capitalist structures, which promote de facto segregation, disenfranchisement, deindustrialization, and "color-blind" racism, even as they enunciate the principle of formal equality de jure. New Orleans shows that in a privatized world, where public services, transport, and infrastructures have been dismantled or degraded, no real equality is possible. At a time when the political Right stridently insists that the era of racial discrimination is over, it is sobering to be reminded by mother nature that this is not so. Hurricane Katrina has forced us to recognize that, for all too many, "separate and unequal" remains the reality, four decades after the great battles for civil rights were supposedly won.

This point has been even more recently reinforced by the Supreme Court decisions and the "Jena Six" cases of 2007. Both offer further proof that race remains very close to the surface of an epoch that often depicts it as an evil that has passed. Thus, we are faced with some striking contradictions with regard to the contemporary relevance of race. At the very moment when a Black man has become president of the United States, the Supreme Court reflects the full fruit of the Reagan and Bush eras. Indeed, the Roberts Court of 2007–2008 has come very close to revoking *Brown v. Board of Education* through a decision that professes opposition to racial discrimination. In Louisville and Seattle, carefully designed programs of school desegregation have been struck down as "unconstitutional" for the sin of simply recognizing the reality of race. Because these two cities were never forced by the courts to correct racial disparities in their school systems, Chief Justice Roberts does not accept that any such disparities can exist. It follows that any attempt to rectify them—however limited and modest—is itself a form of racial discrimination that cannot be allowed.

Although all the chapters in *Race Struggles* were drafted before the above-mentioned events and disasters, we think that the reader will find much in our pages that will help him or her to make sense of the underlying causes of these disturbing developments.[1] It is certainly our aim to contribute to forging a new language in which the hidden social structures and power inequalities that loom behind such seeming accidents and "racial blindness" can be exposed to stringent analysis, critique, and public view. We aim to deconstruct the obfuscations of racial ideologies that deflect attention away from these underlying causes, by blaming looters, agitators, quotas, declining values, or a culture of poverty for the problems of our time. Finally, we hope that *Race Struggles* will make at least a modest contribution to reactivating a new wave of future race struggles, dedicated to holding those responsible for inequality accountable, and to ensuring that such catastrophes never happen again.

To address the multiple goals of this ambitious agenda, we have adopted a number of parallel strategies. We have tried to absorb what is valid from the insights of postmodernism, while avoiding the intellectual incoherence and disengagement that it frequently promotes. We have returned to the explanatory agendas of classical social history and social science, while we have jettisoned the overly rigid, formal theories that were formerly taken to be foundational to those genres. Our premise is that whether or not we want to call our epoch "postmodern," it is still very much *capitalist*. To understand today's world of fully globalized capitalism either on the micro or the macro level, it is necessary to reengage the familiar problems of social history and social science, while learning to interrogate them in novel ways. For reasons that we hope will become evident in these pages, the problem of racial formation and transformation is one of the key areas in which this reinterrogation must proceed.

In addition to the novelty of our intellectual perspective, our book is distinguished from other anthologies on race, in terms of its format and positioning in the field.[2] While each of its chapters constitutes a separate contribution to the scholarly literature, the book has been conceived holistically, as a pedagogical reader, that could be assigned in upper-level undergraduate or graduate courses in history, sociology, psychology, Black Studies, or ethnic studies. As teachers, we have been struck by the absence of adequate texts that bridge the gap between the general anthologies designed for introductory courses and the narrow compendia of specialized articles that only confirmed scholars are likely to appreciate. Moreover, unlike other collections, which simply anthologize reprints, *Race Struggles* is a compilation of cutting-edge research by a mix of senior scholars and rising young practitioners in several disciplines. All of our pieces are new works. Because the essays are sufficiently connected in terms of theme and analysis, an instructor might profitably assign the whole volume. On the other hand, the individual chapters are sufficiently distinct in terms of methodology and orientation that they could also be assigned on their own. The essays are sophisticated enough to give the student (or teacher, or researcher) a good sense of the state of play in the various fields. On the other hand, they are written in a clear, comprehensible, jargon-free manner that should make them accessible to the motivated undergraduate.

To provide our readers with direction and guidance, we have prefaced each part with a brief introduction that frames the individual chapters and then draws out many of the most important points of comparison and contrast. At the end of these introductions, and at the end of the individual chapters, we offer a series of questions that are intended as aids to comprehension. We hope that they will help the reader to identify the main lines of argumentation within the chapters, and to put these individual arguments together (or sometimes juxtapose them) in ways that will make the volume add up to something more than the sum of its individual parts. At the end, we cap our book with a brief conclusion, in which we articulate what we think our collection has accomplished and what we see as the most fruitful directions for future thinking and research.

Notes

1. At key points, either authors or editors will note these connections.

2. For introductory courses, there are five very general readers: Les Back and John Solomos, eds., *Theories of Race and Racism: A Reader* (London: Routledge, 2000); Naomi Zack and Laurie Shrag, eds., *Race, Class, Gender, and Sexuality: The Big Questions* (Malden, Mass.: Blackwell, 1998); Linda Martin Alcoff and Eduardo Medieta, eds., *Identities: Race, Class, Gender, and Nationality* (Malden, Mass.: Blackwell, 2003); Paula S. Rothenberg, ed., *Race, Class, and Gender in the United States: An Integrated Study* (New York: St. Martin's, 1998); and Margaret L. Andersen and Patricia Hill Collins, *Race, Class, and Gender: An Anthology* (East Windsor, Conn.: Wadsworth Press, 2001). At the other end of the spectrum, for Ph.D. candidates and academic professionals, there is the massive three-volume compendium of eighty-one classic journal articles, edited by Malcolm Cross, *The Sociology of Race and Ethnicity* (Cheltenham, England: Edward Elgar Publishing, 2001), which is available only in an expensive hardcover edition. We have positioned our book in between these extremes.

PART 1

Racial Structures

Had this book been written thirty or forty years ago, it would probably have opened with a broad exposition of the theoretical framework(s) on which the subsequent case studies were to be based. These theoretical framework(s) would probably have consisted of some variant of modernization or Marxism. We need to begin, therefore, with a brief consideration of why this approach is no longer viable today. The basic problem is that as our knowledge has increased, our intellectual horizons have widened, and our confidence in the possibility of objective social knowledge has diminished, such frameworks no longer carry the conviction that they formerly enjoyed. The problem is twofold: First, as social historians have become more attentive to the play of contingency, social scientists more cognizant of the complexity of structures, and activists more conscious of the importance of agency, all three have begun to appreciate the inherent limitations of "top-down" social theory, whether as a key to history, a model of society, or a guide to action. Second, however, there have been particular problems in applying such theories to explain the dynamics of race. Modernization, for example, implies some linear pattern of onward development. It predicts the diminution of race as a factor in history, as enlightenment spreads, opportunity expands, and social science is applied to rectify social ills. Once it became clear that these hopes were not being borne out by experience—and that the development of capitalism often augmented rather than diminished the significance of racial discrimination—these hopes for the powers of modernization were dashed.

By contrast, Marxism showed a good deal of initial promise in realizing the explanatory and political potential that modernization had left unfulfilled. Focusing on the contradictions of capitalist development, Marxism was able to explain why the path to progress was so often littered with conflict, prejudice, violence, and hate. Yet because of its tendency to reduce all manifestations of these evils to the fissures of class division and the dynamics of class struggle, Marxism did not provide a very effective theoretical framework for understanding inequalities when they appeared in the form of gender or race.

Of course, as sophisticated Marxists became aware of this problem, they tried to rectify it in a variety of ways. None of these efforts at theoretical revision proved very sustainable over the long run, however. As history advanced, and as the evidence accumulated, it became increasingly evident that *class* consciousness was *not* the overriding feature of capitalist experience, that its significance was diminishing rather than increasing, and that many of the most pervasive manifestations of social inequality, identity, antagonism, and struggle in capitalist societies have actually played out in terms of gender, nationality, ethnicity, or race.

Although this has led many activists and scholars to abandon the insights of Marxism, the authors of the essays in this volume have pursued a different course. We remain impressed with the explanatory power of certain aspects of Marxist theory. We remain convinced of its ability to clarify the contradictions of capitalism and to illuminate *some* dimensions of modern history. At the same time, we are sufficiently troubled by Marxism's many failures and deficiencies (especially on the question of race) to believe that it will take more than minor (or even major) modifications to turn it in into a really viable theory. It is for this reason that we have entitled our first section "Racial Structures," leaving some deliberate ambiguity as to exactly what these structures are, and how they form. Clearly, the structures and formations are rooted in the logic of capitalism, yet we make no assumptions that they can be entirely specified by any predetermined theory. Indeed, we suspect that these structures and formations are so complex, metamorphic, and multidimensional that any attempt to specify them can be only partial, and will depend on the exact nature of that which they are supposed to explain.

Because of this inherent multidimensionality, we begin with four essays that approach racial structures and formations sui generis. Moreover, because the first two have been assigned the task of locating these structures in the broad sweep of capitalist development, they have been allowed a bit of extra space. All four, however, are primarily concerned to situate only the most directly relevant structures within the particular thematic and time-place parameters on which the authors have chosen to concentrate. In our first chapter, Sundiata Keita Cha-Jua's approach is aptly conveyed in his paradoxical title: "The Changing Same: Black Racial Formation and Transformation as a Theory of the African American Experience." On the one hand, U.S. race relations have been repeatedly formed and transformed, in tandem with the dynamics of U.S. capitalism. On the other hand, they have remained depressingly the same, with

African Americans habitually at the bottom of the racial hierarchy, subject to *both* superexploitation at the hands of the master class or caste and hostility and discrimination from other (less abject) racial and social groups.

To resolve this paradox, Cha-Jua builds upon, and substantially revises, Harold Baron's explicitly Marxist three-stage model of racial formation, first formulated in 1985. In Baron's scheme, U.S. racial formations were divided into three distinct periods: Slavery (1619–1865), the Plantation Economy (1865–1965), and Proletarianization-Ghettoization (1910–1979), each of which was supposed to correspond to a distinctive stage of U.S. capitalism. Although Cha-Jua accepts Baron's periodization for the pre-1980 period, and endorses Baron's concept of superexploitation, he shows that Baron's mechanistic model is unable to capture the full range of the African American experience, and largely fails to specify the transformational process whereby one racial formation (that is, period or stage) gave way to the next.

Cha-Jua's chapter is therefore devoted to rectifying these deficiencies in the Baron model, and to characterizing the newest and most recent racial formation, which has been gradually emerging in the quarter century since 1980. He shows how the uneven character of U.S. capitalist development has left repeated openings for the differential operation of race and class. Segregated into the most laborious and worst-remunerated sectors of production, Black people have been subject to continually changing forms of superexploitation, which segregated them from other sectors of the proletariat and prevented them from realizing the "American Dream." Even as one racial formation gave way to another, these underlying racial discriminations remained. Thus, while freedom was obviously an improvement over slavery, the Jim Crow system devised for policing the "free" plantation introduced new brutalities of its own. Correspondingly, while Black proletarianization brought genuine gains during the 1960s, the deproletarianization that the current wave of globalization has unleashed threatens to leave the Black working class even more marginalized and isolated than before.

In Cha-Jua's final section, he offers an extensive analysis of this most recent stage of Black racial formation, which he labels the "New Nadir." Like the original nadir of the 1880s and 1890s, we are in the midst of an era, when many of the gains of earlier freedom struggles are coming undone. Yet, as Cha-Jua shows, the specific dynamics of today's unraveling are rooted in a set of global capitalist dynamics that are fundamentally new. Where Baron saw proletarianization as key to the integration of Black workers, Cha-Jua examines the impact of deindustrialization and deproletarianization on today's Black working class. With the material basis for integration and enfranchisement unraveling, he shows that we are in the midst of a new kind of resegregation and disenfranchisement that no longer draws on the crudities of Jim Crow apartheid. Quite the contrary, it assumes the invidious form of a new kind of "color-blind racism" that wraps itself in the language of ostensible equality. As blame for poverty and marginalization is transferred from the social system onto its victims, a small, upwardly mobile Black middle class has benefited. These benefits have been achieved, however, even as the vast mass of African Americans are again being subject to new forms of marginalization, even more and entrenched and intractable than those they have replaced.

Cha-Jua's bold, sweeping survey of these racial formations and transformations provides a template for many of the essays in this collection. Nevertheless, as the reader will discover, it does not offer a completely exhaustive theoretical framework for everything that we are attempting to accomplish in this book. In particular, Cha-Jua's approach is limited by his selective focus on U.S. history and his exclusion of other differently colored races from an analysis, which is painted primarily in black and white. Some of these complications are considered by Theodore Koditschek in the second chapter, "Capitalism, Race, and Evolution in Imperial Britain, 1850–1900." As the title indicates, this chapter focuses entirely on the moment that Cha-Jua would identify as the transition from "slavery" to the "plantation economy," but it shifts attention from the United States to the British Empire. During this period, as Koditschek points out, it was Britain, rather than the United States, that stood at the center of the world capitalist economy. Seen from this vantage, the shift from slavery to the quasi-coerced plantation was only one of several refigurations of colonial and neocolonial exploitation that were all designed to integrate the labor and loyalty of nonwhite peoples into the emerging world capitalist system.

Like Cha-Jua, Koditschek emphasizes the uneven character of capitalist development, which meant that the onset of an industrial revolution in Britain precipitated demand for a host of raw materials and tropical products that could be produced only in the so-called colored colonies. It was this rapid economic integration of the British Empire, according to Koditschek, that precipitated the emergence of a "new racism" during the second half of the nineteenth century. Taking issue with a dominant historiography, which attributes the "new racism" to the advent of new ideologies of social Darwinism or scientific racism, Koditschek argues that, rather, it reflected metropolitan fears of actual colonial economic resistance, as well as anxieties about the many diverse cultures and races that might someday have to be accommodated within a "Greater British" polity. At a time when the empire was rapidly coming together, the new racism provided a means of cognitive distancing that allowed metropolitan Britons to keep the Other at bay.

It is here, Koditschek contends, that racial ideologies based on scientific (or pseudoscientific) theories of evolution had a crucial role to play. These theories provided the ideological raw materials with which a multitude of different imperial races could be comprehended, rank ordered, and potentially managed, in a manner that suited the interests of imperial administrators and capitalist elites. Invoking principles of biological fixity while actually accommodating historical change, these evolutionary theories offered mechanisms for racial "promotion" and "demotion" by which the rank ordering and putative quality of the races might be changed. In the end, Koditschek shows, this process of racial reordering could never be entirely controlled by imperial elites, as the colonial Others began to devise their own distinctive narratives of racial evolution in order to claim a higher place on the racial hierarchy.

Koditschek's account, which focuses primarily on Britain, Ireland, and India, makes no attempt to carry his story forward beyond the nineteenth century, nor does he have anything to say about the British role in Africa, which became so prominent during the twentieth century. This subject, however, is taken up in our third chapter, by Tola Olu Pearce, "Globalization and the Cycle of Violence in Africa." Pearce shows how the dire conditions that prevail over so much of today's postcolonial Africa have their origins in the colonial hierarchies of race that Koditschek describes. Today, in the context of globalization, these hierarchies may seem to be invisible and color-blind. They are, however, deeply grounded in long-standing historical structures of racial inequality.

Although Pearce does not directly address the *racial* character of these power disparities, she shows how they operate on the ground. Thus, International Monetary Fund and World Bank programs force African countries into the harshest currents of globalization, on terms that would never be tolerated in the West. This produces devastating consequences for the health and welfare of the population, which is left physically enervated and economically marginalized. Political pressure from international institutions to enforce unpopular social policies generates corrupt undemocratic states. Ethnic conflicts and rebellions, conventionally blamed on African tribalism, are, as Pearce demonstrates, often precipitated by severe economic competition for scarce resources that Western-imposed globalization has induced.

Devastating as it is, Pearce's picture of postcolonial Africa is not entirely bleak. Through a combination of international institutions, transnational coalition building, and grassroots movements, she believes that Africans can regain control of their destiny. Yet it is difficult to imagine any of these goals succeeding without an explicit formulation of the ways in which racial discrimination has shaped African history. This challenge of bringing race to the point of visibility under contemporary conditions is peculiarly difficult, not because it is new but because it is asymmetric in scope. It is easy enough to see race as a problem for Africans or African Americans. Less easy is to force white Western capitalists (or even white Western workers) to recognize that the dynamic of racial oppression is the consequence of *their* action (or inaction), and therefore that racial structures must implicate them too.

This recognition, that race is not a thing but a relationship that involves interactions between both whites and blacks, has been greatly enhanced over the past two decades by the genre of "whiteness studies," which has applied many of the insights first advanced by Black scholars to enhance our understanding of the master race. In our fourth chapter, "White without End? The Abolition of Whiteness; or, The Rearticulation of Race," David Roediger, one of the founders of whiteness studies, looks back on the way in which this field has developed in the years since the appearance of his original pioneering work. In *The Wages of Whiteness* (1991) Roediger outlined the economic and psychological benefits that white racial privilege had historically brought to the white American worker. Three years later, his *Towards the Abolition of Whiteness* pointed to the larger racially transformative conditions that would be required to achieve that ultimate goal. In the present chapter, he reaffirms his commitment to "abolitionism," taking issue with those who have recently argued that whiteness should be preserved. In contrast to those "preservationists," who wish to shear whiteness from its racist moorings, Roediger regards this operation as impossible. Given its nature, whiteness cannot be converted from a noxious privilege into a positive identity.

Roediger's case that this transmutation is impossible brings us full circle to the premise of our book: Racial ideologies—or identities—such as whiteness are not free-floating signifiers into which we may impute whatever meaning we choose. They are subject positions inherent in racial-capitalist structures that can be altered only through collective struggles aimed at transforming society as a whole. The problem with whiteness is neither the "cultural debasement" that it signifies nor the "bad attitudes" that it promotes. Rather, it is with the oppressive structures within which it is embedded, and whose perpetuation it underwrites. Outside these structures, Roediger reminds us, "whiteness" is nothing—and when these structures are overturned, it will no longer exist.

PART 1 READING QUESTIONS

1. Although Part 1 focuses explicitly on racial structures, it also points forward toward the racial ideologies and identities that are embedded within them, as well as the racial struggles that their contradictions produce. Focusing particularly on the chapters by Koditschek and Roediger, think about the authors' arguments as to *how* such ideologies are embedded and *where* such struggles are produced. What insights about the relationship between structure, ideology, and struggle do you take with you from Part 1 as you prepare to begin reading the chapters in Part 2?

2. There is a tension in our chapters: Cha-Jua and Roediger envision racial structures as essentially binary in nature, whereas Koditschek posits a graded hierarchy of multiple races. Although it is important to acknowledge the analytical distinctiveness of these two approaches, it may also be useful to think about how they might be combined. For example, if Koditschek were to carry his analysis forward into the twentieth or twenty-first century, when metropolitan Britain became a Herrenvolk democracy, more like the United States, might his analysis of racial

structures be rendered more dichotomous, and translatable into Roediger's generic "white-ness" terms? Conversely, can Roediger's "whiteness" be decomposed into a more multicolored rainbow of several ethnicities, each of which have gravitated into (and perhaps out of) the system of white racial privilege as U.S. social and historical conditions have changed?

3. As we enter the current era, which Cha-Jua labels "globalization," he suggests—in a manner echoed by Pearce and Roediger—that the relationship between racial structures and ideologies has fundamentally changed. Whereas the function of racial ideology during earlier phases of capitalist development was to make race as *visible* as possible, its current function may be to obscure and therefore render *invisible* those structures of oppression that continue to assume a racialized form. What features of today's global deproletarianization might contribute to the creation of this new phenomenon of "color-blind racism," which Helen A. Neville will analyze more fully at the beginning of Part 2?

1

The Changing Same

Black Racial Formation and Transformation as a Theory of the African American Experience

SUNDIATA KEITA CHA-JUA

> Capitalist development in our research settings both preserves and remakes the racial order, extending and reinforcing racial barriers, but also creating new contradictions that paradoxically threaten to dismantle them.
>
> —Stanley B. Greenberg, *Race and State in Capitalist Development*

> The racial history of blacks and whites in the United States can be usefully theorized as a succession of different racial formations.
>
> —Harold Baron, "Racial Oppression Transformed: The Implications of the 1960s"

> The writers and organizers of the study of Negro history have reached a critical stage in their work. They have accumulated an imposing body of facts which demonstrate the active participation of Negroes in the making of American history and, in particular, in the creation of American liberal and revolutionary tradition. . . . But what next? Merely go on accumulating facts? . . . Historical facts, as facts, can do so much and no more. They have to be organized in the light of a philosophy of history. To be quite precise, they have to be consciously organized in the light of a correct philosophy of history.
>
> —C. L. R. James, "Key Problems in the Study of Negro History"

Though written nearly seventy years ago, the epigraph by C. L. R. James establishes the central concern of this chapter, the need for a theory of the African American experience. If historical scholarship is to explain the persistence of antiblack racism or the periodic transmutation of Black racial oppression into new systems of racial control, then empiricism is insufficient. A new conceptual framework is needed. Recently, Black feminist historian Darlene Clark Hine and African American urban and labor historian Joe W. Trotter called for new syntheses of African American history. According to Trotter, enough archaeological work has been done to produce several new historical syntheses. Specifically, addressing the problem of *historical periodization,* Clark Hine proposed, "The new periodization should focus on the four major themes in African American history: Slavery and emancipation, migration, urbanization, and the changing status of Black women." I share Trotter's and Clark Hine's yearning for new conceptual frameworks, including the construction of explicit periodization schemas.[1]

The purpose of this chapter then is to explore how the system of *racism* or Black *racial oppression* and resistance to it have been both *continuous* and *discontinuous* throughout African American history. The questions I pose are mainly historical: If Blacks have been on the "bottom rail" since their forced migration to these shores and remain so currently, in what sense can we claim the system of Black racial oppression has changed over time? What is the relationship between African American agency and transitions and transformations in Black racial formations? How have the structures and discourses of racial oppression and Black resistance changed over time and across geographic regions? What social forces have reinforced or destabilized the system of oppression or facilitated or restrained the Black Liberation movement? Whereas the questions driving this project are historical, and historical examples are used throughout the chapter, the project is mainly theoretical. It is a work of historical synthesis derived from a *historical materialist* reading of the African American experience, as evidenced in textbooks, collections of primary documents, and seminal and recent Black Studies literature—historical, sociological, political theory, and psychological.

In this chapter, I delineate the Black Racial Formation Theory (BRFT) as a framework for analyzing the African American experience as it evolved in conjunction with the development of capitalism and the processes of racial oppression in the United States. I have divided the chapter into three parts: "Theory and Periodization of Black Racial Formations," "Contours, Patterns, and Trends in Black Racial Formation," and "Contemporary Black Racial Formation: The New Nadir." In the first section, I offer a provisional theory of racism or racial oppression and advance the BRFT as a theory and paradigm for conceptualizing African American history. Elaborating on political scientist Alex Callinicos's theory of history, in the second section, I dig into the marrow of the Black experience and use the BRFT paradigm to delineate African American history's basic structure and core components and to chart its contours, coordinates, patterns, motifs, and connections. In the third segment, I use BRFT theory to conceptualize the key features of what is commonly referred to as the post–civil rights era. I advance the argument that the contemporary transformations in the lives of a majority of African Americans are constructing a new racial formation, a new historical period, which I have termed the *New Nadir*.[2]

Theory and Periodization of Black Racial Oppression

Since the eighteenth century, racial oppression and its apparatuses have structured the social position *and* perceptions of African-descended people and people of color in the United States and throughout the world. Racial oppression is a system of *domination, discrimination, and degradation* of people who differ in *some* physical traits from their oppressors. The difference becomes the basis for the social processes of exploitation, appropriation, exclusion, or extermination, or a combination thereof. Except for perhaps the indigenous people, who experienced genocide, it can be argued that African Americans have suffered the most sustained and severe forms of racial oppression in the United States. Black racial oppression *and* resistance to it have been persistent and pervasive, and have permeated every aspect of African Americans' lives. Although it has been ubiquitous, racial oppression has continuously changed. Transformations in the system of racial oppression and our understanding of it have been constant, though not steady. Racial change has recurred throughout U.S. history, particularly during moments of substantial economic restructuring. Over the past forty years the system of racial oppression and our understanding of it have changed in both profound and contradictory ways.[3]

The beginning of the civil rights and Black Power movements dismantled the most overtly offensive aspects of the existing system of Black racial oppression, segregation under the plantation economy. Neoconservatives transmuted the more subtle and supple aspects into a new disciplinary regime. The same contending forces generated an epistemological revolution and counterrevolution in the study of race and racism. I will discuss the transformation to a new Black racial formation in the last third of the essay. At this point, it is important to trace contemporary changes in our conception of racial oppression. From the early 1940s, when Ruth Benedict first identified the concept, until the mid-1960s, racism referred to an explicit ideology, a set of attitudes, values, and beliefs, which posited that racially defined social groups possessed unequal genetically determined intellectual and moral characteristics. According to her, "Racism is the dogma that one ethnic group is condemned by nature to hereditary inferiority and another group is destined to hereditary superiority."[4] In 1967, Kwame Ture (Stokely Carmichael) and Charles V. Hamilton repudiated Benedict's idealism and recast "racism" as the coalescence of institutional power and discourses of racial superiority and inferiority. Writing in *Black Power* they conceptualized racism as comprising two interrelated components: those that are individual and overt and those that are institutional and covert. According to Ture and Hamilton, *institutional racism* "originates in the operation of established and respected forces in society" and "relies on the active and pervasive operation of anti-black attitudes and practices." They initiated the shift from viewing racism as an ideology toward recognizing that it was a *system* of white supremacy. In this system, the normal institutional conventions—hierarchical arrangements, procedures, and policies—are structured to convey *power, privilege, and prestige* on those deemed white, and correspondingly to *dominate* and *discriminate* against those defined as Black, brown, red, yellow, and so on. In conjunction with these forms of structural oppression, darker people are *degraded* via the construction of corresponding discourses that rationalize racial hierarchy. The concept of institutional racism emphasized outcomes, not intentions or opportunities. To reflect the ways in which the Black Power movement transformed our understanding of racism, I will substitute the concept *racial oppression* for that of racism.[5]

By the 1980s, as *social constructivism* gained dominance in cultural studies, the view that race was a social construct—a human invention, which ascribed social meanings to hereditary physical characteristics—had become common sense among physical and social scientists as well as humanities scholars.[6] Social constructionism provided scholars with a powerful but flawed theory to challenge residual essentialist notions, which still posed race as a natural primordial category in which visible traits marked fixed inherited attributes. On the whole, studies of race benefited from the insights of social constructivism, however, because that overused phrase fails to capture the materiality of the historically evolved social relations that exist between groups identified as different races; it also generated negative effects. The constructivist intervention generated two unintended deleterious consequences. First, it shifted the conversation from the system of racism or racial oppression to the race concept. Though often treated as synonymous concepts by social constructionists, the theoretical and social differences between them are significant. This terminological reversal contributed mightily in moving the discussion away from structured inequality back to interpretations of prejudice ideology. Second, on this topic, the logic of social constructivism intersected with the dominant neoconservative discourse on race, color-blind racial ideology. For social constructionists, the deconstruction of race revealed that it was neither natural nor divine but an invention of a particular society at a particular historical moment. In popular parlance, race is not real. These flaws in social constructionism have been pernicious inasmuch as they have dovetailed with the conservative denial of continuing racial oppression. The intersection of social constructivist with conservative arguments came to supersede discussions of racism by focusing on race. Simply, from this logic, race was not real, which implied the denial of racial oppression.[7]

Twenty years after the Black Power revolt, sociologist William Julius Wilson claimed "economic class position" had superseded race as the prime determinate of African Americans' "life chances." Contesting Wilson, political economist Donald J. Harris argued that his thesis was at best premature. Harris claimed Wilson exaggerated a momentary aberration in African American history. He predicted that a lull in the Black Liberation movement "coupled with the role of cyclical and long-term structural factors" would soon erode Blacks' socio-economic position. The current recession supports Harris's argument. Sociologists Martin Bulmer and John Solomos also challenged Wilson's thesis. In a direct refutation of the Wilson thesis, they contended that race and racism had "become more evident during the last thirty years." Furthermore, according to Bulmer and Solomos, as formerly colonized people of color flooded into Europe, spurred by the emerging global economy, "new racisms" were being generated. More recent academic research, public polls, and personal testimony support Harris's and Bulmer and Solomos's suspicions that racism is resurgent in contemporary societies. Contestation over its meaning(s) and racial oppression's continuing power to structure social relations, organize basic institutional functions, and shape ideological discourses in contemporary societies attest to its continuing significance. And our widely divergent understandings of "racism" (is it an ideology, a system of domination, an atavistic remnant, or the primary contemporary contradiction in the United States?) give salience to philosopher Charles Mills's and sociologist Eduardo Bonilla-Silva's arguments that "racism" needs "a sound theoretical apparatus."[8]

Bulmer and Solomos make two significant points: first, political mobilization around racial and ethnic identity or interests has grown in significance over the past generation; second, new forms of racial oppression are being produced as societies accommodate the transition to global capitalism. However, a third point can be gleaned from their discussion. The logic of their argument suggests that racial oppression is dynamic, not static. They view the racial structure as a fluid system that articulates with a society's dominant political economy, social relations, and discourses. Thus, the paradox of racial oppression is that it has been simultaneously *stable yet constantly changing.*

Amiri Baraka's metaphor, the "changing same," best captures the permanence and frequent permutations in the system of racial oppression and the complexities of the *continuities* and *discontinuities* in the African American experience.[9] However, if we are to explicate how the role, position, and status of Blacks in the U.S. political economy, the polity, and civil society have changed since 1619, we must move beyond metaphor. We must offer a theory of racial oppression and, more important, a specific theory of antiblack racism and African American sociohistorical formation and transformation. Such a theory, as Ture and Hamilton argue, is best thought of as a system of oppression in which the *structural* and *ideological* components are *intertwined.*[10]

Black Racial Formation and Transformation Theory posits six hypotheses: (1) Black racial oppression is constitutive of rather than contingent to U.S. social formations; (2) Black racial oppression includes institutional and individual practices, and corresponding ideological discourses; (3) Black racial formations articulate with and follow the logic of the social formations in which they subsist; (4) Black racial formations are dynamic rather than static; (5) Black racial formations represent specific systems of racial control that occur at particular historical moments within specific political-spatial boundaries; thus, Black racial formations constitute particular periods of African American history; and (6) Black racial formations are formed and transformed according to the dialectical interaction between restructuring capitalist political economies, the evolving U.S. federal-state system, U.S. popular culture, and the Black Liberation movement.

The concept "racial formation" was introduced into the scholarly literature in the mid-1980s. The contributions of Michael Omi and Howard Winant are widely known. My approach to racial formation and transformation, however, is derived mainly from sociologist Harold Baron, whose contributions to this theory are less known. I am attracted to Baron's formulation because he offers a materialist model that emphasizes political economy and provides a periodization of African American history. In particular, he argues that over the course of African American history, "the most decisive relationship is between capitalistic development and change in the form of the system of racial control." Baron's racial formations consist of four elements: a dominant group classified as white, a subordinate group defined as black, a racial control system, and the social formation's dominant national mode of production. A racial formation then is a system that operates a racially stratified society with identifiable political and spatial boundaries bound within a particular historical period. Based on the historic interaction among his four components, Baron conceives of three racial formations or periods of African American history. The first, "Plantation Slavery," covers the period from 1619 to 1865. It intersects with the creation of commercial capitalism in the British American colonies, especially those that became the United States in 1787. The second, "Agrarian Ascendancy," covers the period from 1865 to 1965, and corresponds with the advent of industrial capitalism on the national scale. The third, which Baron calls "Advanced Racism," emerged during the 1950s, and corresponds with a rather imprecisely formulated "Advanced Capitalism."[11]

The strength of Baron's rather orthodox Marxist formulation lies in the way he tethers his racial formations and transformations to the major stages of the larger U.S. political economy. This structural reductionism, however, is also Baron's weakness, for the causal lines in his account all flow one way: from structures to ideologies and practices. This understates the extent to which racial structures, grounded in the subjugation of dark bodies, constitute a separate axis of oppression, which cannot be subsumed completely within the national political and economic frame.

My own approach to racial formation diverges from Baron in two ways. First, I subsume the "dominant white racial group," the "subordinate Black racial group," and the "racial control system," Baron's first three components, into two elements: *racialization* and *racial oppression*. By *racialization,* I mean the dialectical process by which social groups—ethnicities, nationalities, and so forth—are reconstructed into races. Both the dominant and the subordinate groups contribute, albeit in unequal ways in the reconfiguration and the use of race to define their own and each other's identity. Because I view the ongoing process of racial identity formation as the central relationship, I combine the "dominant white racial group" and the "subordinate Black racial group" under the category "race." Racial oppression, which is historically concomitant with racialization, produces two processes: institutional racism and racist ideologies, which correspond with one another. My second departure from Baron involves the relationship between the dominant mode of production and the racial formation. I view the broader social formation's "dominant national mode of production" as enveloping and subordinating the racial formation's political economy. Nevertheless, my conceptualization emphasizes the production and social relations dominant in the political economy in which Blacks *actually* labored. The composition of a racial formation then includes processes of racialization; the articulation and disarticulation of class, racial, and gender oppressions; the relationship of its structures and ideologies to practices, events, and consciousnesses; and the relationship between dominant and subordinate political economies.

By focusing on African Americans' actual sociohistorical experiences, most scholars of the Black experience, like Baron, have conceived of three dichotomous experiences: slavery, sharecropping, and industrialization. However, writing in the twenty-first century, it is now clear that the transformation to global capitalism has produced a profound realignment in African Americans' role, position, status, and representation in the U.S. political economy, polity, civil society, and popular culture. Beginning with the recession of 1979 and the conservative Reagan Revolution, a seismic shift occurred in African Americans' condition and future possibilities; this transformation has been of such magnitude that it constitutes a new historical period, a fourth Black racial formation.[12]

Thus, I theorize that African American history consists of a succession of four qualitatively distinct sociohistorical periods. Much about the character of these four periods or racial formations is schematized in table 1.1. Although limitations of space preclude a full discussion of these formations, or the process that transformed one into the next, the following elementary periods can be identified: (1) *Slavery* (1619–1865), from the arrival of Africans and their eventual enslavement to the enactment of the Thirteenth Amendment, during which approximately 92 percent of Africans were enslaved and the remaining 8 percent of quasi-free Blacks existed as outlaws, literally outside the U.S. polity and civil society, and governed by an extra set of slave or Black codes. (2) The *Plantation Economy* (1866–1965), from the passage of the Thirteenth Amendment through the civil rights movement, during which an overwhelming majority of Blacks were southern rural sharecroppers. For most of the period they were denied constitutional rights, and suffered under vituperative white supremacist regimes. (3) *Proletarianization-Ghettoization* (1910–1979), from the labor migrations to the North around World War I through the mechanization of southern agriculture and the U.S. entrance into World War II to the recession of 1979. This was the period in which African Americans made their greatest advances, moving into the urban industrial economy, becoming unionized, making strides toward closing the educational gap, and finally abolishing apartheid. Also during this period, African Americans' gains were eroded and repealed by the transformation to global capitalism, specifically deindustrialization, and assaults by neoliberal policies. My first three periods are similar to Baron's. However, since Baron last addressed this issue, a fourth Black racial formation, the *New Nadir* (1979–present), has taken shape. The *New Nadir* began to emerge during the recession of 1979 and Ronald Reagan's presidency; its outlines were starkly apparent after another recession a decade later. It is a product of global capitalism and represents the impact of that process on Afro-America.

The four periods of African American history or Black racial formation are also roughly congruent with the four accumulation structures of U.S. capitalist development: commercial capitalism, industrial capitalism, corporate capitalism, and globalization conceived by David Gordon, Richard Edwards, and Michael Reich. However, Black racial formations do not fit neatly into the periodization of America's social structures of accumulation. Capitalism developed unevenly across U.S. regions and alternated cycles of prosperity and crisis. Blacks have generally existed in a subordinate political economy. Thus, there existed a lag between the emergence of a new structure of accumulation and the transformation of African Americans' role in the political economy, position in the polity, status in civil society, and participation and depiction in popular culture. By linking the four periods of African American Racial Formation and Transformation with these corresponding structures of U.S. capitalist accumulation, the BRFT model offers a structural theory that articulates the dialectical connections between conditioning structures of racial oppression and the oppositional power of Black agency. It is attentive to ideology and culture, and explicates the processes, agents, and direction of historical change in the African American experience. BRFT is a conceptual model for investigating past and

Table 1.1. Racial formation and transformation: Conceptual schema of the African American sociohistorical experience, 1619–present

Transition	Processes	Transformation	Black Labor/ Core Economy	Racist Ideology	Turning Points	Watershed	Identity
From Africa to America (1607–1858)	Slave trade, slavery, & racialization	Slavery (1619–1865)	Southern chattel slavery/ commercial capitalism	Genetic inferiority (1803–1940s)	Bacon's Rebellion (1676)/ Louisiana Purchase (1803)	1700s & 1830s	African & Colored American
From slavery to freedom (1619–1865)	Civil War, emancipation, Reconstruction, tenancy, & segregation	Southern sharecropping & domestic service/industrial capitalism	Southern sharecropping & domestic service/industrial capitalism	Scientific racism (1880s–1940s)	Civil War, Reconstruction, and Nadir	1860s & 1890s	Colored Negro
From field to factory (1910–1979)	Migrations (1910–1930 & 1940–1970)	Proletarianization & ghettoization (1910–1979)	Urban menial workers & domestic service/corporate capitalism	Cultural deprivation (1940s–2000s)	World War I, World War II, & Civil Rights & Black Power movements	1920s, 1940s, & 1960s	Negro & Black
From plant to penitentiary (1980s–present)	Deindustrialization & political realignment	New Nadir (1980–present)	Subproletarian- ization/global capitalism	Color-blind, racial ideology (1990s–present)	Bakke decision (1978); Reagan presidency (1980s)	1980s & 2000s	Black African American

Source: Partially derived from Baron (1985): 13; Harris (1985), iv; Alaklimat (1987), 24–27; Boston, (1988), 23; Waquant, (2002): 42; and Wilson (2007), 13.

present material conditions and ideological beliefs among African-descended people: demographic patterns, socioeconomic structures, historical processes, institutional arrangements, social movements, material and expressive culture, and psychological attitudes.[13]

BRFT is a theory of history in the sense that it uses general concepts to provide causal explanations for the content, contours, patterns, conversion processes, and course of African American historical development. BRFT is a particular application of historical materialism to African American history. Alex Callinicos contends that classical historical materialism is a theory of history because it offers an account of social transformation. According to him, historical materialism posits "a weak tendency for the productive forces to develop, the consequent likelihood of organic crises and the primacy of structural capacities and class interests in explaining social action." Moreover, he has persuasively argued that theories of history embody theories of *structure, transformation,* and *directionality.* These aspects specify the uniqueness of the social formation being observed and explain the processes by which it has been transformed, and the likely paths of change.[14]

According to BRFT, racial formations have three interrelated and multifaceted aspects: racialization, racial oppression (including institutional, ideological, and individual), and a dominant mode of production with a subordinated secondary sector in which most Blacks labor. Racialization contains two elements: the *idea* of race and the experiences of racial oppression. This latter term signifies the *social relationship* of racial domination manifested in institutional practices, public discourses, and individual behaviors. Yet each racial formation also has a unique configuration. In other words, Blacks have a distinct relationship to the political economy, polity, civil society, and popular culture. Correspondingly, Blacks express their agency through particular consciousnesses, identities, and social movements. Thus, despite continuities in racial oppression from one racial formation to another, the articulation of the elements is quite different in each specific racial formation. Behavior preceded consciousness. Historically, the oppression of African ethnicities has occurred prior to the creation or revision of the race concept to classify different types of humans. However, for the purposes of discussion, I will first explore the concept and then elucidate the sociohistorical context—racial oppression—in which race came to embody a biologically determined hierarchy of ability personified in somatic image.

What is race? We have discussed the social constructivist perspective. Natural scientists view race as a "breeding population." Similarly, philosopher Albert Mosley views it as "a set of characteristics that occurs with greater frequency among its members than among the members of another race." For anthropologist Audrey Smedley, race is "a set of beliefs and attitudes about human differences, not the differences themselves."[15] The essential difference between those who view race as a legitimate social category that specifies real biological differences and those who view it as merely a social construct is embodied in these observations. However, these understandings are not mutually exclusive. Obviously, race is not natural. Human populations have never been completely isolated or reproductively distinct. Nonetheless, real differences in physical appearance do exist. But neither is it purely a social construct. Thus, race has both biological and social dimensions, though it is the sociohistorical relations—the economic, political, and cultural relations—between two different groups of people that predominantly determine racial categories. These morphological characteristics give race an "underlying genetic basis," according to Mosley. This "apparent" correspondence with reality is what gives race, and by extension racial oppression, the appearance of "common sense." Nonetheless, biologists and social scientists have shown that these variations in appearance are not the physical expression of different underlying essences. In and of themselves, distinctions in phenotype and morphology are socially meaningless. "Races" are, in Benedict Anderson's language, "imagined communities." But unlike nations, races are other-determined, at least initially. English colonialists had to designate the indigenous peoples "red" and enslaved Africans "black" before they could declare themselves "white." The meaning(s) of the categories—"blackness" and "whiteness"—were not predetermined but were constructed during the enslavement of African peoples, the specific sociohistorical context in which black-white racialization occurred. However, their meanings were not wholly new inventions. Modern meanings of blackness were elaborated from long-standing antiblack notions ubiquitous throughout European culture. Therefore, although differences in phenotype and morphology between social groups are natural, that is, biologically based, the essential elements constituting the race concept are predominately sociohistorical.[16]

The burgeoning enslavement of Africans in the eighteenth century initiated a process in which "blackness"—or, more precisely, what anthropologist St. Clair Drake distinguished as "Negroidness"—came to supersede religion and ethnicity or nationality as a marker of difference. Many historians focus on Bacon's Rebellion (1676) as the critical incident that sparked this transformation. Specifically, the Virginia gentry responded to the biracial uprising of the poor with a shift of the axis from class, "nation," and religion toward race as the decisive form of oppression. The transformation of Africans to chattel slaves necessitated both new methods of discipline and discursive changes in the meanings of race and nation. Differences that previously had led Europeans to classify Africans into different nations were now deemed insignificant. (See Theodore Koditschek's "Capitalism, Race, and Evolution in Imperial Britain, 1850–1900" in this volume.) Literature scholar Nicholas Hudson's insightful discussion of how European natural scientists and philosophers created the modern definition of race that replaced the term *nation* is helpful here. According to Hudson, prior to the eighteenth century both *race* and *nation* referred to lineage groups. In the context of the explorations and the slave trade, and the exploitation and extermination that followed, *race* was "gradually mutated from its original sense as a people or a nation . . . to its latter sense of a biological subdivision of the human species." Simultaneously, *nation* was recast as a "subdivision" of the revised concept of race, but with a caveat: it now only referred to sophisticated "cultural" or "political" groups; that is, it was reserved for European peoples. Diverse African people were reduced to members of a single unified race in which every person of African descent was deemed below any European, regardless of social class or individual character.[17]

Composing the ruling race, Europeans rationalized their dominance by claiming that the phenotypic features of the oppressed races expressed their innate inferiority. The physical and moral characteristics attributed to "Negroes" in the 1798 edition of the *Encyclopedia Britannica* illustrate the warped combination of physical description and ideological imputations embedded in racist logic: "Round cheeks, high cheek bones, a forehead somewhat elevated, a short, broad, flat nose, thick lips, small ears, ugliness, and irregularity of shape, characterize their external appearance. . . . Vices . . . idleness, treachery, revenge, cruelty, imprudence, stealing, lying, profanity, debauchery, nastiness and intemperance. . . . They are strangers to every sentiment of compassion, and are an awful example of the corruption of man when left to himself."[18] Though the full entry mentions color, it focuses on what Drake called "anti-Negroidness." One caveat, the negative attributes assigned Africans in these *objective* observations, is always a window through which to also detect the central contradiction between masters and the enslaved: the assigned negative traits evidence day-to-day resistance against forced labor and dehumanization.

Racialization is the unfolding of a material social relationship of oppression, but it is also equally a process of cultural construction. The intelligentsia of an elite that controls the state's repressive and ideological apparatuses initially imagines racial categories. The state through the law codifies the material relationship of domination that is created through incorporating the subordinate racial group into the ruling race's political economy. Because Africans were regarded as subhuman, they could be excluded from the polity and subjected to extralegal racialized laws in the form of slave codes and Black laws (for free Blacks). The thirteen colonies and ultimately the United States enacted laws legitimating slavery and affirming the racialization of their populations. Nonetheless, these laws merely confirmed the social relations that were already in existence. For example, Massachusetts's *Body of Liberties* (1641) and Virginia's (1661), Maryland's (1663), and New York's slave laws (1665) codified relations that had materialized somewhat earlier. When the U.S. Constitution was finally written, it was not color-blind. Rather, as Eric Foner maintains, it "strengthened the institution of slavery," and its "federal structure . . . insulated slavery from outside interference." From 1787 until 1965, the U.S. federal state and its southern regional states would remain explicitly "Herrenvolk democracies," that is, white supremacist societies.[19]

Although "race" was invented by Euro-American elites, its continued salience was heavily reinforced by the role of white subordinate classes in consolidating the white supremacist social system and by Africans seeking to resist domination and to refute white assertions against their humanity. The exploited "white" racial classes have often pressured the dominant white "racial class" to organize, preserve, or extend white supremacy. More important, we should not ignore the emancipatory use of "race" by oppressed peoples to organize resistance movements. Nonetheless, it must be emphasized that the dominant racial or class group had to sanction racist practices and ideologies before they could be woven into a social formation's basic institutional fabric.

As we have seen, the essence of race is social; therefore, what is really important is not race per se but racial oppression. Racial oppression's social character means that its material and ideological elements work through both institutions and individuals. Systems of racial oppression also consist of both structural and ideological components. French Marxist philosopher Louis Althusser divided capitalist social institutions into two types: repressive institutions (the police and military) and ideological institutions (the media, popular culture industries, education, the legal system, religion, social organizations, and so on). Althusser's framework is especially useful for analyzing Black racial oppression. The repressive institutions are deployed to police the racial contract, whereas the ideological institutions are arrayed to construct rationalizations and to instruct the entire populace in justifications of the racial order. To a greater and lesser extent all institutions perform functions of coercion and consent building, but in a racial state, institutions, regardless of type, more frequently resort to force against members of the ruled race. Yet repression is acute in a racial state; in the United States, force—state and private racial violence—has been almost as central as economic exploitation in Blacks' oppression.[20]

The material aspects of antiblack racial oppression have, over the years, specifically involved such diverse mechanisms as *superexploitation,* market-based nonexploitative economic oppression, de jure or de facto discriminatory state policies, state terrorism and private racial violence, exclusion from the polity or systematic underrepresentation, and a combination of cultural imposition, appropriation, and commoditization. The production relations in which most Blacks have labored throughout most of African American history can be characterized as superexploitation. Racial discrimination has characterized Black-white social relations, including disproportionate unemployment, but particularly in nonexploitative economic relations, such as consumption and governmental social reproductive spending. The ideological aspect of racial oppression involves imputing imagined differences in intelligence, morality, and beauty onto real physiognomic differences to rationalize a preexisting relationship of domination, discrimination, and degradation. Both during and since slavery, Euro-America's cultural and belief systems have been organized to produce and promote degrading images of African people and to appropriate and mass-market African American creativity.[21]

Both the repressive and the ideological institutions of racial oppression have social and personal effects. Consequently, racial oppression infects and warps all social relationships, especially those that are already predicated on domination, such as class, ethnicity or nationality, and gender. Depending on one's racial designation, individuals are either beneficiaries or victims of the institutional mechanisms and ideological representations of racial domination. Racial oppression privileges those with skin designated white by giving them additional material benefits and what W. E. B. Du Bois termed a "psychological wage." In contrast, those who are deemed black, brown, red, or yellow are penalized and suffer immense monetary losses due to superexploitation and economic discrimination. Additionally, people of color are debased, and racial oppression induces deleterious effects on their mental and physical health, often producing internalized racial oppression and exacerbating illnesses such as hypertension.[22]

Contours, Patterns, and Trends in Black Racial Formation

Racial formations have a complex dialectical relationship to the broader social formations in which they are ingrained. The production process and the corresponding social relations of production prevalent in racial formations differ from, and are subordinate to, the dominant national mode of production. For instance, the mode of appropriation of the surplus in both slavery and sharecropping differed significantly from the appropriation process in the dominant capitalist mode of production. Also, the level of productive forces and the technologies employed in the political economies and industries in which Blacks predominated lagged behind those prevalent in the dominant political economy. Moreover, higher levels of coercion and repression than exist in the core political economy characterize racial formations. Slavery is illustrative. The slave South was part, but a subordinate part, of the evolving U.S. commercial capitalist system. The South was characterized by slavery, the Midwest by small-scale commercial agricultural production, and the Northeast by manufactory capitalism, before the late antebellum period (1840–1860). Prior to the 1840s, midwestern family farmers operated a mode of production that Charles Post describes as "petty-commodity production."[23] It was noncapitalist because these farmers employed few workers, utilized little machinery, produced primarily for subsistence, and sold their meager surplus in regional markets. The South was characterized by a political economy that blended noncapitalist features of slavery, particularly coerced labor, with the bourgeois features of commercial speculation. Slavery's relationship to the other production systems in the U.S. social formation determined the nature and role of the slave system. Although a free wage-labor system existed in the American South, Black slave, not free white, labor produced the cash crops that were the economy's foundation. Slavery was noncapitalist in both its production and its social relations, but in the U.S. social formation it was subordinate to northeastern manufactory capitalism, thus producing commodities for the world capitalist market.[24]

As history is properly conceptualized as the study of change and continuity over time and across space using particular concepts and paradigms, historical theories must explain the mechanism(s) by which both transitions within a society and transformations from one society to another are produced. Racial formations are constantly changing, being transformed either into another stage or into a new racial formation. According to Alex Callinicos, to account for social change theories of history must have embedded in them a theory of transformation.[25]

Historical change is generally explained by two broad types of theories: one that identifies a single leading cause and another that focuses on the combination of several factors. Black racial formation and transformation subscribe to a view that transformations and transitions are overdetermined. In general, I mean that all social phenomena shape all other social phenomena by establishing the sociohistorical context in which they exist. Specifically, I mean that racial formations and racial restructuring, whether a transition or a transformation, are the results of the interaction of multiple social forces. Among the most important social factors, in terms of racial oppression, are the dialectical interactions among technological innovations, economic reorganization, and political conflict, especially Black resistance and the state's responses. The consequence of these interactions with the dominant national mode of production is the development of a new social structure of accumulation. For instance, at the end of the eighteenth century the invention of the cotton gin, the establishment of the federal Constitution enshrining private property and states' rights as its central concepts, the westward expansion, and the closing of the Atlantic slave trade combined to transform U.S. slavery. These processes and events changed U.S. slavery from a decaying patriarchal system of small commercial farms on the Atlantic seaboard into a system of huge prosperous plantations in the Deep South that produced cotton primarily for the international market. The transition to King Cotton drastically changed the slave relations of production. Before the cotton gin's invention it took a slave a whole day to clean a pound of cotton; afterward, that same slave could produce 150 pounds of cotton a day. In this new phase slave owners solidified slavery, intensified exploitation, and increased oppression. A more stringent Fugitive Slave Act was enacted under President George Washington in 1793 and an even harsher one in 1850 under President Millard Fillmore. Enslaved Africans responded by altering their strategies of resistance. Conspiracies and rebellions by slaves became more extensive and elaborate. The most significant revolts, the Prosser Rebellion, Louisiana Uprising, Vesey Conspiracy, Turner Revolt, and New Orleans and Charleston arsons all occurred after 1800. According to C. L. R. James, before 1800, revolters sought to escape slavery; afterward, slave rebels sought to destroy the "peculiar institution."[26]

Industrial capitalism was expanding and transforming both the Northeast and the Midwest simultaneously with the southern transition to the Cotton Kingdom. According to Post, during the 1840s and 1850s, northeastern manufacturers in "leading branches of capitalist industry," such as textile, railroad, meatpacking, and farm equipment production, broke their dependence on merchant capital, revolutionizing both the labor process and the social division of labor. By 1840, 37 percent of U.S. workers were working for wages. The invention of the steam engine and the social forces unleashed by the Industrial Revolution combined with increasing slave resistance and the growth of abolitionism to destroy chattel slavery.[27]

The production and social relations operating in the new racial formation were different from those of the old racial formation and the dominant mode of production. For instance, after slavery was abolished, racial oppression was recast, and slowly a new rationalization was created to buttress the new system of racial domination. Most freedmen were incorporated into the ambiguous and highly oppressive economic system of tenancy, particularly sharecropping, its lowest rung. The production and social relations of sharecropping were both different from and similar to those of slavery. And they deviated sharply from those operative in northern industrial capitalism. Sharecropping shared "characteristics with both capitalist and noncapitalist farms," according to Susan A. Mann. It was semiproletarian in its work relations; tenants received payment in part of the crop rather than in money wages, and the labor contract characterized by the "black codes" was constructed on coercive rather than free labor relations. Meanwhile, Black women were proletarianized as lowly paid domestic servants. And although African American men were initially incorporated into the polity, by 1900 they had been driven out of electoral politics by legal chicanery and extralegal violence.[28]

The basic premise of the BRFT paradigm is that the mode of capital accumulation conditions the historical form in which racial oppression is manifested. Racial formations or different periods of African American history are created by the dominant conditions (material and ideological) of African American life. BRFT acknowledges the conditioning capacity that structures have on agency in the historical process. I theorize that transformations between periods of racial formation and transitions between stages within a racial formation are based on complex interactions between U.S. capitalist political economies (dominant and subordinate), institutions and ideologies of racial domination, and the self-liberatory praxis of African Americans.

Theories of history, according to Callinicos, must also include a theory of directionality. He contends that theories of structure and transformation necessitate an attempt to chart the course and pattern of sociohistorical development. Finally, Callinicos posits that a theory of directionality needs to do two things. First, it must identify the properties by which it calculates progression or regression. Second, it must specify whether history's tendency is toward progress, regression, or repetition.[29]

Black labor, or, more precisely, the degree of incorporation and the nature of the production relations in which African Americans work, has been the key variable determining the character of Black racial formations. In what sectors of the political economy are Blacks predominately located? How are Blacks distributed throughout the class structure, and what is the composition of Afro-America's class structure? In what *class fractions* within each class are Blacks mainly found? This is not to negate the importance of questions of political rights, cultural representation, autonomy, and influence but to establish the context in which they operate. As Harold Baron has argued, changes in the dominant mode of production have preceded transformations in racial formations and establish the framework within which new racial formations are consolidated. Because Blacks have had a more tenuous relationship to the primary economy, they experience the positive trends last and the negative trends first, and usually with more severity—hence the aphorism, "When America gets a cold, Blacks get double pneumonia."[30]

Baron claims that the transformation from one racial formation to another resulted from catastrophic events: revolution, depression, or war. The transformation to a new racial formation, however, should not be viewed as spontaneous or the product of a single dramatic event. The transformation to a new racial formation develops over time through several transitional stages that characterize historical moments of one or several decades. Baron does not envision transitional stages within his historical periods. Yet without the conceptualization of transitional stages, a racial formation appears as one long undifferentiated moment. The historical process requires that each period undergo historical development. Each period begins, develops, reaches its apex, undergoes transformation, and is eventually transformed into another historical period.[31]

What causes transitions and transformations to occur in racial formations?

Baron views "the demand for black labor," the degree to which Blacks were in-corporated into the political economy, as the main source of change. His stress on labor inclusion implies much more than rates of employment and unemploy-ment. It suggests specific contradictions between the production relations under which Blacks worked and the production relations in the primary economy. Baron's model delineates the articulation between major technological advances and economic restructuring and transformations in the corresponding racial formation. Nonetheless, his stress on structural factors leaves the significance of African American agency undertheorized. For example, under the pressure of the Great Depression, the New Deal, and World War II, between 1940 and 1960 the federal government and northern industrialists rapidly restructured the southern economy, transforming southern society, shifting it from a rural society with power located in the hands of plantation barons to an urban indus-trial society. The weight of these changes reverberated throughout the South. In 1940, 35 percent of southerners lived in towns and cities, while 23 percent still dwelled on farms. By 1960, 58 percent of southerners resided in urban areas, and farm dwellers had declined to 11 percent. During the 1940s, African American agricultural workers declined by a third, 450,000 people. Simultaneously, a half-million Blacks gained employment in southern manufacturing, and more than 350,000 moved into commerce. The resulting wage increases elevated Blacks' median family income from $489 in 1939 to $3,088 in 1963. Consequently, Black consumers became a critical sector of the economy of large southern cities—15 percent in Houston, 17 percent in Atlanta, and 24 percent in Memphis. Yet al-though southern industrialization, the New Deal, and World War II generated broad socioeconomic changes—freeing significant numbers of Blacks from the domination of the social relations of the plantation economy, producing new political opportunities, and increasing the power of Black civil society to take full advantage of these social changes—Blacks had to galvanize their autono-mous social and cultural capital into a mass movement to end segregation. The central force determining African American historical development has been the U.S. capitalist political economy's "demand for Black labor" in dialectical interaction with the state's racial policies, the academy's and popular culture's representations of Blacks, and the character and robustness of Black agency.[32]

Contemporary Black Racial Formation: The New Nadir

In 1865, Frederick Douglass speculated that emancipation would witness the metamorphosis rather than the end of "slavery." According to Douglass, "Slavery has been fruitful in giving itself names. It has been called the 'peculiar institu-tion,' the 'social system,' and the 'impediment.' It has been called by a great many names, and it will call itself by yet another name; and you and I and all of us had better wait and see what new form this old monster will assume, in what new skin this old snake will come forth next."[33] That "old snake" Douglass spoke of so eloquently has undergone another transformation.

As we enter the twenty-first century, advances by the civil rights and Black Power movements have been nullified, America has retreated from racial justice, racial violence is surging, and old rationalizations of Black inferiority are being rehabilitated even as new ones are being constructed. The combination of economic restructuring and political realignment has plunged African Americans into a *New Nadir*. The fourth Black racial formation, what I am calling the New Nadir, is a consequence of the combination of market forces and the calculated malevolent decision making of right-wing corporate executives and neoliberal politicians in both major political parties. A product of global capitalism, the New Nadir follows its general strategic division into two interrelated constituent parts: economic marginalization and political destabilization.[34]

From the recession of 1979 to the initial years of the new millennium, the African American community has experienced the economic marginalization and political destabilization of its Black working-class majority and since 1992 the economic and political incorporation of its small but expanding bourgeois and petty-bourgeois classes. Economic marginalization and incorporation involve the following five features: deproletarianization and subproletarianization, hypersegregation, a new illiteracy, incorporation of the Black elite, and acceleration of class stratification in Afro-America. Collectively, these economic changes established the foundation for a broader political fragmentation of Black America along class lines.

Contemporary political policies are intertwined with and both mirror and shape current economic strategies toward Afro-America. Since 1980, the state's dominant strategy toward Black politics has included the following five processes and policies: racialized incarceration, resurgence in state terrorism and private racial hate crimes, new disfranchisement, demographic diversification, and political fragmentation. The economic and political strategies of the new Black racial formation are integrated and mutually reinforcing. These structural adjustments, economic and political processes, and policies are united and organized by "color-blind racism," a new rationalization for racial oppression. Color-blind racism denies the salience of racism in U.S. society.

THE NEW NADIR: ECONOMIC MARGINALIZATION AND INCORPORATION

The neoliberal retreat from racial justice in the context of deindustrialization, deproletarianization, and subproletarianization produced a comprehensive economic, political, social, cultural, and ideological restructuring of African Americans' relationship to U.S. society. The Black population has been disproportionately affected by corporate locational decisions and state policies that have excluded large sectors of Blacks from the legitimate workforce. Yet, simultaneously, the state pursued other policies that worked to incorporate a small sector of Afro-America into the U.S. capitalist political economy as entrepreneurs.

African Americans' concentration in the inner cities of Rust Belt states, where the greatest job losses occurred, was a major contributing factor in their marginalization. Between 1966 and 1973, corporations relocated more than two million manufacturing jobs overseas or to the South from the Northeast and Midwest. Corporations' locational decisions affected African Americans in another negative way. According to Betsy Leondar-Wright, communications director for United for a Fair Economy, the movement of jobs from U.S. cities to the suburbs was as dramatic as their relocation from North to South or overseas. Occasionally, corporate executives even admitted their locational decisions were sometimes motivated by a desire to evade Blacks. Even the federal government colluded with this strategy; between 1966 and 1973, federal jobs in inner cities declined by more than 41,000. Consequently, between 1970 and 1993, African Americans lost ground in nearly every economic category. The percentage of unemployed African Americans soared from 5.6 percent in 1970 to 12.9 in 1993. After 1993, Blacks' employment and income appeared to improve as the country recovered from the 1989 recession. For instance, by 1999, African Americans' unemployment fell to a record low of 7 percent. Blacks' median family income rose 20 percent between 1993 and 1997, from $23,927 to $28,602. This trend occurred in the area of poverty as well. In 1997, at 26.5 percent, the percentage of Blacks below the poverty line was the lowest recorded in the thirty-seven years the government had collected poverty data. Overall, during the 1990s, the economic condition of African Americans improved slightly.[35]

If the situation was mixed during the 1990s, by 2001, when "the economy began to shrink," the sharp downward path of African Americans relative to whites was crystal-clear. By 2000, African American unemployment had risen to 8.4 percent from its record low of 7 percent the previous year. Within a year, it had increased sharply to 10.2 percent, twice that of whites. By 2003, Blacks' unemployment rate had grown to 10.8 percent, again double the white rate of 5.2 percent. As of April 2007, the unemployment rate for Blacks had decreased to 8.2 percent, but with whites' at 3.9 percent, the gap between them remained the same. Since the Reagan regime, the Black-white differential has been about a factor of 2.5. Initially, Blacks' poverty level continued to decline, falling to 24.1 percent in 2002, the lowest recorded in forty-two years. Yet with whites' at 8 percent, the disparity between them actually increased. By 2006, both white and Black poverty rates had risen slightly, to 8.2 and 24.3 percent, respectively.[36]

African Americans remain on the "bottom rail," with vast economic disparities between them and whites. Income, the traditional measure of economic well-being, reveals stark inequalities between Blacks and whites. For example, in 2002, Black households' median income was $29,982, Latino/as $33,946, and whites $47,194. By 2005, white households' median income had increased to $52,449, Latino/as to $37,146, and Blacks' to $31,870. After gradually rising from 55 percent that of whites in 1988, in 2000 Blacks' median household income reached a contemporary high at 65 percent that of white households. Yet at 60.7 percent that of whites in 2006, it was lower than the percentage in 1969! This trend continued in per capita income. In 2001, Black per capita income was 57 cents for each dollar of white per capita income. In 2006, whites' per capita income was $30,431, Latino/as' was $15,421, and Blacks' was $17,902. As a percentage of white per capita income, Blacks' had increased slightly to 58.8 percent. Despite these disparities, reliance on income as the dominant measure of financial well-being masks the true gap between the rich and the poor and especially between African Americans and Americans of European descent.[37] Wealth unmasks depths of inequality camouflaged by income.

According to sociologist Lisa A. Keister, "Wealth is measured as net worth, defined as total assets . . . minus total liabilities." Wealth also reveals the inter-generational transfer of assets within families, which is at the crux of the wealth differential between Black and white families. Sociologist Thomas Shapiro contends, "Racial inequality appears intransient because the way families use wealth transmits advantages from generation to generation."[38] By exposing inheritance and other intergenerational transfers, the wealth index calls attention to the past, to previous periods of racial domination and asset accumulation. In doing so, it reminds us that racial inequality is structural.

The wealth gap between Blacks and whites, according to sociologist Dalton Conley, "is wider than the racial gap in any other socioeconomic measure." In 1995, Black households' median net wealth, including home equity, was only $7,400, about 15 percent of the more than $49,000 median wealth of white households. In 2000, African Americans' net wealth rose $100 to $7,500, compared to $9,750 for Latino/as and $79,400 for whites. By 2002, Blacks' and Latino/as' median net wealth had fallen 27 percent, whereas whites' had increased 2 percent. Based on U.S. Census Bureau data, the Pew Hispanic Center reported that in 2002 Blacks' median net wealth had declined to $5,998, compared to $7,932 for Latino/as and $88,651 for whites. Much of the disparity in wealth is tied to the disparity in home ownership. Conley argues, "In contemporary America, race and property are intimately linked and form the nexus for the persistence of black-white inequality." The fact that fewer than half of African Americans own their homes while nearly three-quarters of European Americans do (47.7 percent to 74.3 percent) underscores Conley's point. Moreover, the gap in Black-white home ownership at 28 percent in 2000 was greater than the gap in 1940 at 23 percent! Furthermore, the worth of African American–owned homes average only $80,000, compared to $105,000 for Latino/as and $123,400 for whites.[39]

As Conley alludes, a dialectical link exists between wealth, race, and residence. The new racial formation is characterized by resegregation, as the move toward greater-integrated housing patterns of the 1960s and 1970s have halted and new patterns of residential segregation have asserted themselves. Discussing the transformation to a *new segregation,* David Theo Goldberg identifies three historical eras of residential segregation: "(1) 1880 to the early 1930s, or roughly the post Reconstruction era to the beginning of the New Deal; (2) the 1930s to the late 1960s, or from the New Deal to the end of the Civil Rights Movement; and (3) 1968 to the present," in which, according to him, "whites and blacks tend not only to live, work, school, and die in different neighborhoods but in different cities."[40]

Douglas S. Massey and Nancy A. Denton's concept of *hypersegregation* reflects Goldberg's thesis. Their analysis of 1980 and 1990 census data uncovered sixteen and twenty-nine metropolitan areas, respectively, that met the criteria of their *hypersegregation* index for Blacks and whites. According to them, about 35 percent of Blacks have almost no day-to-day contact with nonblacks, particularly Euro-Americans. In the most extensive analysis of housing data from the 2000 census, Rima Wilkes and John Iceland discovered no change in the number of hypersegregated communities. Summing up progress in housing desegregation, a 2007 report by the National Fair Housing Alliance concluded, "America's metropolitan areas remain far more segregated than they were in 1980." Not surprisingly, there is a 12 percent rise in housing-discrimination complaints filed with the Department of Housing and Urban Development; in fact, the 10,328 complaints filed in 2006 are the highest number since the department began keeping such data in 1990. For African Americans, this racial segregation transcends class. By 1998, 31 percent of African Americans lived in suburbs, yet even after "differences in family size and education" were controlled for, they remained largely segregated. Historian Andrew Wiese contends that "most black suburbanites in the 1990s lived in older inner-rung suburbs, which exhibited a variety of fiscal shortcomings, such as high taxes, mediocre services, low performing schools, commercial disinvestment, and anemic rates of property appreciation."[41]

The contemporary coupling of class, race, and place has further isolated African Americans in inner-city neighborhoods thereby increasing school segregation. Wealth, education, jobs, and almost all other public goods have come to correspond to the new municipal apartheid. Thus, by 2005, resegregation was increasing in the southern and border states that had been under court order to desegregate, and segregation was growing in degree and complexity in the metropolitan areas of the Northeast, Midwest, and West, where desegregation had made little headway, according to Gary Orfield and Chungmei Lee. Since the Supreme Court reauthorized segregated neighborhood schools in 1991, the percentage of Black students in predominately nonwhite schools has increased from 66 to 73 percent. More significantly, the percentage of Black students in "intensely segregated schools," schools with 10 percent or fewer white students, has grown nationally from 34 to 38 percent, and currently is 51 and 46 percent in the Northeast and Midwest, respectively. "Apartheid schools," schools with fewer than 2 percent white students, decreased from 19 to 17 percent, but composed 26 and 23 percent of Black students' schooling in the Midwest and Northeast, respectively. Resegregation of public education threatens the advances African Americans have made in closing the attainment gap over the past forty years.[42]

Since the civil rights and Black Power movements' destruction of the legal structure of the old racial formation, African Americans had rapidly eliminated the educational gap separating them from whites. By 1998, 88 percent of African Americans aged twenty-five to twenty-nine had graduated from high school, and approximately 15 percent had completed at least a bachelor's degree. The latter is almost four times the percentage it was in 1960! Yet by 2006, the percentage of Blacks aged twenty-five to twenty-nine that had graduated from high school had slipped to 85.6 percent, though those completing a bachelor's degree had grown to 19 percent. The gender differences are stark for both high school and college graduates: 87.7 percent of Black women have graduated from high school compared to 83.3 percent for Black men. The gender gap is vastly greater for college graduates, with 22.4 percent of Black women holding a bachelor's degree compared to only 15 percent for Black men. Yet by 2006, Blacks had obtained parity with whites in high school graduation, 85.6 to 86 percent, but trailed in bachelor's degrees, 19 to 28.1 percent.[43]

Just as African Americans were closing the gap in traditional educational attainment, economic restructuring, resegregation, and technological advances conjoined to undermine their educational and socioeconomic advances. Specifically, the revolution in computer technology has made the possession of higher-level mathematics and computer skills necessary for future job acquisition. Although more Blacks are online than the mainstream media report, computer and Internet access has followed established racial-class niches. Suburban schools have a much higher computer-to-student ratio than inner-city schools. Disparities in school-district computer ownership and Internet access mirror home computer ownership, reflecting race, income, and education. In 1999, Thomas P. Novak and Donna L. Hoffman discovered that 44.2 percent of white households had home computers, compared to only 29 percent of African Americans. Six years later, in 2005, Robert Fairlie found that Blacks' computer ownership rates had risen substantially, to 50.6 percent, but because whites' had grown to 74.6, the digital divide had actually increased. Fairlie also discovered that Blacks' Internet access, at 40.5 percent, lagged considerably behind whites' 67.3 percent. Like Novak and Hoffman, Fairlie found that "lower levels of income" accounted for the greatest portion of the difference in home computer ownership and Internet access. The gap between Black and white students' acquisition of higher-level math skills reflects the existing racial-class chasm and also works to accelerate the "digital divide." White high school students take calculus at two and a half times the rate of Black high school students. Consequently, the race- and place-based inequalities in schooling have produced what Black Studies scholar Abdul Alkalimat has called a *new illiteracy*.[44]

Among the most significant transformations of the *New Nadir* have been the incorporation of the new Black political-professional-entrepreneurial elite and the acceleration of class stratification among Blacks. The major paradox of the African American predicament is that the limited political and economic incorporation of Blacks has produced a powerful Black elite, though largely only in relationship to the Black community. Political scientists Robert C. Smith, Stanley Rothman, and Amy E. Black found that African Americans are largely excluded from the highest circles of decision making—the major corporations, executive branch, and the public interest institutions (philanthropic foundations, educational institutions, major law firms, cultural institutions, and so on). Even in politics, Blacks have been only marginally incorporated into the middle (Congress) and bottom rungs (local elected office) of the U.S. state. According to Smith, of the 7,314 decision-making positions within America's elite institutional network, Blacks occupied only 284, or 3 percent. In the realm of electoral politics, the number of Black elected officials has grown from 1,469 in 1970 to 8,015 in 1990, 9,101 in 2001, and 9,500 in 2006. Yet they still only represent 1.5 percent of the 500,000 elected offices in the country! Nonetheless, amazingly, according to Richard L. Zweigenhaft and G. William Domhoff, America's power elite is more racially diverse than ever.[45]

Since the end of the civil rights and Black Power movements, the richest quintile of African Americans has dramatically increased its share of the aggregate income of Black families. Over the same thirty-year period, 1968–1998, the Black middle class's (the fourth quintile) share has remained roughly the same. Meanwhile, the Black working class's and the poor's (the third, second, and lowest quintiles) share of Black families' aggregate income plummeted. A generation ago, in 1968, the poorest fifth of Black families received 5 percent, the wealthiest fifth 42.7 percent, and the top 5 percent 15 percent of the aggregate Black family income. By 1998, the poorest fifth received 3.4 percent, while the richest fifth received 47.6 percent and the top 5 percent of Black families now claimed 17.8 percent of the aggregate share of Black family income. The surging growth of the Black elite, the stagnation in the Black middle class, and the dramatic decline of the working class and poor have drastically exacerbated wealth disparities among Black people. The concentration of African American family income and wealth into the hands of the Black elite reflects a broader problem, the consolidation of power into a smaller percentage of the Black community.[46]

Table 1.2. Share of aggregate income received by each fifth and top 5 percent of Black families: 1968, 1978, 1988, and 1998

Year	Number (thousands)	Lowest fifth	Second fifth	Third fifth	Fourth fifth	Highest fifth	Top 5 percent
1998	12,579	3.1	8.2	14.8	24.4	49.5	19.1
1988	10,561	3.3	7.7	14.6	24.7	49.7	18.7
1978	8,066	4.0	8.7	15.6	25.3	46.4	16.3
1968	5,728	4.0	9.8	16.3	25.1	46.7	15.9

Note: Created from Table F-1B, "Income Limits for Each Fifth and Top 5 Percent of Black Families: 1966 to 1998," http://www.jointcenter.org/DB/table/databank/income/incomei/ilef1/66-98.txt.

Collectively, the combination of de- and subproletarianization of Black workers, hypersegregation, the new illiteracy, incorporation of the Black elite, and increasing class stratification has completely reframed African Americans' economic position in the United States. These transformations have pushed many socioeconomic indicators back to their 1950s and 1960s levels. It is not just in the political economy that African Americans are witnessing a declining presence and power. Blacks are also experiencing a significant decline in their political status.

THE NEW NADIR: POLITICAL DESTABILIZATION, INCORPORATION, AND FRAGMENTATION

The transition to global capitalism initially manifested itself in devastating neoliberal economic and political policies against Afro-America. During the twelve years of Ronald Reagan's and George Bush's presidencies, the federal state attacked African Americans with malignant intent. In addition to pursuing aggressive policies aimed at destabilizing Black political mobilization, the Reagan and Papa Bush regimes also ignored racial assaults, whether in employment, housing discrimination, or savage acts of racial violence. The eight years of Democratic presidential leadership under Bill Clinton reversed some and slowed the pace of other deprivations visited by the Republican demagogues, but Clinton's administration also accelerated others. The selection of George W. Bush in 2000 inaugurated another eight years of economic decline and deterioration of Blacks' political position and social status.[47]

The major political change in Afro-America over the past forty years has been the massive increase in incarceration. Since the early 1970s, the number of persons incarcerated has increased a staggering 500 percent! The brunt of this extraordinary increase has been borne by Blacks. Global capital has deemed the deproletarianized, particularly those in Black and other communities of color, as surplus populations. According to criminologist Richard Quinney, "Criminal justice is the modern means of controlling this surplus population produced by late capitalist development. . . . A way of controlling this unemployed population is simply and directly by confinement in prisons." American drug policy largely accounts for the dramatic rise in U.S. incarceration rates. President Ronald Reagan created the policy architecture underlining contemporary control of the superfluous populations. On September 14, 1986, Reagan declared the "War on Drugs." Six weeks later, on October 27, at his urging, Congress passed the first Anti–Drug Abuse Act, appropriating $1.7 billion. Nearly two years afterward, they enacted a second antidrug act, this time increasing the appropriation by more than a billion dollars, to $2.8 billion. Law enforcement and prison construction received almost all of the monies. Global capitalism's drastic constriction of economic opportunity and social mobility necessitated a new social structure of control; the prison industrial complex emerged as that edifice. Between 1979 and 2000, the number of prisons grew from 592 to 1,023, an increase of nearly 72.8 percent, and state spending on prisons soared from approximately $17 billion to $29 billion between 1990 and 1997.[48]

The "War on Drugs" rationalized racial profiling, targeting of urban areas, "antigang laws," mandatory minimum sentencing, and zero-tolerance legislation, policies that criminalized Black youth and hip-hop culture. Its focus on "crack cocaine," urban neighborhoods, and street dealers rather than suburban and rural drug abusers, importers, and major distributors distorted drug abuse by misrepresenting African Americans' involvement. The effect of this disparity in policy and enforcement served to reverse the ratio of Blacks to whites in prisons. A year before Reagan's Anti-Drug Abuse Act, 16,600 Blacks were in state penitentiaries, compared to 21,200 whites. A decade after its passage, 134,000 Blacks and 86,100 whites were incarcerated in state prisons. By 2002, Blacks constituted 43.7 percent of all prisoners, more than three and a half times their representation in the population. In 2005, Blacks composed 900,000, or 41 percent, of the nation's 2.2 million incarcerated persons. This meant that 2.3 percent of all Blacks were incarcerated, compared to 0.4 percent for whites and 0.7 percent for Latino/as.[49]

At a moment when 8 percent of Black males are incarcerated on any given day, perhaps, contradictorily, the "War on Drugs" has degendered imprisonment. Some have characterized the "War on Drugs" as a "war on Black women." Evidence suggests that this contention has merit. Since the passage of Reagan's antidrug laws in 1986, Black women's incarceration rate has soared 800 percent! Three decades ago, in 1979, only 10 percent of women in prison were incarcerated for drug offenses, whereas in 2007, 38 percent were. In 2004, Black women were incarcerated at four and a half times the rate of white women.[50]

In the era of global capitalism, police brutality and racial hate crimes along with racialized incarceration can be understood as a strategy of racial repression. During the 1990s, police brutality reached epidemic proportions. The brutalization of Abner Louima and the murders of Tynisha Miller, Amadou Diallo, Bobby Russ, and Latanya Haggerty (Chicago) or the more recent killings of Kathryn Johnson (Atlanta) and Sean Bell (New York) remind us that race remains the central factor in the police's use of excessive and deadly force. The Bureau of Justice reported that police used force 3.2 more times against Blacks than whites in 2002. In 172,660 instances, 3.5 percent, police used force against Blacks. This compared to 373,850 cases, or 1.1 percent, of incidents in which police used force against whites. By 2005, the racial gap in the police's use of force had increased to 3.7 times. Police used force in 401,610 instances, or 1.2 percent, against whites and 186,060 occurrences, or 4.4 percent of cases, against Blacks. Blacks composed 39 percent of the 370 persons killed by police in 2006. The extent of state-sanctioned brutality and murder underscores superfluousness of Black life in the United States.[51]

Private racists decoded the state's signals and acted accordingly. Racially motivated violence increased at an alarming rate in the 1990s. During the 1990s, hate crimes surged 58 percent, from 4,558 in 1991 to a high of 8,759 in 1996, and closed the decade with 7,876 incidents. The vast majority of hate crimes in the United States are motivated by racial antipathy. Racially motivated incidents (2,963) composed 62.3 percent of all hate crimes in 1991. And predictably, the vast majority of racially motivated crimes resulted from antiblack racism. The 1,689 antiblack incidents composed 35.5 percent of all hate crimes and 58 percent of racially motivated crimes in 1991. Although the frequency of hate crimes has declined since the enactment of the Hate Crimes Statistics Act of 1990, antiblack offenses as a percentage of all hate crimes have remained remarkably consistent over the fifteen-year period. More important, antiblack incidents as a percentage of racially motivated offenses increased 9 percent, rising from 58 to 67 percent during the period. Finally, in the wake of the Jena Six protests, the lynch noose is rapidly replacing the Klan's burning cross as the preferred racial terrorist symbol.[52]

The increase or intensification of antiblack hate crimes represents the failure of the government to control private racial violence; however, in other areas, such as political representation, the government has not simply retreated from racial justice but rather has accelerated the judicial assault on the gains from the civil rights and Black Power phases of the Black Liberation movement. The *new disfranchisement,* a term first used by Abdul Alkalimat in 1979 to characterize the use of the census undercount to reduce Blacks' voting power, was reconceptualized in 1998 by Winnett Hagens and Ellen Spears. They contrasted its subtle and apparently color-blind techniques with the crude racist policies of the "old" disfranchisement of the Reconstruction and Nadir eras. For them, it described how redistricting and white bloc voting dilute the power of the Black vote and deny African Americans the right to elect candidates and representatives of their choice.[53]

The *new disfranchisement* is the result of conservative white voters' successful challenge to increase majority-minority congressional districts, from 27 to 52, as a result of the 1990s' reapportionment and redistricting process. Correspondingly, the number of Black and Latino/a elected officials reached their highest numbers ever, more than 8,000. Majority-minority legislative districts also increased substantially, as was particularly apparent in the South, where the number of majority-minority congressional districts grew by 17, the number of Blacks elected to state senates rose from 43 to 67, and state representatives increased from 159 to 213.[54]

White voters responded to the growth of Black and brown political power by challenging the constitutionality of majority-minority districts. In *City of Mobile v. Bolden* (1981), *Shaw v. Reno* (1993), and *Miller v. Johnson* (1995), the Supreme Court initiated a process that undermined the Fifteenth Amendment and the Voting Rights Act. By ruling that plaintiffs must prove "discriminatory intent" as well as "discriminatory effect," *Mobile v. Bolden* imposed a difficult, though not impossible, standard of proof. However, in *Shaw* the Supreme Court did not require white conservatives to demonstrate a "discriminatory effect." A majority of the justices accepted the plaintiffs' allegation that "racial gerrymandering" was the "only" explanation for the "bizarre shape" of a North Carolina district. *Miller* extended the attack on majority-minority districts. Here the Court ruled that plaintiffs had to demonstrate only that race was a substantial factor in redistricting. Since the success of *Shaw v. Reno,* white voters have extended their attack to state legislative districts, and the lower courts have joined the attack, dismantling 10 majority-minority districts in seven states. Collectively, these decisions not only restrict the growth of Black and brown political power but also seem aimed at denying African Americans and Latinos their right to self-representation.

Another major aspect of the new Black racial formation is demographic transformation, as the immigration of black people from the Caribbean and Africa is remaking the U.S. black population. Until recently, the percentage of foreign-born blacks remained minuscule. As late as 1960, foreign-born blacks constituted only 1 percent of the U.S. black population. During the mid-1990s, their percentage soared to 7.4 percent; however, by the 2000 census, it had declined to 6.1 percent. Second and as important as increasing numbers are their relations with African Americans and engagement with U.S. racial politics. Most new immigrants come to the United States with traditional immigrant optimism. They also have a poor comprehension of U.S. antiblack racism and generally accept racist stereotypes of African Americans as lazy and violent. Also, many immigrants, especially those from African countries, are middle class, possessing valuable human capital. Describing the typical African immigrant, Sylviane A. Diouf, a historian and researcher at the Schomburg Center for Black History and Culture, comments, "They are better educated, they're here to work, to prosper, they're more compliant and don't pose a threat." Elaborating on Diouf's comments, Howard Dodson, director of the Schomburg Center, states, "They're not politically mobilized as yet and not as closely tied to the African-American agenda." Nonetheless, political scientist Reuel Rogers anticipates racial discrimination radicalizing black immigrants. Linguist Flore Zephir finds supporting evidence for this thesis among second-generation Haitian immigrants.[55]

Though important, ethnic diversification has not been the only factor in political fragmentation. The presence of black conservatives has also increased. At the heart of political fragmentation, however, has been accelerating class stratification. A major consequence of class stratification has been the emergence of a small but significant class of African Americans who reside in predominately white neighborhoods and whose children, if not largely assimilated into mainstream white American civil society, certainly are alienated from Black civil society. Consequently, they have been socialized largely outside of Black civil society, especially beyond the politicalization of the Black counterpublic sphere. It is mainly among these relatively affluent African Americans that right-wing recruitment initiatives have had some success, especially among second-generation suburbanites and religious fundamentalists.

Although conservatism is a long stream in the river of the Black intellectual tradition, the roots of contemporary Black neoconservatives are best traced to the incorporative mechanisms of the Reagan regime. Black neoconservatives articulate better with their white ideological colleagues than any other African American ideological group. Like its white conservative counterpart, Black neoconservative philosophy advocates the rule of the market, decimating public expenditures for social services, deregulation, privatization, and shifting the discourse from the "public good" or "community well-being" to personal responsibility. Black neoconservatives blame the dislocations endemic to poverty on welfare and government subsidies. According to them, the Great Society created dependent personalities and an antiachievement-oriented culture in the Black community. Thus, they contend that the African American poor are afflicted by a "culture of dependency" and practice a politics of victimology. Although conservatives compose a small percentage of the African American population, since the Reagan administration, their Republican patrons have conveyed visibility and prestige upon them far out of proportion to their numbers or influence in the Black community.[56]

Concomitant with economic, social, political, and cultural changes in the system of domination has come a new rationalization of racial oppression, *color-blind racial ideology,* whose advocates claim race (read: racism) has declined and is no longer salient, nor should it be, in U.S. society. Over the past quarter of a century, theorists have attempted to conceptualize the transition to a sophisticated and subtle form of racism. Scholars have termed the new racism variously "advanced racism," "modern racism," and "symbolic racism." Recently, social scientists and journalists have coalesced around the concept of "color-blind racism." According to Helen A. Neville and associates (hereafter referred to as

Neville), color-blindness rejects race consciousness and entails beliefs that race ought to be irrelevant in U.S. social relations. More specifically, in one of the few empirical studies of color-blind racial attitudes, Neville found that persons who hold color-blind racial attitudes deny the existence of white privilege and racial oppression and reject the need for ameliorative social programming. Additionally, she discovered that color-blind racists might acknowledge past discrimination but believe that racism "is not an important problem today." Yet, contradictorily, Neville found that individuals who adopt a "color-blind" perspective believe race-conscious remedial policies such as affirmative action discriminate against whites.[57]

Conclusion

The most pressing task for African American activist intellectuals is to explain racial oppression and the historic and contemporary transformations to new racial formations. To do so requires the development of a theory of racial oppression and the construction of a theory of African American history. Racial Formation and Transformation Theory argues that racial formations are structured by the dialectical relationship between processes of racialization and modes of production. Racial oppression is viewed as a relationship of domination in which labor exploitation has historically been its animating feature. It has also produced corresponding ideological rationalizations and representations. In the contemporary conjuncture, color-blind racial ideology has emerged as the contemporary rationalization of the deproletarianization and subproletarianization attendant to global capitalist restructuring.

The term *racial capitalism* conveys the centrality of racial oppression to the development and maintenance of capitalism in the United States. Racial oppression has been integral to the development of the U.S. social formation since the country's inception as thirteen British colonies. It has also been dynamic, extremely adaptable, and capable of transforming itself into newer racial formations. Each new racial formation took shape in a specific sociohistorical context and constituted a particular racist arrangement of repressive and ideological institutions and individual behavior. It has been undying and constantly changing, shedding its old skin as Douglass said it would and reappearing in ever newer forms: slavery, sharecropping, proletarianization, and labor marginalization.

Racial Formation and Transformation Theory argues that change in African Americans' relationship to the political economy, the state, and civil society has multiple sources. Transitions and transformations in racial formations are the consequence of technological innovations, economic reorganization, and political conflict. Specifically, change results from the dialectical interactions between the dominant U.S. mode of production, the subordinate political economy in which Blacks are located, the structures and ideologies of Black racial oppression, and African American agency. Racial Formation and Transformation Theory also posits that the nature and extent of African Americans' incorporation into the labor force have been the central factors in determining whether their quality of life is improving, static, or regressing. The theory self-consciously repudiates objectivity and offers a metanarrative that facilitates the construction of radical readings of the African American experience that reconstruct the past into arguments for Black liberation and socialist construction.

CHAPTER 1 READING QUESTIONS

1. How does Cha-Jua's approach to Black racial formations and transformations compare with the earlier work of Harold Baron? What changes has Cha-Jua made to Baron's schema, and why has he made them? What are the advantages of Cha-Jua's approach?

2. How does Cha-Jua understand the relationship between racial structures, capitalism, and racial ideologies? How does he see this relationship playing out in each of the four racial formations that he identifies?

3. Reflecting on Cha-Jua's title, "The Changing Same," compare his account of the "New Nadir" that he discusses with the original "Jim Crow" Nadir of the late nineteenth century.

4. As Cha-Jua conceptualizes the New Nadir of the twenty-first century, how does he characterize the relationship between subproletarianization, racialized incarceration, the new disfranchisement, and the incorporation of the Black elite? What does this tell us about the relationship between race and capitalism in our time?

5. In table 1.1, Cha-Jua offers a schematization of the main features of each of his four racial formations and transformations. Due to limitations of space he is unable to fully characterize all the listed features in his discussion. Using the table and the discussion that he does provide, see if you can "fill in the blanks" and come up with your own formulation of the way Black racial formations and transformations have played out in U.S. history.

Notes

1. Scott McLemee, ed., *C. L. R. James on the Negro Question* (Jackson: University Press of Mississippi, 1996), 123–24; Sundiata Keita Cha-Jua, *Sankofa: Racial Formation and Transformation: Toward a Theory of African American History* (Pullman: Washington State University Press, 2000), 1; Darlene Clark Hine, "Paradigms, Politics, and Patriarchy in the Making of a Black History: Reflections on *From Slavery to Freedom*," *Journal of Negro History* 85 (Winter–Spring 2000): 18; Joe W. Trotter Jr., "African-American History: Origins, Development, and Current State of the Field," *OAH Magazine of History* 7, no. 4 (Summer 1993): 18; Cedric Robinson, *Black Marxism: The Making of the Black Radical Tradition* (London: Zed, 1984), 2–3. Because I use *Black* as a synonym for *African American*, that is, as a designator of ethnicity or nationality, I capitalize it. When I use it as a racial designator, I use the lowercase. See Robert S. Wachal, "Capitalization of 'Black' and 'Native American,'" *American Speech* 75, no. 4 (Winter 2000): 364–65.

2. I argue that the new racial formation is the second nadir. On the nadir, see Rayford Logan, *The Betrayal of the Negro: From Rutherford B. Hayes to Woodrow Wilson* (New

York: Collier Books, 1965). On the theory of history, see Alex T. Callinicos, *Making History: Agency, Structure, and Change in Social Theory* (Ithaca: Cornell University Press, 1988). See also Sundiata Keita Cha-Jua and Clarence Lang, "Strategies for Black Liberation in the Era of Globalism: Retronouveau Civil Rights, Militant Black Conservatism, and the Black Radicalism," *Black Scholar* 29, no. 4 (Winter 1999): 25–47; and Sundiata Keita Cha-Jua, "Racial Formation and Transformation: Toward a Theory of Black Racial Oppression," *Souls: A Critical Journal of Black Politics, Culture, and Society* 3 (Winter 2001): 25–60.

3. Oliver Cromwell Cox, *Caste, Class, and Race: A Study in Social Dynamics* (1948; reprint, New York: Modern Reader, 1970); Audrey Smedley, *Race in North America: Origin and Evolution of a Worldview* (Boulder: University Press of Colorado, 1998), 66; Theodore W. Allen, *The Invention of the White Race*, vol. 1, *Racial Oppression and Social Control* (London: Verso, 1994).

4. Ruth Benedict, *Race: Science and Politics* (New York: Viking Press, 1943), 153. Oliver C. Cox delivered a devastating critique of Benedict, Robert Park, Gunnar Myrdal, and the other liberal idealist race theorists. See Cox, *Caste, Class, and Race*, 463–538.

5. E. J. San Juan Jr., *Racism and Cultural Studies: Critiques of Multiculturalist Ideology and the Politics of Difference* (Durham: Duke University Press, 2002), 43; Kwame Ture [Stokely Carmichael] and Charles V. Hamilton, *Black Power: The Politics of Liberation in America* (1967; reprint, New York: Vintage Press, 1992), 4–6; St. Clair Drake, *Black Folk: Here and There* (Berkeley and Los Angeles: University of California Press, 1987), 1:32–38.

6. Political scientist Charles Murray and psychologists Arthur Jensen, William Shockley, Richard Herrnstein, and J. Philippe Rushton continue to view race as indicative of inherent fixed traits, especially intelligence and morality. Rushton argues that Africans are "borderline retarded"! Their counterparts in the Afrocentric community argue that greater levels of melanin make African-descended people superior to other humans. Psychiatrist Frances Cress Welsing is representative of this perspective. She attributes George Washington Carver's success as a scientist to melanin, which she claims "enabled him to communicate with energy frequencies from plants" (*The Isis Papers: The Keys to the Colors* [Chicago: Third World Press, 1991], 233). Arthur Jensen's, William Shockley's, and Richard Herrnstein's views can be found in N. J. Block and Gerald Dworkin, *The IQ Controversy* (New York: Random House, 1976); and Richard Herrnstein and Charles Murray, *The Bell Curve: Intelligence and Class Structure in American Life* (New York: Free Press, 1996). Rushton's comments are reported in Peter Novobatzy, "Bigots in Jackets and Ties: The 2000 American Renaissance Conference," *Journal of Blacks in Higher Education* 28 (Summer 2000): 117–21, 129.

7. For a discussion of the importance of distinguishing between race and racial oppression, see Satyananda Gabriel, "The Continuing Significance of Race: An Overdeterminist Approach to Racism," *Rethinking Marxism* 3 (Fall–Winter 1990): 66–67.

8. William Julius Wilson, *The Declining Significance of Race: Blacks and Changing American Institutions* (Chicago: University of Chicago Press, 1978), 1, 17–18; Donald J. Harris, "Economic Growth, Structural Change, and the Relative Income Status of Blacks in the U.S. Economy, 1947–78," *Review of Black Political Economy* 12, no. 3

(1983): 91; Martin Bulmer and John Solomos, "Introduction: Re-thinking Ethnic and Racial Studies," *Ethnic and Racial Studies* 21 (September 1998): 819, 825; Charles Mills, *Blackness Visible* (Ithaca: Cornell University Press, 1998), 67–68; Eduardo Bonilla-Silva, "Re-thinking Racism: Toward a Structural Interpretation," *American Sociological Review* 62 (June 1996): 465 and *White Supremacy and Racism in the Post–Civil Rights Era* (Boulder: University Press of Colorado, 2001), 19n54; David Theo Goldberg, "The Social Formation of Racist Discourse," in *Anatomy of Racism* (Minneapolis: University of Minneapolis Press, 1990), 295.

9. Amiri Baraka coined the term *changing same* to describe the continuities and discontinuities in Black music, specifically rhythm and blues music (William J. Harris, *The Leroi Jones/Amiri Baraka Reader* [New York: Thunder's Mouth Press, 1991], 186).

10. Ture and Hamilton, *Black Power*, 4–6.

11. Harold Baron, "Racism Transformed: The Implications of the 1960s," *Review of Radical Political Economics* 17 (Fall 1985): 11, 12–14.

12. Thomas Holt, "African-American History," in *The New American History*, edited by Eric Foner (Philadelphia: Temple University Press, 1990), 212; Baron, "Racism Transformed," 11. A few scholars have proposed models different from the standard three-period framework. Abdul Alkalimat's periodization stresses the transformation between four periods of social cohesion (Traditional Africa, Slavery, Rural Life, and Urban Life) and four periods of social disruption (Slave Trade, Emancipation, Migration, and Crisis) (see Alkalimat and associates, *Introduction to Afro-American Studies: A Peoples College Primer* [Chicago: Twenty-first Century Books, 1987], 24–27). Loic Waquant's schema involves four "peculiar institutions: Chattel Slavery, Jim Crow, the Ghetto, and the contemporary Hyperghetto and Prison ("From Slavery to Mass Incarceration: Rethinking the Race Question in the U.S.," *New Left Review* 13 [January–February 2002]: 41–60). David Wilson's is an elaboration of Waquant's by adding a fifth peculiar institution, what he calls the "Local Ghetto" (*Cities and Race: America's New Black Ghetto* [London: Routledge, 2007], 12–18). Intriguingly, Thomas D. Boston moves in the opposite direction of these theorists, proposing a two-period model, "Slavery" and "Free Labor" (*Race, Class, and Conservatism* [London: Routledge Press, 1988], 22–53). For earlier periodization schemas, see Joe F. Feagin, "Slavery Unwilling to Die: The Background of Black Oppression in the 1980s," *Journal of Black Studies* 17 (December 1986): 173–200; Sidney Willhelm, "The Economic Demise of Blacks in America: A Prelude to Genocide?" *Journal of Black Studies* 17 (December 1986): 201–54; W. J. Wilson, *Declining Significance of Race*, 2–3; Lloyd Hogan, *Principles of Black Political Economy* (Boston: Routledge 1984); and Robert L. Harris, *A Framework for African American History* (Washington, D.C.: American Historical Society, 1990).

13. Baron, "Racism Transformed," 14; David Gordon, Richard Edwards, and Michael Reich, *Segmented Work, Divided Workers: The Historical Transformation of Labor in the United States* (New York: Cambridge University Press, 1982). I characterize my second period as the "Plantation Economy," a term I borrow from Jay Mandle, though I use it differently. Mandle views Slavery and Sharecropping as specific moments within the broader Plantation Economy period. For me, it characterizes the production and social relations of tenancy. See Mandle, *The Roots of Black Poverty: The Southern Plantation*

Economy after the Civil War (Durham: Duke University Press, 1978) and *Not Slave, Not Free: The African American Economic Experience since the Civil War* (Durham: Duke University Press, 1992).

14. Alex T. Callinicos, *Theories and Narratives: Reflections on the Philosophy of History* (Durham: Duke University Press, 1995), 98; Callinicos, *Making History,* 94–95.

15. Albert Mosley, "Are Racial Categories Racist?" *Research in African Literatures* 28 (Winter 1997): 105; Smedley, *Race in North America,* xi.

16. Ruth Benedict and Gene Weltfish, *The Races of Mankind* (Washington, D.C.: Public Affairs Committee, 1943), 5; Benedict Anderson, *Imagined Communities* (London: Verso, 1983), 3. Benedict believed race was a scientific fact but that racial differences were located in "nonessential" physical attributes. See also Lucious Outlaw, "Toward a Critical Theory of 'Race,'" in *Anatomy of Racism,* edited by Goldberg, 68; Harry Chang, "Toward a Marxist Theory of Racial Oppression: Two Essays by Harry Chang," edited by Paul Liem and Eric Montague, *Review of Radical Political Economics* 17, no. 3 (Fall 1985), 38; Mosley, "Are Racial Categories Racist?" 105; and Vilna Bashi, "Racial Categories Matter Because Racial Hierarchies Matter: A Commentary," *Ethnic and Racial Studies* 21 (September 1998): 959–68.

17. Recognizing that Europeans' negative attitude toward the dark or blackness in general and disparaging aesthetic assessment of sub-Saharan Africans' physical features in particular were combined into what became a doctrine of white racism, Drake nonetheless argues the importance of disentangling these two aspects (*Black Folk,* 13–14). See also T. H. Breen, "A Changing Labor Force in Virginia, 1660–1700," *Journal of Social History* 7 (Fall 1973): 3–25; Allen, *Invention of the White Race,* 1:28; Edmund Morgan, *American Freedom/American Slavery: The Ordeal of Colonial Virginia* (New York: W. W. Norton, 1975), 295–454; and Nicholas Hudson, "From 'Nation' to 'Race': The Origin of Racial Classification in Eighteenth-Century Thought," *Eighteenth Century Studies* 29, no. 3 (1996): 258.

18. Emmanuel Chukwudi Eze, ed., *Race and the Enlightenment: A Reader* (Cambridge, Mass.: Wiley-Blackwell, 1997), 3.

19. John Hope Franklin, *From Slavery to Freedom,* 8th ed. (New York: Alfred A. Knopf, 2000), 102, 72, 90; Stephen Middleton, *The Black Laws: Race and the Legal Process in Early Ohio* (Athens: Ohio University Press, 2005); Eric Foner, "Blacks and the U.S. Constitution, 1789–1989," *New Left Review* 183 (1990): 65–66.

20. Louis Althusser, "State Ideological and Repressive Apparatuses," in *Lenin and Philosophy, and Other Essays* (New York: Monthly Review Press, 1972), 127–86.

21. Thomas M. Shapiro, *The Hidden Cost of Being African American: How Wealth Perpetuates Inequality* (New York: Oxford University Press, 2004); George Lipsitz, "Law and Order: Civil Rights Laws and White Privilege," in *The Possessive Investment in Whiteness: How White People Profit from Identity Politics* (Philadelphia: Temple University Press, 1998), 24–46; Donald G. Nieman, *Promises to Keep: African-Americans and the Constitutional Order, 1776 to the Present* (New York: Oxford University Press, 1991); Richard Delgado and Jean Stefancic, "Cultural Imagery," in *Race and Races: Cases and Resources for a Diverse America,* edited by Juan Perea, Richard Delgado, Angela P. Harris, and Stephanie Wildman (St. Paul: West Group, 2000), 959–74.

22. W. E. B. Du Bois, *Black Reconstruction in the United States, 1860–1880* (1935; reprint, New York, 1977), 700–701; D. R. Williams, Y. Yu, J. S. Jackson, and N. Anderson, "Racial Differences in Physical and Mental Health," *Journal of Health Psychology* 2 (1997): 335–51; Robert M. Sellers, Cleopatra H. Caldwell, Karen H. Schmeelk-Cone, and Marc A. Zimmerman, "Racial Identity, Racial Discrimination, Perceived Stress, and Psychological Distress among African American Young Adults," *Journal of Health and Social Behavior* 44, no. 3, special issue, *Race, Ethnicity, and Mental Health* (September 2003): 302–17; Deidre Franklin-Jackson and Robert T. Carter, "The Relationships between Race-Related Stress, Racial Identity, and Mental Health for Black Americans," *Journal of Black Psychology* 33, no. 1 (February 2007): 5–26.

23. John Ashworth finds the term *petty-commodity production* problematic because these independent farmers were only marginally involved in commodity production. But he agrees with Charles Post's description of the three modes of production that existed in early America. See Ashworth, *Slavery, Capitalism, and Politics in Antebellum Republic,* vol. 1, *Commerce and Compromise, 1820–1850* (Cambridge: Cambridge University Press, 1995), 83n5; and Post, "The American Road to Capitalism," *New Left Review* 133 (May–June 1982): 44.

24. Charles Post, "The 'Agricultural Revolution' in the United States: The Development of Capitalism and the Adoption of the Reaper in the Antebellum U.S. North," *Science and Society* 61 (Summer 1997): 216–28; Post, "American Road," 34–39; Clarence J. Munford, *Production Relations, Class, and Black Liberation: A Marxist Perspective in Afro-American Studies* (Berlin: Gruner, 1978), 32. See also Sue E. Headlee, *The Political Economy of the Family Farm: The Agrarian Roots of American Capitalism* (Westport, Conn.: Praeger. 1991); and Allan Kulikoff, *The Agrarian Origins of American Capitalism* (Charlottesville: University Press of Virginia, 1992).

25. Callinicos, *Theories and Narratives,* 100–101.

26. C. L. R. James, "Stalinism and Negro History," in *C. L. R. James and Revolutionary Marxism: Selected Writing of C. L. R. James, 1939–1949,* edited by Scott McLemee and Paul LeBlanc (Atlantic Highlands, N.J.: Humanities International Press, 1994), 190.

27. Post, "American Road," 34–37; Post, "'Agricultural Revolution,'" 216–28.

28. Susan A. Mann, "Sharecropping in the Cotton South: A Case of Uneven Development in Agriculture," *Rural Sociology* 49 (Fall 1984): 414. See also Evelyn Nakano Glenn, "From Servitude to Service Work: Historical Continuities in the Racial Division of Paid Reproductive Labor," *Signs* 18 (Autumn 1992): 1–41; Sharon Harley, "When Your Work Is Not Who You Are: The Development of a Working-Class Consciousness among Afro-American Women," in *We Specialize in the Wholly Impossible: A Reader in Black Women's History,* edited by Darlene Clark Hine, Wilma King, and Linda Reed (New York: New York University Press, 1995), 25–37; Tera W. Hunter, *To Joy My Freedom* (Cambridge: Harvard University Press, 1997); Elizabeth Clark-Lewis and Deborah Baker, eds., *Living in, Living Out: African American Domestics and the Great Migration* (New York: Kodansha International, 1996); and Stephanie J. Shaw, *What a Woman Ought to Be and to Do: Black Professional Women Workers during the Jim Crow Era* (Chicago: University of Chicago Press, 1996).

29. Callinicos, *Theories and Narratives,* 102–4.

44 · SUNDIATA KEITA CHA-JUA

30. Baron, "Racism Transformed," 15.

31. Daniel Scott Smith, "Recent Change and Periodization of American Family History," *Journal of Family History* 20, no. 4 (1995): 342; Cha-Jua, *Sankofa*.

32. Harold Baron, *The Demand for Black Labor: Historical Notes on the Political Economy of Racism* (Somerville, Mass.: New England Free Press, 1971); Baron, "Racism Transformed," 12–14; Jack M. Bloom, *Class, Race, and the Civil Rights Movement* (Bloomington: Indiana University Press, 1987), 60.

33. Speech by Frederick Douglass, May 9, 1865, in Lerone Bennett, *The Shaping of Black America* (Chicago: Johnson Publishing, 1983), 207.

34. Logan, *Betrayal of the Negro;* Bruno Amoroso, *On Globalization: Capitalism in the 21st Century* (New York: Palgrave Macmillan, 1998), 3.

35. Betsy Leonard-Wright, "Black Job Loss De'Javu," *Dollars and Sense* (May–June 2004): http://www.dollarsandsense.org/archives/2004/0504leondar.html; Victor Perlo, *Economic of Racism, II: The Roots of Inequality, USA* (New York: International Publishers, 1996), 27, 82; Joint Center for Political Studies, http://www.jointcenter.org/databank/factssht/famincm.html; U.S. Bureau of the Census, http://www.census.gov/Press-Release/cb98-127.html; http://www.census.gov/Press-Release/cb95-219.html; http://www.census.gov/Press-Release/cb98-176.html.

36. Geralda Miller, "Minorities behind in Economic Boom," Associated Press (AP-NY-02-22-01 1525EST); Deborah Kong, "Recession Toughest for Minorities" (AP-NY-01-09-02 0251EST); Leonard-Wright, "Black Job Loss"; U.S. Census Bureau, table 16, "Poverty Status of the Population by Sex, Age, Race, and Hispanic Origin," March 2002, Current Population Survey, Racial Statistics Branch, Population Division, Internet release date April 25, 2003; Dedrick Muhammad, Attieno Davis, Meizhu Lui, and Betsy Leonard-Wright, *The State of the Dream, 2004: Enduring Disparities* (Boston: United for a Fair Economy, 2004), 1, 10; Carmen DeNavas-Walt, Bernadette D. Proctor, and Jessica Smith, *Income, Poverty, and Health Insurance Coverage in the United States, 2006* (Washington, D.C.: U.S. Government Printing Office, 2006), 12, table 3.

37. U.S. Census Bureau, *Income of Households by Race and Hispanic Origin Using 2- and 3-Year Averages, 2000–2002* (2002) (median income and confidence intervals in 2002 dollars), http://www.census.gov/hhes/www/income/income02/3yr_avg_race.html; *New Report: State of the Dream, 2005: Under Bush, People of Color Slide Further from King's Dream,* press release from United for a Fair Economy, January 10, 2005, http://www.faireconomy.org/press/2005/StateoftheDream2005pr.html; Victor Perlo, "Deterioration of Black Economic Conditions in the 1980s," *Review of Radical Political Economics* 20, no. 2 (1992): 55–60; DeNavas-Walt, Proctor, and Smith, *Income, Poverty, and Health Insurance Coverage,* 6, table 1.

38. Shapiro, *Hidden Cost of Being African American,* 131.

39. Dalton Conley, "The Racial Wealth Gap: Origins and Implications for Philanthropy in the African American Community," *Nonprofit and Voluntary Sector Quarterly* 29, no. 4 (December 2000): 530; Shawna Orzechowski and Peter Sepielli, *Net Worth and Asset Ownership of Households* (Washington, D.C.: U.S. Bureau of the Census, May 2003), 13, fig. 6; "African Americans Have Less Wealth and More Debt than White Americans," United for a Fair Economy, http://www.faireconomy.org; Pew Hispanic Center, "Wealth

Gap Widens between Whites and Hispanics," October 18, 2004, http://pewhispanic.org/newsroom/releases/release.php?ReleaseID=15; Dalton Conley, *Being Black, Living in the Red: Race, Wealth, and Social Policy in America* (Berkeley and Los Angeles: University of California Press, 1999), 5; Meizhu Lui, "Doubly Divided: The Racial Wealth Gap," http://www.racialwealthdivide.org/documents/doublydivided.pdf, 42; and William J. Collins and Robert A. Margo, "Race and Homeownership: A Century-Long View," *Explorations in Economic History* 38, no. 1 (2001): 68–92.

40. Ronald Smothers, "Housing Segregation: New Twists and Old Results," *New York Times,* September 25, 2007, 1; David Theo Goldberg, "The New Segregation," *Race and Society* 1, no. 1 (1998): 16.

41. Douglas S. Massey and Nancy A. Denton, *American Apartheid: Segregation and the Making of the Underclass* (Cambridge: Harvard University Press, 1993), 77–78; Rima Wilkes and John Iceland, "Hypersegregation in the Twenty-first Century," *Demography* 41 (February 2004): 23–36; National Fair Housing Alliance, "The Crisis of Housing Segregation, 2007: Fair Housing Trends Report," April 30, 2007, http://www.national fairhousing.org/resources/newsArchive/2007%20Fair%20Housing%20Trends%20 Report.pdf, 40; *Race Relations Reporter Weekly Bulletin* (New York), October 10, 2007, 1; Andrew Wiese, *Places of Their Own: African American Suburbanization in the Twentieth Century* (Chicago: University of Chicago Press, 2004), 258.

42. Gary Orfield and Chungmei Lee, *Racial Transformation and the Changing Nature of Segregation* (Cambridge: Harvard University Press, 2006), 2, 9, 10.

43. U.S. Bureau of the Census, "Percent of High School and College Graduates of the Population 15 Years and Older, by Age, Sex, Race, and Hispanic Origin," 2006, detailed table, 1a; U.S. Bureau of the Census, http://www.census.gov/Press-Release/cb98-221 .html.

44. Thomas P. Novak and Donna L. Hoffman, "Bridging the Digital Divide: The Impact of Race on Computer and Internet Use," http://www2000.ogsm.vanderbilt.edu; Robert Fairlie, "Are We Really a Nation Online? Ethnic and Racial Disparities in Access to Technology and Their Consequences," report for the Leadership Conference on Civil Rights Education Fund (2005), 2; Abdul Alkalimat and Kate Williams, "Social Capital and Cyberpower in the African American Community: A Case Study of a Community Technology Center in the Dual City," in *Community Informatics: Community Development through the Use of Information and Communications Technologies,* edited by Leigh Keeble and Brian Loader (London: Routledge, 2001), 1. See also Gerald Mc-Worter [Abdul Alkalimat], "Racism and the Numbers Game: A Critique of the Census Enumeration of Black People and a Proposal for Action," in *Black People and the 1980 Census,* edited by Ronald Bailey (Chicago: Peoples College Press, 1979), 143, 143–47, 85–155; and Malik Miah, "Digital Divide and Racial Capitalism: A High-Tech Colorblind Economy?" *Against the Current* 84 (January–February 2000): 14–16.

45. Robert C. Smith, *We Have No Leaders: African Americans in the Post–Civil Rights Era* (Albany: SUNY Press, 1996), 127–37; Stanley Rothman and Amy E. Black, "Who Rules Now? American Elites in the 1990s," *Society* 35, no. 6 (September–October 1998): 17–21; David Bositis, *Black Elected Officials: A Statistical Summary, 2001* (Washington, D.C.: Joint Center for Political and Economic Studies, 2001), 5, and "Political Report: Few

Gains Likely among Black Legislators," *Focus* (March 2002): 5; Ralph Everett, "Number of Black Elected Officials Increases, but Not by Much," *Joint Center Journal* (Washington, D.C.) (October 16, 2007), http://jointcenterjournal.squarespace.com/; Richard L. Zweigenhaft and G. William Domhoff, *Diversity in the Power Elite: Women and Minorities in the Higher Circle* (New Haven: Yale University Press, 1998) and *Blacks in the White Establishment: A Study of Race and Class in America* (New Haven: Yale University Press, 1991).

46. In 1998, 23 percent of African American women and 17 percent of African American men were employed in the traditional professions or in the new managerial and technical class. Between 1987 and 1992, African American–owned businesses increased from 424,165 to 620,912, or 46 percent. And their revenue jumped 63 percent, from $19.8 billion to $32.2 billion. See http://www.jointcenter.org/databank/databank/income.html. See also Salim Muwakkil, "So Goes the Movement," *In These Times* (September 6, 1998): 17–18.

47. Cha-Jua and Lang, "Strategies for Liberation," 36–37.

48. Richard Quinney, *Class, State, and Crime: On the Theory and Practice of Criminal Justice* (New York: Longman Publishing Group, 1977), 131–37; Doris Marie Provine, *Unequal under the Law: Race in the War on Drugs* (Chicago: University of Chicago Press, 2007), 15–36.

49. Kim Strosnider, "Anti-gang Ordinances after *City of Chicago v. Morales:* The Intersection of Race, Vagueness Doctrine, and Equal Protection in the Criminal Law," *American Criminal Law Review* 39 (Winter 2002): 101–47; Eric Schlosser, "The Prison-Industrial Complex," *Atlantic Monthly,* August 1998, 51–77; Timothy Egan, "The War on Crack Retreats, Still Taking Prisoners," *New York Times,* February 28, 1999, 20–21; Human Rights Watch, "Race and Incarceration in the United States," February 27, 2002, http://www.hrw.org/legacy/backgrounder/USA/race, tables 2a, 3, 4; Marc Mauer and Ryan S. King, *Uneven Justice: State Rates of Incarceration by Race and Ethnicity* (Washington, D.C.: Sentencing Project, July 2007), 1, 4.

50. American Civil Liberties Union, "Women in Prison: An Overview," http://www.aclu.org/womensrights/violence/25829res20060612.html; Helen A. Neville and Jennifer Hamer, "'We Make Freedom': An Exploration of Revolutionary Black Feminism," *Journal of Black Studies* 31 (March 2001): 448, 437–61; S. R. Bush-Baskette, "The War on Drugs as a War against Black Women," in *Crime and Women: Feminist Implication of Criminal Justice Policy,* edited by S. I. Miller (Thousand Oaks, Calif.: Sage Publications, 1998), 113–29; Human Rights Watch, "Race and Incarceration," table 2b.

51. Matthew R. Durose, Erica L. Smith, and Patrick A. Langan, *Contacts between Police and the Public, 2005* (Washington, D.C.: U.S. Department of Justice, April 2007), 8, table 9; Human Rights Watch, "Shielded from Justice: Police Brutality and Accountability in the United States," http://www.hrw.org/reports98/police/uspo17.htm; "Black America in Uproar over Police Brutality," *Jet,* June 28, 1999; Dan Berry, "Officer Charged in Man's Torture at Station House," *New York Times,* August 14, 1997, A1; Lori Leibovich, "The Mysterious Death of Tyisha Miller," February 8, 1999, http://dir.salon.com/story/news/feature/1999/02/08/cou_08news; "Law Enforcement: Rev. Al Sharpton Calls for Congressional Hearings into Police Killings of Civilians," *Drug War Chronicles* 464 (December

8, 2006), http://stopthedrugwar.org/chronicle/464/reverend_al_sharpton_calls_for_congressional_hearings_on_police_killings; Kit R. Roane, "3 of the Officers Were Involved in Shootings in the Last 2 Years," *New York Times,* February 5, 1999; Robert D. McFadden, "Police Kill Man after a Queens Bachelor Party," *New York Times,* November 26, 2006, http://www.nytimes.com/2006/11/26/nyregion/26cops.html; Jeffry Scott and S. A. Reid, "Woman, 92, Fatally Shot as 3 Atlanta Officers Wounded," *Atlanta Journal-Constitution,* November 21, 2006, A1.

52. Corrine Yu, *Cause for Concern: Hate Crimes in America, 2004 Update* (Washington, D.C.: Leadership Conference on Civil Rights Education Fund, August 2004), appendix B, C, http://www.civilrights.org/publications/reports/cause_for_concern_2004/cause_for_concern.pdf; U.S. Department of Justice, "Hate Crime: Statistics, 2005," table 1, http://www.fbi.gov/ucr/hc2005/; U.S. Department of Justice, "Hate Crime: Statistics, 2004," table 1, http://www.fbi.gov/ucr/hc2004/; Darryl Fears, "In Jena and beyond, Nooses Return as a Symbol of Hate," *Washington Post,* October 20, 2007.

53. Winnett Hagens and Ellen Spears, "The 'New' Disfranchisement," *Southern Changes* 20, no. 3 (1998): 3–4.

54. "Race, Voting, and Participation in Democracy," in *Race and Races,* edited by Perea et al., 590–614; Delia Grigg and Jonathan N. Katz, "The Impact of Majority-Minority Districts on Congressional Elections," paper presented at the Midwest Political Science Association, Chicago, April 4, 2005.

55. Jesse D. McKinnon and Claudette E. Bennett, *We the People: Blacks in the United States,* Census 2000 Special Report (Washington, D.C.: U.S. Bureau of the Census, 2005), 7, fig. 5; Sam Roberts, "More Africans Enter U.S. than in Days of Slavery," *New York Times,* February 21, 2005, A1, A18; Reuel Rodgers, "Afro-Caribbean Immigrants, African Americans, and the Politics of Group Identity," in *Black and Multiracial Politics in America,* edited by Yvette M. Alex-Assensoh and Lawrence J. Hanks (New York: New York University Press, 2000), 42; Flore Zephir, *Haitian Immigrants in Black America: A Sociological and Sociolinguistic Portrait* (Westport, Conn.: Bergin and Garvey, 1996), 44.

56. Angela Dillard, *Guess Who's Coming to Dinner Now? Multicultural Conservatism in America* (New York: New York University Press, 2001); Leon Newton, "The Role of Black Neo-Conservatives during President Ronald Reagan's Administration," *White House Studies* 6, no. 1 (Winter 2006): 3–14; Seth N. Asumah and Valencia C. Perkins, "Black Conservatism and the Social Problems in Black America: Ideological Cul-de-sacs," *Journal of Black Studies* 31, no. 1 (September 2000): 51–73.

57. Helen A. Neville and associates conducted five empirical studies on the Color-Blind Racial Attitudes Scale (CoBRAS) involving 1,143 subjects (Helen A. Neville, Roderick L. Lilly, Richard M. Lee, Georgia Duran, and LaVonne Browne, "Construction and Initial Validation of the Color-Blind Racial Attitudes Scale (CoBRAS)," *Journal of Counseling Psychology* 47, no. 1 [2000]: 68; Baron, "Racism Transformed," 11). See also Ellis Cose, *Color-Blind Racism: Seeing beyond Race in a Race-Obsessed World* (New York: Harper Collins, 1997); D. R. Williams et al., "Racial Differences," 335–51; D. R. Kinder and David O. Sears, "Prejudice and Politics: Symbolic Racism versus Racial Threats to the Good Life," *Journal of Personality and Social Psychology* 40 (1981): 414–31.

2

Capitalism, Race, and Evolution in Imperial Britain, 1850–1900

THEODORE KODITSCHEK

There are certain moments in the development of modern capitalist society when racial ideologies precipitously change. One such moment came in the 1950s and 1960s, when movements for civil rights and decolonization broke down prevailing norms of racial inequality and segregation and replaced them with the ostensible color-blindness of today. Another such moment came a century earlier, with the creation of that system of racial segregation and formal inequality that the movements of the 1950s and '60s dethroned.

Before 1850, much white European public discourse on the subject of race had been shot through with tones of paternalistic condescension: People of color were depicted as backward but innocent children of Adam who stood in need of protection and instruction from their more advanced, lighter-skinned siblings. Allegedly stronger, smarter, and more culturally developed, these white people were morally enjoined to assist their less fortunate brethren. Armed with the blessings of Christianity and the lessons of civilization, the white man would reform and improve his darker brother, preparing him for the competitive conditions of the modern market age.[1] During the decades after 1850, however, the tenor of white racial discourse rapidly changed. The colored innocent was refigured as a dangerous savage. As sympathy evaporated, and the discourse hardened, the older spirit of philanthropic patronage was replaced by a new language of denunciation and vituperation, which denied any kinship or sense of obligation between black and white. The races were classified in different categories, separate and unequal, which had to be more or less indefinitely maintained.[2]

How is this great watershed in racial ideologies to be explained? Most explanations stress the ascendancy of "scientific racism" during the second half of the nineteenth century—a new and harsher doctrine of biological reductionism and genetic determinism, often associated with "social Darwinism" or other theories of evolutionary struggle.[3] This explanation is inadequate, for the term *scientific racism* takes for granted precisely that which it purports to explain— the appearance of hateful and disparaging ideas about people of color. My own starting point is the contrary presumption that fundamental shifts in ideas are not sui generis but must be explained with reference to the fundamental processes of societal change.

Racial Change and Structural Change: The Problem of Imperial Britain

In this chapter, I will show how the new racial ideologies of the second half of the nineteenth century had their roots in changes in the reorganization of British capitalism, and in the restructuring of the British Empire. I argue that the new racial ideas were devised as ways of managing these structural changes and legitimating them in naturalistic terms. Although this project did draw opportunistically on the new evolutionary theories of the Victorian era, it is misleading to attribute changes in racial thinking to this scientific (or pseudo-scientific) work.

Thus, like Sundiata Keita Cha-Jua's opening chapter, my starting point is the premise that one must begin by interrogating the shape and dynamics of racial structures before racial ideologies and racial struggles can be explained. Yet the racial structures explored by Cha-Jua's analysis are limited to the history of the United States. He shows how American racial structures changed in tandem with American capitalism. But American capitalism constituted only one corner of world capitalism in the nineteenth century. How might racial structures, ideologies, and struggles look from this broader vantage point?

I would argue that one way to apprehend this larger context might be to shift our focus from the United States to the British Empire. As everyone knows, the United States began its life as a part of the British Empire. Indeed, the plantation economy, which is at the center of Cha-Jua's analysis, was originally designed as one component of a larger mercantilist system. In this system, such peripheral regions would produce and export raw materials in return for British manufactured goods.[4] After 1776, when the plantation South switched allegiance from Britain to the new American Republic, the old mercantilist empire was dealt a fatal blow. The center of gravity of the entire slave system shifted from mercantilist Britain to this vaunted, experimental "land of liberty."[5] Yet the demise of mercantilism and the loss of the thirteen colonies did not destroy the British Empire. Over the next century and a quarter, a second "postemancipation" and "free-trading" British Empire arose in its place. By 1849, Britain stood again at the center of a new international capitalist system that was even more far-reaching and effectively integrated than the one it replaced.[6]

In this chapter, I will argue that it is only by examining the creation and transformation of this new global industrial capitalist system—sustained by Britain's "second" empire of free trade—that we can understand the watershed in race ideologies and race relations that occurred during the second half of the nineteenth century.[7] Cha-Jua's American story of slave emancipation and reconstitution of the plantation economy is, indeed, a part of this story. But it is only one strand in a larger picture of global capitalist organization and reorganization in which social relations were everywhere becoming far more multifarious and complex. Seen in this context, the abolition of slavery was a considerably more protracted affair. In the British Empire, the trajectory of development was profoundly influenced by the fact that emancipation came relatively early, and was physically separated from the decision-making imperial center.[8]

During the 1850s and 1860s, while the United States was swept by sectional crisis and Civil War, British elites seemed, superficially, untroubled and secure. Following Cha-Jua's materialist argument, it is easy to see why race relations became so contested in the bellum and postbellum United States. But why did so many British elites turn in the same direction as their American kindred? It is difficult to understand why British opinion makers were so quick to give up their philanthropic racial liberalism and fall prey to vituperative hostility toward the "lesser breeds." No wonder so many historians have turned to the realm of ideology to explain this striking volte face.[9] We should, however, resist this temptation to acquiesce in assumptions about the autonomy of ideology, and seek the deeper structural forces that almost always undergird major intellectual change. This does not mean that ideas are unimportant. It does mean that they must be restored to their original social context and understood as dynamic discursive practices—strategies consciously or unconsciously deployed by structurally constrained actors who were seeking simultaneously both to reflect and to transform their existing world.

In Cha-Jua's nineteenth-century America, these structural constraints were obvious. In nineteenth-century Britain, they seem initially more amorphous and obscure. However, if we view the empire as a whole, this obscurity diminishes. As in the United States (albeit more slowly and less dramatically), the replacement of slavery with other postmercantilist forms of labor management and colonial social organization necessitated the search for new conceptual frameworks of control. Some new principle had to be devised so as to classify imperial Britain's diverse inhabitants, to integrate them into wage labor, and to justify their position in the imperial hierarchy. During the decades after 1850, the category of "race" emerged to play these roles.[10]

Industrial Capitalism and the Second British Empire

In 1850, the British Empire encompassed approximately 350,000,000 inhabitants and 6,539,685 square miles, not including the 20,817,000 who lived in the home isle. This empire was an odd assortment of miscellaneous dependencies that had been acquired at various times during the previous three hundred years: Ireland (sixteenth century), the West Indies (seventeenth century), Canada, India, West Africa (eighteenth century), Australia, New Zealand, South Africa, Burma, Hong Kong (nineteenth century), and so on, each of which had its own distinctive political and economic relationship to the mother country.[11] The overwhelming majority of people in most of these colonies were either subsistence peasants or economically marginal tribesmen who lived much as their ancestors had for thousands of years.

By contrast, within Britain itself, the 1775–1850 period had a very distinctive character, as much of the nation was drawn up in an accelerating vortex of revolutionary economic and demographic change. During this period, the population more than doubled, the (real) national income tripled, and labor productivity jumped by leaps and bounds. An urban industrial revolution was beginning to reshape the face of the land. Step by step, textiles, mining, metallurgy, and transportation were swept up in a process of mechanization that transformed Britain into the workshop of the world. Alongside London, which had been the world's commercial capital for more than a century, the industrial North was now rising up as a second Leviathan, further consolidating Britain's hegemonic place in the world economy.[12]

It would be an oversimplification to say that the empire lost its significance during this period, but it is certainly true that the sinews of the old mercantilism were coming unglued. As Britain became increasingly committed to the new free-trade system—benefiting spectacularly by its open-market rules—the value of imperialism, as a distinctively economic system, was fundamentally cast into doubt.[13] To be sure, the 1,562,612 square miles of territory that were added to the British dominions during this period were not acquired in a fit of absence of mind.[14] Nevertheless, these annexations were made almost entirely for military or strategic reasons, to secure the borders, and to extend the frontiers of existing colonies. Here an almost countereconomic logic was at work, as the protection of one colony led to the acquisition of the next, with insufficient attention paid to cost. Given the British taxpayers' reluctance to pay for these adventures, it was hoped that these colonies could be reorganized to pay for themselves.[15]

For aristocratic younger sons in search of employment, these conquests provided a path to glory, economic security, and early retirement. A vast colonial-military establishment of some four to five hundred thousand British troops and officials (including the native sepoys of the Indian army) settled in as a more or less permanent military-colonial complex, raising revenue, administering provinces, and defending frontiers. For free-trading liberals absorbed in the drama of industrialization at home, these colonies might well seem little more than millstones around the nation's neck.[16] To dragoon and tax hundreds of millions of Asian peasants for the privilege of being governed by a few thousand superfluous English, Scottish, and Irish gentlemen who could find no gainful employment at home seemed a dubious and potentially dangerous proposition— threatening to liberty both in Asia and in the mother country. True Britons, most liberals acknowledged, had a moral responsibility to liquidate the disaster of New World slavery that their ancestors had created. But the emergence of an ever enlarging Asian and African empire left most of them cold.[17]

This diffidence at the prospects for a liberal empire hinged on serious doubts about its economic value. With the dismantling of the old mercantilist protections, and Britain's industrial takeoff under the new regime of free trade, it was difficult to see the economic benefits of distant colonies. The dim prospect that they might afford new markets for British industry was almost always outweighed by the heavy cost of bringing (and keeping) them under political control.[18] A large part of the problem lay in the sheer distances that would be involved in binding together such a miscellaneous assemblage of far-flung lands. In the 1830s, it took five to eight months to sail from London to Calcutta. The journey to Australia or New Zealand occupied the better part of a year. Under these circumstances, the transfer of people, information, and goods was too intermittent and too expensive for these globe-spanning provinces to cohere in any meaningful way. Visionaries might dream of a globalized future in which millions upon millions of Asians, Africans, and Americans would be integrated into Britain's industrial economy, but under early-nineteenth-century conditions, this was a quixotic pipe dream.[19]

There were, however, a few far-distant regions that were, even before 1850, already impacted by the long arm of Britain's domestic industrial takeoff. The first was the American South, whose cotton plantations were being converted into feeder farms for Lancashire's factories at the very moment when political independence was removing them from the sovereignty of the Union Jack.[20] No less significantly, the demographic explosion, which reverberated throughout the home islands (including Ireland), led many observers to look to the empire as a critical safety valve onto whose "empty" spaces the surplus people could be discharged. The agglomeration of an industrial proletariat in Britain's slum-ridden industrial cities (or Ireland's densely packed cottage plots) led many elites to look to Canada, Australia, and New Zealand as transoceanic outlets where Anglo-Saxon wage laborers (or Irish peasants) could become respectable farmers, property owners, and customers for British industrial goods. Given the distance of these "New Britains," it was assumed that they would eventually achieve de facto self-government and independence, preferably within the perimeter of the formal empire.[21]

The paternalistic racial theories of the early nineteenth century reflected these metropolitan and colonial realities. There was a cognitive no less than a physical gap between the lofty, idealistic philanthropists in the home island and the colonial planters and settlers who were determined to exact labor from resistant slaves or land from peripatetic aborigines.[22] For bourgeois liberals who were embarrassed by conditions in Britain's factories, it was very convenient to deflect attention to the evils of slavery across the seas. When feckless white paupers and working-class Chartists erupted in class resistance in the mother country, it was pleasant to dream of dramatic and rapid racial progress among more tractable dark-skinned peoples on the imperial periphery.[23] Yet these illusions were soon to be shattered. During the second half of the nineteenth century, the socioeconomic dynamism, which had previously been confined to the home island, dramatically spread to even the most distant colonies. Within a few decades, the empire was integrated, and unified, in hitherto unimaginable ways. Yet as liberals began to understand the economic value of colonies, they discovered that the challenges of managing them were greatly exacerbated, and the resistance of their native inhabitants grew more effective and intense. As a result, social conflicts, which had previously manifested themselves as domestic class struggles, began to resurface in a novel form, as racial formations and transformations, playing themselves out on a global, imperial stage.[24]

Capitalist Transformation in the British Colonies, 1850–1900

If the driving forces of the early Industrial Revolution in Britain were the factory and the steam engine, it was the railroad, the steamship, and the electric wire that transmitted their kinetic energy to the colonial hinterlands during the second half of the nineteenth century. The railroad had transformed the face of Britain during the 1840s. Between the 1850s and the 1880s, it transformed the face of the colonies. Between 1850 and 1900, 25,936 miles of track were laid in India alone. Canada and Australia (as well as Argentina and the United States) metamorphosed from vast wastelands, served by a few coastal outposts, into huge granaries and ranches that would come to feed a world market in animal products and food.[25] Following fast behind the railroad was the steamship, turning the world's oceans from barriers into highways for the rapid transport of people, raw materials, and manufactured goods. During the 1850s, the voyage from London to Calcutta had been reduced from about half a year to a mere forty-five days. The opening of the Suez Canal, in 1874, further diminished this travel time by half. By the 1870s and 1880s, the transoceanic transfer of bulk commodities was becoming ubiquitous, and freight and passenger rates began to drop.[26]

Of all the transportation and communication innovations of the second half of the nineteenth century, none was more striking or consequential than the advent of the telegraph. The rapid spread of overland lines during the 1840s and 1850s was supplemented by a thickening web of undersea cables, laid during the 1860s and 1870s, that facilitated almost instantaneous communication between one continent and the next. By the 1870s, the direct line between England and India had become fully operational, and telegraphic communication was becoming routine. Two million messages were transmitted along this route in 1895 alone. It would be difficult to overstate the significance of this revolution in communication in transforming the second British Empire from an agglomeration of miscellaneous dependencies into an integrated whole. The ability to move not only people and goods but also troops and information greatly diminished the isolation of local authorities and strengthened the reins of central control. For the first time, it was possible for the Colonial or India Office to know what was actually happening in even the remotest province of the empire, and to affect the outcome in a timely way.[27]

Of course, the impact of this transportation and communications revolution was not limited to the British Empire. It quickened the circulation of trade and the synapses of interconnection between nations and regions all around the globe. With the advent of freer trade and industrialization in continental Europe and the United States, the volume of trade between Britain and the other developed regions began to accelerate at a breakneck pace. From the perspective of British manufacturers and British investors, these places, with all the amenities of civilization, afforded many of the most attractive outlets for commerce and capital export without the costly necessity of direct political management or imperial control. It was only in the period after 1875 that the empire began to exercise disproportionate sway as the preferred target for British exports and British investments. It is for this reason that most historians date the "New Imperialism" only from the 1870s or the 1880s.[28]

This, however, is to conceive the "New Imperialism" too narrowly. If its centrality as a target for British exports and capital mushroomed primarily in the late Victorian period, its centrality as a source of raw materials and human labor began a few decades earlier. A good symbolic starting point might rather be the discovery of gold in Australia in 1849. Almost instantly, speculators, adventurers, and laborers from around the world gathered in the province of Victoria, which rose from almost nothing to five hundred thousand inhabitants in the space of a few years.[29] Gold, of course, was merely a lubricator of commerce. But there were many other extractive and agricultural products that were becoming absolutely essential, both for the European consumer market and for the process of industrial production itself. Outside of coal and iron, which were extensively mined within Europe, most of these raw materials had to be obtained from other continents, especially from tropical regions that were now within Britain's formal, or informal, empire. It is not too much to say that the second half of the nineteenth century witnessed a veritable revolution in the way these primary products were harvested and distributed to meet the rapidly expanding demand of the industrial-core regions.[30]

With slavery gradually eliminated from all the old plantation regions, it was necessary to create new systems of labor recruitment and control in its place. Generally, this involved reorganizing the plantations into large capitalistic units, or "factories in the field." The old planters either faded away or learned to compete in the global free market, where prices and profits could fluctuate rapidly. When former slaves discountenanced the working conditions that they were offered, they were either coerced by indirect methods or unceremoniously replaced by impoverished indentured laborers shipped in from India, China, or other parts of the empire where labor was cheap.[31]

Even more striking than this reorganization of the old plantations was the way they formed a prototype for a vast new system of raw-material procurement that transferred people and plants to new points of production that extended to the farthest reaches of the globe. Sugar declined in Jamaica only to reappear in Mauritius, Guiana, and Fiji. American cotton was supplemented (and eventually supplanted) by more reliable operations in Egypt, India, and Kenya. Coffee, tea, and cocoa, demanded in ever increasing quantities by European consumers, spread the plantation system through East India, Assam, Ceylon, Burma, Ghana, and Brazil. In other areas, traditional peasants could be transformed by debt peonage into sharecropping market farmers, producing staple crops of every kind for the factories and dinner tables of the industrial North.[32]

In these advanced capitalist countries, ever more sophisticated machinery required regularly expanding supplies of new materials, such as Brazilian rubber, Malayan gutta-percha, Indian indigo, and West African palm oil. High-yield agriculture demanded a steady flow of Chilean nitrates. The discovery of gold and diamonds in South Africa turned Transvaal, Witwatersrand, and Natal into a vast mining camp with 173,000 laborers. The huge construction projects involved in railway building, irrigation, and other infrastructure demanded huge armies of unskilled laborers to move earth, lay tracks, and carve stone. Railroad magnate Thomas Brassey was reputed to employ 80,000 men on five continents. India's railways employed 185,736 in 1882 and nearly 400,000 by the end of the century. The construction of the Suez Canal, in the late 1860s and early 1870s, required the labor of a quarter-million Egyptian peasants, each of whom put in a month of annual service before returning to his land.[33]

Thus, the second half of the nineteenth century was an era of indigenous peoples in motion, as peasants were drawn (or forced) into the market, and once remote groups were expropriated from their lands. This was at once both an extension of the first (British) stage of industrialization and a novel manifestation of a new process of combined and uneven development between periphery and core. In the developed metropolis, the industrial takeoff had vastly amplified labor productivity and consumer demand. Yet these developed sectors had to be fed by extractive enterprises on the underdeveloped periphery that were still worked by naked human muscles and hands. The result was a vast increase in the number of proletarianized (or semiproletarianized) laborers in the colonies. For the first time, significant numbers of Asian and African peasants were being mobilized and integrated into the world economy. At the same time, huge tracts of undeveloped land in Canada, Australia, New Zealand, Latin America, the United States, and South Africa were being expropriated from their indigenous occupiers to make way for the vast ranches and granaries that were feeding and clothing Europe's factories and people.[34]

Racial Resistance and the Problem of Colonial Management

One might think that this rapid forward march of socioeconomic modernization would have made these indigenous peoples more congenial to metropolitan Britons. In fact, the opposite was often the case. If the early-nineteenth-century paeans to the brotherhood of man were attempts to establish moral connections with people who seemed exotically distant, the new proximity of these colonial ethnic and religious others precipitated new and increasingly racialized distancing mechanisms for cognitively keeping them at bay. When white Britons used soap and ate fertilized crops, when they sent telegraph messages, when they wore diamonds, when they rode in vehicles with tires, and when they consumed sugar, coffee, cocoa, or tropical fruit, they made themselves dependent on peoples of color in ways that many found painful to contemplate.[35]

I would argue that the new racism was primarily fueled by white Britons' desire to perpetuate the dependence of distant colonial producers, and to avoid recognizing their own dependence on such colonial agricultural and extractive work. By refiguring the colonial subaltern as a savage, backward other, it was possible to mask the extent to which he or she was integrated alongside the metropolis into a global capitalist milieu. Given the spread of the new connective communications media, it was now possible to disseminate grotesque, derogatory, and xenophobic images of racial difference and distance far more quickly and effectively than had previously been the case. Sensational newspapers such as *Reynold's Miscellany* and popular magazines such as *Punch* became venues for the circulation of lurid representations of Indians and Africans (and sometimes Irishmen) that conveyed messages of sexual danger and racial disorder in an imperial universe where the old distinctions of fixed status had become destabilized. In that sense, the new racism was also a product of the new imperialism—one of the most toxic commodities exported from the metropolis in return for the goods and services of colored peoples on the periphery. One of the most striking features of this new racism—at least in its cruder and more sensationalist manifestations—was the way in which it displaced concerns about land and labor onto anxieties about violence and rape. Despite slight differences of circumstances and color, these images were remarkably similar: a dark, hairy, prognathic male figure with enlarged fangs, distended muscles, and a bloodthirsty grin stood poised to commit some act of unspeakable brutality against defenseless white female flesh.[36]

This obsession with bomb-throwing terrorists and oversexed brutes was initially a response to the horror stories that emerged from the Indian Revolt of 1857, when the British-Indian army briefly lost control of much of the subcontinent. It was greatly exacerbated, over the next decade, by colonial rebellions in New Zealand and Jamaica, and by the emergence of Fenianism in the Irish diaspora. The great drama on the other side of the Atlantic—sectional crisis, Civil War, emancipation, Reconstruction, and redemption—only reinforced the sense that some great moment of racial reckoning was at hand.

Such events and episodes resonated with the mass media because they were so easily taken out of context and reduced to a handful of gruesome, sensationalized tropes. Yet these images were profoundly misleading. In highlighting the alien character of the racial and colonial other, they almost deliberately obscured the ways in which he and the metropolitan self were becoming more alike. To depict the Indian sepoy as a brutal monster was to disguise his real existence as a trained British soldier, often from a family that had collaborated with the Raj for more than a century. His dramatic gesture of disloyalty was no simple repudiation of Britishness but a reflection of his anxiety at the manner in which rapid modernization and Anglicization were threatening his traditional religion and way of life. Over the long run, the assertive loyalty of the Western-educated Bengali would prove to be even more disturbing than the momentary mutiny among the troops. Both cases foreshadowed (albeit in different ways) a more egalitarian imperial future in which Greater Britishness might have to break from its metropolitan moorings and assume a decentered Hindu or Muslim frame. The image of the raving black rapist forestalled the necessity of such a thought.[37]

A similar ambiguity lurked beneath the derogatory caricatures of "Paddy," which accompanied every report of Fenian outrage, and swelled with the advent of aggressive nationalism. The more astute British observers well understood that the real power of Irish nationalism lay not in escapades and bombings but in its capacity to sustain a mass political movement for Home Rule. Such nuances were lost, however, on the increasingly conservative British public, which found it much easier to demonize "Paddy" than to contemplate the new kind of democratic, devolutionary empire that would be necessary to secure his continued allegiance to the Union Jack.[38] If the oldest dominions of the empire were renegotiating their relationship to the metropolis from the 1860s onward, a comparable ferment was brewing on the imperial frontier, where land rather than loyalty was at stake. In New Zealand and South Africa, the land hunger of British settlers was meeting the resistance of a new kind of armed, savvy native, who knew how to adopt the weapons of modernity to defend his traditional ways.[39]

Needless to say, such expressions of colonial subaltern agency did not produce a unanimously racialized metropolitan reaction, but the "Jamaica Revolt" of 1865 showed how and why such racialization usually became the predominant consensus view. As many white Britons were initially willing to recognize, the Jamaica affray was the product of long-standing tensions between the island's emancipated freedmen and its planter elites. Whereas the former wished to acquire land and economic independence, the latter were determined to force them back into plantation work. Under the leadership of progressive elements in Jamaica's mulatto bourgeoisie, large numbers of black peasants were becoming politically mobilized. These insurgent forces were, however, increasingly frustrated at their inability to translate their numerical preponderance into control of established colonial institutions. Matters came to a head in October 1865, when a small, shadowy conspiracy, in a remote outpost, Morant Bay, became the occasion for a massive military repression, organized by the hated governor, Edward Eyre. This police riot left thousands homeless and 439 black and colored Jamaicans dead.[40]

Horrified by preliminary reports of this carnage, the initial metropolitan reaction was by no means favorably disposed toward Governor Eyre. It was only after a small group of radicals proposed to hold the governor legally responsible for his mayhem that public opinion turned in his favor. To justify Eyre's brutal measures, the original riot was retrospectively magnified into a full-scale rebellion, and the victims were blamed for his disorder and misrule. The governor's panicked loss of self-control was now transformed into manly resolution: had he hesitated, or succumbed to flaccid liberal scruples, it was now opined, a fearful massacre of whites would have resulted.[41]

Had the Jamaican uprising occurred a century earlier, its outcome would have been straightforward: the black slaves would have been forced back into plantation labor, while the mulattoes—consigned to the purgatory of an intermediate caste—would have been easily divided and ruled. In 1866, these simple approaches were no longer possible. The "rebels" were free British subjects, mostly Independent Baptists, who aspired to economic independence and social respectability. They had the audacity to think that their hybrid African-influenced version of Christianity was as valid as that of European Protestants. Even worse, they had the temerity to believe that the rights of the "freeborn Briton" applied to them as well.[42] For more than three decades they had watched as metropolitan subjects had gradually transformed themselves into self-governing citizens. In 1832, much of the English and Scottish middle class had been enfranchised, and in the late 1830s and 1840s, working-class Chartists had demanded a further extension of the vote. Although these latter demands had been successfully resisted, "responsible government" by a very broad adult male suffrage was simultaneously granted (as if by way of compensation) in the white settler colonies of Canada, Australia, and New Zealand.[43]

How could these civic rights be denied to black or colored colonials while such dramatic strides were being made in the direction of white democracy? In an age when the lines between imperial center and periphery were blurring, this was a matter not merely of justice for Jamaicans but also of self-protection for English liberties. Failure to punish Eyre for his tyrannical, illegal actions would set a dangerous precedent, Frederick Harrison worried. "What is done in a colony today may be done in Ireland tomorrow, and in England, hereafter."[44] Even worse, what was done yesterday in Britain and the white dominions (namely, extending the franchise) would probably someday have to be done in India and Jamaica. The only way in which these equalizing trends could be resisted would be to impose formal, legal discriminations on the basis of race.[45] But in an imperial world based on liberal principles. how were such racial discriminations to be defended and sustained?

"Race" and the Management of Imperial Social Relations

As readers of Cha-Jua's essay will recognize, one way, devised in the Jim Crow United States, involved erecting a statutory system of racial segregation that defined certain people as inherently inferior on the basis of blood or color. No longer subject to the discipline of the whip, freedmen would be kept dependent by debt peonage and denied any entrée to political power. By proscribing such "inferiors" from public life, white democracy could safely be granted and class divisions could be forestalled by racial exclusions.[46] In such a system, as David Roediger has demonstrated, access to citizenship became a function of "whiteness," which became the ticket of entry into full civic rights in the postbellum United States.[47]

Could such a system be transposed onto the very different circumstances of imperial Britain? Clearly, many government and imperial officials hoped that it could: the "white" dominions (Canada, Australia, New Zealand, and Britain itself) would become federated self-governing states on the American model, and meanwhile the colored colonies would be reorganized as centrally managed dependencies. With the tightened control made possible by the new communications technologies, they would be consigned to the more or less permanent wardship of metropolitan rule. The conversion of India into a Crown colony after 1857, and Jamaica after 1865, clearly indicates that such a strategy was at work: the whole constitutional structure of the empire was to be simplified and dichotomized into self-governing white dominions and dependent Crown colonies.[48]

Yet there were many reasons this simple bifurcation proved inherently unstable. The first and most important was that much of the white working class in Britain remained disenfranchised for most of this period. In sharp contrast to their American cousins, British elites were by no means uniformly reconciled to the prospect of Herrenvolk democracy. So long as many whites at home (indeed, the numerical majority) remained second-class citizens, it was scarcely possible to invoke this condition as a specific marker of racial inferiority.[49] Yet even in the colonies themselves, there remained too many political ambiguities—and too many socioeconomic anomalies—for this simple racial dichotomy to be enforced. The first anomaly, of course, was Ireland, which remained in some ways a neocolonial dependency even as it was being constitutionally integrated into Britain itself. In India, moreover, the abolition of the East India Company, and the advent of Crown government, did nothing to end the patchwork quilt of British-run provinces and princely native states, each of which harbored a different economic base and its own peculiar hierarchies of caste color and creed.[50]

Further undercutting the prospects for a neatly dichotomous racial division was the fact that none of the "white" settler colonies was exclusively white. Indeed, Canada, Australia, and New Zealand all contained more or less sizable populations of indigenous peoples, as well as fresh infusions of colored immigrants from China or the Indian subcontinent. Unable to exclude these racial and ethnic minorities categorically from democratic rights that were ostensibly being extended to all adult men, the governments of these colonies were driven to radical (and often contested) expedients of trying to resettle such peoples on tribal reservations, or to otherwise forestall their ability to participate in political life.[51] In the South African colonies of the Cape and Natal, the situation was even more complex. There "responsible government" meant that a minority of British settlers was able to dominate a diverse, multiracial society, albeit with significant oversight and direction from the Colonial Office in London. This was possible because so many of the majority Boers had removed themselves to their own landlocked interior republics, and because the surrounding African ethnic groups were forcibly disarmed and confined to Bantustans, where democratic principles were presumed to be irrelevant. In this manner, under the guise of "representative government," the outlines of what would become twentieth-century apartheid were already beginning to emerge.[52]

Finally, amid these kaleidoscopic hierarchies of caste and color was the liberal principle of political equality itself. In the dynamic context of late Victorian imperial capitalism, it was neither possible nor desirable to maintain fixed racial barriers, as the needs of labor organization, land commodification, and political mobilization shifted markedly from one decade to the next. Under these circumstances, it generally made sense to pay lip service to egalitarian principles, even as they were belied by a far more heterogeneous reality. In the very same proclamation with which Queen Victoria consigned India to Crown colony status, she also proclaimed that "all shall alike enjoy the equal and impartial protection of the law," and that "our subjects of whatever race or creed shall be freely and impartially admitted to office in our service."[53] The Governor Eyre controversy is often invoked as a milestone in converting British liberals into racists. Yet its effect was also to convert an influential minority of advanced thinkers, such as J. S. Mill, Charles Darwin, T. H. Huxley, and Frederick Harrison (quoted earlier) into racial progressives who saw that as long as colored colonials were subject to legal discrimination, there could be no guarantees at home for English liberty.[54] Few, if any, of these men believed that colored colonials were actually the equals of white Britons. They merely recognized that, in a liberal capitalist society, attempts to enforce segregationist laws or marks of inferior status were bound to be counterproductive over the long run.

If the law had little useful contribution to make to racial classification, these men were apt to put a great deal of faith in science. It is important to recognize that this turn to science as the basis for racial knowledge was not only (or even primarily) the work of reactionaries who were looking for ammunition with which to demonize the other and consign him to some eternal subhuman purgatory. More significantly (and with more lasting consequence), the scientization of race was the work of late Victorian liberals and moderates, who felt impelled by the new imperial realities to question the sentimental humanitarianism of their parents' generation but were too sophisticated to fall prey to the sensationalist demonization of the gutter press. These men saw race primarily as a problem of management: How were the multifarious subordinate races that had come within the purview of Greater Britain to be constructively integrated into its thickening networks of capitalist interconnection? How could they be assimilated without either overestimating their potential for progress and civilization or confining them unnecessarily to a servile place?

A good example of this new kind of liberal (or postliberal) scientific managerialism can be seen in an article, "The Economic Value of Justice to the Dark Races," which appeared in the *Economist* in 1865, just as news of the "Jamaica Revolt" was trickling in. In sharp contrast to the sensationalist magazines, with their images of savage mayhem, this journal resisted the impulse to demonize the rebels, advocating a more constructive and intelligent approach. In an era when slavery was no longer viable, justice and market incentives would be necessary to lure black peasants into the maws of economic imperialism. Yet given the urgent need for tropical products and cheap labor, such "justice" could be defined not by British standards but rather by those deemed appropriate for this or that particular "dark race." Thus, "an Asiatic does not deny the justice of allowing his employer to fine him . . . [whereas] an African is not irritated because larceny is punished with a flogging, though an Asiatic is."[55]

According to the *Economist,* every group had its own distinctive character, culture, hopes, and expectations that might decompose into sullen resentment or explode into angry revolt. On the other hand, these hopes and expectations could be harnessed to meet the needs of a globalizing marketplace. The challenge of mobilizing and managing these various "backward" peoples who had come within the range of British capitalism and administration required a new kind of racial knowledge and understanding that would enable the empire to enlist their (quasi)-voluntary compliance while keeping them firmly in a tutelary place. For the British newspaper reader it was perhaps sufficient to fulminate against the ingratitude of the Indian, Jamaican, or Irish rebel. The imperial managers and administrators of these subject peoples required more nuanced and authoritative discourses that could reenlist the subject in the Greater British project without including him or her in entitlements that were beyond his or her supposed capabilities and needs.

This scientific, managerial approach to race was a way of avoiding the necessity of negotiating with the colonial other. If it eschewed the quasi-pornographic pleasures of unconditional demonization, it left the demarcation and elucidation of racial difference always firmly in the hands of the metropolitan scientific elite. It is no accident that the economic globalization of British capitalism was swiftly followed by a corresponding enlargement of British natural science and ethnology. Between the 1840s and 1870s, a series of anthropological associations were founded, as imperial scholars rose to the challenge of reclassifying a host of alien others whose newfound proximity was rendering them essential to the realization of the Greater British scheme. "England," the London Ethnological Society editorialized, "encircles the globe in glorious enterprise: her sons come in contact with the Eskimaux of the Arctic Seas, with the red hunter of North America, with the cunning Chinese, with the mild Hindoo, and with the mountaineer of Afghanistan."[56] In the old era of slaveholding and mercantilism, such peoples could be encased in a fixed legal status that would define their political positions and economic roles. Now, in the era of free-trading imperialism, it was necessary to devise a naturalistic (but not inflexible) category that could cognitively locate them in their proper (but actually changing) colonialized place. Armed with new naturalistic discourses on "race," British ethnologists could construct the racial character of the host of subordinate, resistant peoples who had suddenly fallen under their lofty, panoptic gaze.

Evolutionary Theory and the (Re)-classification of Victorian Races

In 1859, Charles Darwin published *On the Origin of Species,* and Hugh Falconer discovered the bones of prehistoric ape-men commingled with those of extinct animals in Brixham Cave.[57] It was fortuitous that these two revolutions in science commenced at the very moment when the revolutions in imperial communication, tropical production, and racialized social relations were getting under way, for the first pair of intellectual revolutions would become interwoven with the second set of social revolutions in a host of intriguing ways.

The first imperial service that Darwinian theory performed, however, was to undercut the crudest and least-tenable versions of the new racial science, which had been receiving wide publicity during the 1850s. The main impresarios of these untenable theories were two down-on-their-luck physicians, Robert Knox and James Hunt. The work of these two men had gained them brief notoriety, not because of their scientific bona fides but because they corresponded so well with the sensationalized images of deranged black monsters that were circulating furiously in the popular press. Boldly disputing the humanitarian pieties of the previous fifty years, Knox and Hunt insisted that mankind was divided into a few primary races that were absolutely different and biologically fixed. Whites and Blacks, they contended, were separate species, created of different material. Any attempts to hybridize these antipathetic races, either genetically or culturally, could lead only to a sterile, monstrous dead end.[58]

As we have seen, this fantasy of a pure Anglo-Saxon race, uncontaminated by the blood of darker peoples, fixed at its eternal summit of racial superiority, clearly did attract some bewildered metropolitans who sensed the alarming proximity of colored colonialized peoples yet wished to keep the looming menace intellectually contained. But among those who were actively involved in managing, or even thinking about, the empire, this blanket exclusion seemed both erroneous and dangerous. To Darwin and other liberal members of the scientific establishment, the myth of separate racial creations was not only incompatible with the fundamental premise of evolution but also a thinly veiled justification for the brutality of American slave drivers and the mad Governor Eyre. For these reasons, it had to be controverted on both scientific and political grounds.[59] Indeed, informed observers, such as the mid-Victorian ethnologist John Crawfurd or the historian Herman Merivale, felt compelled to acknowledge that the British Empire itself was a powerful agent of racial mongrelization, contributing new mixtures and intermediate shadings where none had existed before.[60]

But what new racial knowledge was to replace these untenably dichotomous schemes? The requisite "truths" were painstakingly unearthed from within the discourses of incremental evolutionary development that followed in the wake of Darwin's and Falconer's discoveries.[61] The new evolutionism was rooted in genuine science, but it was diverted for ideological ends. It sought to naturalize the new lines of racial hierarchy and inequality. Yet it allowed for the realities of racial miscegenation and interchange. It accepted that all races were fluid and subject to growth, advancement, or degeneration by multiple mechanisms of biosocial transmutation.[62] In this regard, it is important to distinguish the evolutionary theories of the post-1859 period from those that had been proposed before the Victorian age. In the eighteenth century, evolutionary theory had tended to downplay biology, focusing primarily on processes of social evolution in which environment reigned supreme. Tracing a logical trajectory from hunting (savagery) to pastoralism (barbarism) to agriculture (early civilization) to commerce (advanced civilization), such theories hypothesized that all human societies had passed through these same four stages, albeit with varying success and at differing rates.[63]

On one level, the post-Darwinian theories of racial evolution were not really so different from those of the earlier period. Both took a historical approach to the question of racial formation, in contrast to the absolutist and ahistorical doctrines of Knox and Hunt.[64] There were, however, two crucial innovations in the new evolutionary theories that not only rendered them scientifically respectable but also fitted them for the imperial challenges of the day. The first, of course, was Darwin's theory of natural selection. Yet the influence of this theory is easily overstated. Most biologists and ethnologists, including Darwin himself, still believed that some acquired characteristics could also be inherited—thus leaving open the door to the possibility that environmental changes could become encoded in hereditary bloodlines and that cultural improvement could continue to alter the biology of race.[65]

A more fundamental change was the shift from the six thousand–year time line of Genesis to the almost limitless expanse of geological time that the new paleontological discoveries implied. In terms of the old eighteenth-century categories, the fossils indicated that the earliest stage of hunting had been vastly elongated, and that most humans, and prehumans, had subsisted in a state of protracted savagery throughout their development. Indeed, savagery was now divided into a number of substages, based on archaeological and paleontological evidence. In the earliest stage transitions (that is, Neanderthal to Cro Magnon), skeletal alterations suggested that biological transmutation was the primary agent of change. Thereafter, human skeletons varied only slightly, while the growing sophistication of stone tools (that is, Soultrean to Magdalenian) suggested a combination of both social and biological transmutation. Finally, the advent of metal technologies (first bronze, then iron) was correlated with the more familiar social transition from hunting to pastoralism and early agriculture. This in turn opened the way to writing, civilization, and the era of recorded history.[66] The fact that so much of human history had been passed in various stages of savagery was oddly reassuring, as it explained why "savages," of one kind or another, still predominated in most portions of the globe. That these savages were actually being drawn into the world capitalist economy, in ways that were empowering them to act and to resist, only added to the discursive pressure on evolutionary theory to reinscribe them cognitively in their primordial savage state. The hierarchy of races was not some arbitrary invention but a truth documented in the sedimentary deposits of flints and bones.

In his book *Cave Hunting,* amateur paleontologist Boyd Dawkins purported to demonstrate, from fossil evidence, that only the severest pressure of Darwinian selection had enabled British Anglo-Saxons to achieve their uniquely elevated civilizational pinnacle. European history, he hypothesized, had been driven by successive waves of invasion, in which a superior race, with a more advanced technology, supplanted its more primitive predecessor. In this manner, the brow-ridged Neanderthals (Mousterian tools) had been replaced by a "dark-haired swarthy" (Bronze Age) race of people, whom Dawkins identified as the ancestors of the Basques. During the Iron Age, these primitive peoples were replaced by the Celts and the Belgae, and then finally by the Germans, whose conquests ushered in the age of written historical records.[67] It was left for the reader to draw the implication that Britain's global and imperial ascendancy was deeply encoded in its racialized history. In Asia, Africa, and indigenous America, where selection had been less rigorous, primitive dark men still subsisted in a Stone or Bronze Age mentality. By contrast, British history had been a Darwinian proving ground where the weaker (darker, lower tech) had repeatedly perished and only the strongest (blondest, highest tech) had survived.

The problem with this theory (as Dawkins himself half-realized) was that, even in Britain, none of his "unfit" races (except perhaps the Neanderthal) had been entirely wiped out.[68] To the less dogmatic ethnologists and race commentators, this evidence showed that cultural exchange and biological miscegenation had always been an important motor of evolutionary progress. Instead of denying the evidence of biological and cultural miscegenation, they preferred to concentrate on the ways in which the imperial infusion of superior culture into backward regions might enable inferior races to improve their bloodlines—very gradually—albeit at some risk of a weakening and dilution of the superiority of the master race.[69]

A good example of this kind of historicized thinking can be found in Sir John Lubbock's enormously influential treatise *Pre-historic Times* (1865). To Lubbock, the scientific interest of the modern savage was that his culture had preserved in evolutionary amber the same kind of primitive social structures and cultural belief systems that had prevailed in Britain during the Neolithic and Paleolithic epochs. Yet if the modern savage represented the past of the modern Briton, modern British industrial capitalism represented the future to which the modern savage had to adjust. Where the earlier generation of abolitionists had figured the savage or slave as a shackled suffering brother, Lubbock refigured him as a wayward refractory child. The adult savage, Lubbock repeatedly argued, exhibited the same behavior as a typical English child. He was moody, undisciplined, attracted to baubles, and mired in dirty habits and gross, superstitious beliefs. Lubbock's analogy was by no means original, and many other ethnologists repeated the observation that although colored children might be as intelligent as their English counterparts, from adolescence onward their development was arrested, and they became fixed as mental children for the remainder of their lives.[70]

Among those savages (like those children) that were destined for survival, childish behavior manifested itself in several ways.[71] Some children were obedient, and some were naughty. Some had to be punished, corrected, and disciplined, whereas others were responsive to incentives and rewards. The important thing was to be patient, purposeful, and paternalistic, without any illusions that those whom one held in a state of wardship could instantly develop, advance, or progress. At some distant point in the *longue durée* of racial evolution, self-control, and even self-government, might become a possibility. This time, however, lay far away in an unknown hereafter. For the present, and the foreseeable future, imperial rule had to be the order of the day.[72]

The problem, of course, was precisely that these colonial children were developing at an alarming and ever accelerating pace. Catalyzed by the dynamic of industrial capitalism, this development was precipitating dangerous outbursts in the nursery, where the children were getting too many ideas of their own. The utility of evolutionary theory lay in the way it provided an ideological rheostat to regulate colonial cultural development, even as unbridled capitalism was taking economic control. Yet given the complexity of colonial cultures, and the diversity of colonial peoples, evolutionary theory could not accomplish this work of racial stabilization on its own. It was, rather, the interaction of evolutionary theory with three other racialized discourses that made it possible to identify the precise cultural coordinates of any given ethnic group or colonized people, and the exact pace at which they could be allowed or encouraged to progress.

In the remainder of this chapter I will examine the way in which the new post-Darwinian evolutionism played itself out in connection with two of these other racial discourses—Aryanism and racial degeneration—to produce a new body of racial and ethnological knowledge designed to help British metropolitan elites and colonial managers in realizing their projects of capitalist integration and colonial control.[73] In fact, because there was never complete agreement among these elites, who came with divergent goals and agendas, these racial and evolutionary discourses became sites of ambiguity and contestation, as rival interpretations turned them in different directions at once. Moreover, by the 1880s and 1890s, some of these discourses themselves were being appropriated by colonial others, who had figured out how to use them to question white metropolitan domination and to assert insurgent objectives of their own.

"Aryanism" and the Evolution of Victorian Races

The "Aryan" hypothesis had been first formulated by the Anglo-Indian jurist Sir William Jones in 1786. Noticing striking resemblances between Sanskrit and the major European languages, he hypothesized that these languages were all remotely descended from a common "Aryan" root. Because Irish and native Indian languages were almost all Aryan, Jones's theory had obvious imperial implications. Not surprisingly, from the 1840s onward, these arguments about the descent of language, culture, and mythology were transmuted into debates about the descent of blood and race.[74] Clearly, not all Aryan speakers were racially Aryan, so attention had to be paid to physical attributes such as skin color, behavior, and physiognomy. Nevertheless, because the exact relationship between biological and cultural attributes was obscure, the history of their interaction was largely conjectural, and could be used to justify several different imperial visions of hierarchy. The point was to come up with a scenario in which the British stood at the top, as pure Aryans. Favored others would be cast as more or less adulterated admixtures, while the laboring masses would be identified as lesser breeds entirely.[75]

The place where the Aryan hypothesis was developed most fruitfully was in India, for there it offered a comprehensive explanation of the existing caste system as well as an Anglo-friendly rendering of Indian history. According to this analysis, caste distinctions had been created by the original light-skinned Aryan invaders (ca. 1500 BC) in a partially abortive effort to preserve their racial purity. To this end, the black "Dravidian" indigenes, whom they conquered, were corralled into the lowest, most menial castes. When miscegenation blurred these racial boundaries, the resultant half-breeds were assigned to intermediate castes, which grew ever more numerous, specialized, and complex. Eventually, as classical Indian civilization faltered, even the highest-caste Brahmans began to darken, as their ranks were adulterated with tainted blood. From this perspective, the British could regard themselves as the new Aryan master caste, destined to advance a stagnant Indian civilization by bracing infusions of their fresh Aryan culture (if not blood).[76] Inasmuch as caste had originally developed as a system of social and labor management, the British could now refurbish it to secure their own aims.

Given the speculative nature of this tenuously grounded historical argumentation, it could be molded to support almost any racial or caste hierarchy that one chose. Thus, a liberal like Friedrich Max Müller, who minimized the significance of skin color, might urge the British to regard nearly all Indians as at least distant racial cousins. Conservatives, like H. H. Risley, on the other hand, would reserve Aryan honors for the highest castes alone. Those in the market for cheap indentured labor often tended to favor the darkest, least-Aryan Dhangars, or "Hill Coolies," who were deemed especially suited to plantation work. For Sir Henry Maine, primarily concerned with the compliance of India's millions of landed peasants, the Aryan connection remained important. Nevertheless, he insisted that these peasants, with their large admixture of primitive blood, were evolutionary throwbacks, deeply attached to collective values and village institutions that English workers had jettisoned centuries earlier.[77]

By far, the most urgent concern for the British in India was to find collaborators among indigenous elites who would help them in the day-to-day running of the subcontinental empire. Initially, they fastened on the Bengali Brahmans, whose Western educations made them the most likely candidates for the job of diffusing British civilization to the masses below.[78] After the 1857 revolt, as we have seen, this strategy began to change. The "Bengali Babu" had now become too Westernized and independent to be trusted. Increasingly, he was caricatured as garrulous, overrefined, deceptive, and effeminate. He was compared unfavorably not only with the "manly Englishman" but also with the traditional Maharajas and northwest frontier "martial castes," which were now increasingly favored as the bulwarks of British rule.[79] Given the importance of race in imperial thinking, however, it was necessary to drain the Aryan blood that had formerly coursed in the Bengali Brahman. Somehow it had to be transfused into those Gurkha or Sikh tribesmen, who had previously been dismissed as borderland pests. When skin color alone did not provide the basis for this operation, other physical indicators of Aryan status—facial angle, cephalic index, or cranial capacity—could be applied. In a pinch, culture could be rehabilitated as an agent of progression or retrogression among those whose true racial status could not otherwise be ascertained.[80]

The utility of this kind of racial and evolutionary classification lay in the way it articulated a graduated hierarchy in which every group in Indian society could be assigned a British place. Radiating the appearance of solidity, inexorability, and biological predestination, such racial classifications were, in reality, highly fluid, transmutable, and easily adapted to whatever racial promotions or demotions the imperatives of capitalist and imperial rule might require. Such malleability was acceptable, however, only when it corresponded to the agenda of British imperial elites. When it was taken up by colored peoples to advance their own interests, it met with concerted hostility and opposition.

In the end, however, the Bengali Babu did get his revenge. Like other rising middle-class colonial groups—prosperous Catholics in Ireland or mulattoes in the West Indies—he began to learn how to formulate Aryan claims of his own. In the hands of creative intellectuals, like Bankimchandra Chattopadhyay, Swami

Vivekananda, or the Irishmen Ulick Bourke and W. B. Yeats, an argument was crafted along the following lines: The ancient Celts and Hindus, no less than the ancient Anglo-Saxons, had once been in the vanguard of the Aryan race. In ancient times, the great Aryan family had split up into eastern and western branches. The western Anglo-Saxons had achieved mastery in the realms of war and government, and in these arenas they had become the undisputed masters of the world. By contrast, the eastern branches (somehow mysteriously including the Celts) had become avatars of the spiritual realm. In the British Empire, these two great Aryan branches had rediscovered one another. Rather than squabbling over superior status, they ought to establish a working division of labor in which the British would retain the powers of government but would recognize the supremacy of Irish and Indian intellectuals in the realms of literature, religion, and morality.[81]

"Racial Degeneration" and Victorian Society

Given the way in which Aryanism was providing unexpected openings for the racial self-promotion of nonwhite others, it is not surprising that the discourses of demotion, exclusion, and limitation were increasingly shifting to ideologies of racial degeneration during the last few decades of the nineteenth century. Given the general evolutionary framework, it was, of course, quite logical to assume that a race could degenerate as well as advance. As we have seen, racial degeneration (often associated with miscegenation) had often been invoked to explain the deterioration of India's or Ireland's Aryans and to justify why they needed the benefits of British rule.[82] When connected to discourses on "savagery," the discourse of degeneration would play an even more critical role in addressing the problems of "third world" labor control, discussed earlier in this chapter. According to this way of thinking, labor in distant mines or tropical plantations was deemed a civilizing experience for black savages, who would otherwise have remained mired in primitive misery. According to this view, slavery—for all its undoubted horrors—had been a civilizing force for the Afro-Americans and Afro-Caribbeans who had been involuntarily dragooned into it. Abolition had been a practical and ethical inevitability, but it had left the incompletely civilized freedmen to lapse back into their "natural" condition of backwardness and savagery. For Greater British entrepreneurs in the new tropical extractive industries, as well as for defenders of Governor Eyre, or the U.S. plantation masters, such arguments were key to justifying the new forms of indentured labor and debt peonage that were coming to replace the old discredited system of chattel slavery.[83]

By the 1870s, the discourse of racial degeneration began to be turned on the metropolis itself, as urban industrial Britain showed a new and increasingly savage underside. During the 1840s, when the metropolitan language of class division and class conflict was pervasive, the notion that certain sectors of the Anglo-Saxon proletariat might be racially degenerating would not have been taken seriously. There were simply too many poor people, too obviously impoverished by circumstances beyond their control, for economic failure to be interpreted in racial terms. In the 1860s, however, social investigator Henry Mayhew began to suggest that there might be a racial element to the dysfunctions of the British poor. Over the generations, their behavior was growing more feckless, their lifestyle was becoming more "Irish," and their vigor was diminishing. Even their skin color seemed to darken, as they came to constitute a permanently inferior underclass.[84] Given the prevailing neo-Lamarckian assumptions about the inheritance of acquired characteristics, this line of thinking did not seem absurd. After all, if the "lesser breeds" could become more or less Aryanized, then degenerate Aryans could become a kind of postlapsarian lesser breed. In both cases, the change was not perceived to have occurred overnight. But over a period of many generations, nature (when reinforced by inadequate nurture) would have its way.

From the 1870s onward, this racialization of the English lower classes became more common, as the language of race became increasingly pervasive, and as the incorporation of respectable workers into the political system made it easier to isolate a degraded underclass. Whether this racialization was taken in a liberal or a reactionary direction depended in large measure on the evolutionary vision in which it was framed.[85] In his best-selling exposé, *In Darkest England,* William Booth explicitly played on the parallelism between England and Africa. England's jungle is an impassable moral thicket of profligate ignorance and economic cannibalism. The predatory ivory and slave traders of the African jungle have their counterparts in the publicans, slumlords, and sweat masters of the metropolis. Whereas African pygmies are stunted by protein deficiencies and malarial fevers, England's pygmies are deformed by inadequate wages, debauched habits, and the contagions of the slum.[86]

Needless to say, the preferred solution to this problem of domestic racial degeneration varied, depending on one's political point of view. For evangelicals like Booth, the solution was home missionaries, Christian conversion, and labor colonies. For conservatives like J. A. Froude or Cecil Rhodes, the solution was more emigration to Australia, New Zealand, and South Africa, where the Saxon yeoman could renew his hereditary vigor and reclaim his racial supremacist legacy.[87] For the New Liberals of the 1890s, racial regeneration became the pretext for the kind of progressive social reform and environmental improvement that would have been couched, fifty years earlier, in the language of class amelioration.[88] The language of race was becoming increasingly promiscuous, and the more it became the sine qua non of political identity and sociological investigation, the more unstable racial categories began to seem. Radicals and reactionaries, visionaries, and demagogues all wrapped themselves in a discourse so protean and vacuous that it was no longer clear what the word itself meant.

Conclusion

In this chapter, I have tried to show how the racialized discourses that proliferated rapidly in the post-1850 British Empire were products of material transformations occurring in the capitalist and imperial political economy. This was a period of profound structural change, when Greater Britain was integrated by a transportation and communication revolution, while the imperatives of free-market capitalism made deep inroads into traditional social relations all around the globe. With the abolition of fixed ranks (that is, in mercantilism and slavery), it was necessary to find another way of regulating proletarianization. With the increasing ability of colored others to demand the civic rights that were accruing to white middle- and respectable working-class groups in the imperial metropolis, it was necessary to devise some alternative framework for justifying political exclusion and naturalizing the larger imperial social hierarchy.

The new discourses on race, I have argued, performed these functions. In order to do so, however, they had to repudiate absolutist and ahistorical anathemas, and reconstitute themselves in the language of evolutionary theory. In part, this was because evolutionary theory had suddenly become a fertile area of inquiry, where genuine scientific discoveries were rapidly being made. However, it was also because the intellectual content of these theories powerfully resonated with the imperial problems and agendas of the day. The evolutionism characteristic of this era was an odd and unstable mix of Darwinism, neo-Lamarckism, and sociohistorical analysis. When conjoined with the older racial and historical discourses of savagery, Aryanism, and degenerationism, it provided a flexible and malleable framework onto which hierarchies of natural superiority or inferiority could be mapped.

Understood in this manner, race was no stark black-and-white bifurcation but an almost infinitely graded array of mixed color shadings. It was a palette of power from which the rulers of Greater Britain could paint new designs of social containment, or labor mobilization, and devise new strategies of "divide and rule." These languages of evolution were attractive because they provided a storehouse of *longue durée* historical narratives that purported to explain how the various races had achieved their present position and what they stood to gain from continued British rule. As capitalist time dramatically shrank in the globalizing markets of the late Victorian period, evolutionary time lengthened in a manner that kept colonial others at bay. The value of these evolutionary theories lay in their promise to bring at least the appearance of racial stabilization, and containment, in an era of extremely rapid socioeconomic change.

In fact, such stability was not only impossible but also not even entirely in the interests of the imperial rulers themselves. By manipulating the evolutionary discourses of savagery, degeneration, Aryanism, and Anglo-Saxonism, these rulers were able to demote, or promote, supposedly fixed racial groups in ways that can be seen, in retrospect, as extraordinarily opportunistic. But this ability to manipulate racial discourses to serve pragmatic interests could also be taken up by racial others. Here the languages of savagery, degeneration, and Aryanism could be reoriented to contest exclusionary judgments, and to mount new demands for political inclusion, in a shifting Greater British constitutional frame. Yet so long as such inclusionary movements were couched in the racialized language of the imperial masters, they too entailed the exclusion of other others, such as Africans, African Americans, and those Asians who could not invoke the badge of Aryan ancestry. In this manner, the Victorian racial discourses outlined in this chapter would continue to cast their toxic shadow over the twentieth century.

CHAPTER 2 READING QUESTIONS

1. According to Koditschek, why did the liberal British Empire that emerged in the nineteenth century experience problems of legitimation that its mercantilist predecessor had escaped? Why and how was "race" a solution to these problems?

2. What economic changes in the character of British capitalism after 1850 suddenly made this new "liberal" free-trading empire central to Britain's economic development and welfare?

3. Given that Koditschek downplays the significance of crude notions of "social Darwinism" or "scientific racism," why does he place so much emphasis on evolutionary discourses in the construction of the new post-1850 ideologies of race? How did these evolutionary discourses differ from completely ahistorical, purely biological definitions of "race"? What made these evolutionary discourses particularly well suited to the needs of the British Empire?

4. Do you think that Koditschek's multiracial model of imperial Britain might have any relevance to the United States, either historically or in our own time? Does Makalani's chapter in Part 2 give you any hints along these lines?

Notes

I would like to thank Kerby Miller and Sundiata Keita Cha-Jua for their extremely useful comments on earlier drafts of this chapter.

1. Reginald Coupland, *The British Anti-slavery Movement* (London: Cass, 1964); Roger Anstey, *The Atlantic Slave Trade and British Abolition, 1760–1810* (Atlantic Highlands, N.J.: Humanities International Press, 1975).

2. Douglas Lorimer, *Colour, Class, and the Victorians: English Attitudes towards the Negro in the Mid-nineteenth Century* (Leicester: Leicester University Press, 1978); Robert J. C. Young, *Colonial Desire: Hybridity in Theory, Culture, and Race* (London: Routledge, 1995).

3. Nancy Stepan, *The Idea of Race in Great Britain, 1800–1960* (London: Macmillan, 1982); Christine Bolt, *Victorian Attitudes towards Race* (London: Routledge, 1971);

Ivan Hannaford, *Race: The History of an Idea in the West* (Baltimore: Johns Hopkins University Press, 1996).

4. See the Glossary.

5. Edmund Morgan, *American Slavery, American Freedom: The Ordeal of Colonial Virginia* (New York: W. W. Norton, 1975). See also Theodore W. Allen's monumental *Invention of the White Race,* 2 vols. (London: Verso, 1994, 1997), which traces the emergence of "whiteness" back to the legal discrimination and juridical labor divisions of the old mercantilist empire. For an analysis that disputes the relevance of "race" to prenineteenth-century Anglo-America, see Colin Kidd, *British Identities before Nationalism: Ethnicity and Nationhood in the Atlantic World, 1600–1800* (Cambridge: Cambridge University Press, 1999).

6. The Navigation Acts limited colonial trade to British ports and British shipping. They were, therefore, the principal mechanisms through which the mercantilist system was enforced. See Klaus Knorr, *British Colonial Theories, 1570–1850* (Toronto: University of Toronto Press, 1944); and Robert Livingston Schuyler, *The Fall of the Old Colonial System: A Study in British Free Trade, 1770–1870* (London: Oxford University Press, 1945).

7. For a general introduction to Britain's nineteenth-century imperialism of free trade, see Ronald Hyam, *Britain's Imperial Century: A Study of Empire and Expansion* (New York: Barnes and Noble, 1976); Andrew Porter, ed., *The Oxford History of the British Empire: The Nineteenth Century,* vol. 3 (Oxford: Oxford University Press, 1999); and the essays in A. G. L. Shaw, ed., *Great Britain and the Colonies, 1815–1865* (London: Methuen, 1970). On the role of slavery in the world economy, see Robin Blackburn, *The Overthrow of Colonial Slavery, 1776–1848* (London: Verso, 1988).

8. Catherine Hall, *Civilising Subjects: Metropole and Colony in the English Imagination, 1830–1867* (Chicago: University of Chicago Press, 2002); Thomas Holt, *The Problem of Freedom: Race, Labor, and Politics in Jamaica and Britain, 1832–1938* (Baltimore: Johns Hopkins University Press, 1992); David Brion Davis, *The Problem of Slavery in the Age of Revolution* (Ithaca: Cornell University Press, 1975).

9. Bolt, *Victorian Attitudes;* Stepan, *Idea of Race.*

10. For our purposes, it is important to understand that superimposed on mercantilism's geopolitical distinctions between metropolis and periphery were a series of legally enforceable divisions between different classes of people, based on a combination of rank, religion, location, and ethnic origin. At the apex of this ad hoc hierarchical structure were the metropolitan landed aristocrats and protected merchants, who controlled the imperial state. Just below them were the metropolitan gentry, colonial planters, and urban merchants, who were outside the charmed circle of government but possessed representative institutions of their own. Other white male Protestant householders were only tenuously represented in national or imperial politics, but (at least after 1688) they enjoyed basic protections and civil rights. Irish Catholics, by contrast, suffered severe civil disabilities, as did women, indentured servants, and household dependents of every kind. At the bottom were black slaves, who had no legal rights, even to their own bodies, and Native Americans, who were treated as nuisances to be removed. The great achievement of the age of revolutions was to destroy this system of differential privilege. In the second British Empire, which arose during the nineteenth century, however, they were

supplanted by more streamlined distinctions based on supposedly naturalistic distinctions of gender and race. My argument here focuses entirely on the question of racial formation. Discussion of the role of gender will have to await a further occasion.

11. Calculated from information in Henry C. Morris, *The History of Colonization,* vol. 2 (New York: Macmillan, 1904), 83–91; and B. R. Mitchell, *Abstract of British Historical Statistics* (Cambridge: Cambridge University Press, 1962), 5–7.

12. Phyllis Deane and W. A. Cole, *British Economic Growth, 1688–1959* (Cambridge: Cambridge University Press, 1969), 6–8, 278–85.

13. Schuyler, *Fall of the Old Colonial System.* See also the Glossary.

14. Calculated from Morris, *The History of Colonization,* 89. These figures are an understatement, since they exclude British India, where the most extensive annexations were occurring during this period. See also Christopher Bayly, *Imperial Meridian: The British Empire and the World, 1780–1830* (London: Longmans, 1989).

15. Percival Spear, *The Oxford History of Modern India, 1740–1975* (Oxford: Oxford University Press), 1–177.

16. Patrick Colquhoun, *A Treatise on the Wealth, Power, and Resources of the British Empire* (London: Mawan, 1815), appendix, 51, 55; G. R. Porter, *The Progress of the Nation* (1836; reprint, Kelley, 1970), 324.

17. I am examining the idea that imperialism was relegitimated during the nineteenth century in distinctively liberal terms in *Liberalism, Imperialism, and the Historical Imagination: Vision of Greater Britain, 1800–1900* (Cambridge: Cambridge University Press, forthcoming). Suffice it to say that evangelical Protestantism played an important role in the early stages of this process. For a good example of how this might work in different colonial settings, see Zachary Macaulay's various essays in the *Christian Observer* 8 (1809).

18. See essays by John Gallagher, Ronald Robinson, and Oliver MacDonagh in *Great Britain and the Colonies,* edited by Shaw, 142–83.

19. Daniel E. Headrick, *The Tools of Empire: Technology and European Imperialism in the Nineteenth Century* (Oxford: Oxford University Press, 1981), 130.

20. Eugene Genovese, *The Political Economy of Slavery* (Middletown, Conn.: Wesleyan University Press, 1989).

21. Edward Gibbon Wakefield, *England and America* (New York: Harpers, 1834); Reginald Coupland, ed., *The Durham Report* (Oxford: Oxford University Press, 1945).

22. Hall, *Civilising Subjects;* Jean Comaroff and John Comaroff, *Of Revelation and Revolution, Christianity, Colonialism, and Consciousness in South Africa,* vol. 1 (Chicago: University of Chicago Press, 1991).

23. Davis, *Problem of Slavery;* Seymour Drescher, *Capitalism and Antislavery: British Mobilization in Comparative Perspective* (Oxford: Oxford University Press, 1986).

24. François Crouzet, *The Victorian Economy* (London: Methuen, 1982); Peter Mathias, *The First Industrial Nation: An Economic History* (London: Routledge, 1983); David Landes, *The Unbound Prometheus: Technological Change and Industrial Development in Western Europe* (Cambridge: Cambridge University Press, 1972).

25. Headrick, *Tools of Empire,* 187; Douglas P. McCallan, *Planting the Province: The Economic History of Upper Canada* (Toronto: University of Toronto Press, 1993); Donald

Denoon, *Settler Capitalism: The Dynamics of Dependent Development in the Southern Hemisphere* (Oxford: Oxford University Press, 1983).

26. E. J. Hobsbawm, *The Age of Capital, 1848–1875* (London: Weidenfeld and Nicholson, 1975), 48–68; Headrick, *Tools of Empire,* 130, 155.

27. Hobsbawm, *Age of Capital,* 48–68; Headrick, *Tools of Empire,* 160; Christopher Bayly, *Empire and Information: Intelligence Gathering and Social Communication in India, 1780–1870* (Cambridge: Cambridge University Press, 1996).

28. Harrison M. Wright, ed., *The "New Imperialism" Analysis of Late Nineteenth Century Expansion* (Lexington, Mass.: D. C. Heath, 1976); D. K. Fieldhouse, *Economics and Empire, 1830–1914* (Ithaca: Cornell University Press, 1973).

29. William Westgarth, *The Colony of Victoria: Its History, Commerce, and Gold Mining; Social and Political Institutions* (London: Sampson, Low, 1864), 12–285.

30. Eric Wolf, *Europe and the People without History* (Berkeley and Los Angeles: University of California Press, 1982), 310–53.

31. Ibid., 354–83; Denoon, *Settler Capitalism;* Hugh Tinker, *A New System of Slavery: The Export of Indian Labour Overseas* (Oxford: Oxford University Press, 1974).

32. Wolf, *People without History,* 310–53; Laxman D. Satya, *Cotton and Famine in Berar, 1850–1900* (Delhi: Manohar, 1997); Lucille H. Brockway, *Science and Colonial Expansion: The Role of the British Botanical Gardens* (New Haven: Yale University Press, 2002), 1–60.

33. Headrick, *Tools of Empire,* 150–56; Hobsbawm, *Age of Capital,* 56; Wolf, *People without History,* 346–47, 367; Rai Saheb Chandrika Prasada, *The Indian Railway* (Ajmer, India: Scottish Mission, 1921), 134.

34. Hobsbawm, *Age of Capital,* 173–92; James Belich, *Making Peoples: A History of New Zealanders* (Honolulu: University of Hawaii Press, 1996), 212–72; Samir Amin, *Accumulation on a World Scale: A Critique of the Theory of Underdevelopment* (New York: Monthly Review Press, 1974), 1–36; Sumit Sarkar, *"Popular" Movements and "Middle Class" Leadership in Late Colonial India: Perspectives and Problems of a "History from Below"* (Calcutta: K. P. Bagchi, 1983), 1–37.

35. Sidney W. Mintz, *Sweetness and Power: The Place of Sugar in Modern History* (New York: Viking, 1985); Laxman Satya, *Cotton and Famine in Berar;* V. B. Singh, ed., *Economic History of India, 1857–1956* (New Delhi: Allied Publishers, 1965); Dharma Kumar, ed., *The Cambridge Economic History of India* (Cambridge: Cambridge University Press, 1983).

36. Roy Foster, *Paddy and Mr. Punch: Connections in Irish and English History* (London: Lane, 1993); H. L. Malchow, *Gothic Images of Race in Nineteenth-Century Britain* (Stanford: Stanford University Press, 1996); Patrick Brantlinger, *Rule of Darkness: British Literature and Imperialism, 1830–1914* (Ithaca: Cornell University Press, 1988), 199–226.

37. Thomas Metcalf, *The Aftermath of Revolt* (Princeton: Princeton University Press, 1964); Tapan Raychaudhuri, *Europe Reconsidered: Perceptions of the West in Nineteenth Century Bengal* (New Delhi: Oxford University Press, 1988).

38. D. George Boyce, *Nationalism in Ireland* (New York: Routledge, 1995); Tom Garvin, *The Evolution of Irish Nationalist Politics* (New York: Holmes and Meyer, 1981); Perry Curtis, *Anglo-Saxons and Celts* (Bridgeport, Conn.: Conference on British Studies,

1968); D. G. Paz, *Popular Anti-Catholicism in Mid-Victorian England* (Stanford: Stanford University Press, 1992).

39. Wolf, *People without History,* 346–50; Byron Farwell, *Queen Victoria's Little Wars* (New York: W. W. Norton, 1972); James Belich, *The New Zealand Wars and the Victorian Interpretation of Racial Conflict* (Oxford: Oxford University Press, 1986); Belich, *Making Peoples,* 236.

40. Holt, *Problem of Freedom,* 115–312; Hall, *Civilising Subjects,* 140–264.

41. Bernard Semmel, *The Governor Eyre Controversy* (London: McGibbon and Kee, 1962).

42. Hall, *Civilising Subjects,* 140–264; Holt, *Problem of Freedom,* 115–312.

43. Catherine Hall, Keith McClelland, and Jane Rendall, *Defining the Victorian Nation: Class, Race, Gender, and the British Reform Act of 1867* (Cambridge: Cambridge University Press, 2000); Coupland, *The Durham Report.*

44. Semmel, *The Governor Eyre Controversy,* 131.

45. "I decline accepting the Negro as the equal of the Englishman," zoologist John Tyndall protested, "nor will I commit myself to the position that a Negro and an English insurrection ought to be treated in the same way" (quoted in ibid., 125).

46. See Cha-Jua's essay in this volume. See also Joel Williamson, *The Crucible of Race: Black-White Relations in the American South since Emancipation* (Oxford: Oxford University Press, 1984), 1–324.

47. David Roediger, *The Wages of Whiteness: Race and the Making of the American Working Class* (New York: Verso, 1991), 95–184.

48. Peter Borroughs, "Imperial Institutions and the Government of Empire," in *Oxford History,* edited by A. Porter, 170–97.

49. Even after the Reform Act of 1867, only 33 percent of British adult males possessed the parliamentary franchise. Only in 1885 did the electorate rise to 65 percent of the adult male population. Calculated from Chris Cook and Brendan Keith, eds., *British Historical Facts, 1830–1900* (New York: St. Martin's, 1975), 115–17; and Mitchell, *British Historical Statistics,* 12–15.

50. Oliver MacDonagh, *Ireland* (Englewood Cliffs, N.J.: Prentice-Hall, 1968); C. A. Bayly, *Indian Society and the Making of the British Empire* (Cambridge: Cambridge University Press, 1988).

51. Belich, *Making Peoples;* Jean Burnet and Harold Palmer, *"Coming Canadians": An Introduction to a History of Canadian Peoples* (Toronto: McClelland and Stewart, 1988); Beverley Kingston, *Oxford History of Australia,* vol. 4 (Melbourne: Oxford University Press, 1988).

52. Leonard Thompson, *A History of South Africa* (New Haven: Yale University Press, 1995), 1–109; N. Bhebe, "The British, Boers, and Africans in South Africa," in *Africa in the Nineteenth Century, until the 1880s,* edited by J. T. Ade Ajaayi (Berkeley and Los Angeles: University of California Press, 1989), 144–78; Mahmood Mamdani, *Citizen and Subject: Contemporary Africa and the Legacy of Late Colonialism* (Princeton: Princeton University Press, 1996).

53. Quoted in Anthony Read and David Fisher, *The Proudest Day: India's Long Road to Independence* (New York: W. W. Norton, 1999), 56.

54. Holt, *Problem of Freedom,* 303–4.

55. *Economist* 12, no. 9 (1865): 1487–89.

56. *Journal of the Ethnological Society of London* 1 (1848): 21.

57. Peter J. Bowler, *Theories of Human Evolution: A Century of Debate, 1844–1944* (Baltimore: Johns Hopkins University Press, 1986); Donald Grayson, *The Establishment of Human Antiquity* (New York: Academic Press, 1983).

58. Robert Knox, *The Races of Man: A Philosophical Enquiry* (1850; reprint, London: Renshaw, 1862); James Hunt, *On the Negro's Place in Nature* (London: Tuebner, 1863).

59. George W. Stocking Jr., "What's in a Name? The Origins of the Royal Anthropological Institute," *Man,* n.s., 6, no. 3 (1971); Stocking, *Victorian Anthropology* (New York: Free Press, 1987), 239–73.

60. This, in spite of the fact that Crawfurd did not think highly of the capabilities of most colored people. See his many articles in the *Transactions of the Ethnological Society of London* (1861–1867); and Herman Merivale, *Lectures on Colonies and Colonization* (London: Longman, Green, 1861).

61. For social Darwinism, see Richard Hofstadter, *Social Darwinism in American Thought* (Boston: Beacon, 1944). But see also Roger Bannister's powerful critique, which shows that "social Darwinism" was primarily an epithet, and that few nineteenth-century writers actually subscribed to any such doctrine (*Social Darwinism: Science and Myth in Anglo-American Social Thought* [Philadelphia: Temple University Press, 1979]).

62. John Beddoe, *The Races of Britain* (Bristol: J. W. Arrowsmith, 1861). Men like Beddoe explained their findings by drawing a distinction between "eugenisic" races (that is, white Europeans) who could interbreed successfully and "paragenisic" or "dysgenisic" races (Blacks and whites) who could produce only sterile offspring.

63. James Cowles Prichard, *Researches into the Physical History of Man* (Chicago: University of Chicago Press, 1973). The classic studies of eighteenth- and nineteenth-century social evolutionary theories are Ronald Meek, *Social Science and the Ignoble Savage* (Cambridge: Cambridge University Press, 1976); John Burrow, *Evolution and Society: A Study in Victorian Social Theory* (Cambridge: Cambridge University Press, 1966); and Stocking, *Victorian Anthropology.*

64. This is a key point that is ignored in most of the existing literature on "scientific racism"—for example, Stepan, *Idea of Race;* and Bolt, *Victorian Attitudes.* I am developing it more fully in my *Liberalism, Imperialism, and the Historical Imagination.*

65. Peter J. Bowler, *The Eclipse of Darwinism* (Baltimore: Johns Hopkins University Press, 1983).

66. Bowler, *Theories of Human Evolution.*

67. Boyd Dawkins, *Cave Hunting: Researches on the Evidence of Caves Respecting the Early Inhabitants of Europe* (London: Macmillan, 1974).

68. Ibid.

69. See, for example, Merivale, *Lectures on Colonies,* 535–40; James Bryce, *The Relations of the Advanced and the Backward Races of Mankind* (Oxford: Oxford University Press, 1903); and Charles W. Dilke, *Greater Britain: A Record of Travel in English Speaking Countries* (New York: Harper Bros., [1868]), 41–43.

70. John Lubbock, *Pre-historic Times, as Illustrated by Ancient Remains and Modern Savages,* 2d ed. (London: Williams and Norgate, 1869).

71. Merivale, *Lectures on Colonies,* 524–53.

72. Dilke, *Greater Britain*, 475–534. The most succinct and powerful statement of this position is Rudyard Kipling's famous poem "The White Man's Burden."

73. Limitations of space prevent me from considering several other important Victorian discourse of racial evolution, those of miscegenation, Anglo-Saxonism, and arrested development. I hope to repair this deficiency in future work.

74. J. Marshall, ed., *The British Discovery of Hinduism in the Eighteenth Century* (Cambridge: Cambridge University Press, 1970). Sir William Jones himself never used the word *Aryan,* which was coined by German philologists in the early nineteenth century. Once the leap had been made from language to race, the doctrine became an important classificatory tool in identifying groups with claims (however attenuated) to racial superiority. Indeed, some ethnologists and sociologists, with more imperial enthusiasm than scientific skepticism, tried to apply it to the "higher races" of South Asia and Oceana. See Tony Ballyntine, *Orientalism and Race: Aryanism in the British Empire* (New York: Palgrave, 2002).

75. Thomas R. Trautmann, *Aryans and British India* (Berkeley and Los Angeles: University of California Press, 1997). See also Martin Bernal, *Black Athena: The Afroasiatic Roots of Classical Civilization*, vol. 1, *The Fabrication of Ancient Greece* (New Brunswick: Rutgers University Press, 1987).

76. Thomas Metcalf, *Ideologies of the Raj* (Cambridge: Cambridge University Press, 1994); H. H. Risley, *The Tribes and Castes of Bengal: An Ethnographic Glossary, in Two Volumes* (Calcutta: Bengal Secretariat, 1891).

77. Henry Maine, *Ancient Law* (1861; reprint, n.p.: Dorset Press, 1986); Henry Maine, *Village Communities in the East and West* (New York: Holt, 1876); H. H. Risley, *The People of India* (Calcutta: Thacker, Spink, 1908); Susan Bayly, *Caste, Society, and Politics in India* (Cambridge: Cambridge University Press, 1999).

78. David Kopf, *British Orientalism and the Bengali Renaissance: The Dynamics of Indian Modernization* (Berkeley and Los Angeles: University of California Press, 1969); David Kopf, *The Brahmo Samaj and the Shaping of the Modern Indian Mind* (Princeton: Princeton University Press, 1979); Nicholas Dirks, *Castes of Mind: Colonialism and the Making of Modern India* (Princeton: Princeton University Press, 2001), 127–228.

79. Mrinalini Sinha, *Colonial Masculinity: The "Manly Englishman" and the "Effeminate Bengali" in the Later Nineteenth Century* (Manchester: Manchester University Press, 1995); Indira Chowdhuri, *The Frail Hero and Virile History: Gender and the Politics of Culture in Colonial Bengal* (Delhi: Oxford University Press, 1998); Linda Colley, *Britons: Forging the Nation, 1707–1837* (New Haven: Yale University Press, 1992); Metcalfe, *Ideologies of the Raj*, 125–27.

80. Risley, *The People of India*, 1–123.

81. Raychaudhuri, *Europe Reconsidered*; R. F. Foster, *W. B. Yeats, a Life: The Apprentice Mage, 1865–1914* (Oxford: Oxford University Press, 1997); W. B. Yeats, *Celtic Twilight* (London: Bullen, 1912); Ulick Bourke, *The Aryan Origins of the Gaelic Race and History* (London: Longmans, 1875). See also Ernest Renan, *Poetry of the Celtic Races, and Other Essays* (London: Scott, 1896); and Matthew Arnold, *Mixed Essays, Irish Essays, and Others* (New York: Macmillan, 1924).

82. Daniel Argov, *Moderates and Extremists in the Indian National Movement, 1883–1920* (New Delhi: Asia Publishing, 1967); Boyce, *Nationalism in Ireland*, 144–227.

83. I am developing this theme more fully in another article, "The Degeneration of Savagery" (in progress).

84. Henry Mayhew, *London Labour and the London Poor, in Four Volumes* (London: Griffin, Bohn, 1861–1862), 1:1–7, 4:23–27.

85. Gareth Stedman Jones, *Outcast London: A Study in the Relationship between the Classes in Victorian Society* (New York: Pantheon, 1971); Gertrude Himmelfarb, *Poverty and Compassion: The Moral Imagination of the Late Victorians* (New York: Vintage, 1991).

86. William Booth, *In Darkest England, and the Way Out* (New York: Funk and Wagnall, 1891).

87. Ibid.; James Anthony Froude, *Oceana; or, England and Her Colonies* (New York: Scribner's, 1886); Vladimir I. Lenin, *Imperialism: The Highest Stage of Capitalism* (Moscow: Foreign Languages Publishing, 1947), 79.

88. Anna Davin, "Imperialism and Motherhood," *History Workshop* (May 1978): 1–65; Bernard Semmel, *Imperialism and Social Reform: English Social-Imperial Thought, 1895–1914* (London: Allen and Unwin, 1960).

3

Globalization and the Cycle of Violence in Africa

TOLA OLU PEARCE

Each year countless organizations and groups report on the state of the world's people. When the searchlight is turned on Africa, serious concerns surface, including concerns about Africa's economic progress and frequent violence. The two are not unrelated, as we will see shortly. Relative to other regions of the world, Africa is making very little progress on the standard indicators of "development" such as health-care delivery, maternal mortality, life expectancy, technical education, and per capita income. For instance, the "Human Development Index" is a composite measurement developed by the United Nations to assess the control people have over their lives as measured by access to health, education, and income. In 2001, thirty-four countries received very low scores ("Low Human Development"), and of these, thirty were African nations. Further, the *Human Development Report* predicted that it is unlikely much of Africa would meet the eight (new) Millennium Development Goals, meant to eradicate the worst problems facing poor nations, by 2015.[1] Unfortunately, problems have continued to grow. At the end of the 1990s, sub-Saharan Africa was 5 percent poorer than it had been at the beginning of that decade.[2] Between 1975 and 2000, its per capita income had dropped from one-sixth of the per capita income in the developed world to one-fourteenth. At the same time, HIV/AIDS is still a growing problem. Of the 39.5 million people worldwide estimated to be living with HIV/AIDS at the end of 2006, 63 percent were in sub-Saharan Africa.[3] Other problems such as infant mortality and maternal health also remain significant.

In addition to all of this, there has been civil unrest, international conflicts, and genocidal wars in many countries: the Congo, Rwanda, Liberia, Sierra Leone, Zimbabwe, Nigeria, and others. All over Africa, local communities have become disenchanted with postcolonial (and postapartheid) governments, and this has sparked strikes, protests, and general political instability. Even though

Africa's present predicament did not begin with globalization, the process has certainly deepened preexisting crises. In this chapter, I review the links between globalization and the constant violence that occurs in the economic, political, and domestic lives of people in Africa. I begin with a discussion of what globalization has come to mean for Africa, and then outline its connection to the escalation of violence. Hidden behind this bleak picture are unstated but implicit assumptions and practices grounded in notions of race.

Globalization and Its Discontents in Africa

Although most would agree that societies are undergoing rapid change, that things are very different from the way they were in the 1950s, there are debates on how these changes should be understood. Here, I will discuss just two issues on globalization. I focus specifically on economic globalization (global capitalism) rather than the political, religious, or cultural dimensions of the process, even though all are related. The first debate deals with the meaning of economic globalization: how is it to be understood? The second is on whether this process is beneficial or predatory. Given my focus on Africa, it is important to contextualize these debates. These discourses are only the latest in the history of debates about the types of social change hoisted on Africa over the past two hundred or so years.

Colonization, development, and modernization were also externally initiated processes over which there have been controversies. Colonization was said to be Africa's ticket to "civilization." Colonization brought with it the idea of the "civilizing mission."[4] It was followed by modernization and development, two processes suggested as the next step to ensure that Africa caught up with the West. It was argued that modernization could occur only with the diffusion of Western values, technology, institutions, and money.[5] With each new concept, mainstream scholars assumed that these processes would bring about the necessary transformations in Africa. However, these models of change have been strongly criticized by other scholars as frameworks for domination.[6] In line with these scholars, A. Escobar has pointed out that change does not occur in a vacuum.[7] Power relations are crucial in assessing both the changes and the meanings attached to them. Power makes it easier for some to construct "facts" and define reality for others. He believes that, for the most part, the "development" framework as constructed by the West for third world countries has been inimical to progress—particularly for the former colonies. As a result of "development programs," many policies, trade agreements, and projects turned out to be detrimental to those on the receiving end.

Today we are at similar crossroads with the *globalization* model of change. There are strong disagreements over what globalization really means and also over its impact. Regarding its meaning, the split is between those who view the process as something new and those who dispute this idea. The latter argue that economic globalization (on which the other dimensions of globalization rest) merely represents capitalism's success in its bid for global reach.[8] This is viewed as the logical outcome of a process that has been unfolding for centuries, and today we are simply experiencing levels of connectedness that were unimaginable in the past. The use of computer technology and the speed of information processing have shrunk the world so that people living in different time zones now have instant connection. This allows for the rapid exchange of material, knowledge, and cultural ideas. In opposition to this view, others argue that a lot has changed in the organization of capitalism itself. According to P. McMichael, J. Mittelman, F. Piven, and others, globalization signals a new and distinct phase of capitalism.[9] Throughout its history, each phase (mercantile, industrial, imperial-colonial) creates new and distinct structures or relationships that must be carefully analyzed. For McMichael, the present phase of capitalist growth (global capitalism or economic globalization) requires that nations produce for global markets by becoming part of the "World Factory." Global capitalism "concerns the attempt to promote and manage global markets to sustain the Western lifestyle (which also means incorporating, eliminating, or containing alternatives)." This project is accomplished in ways that set it apart from earlier phases of capitalist growth. During the preceding era of industrial capitalism, emphasis was on nation building in an effort to integrate and expand the domestic markets of each nation. Global capitalism demands that a country finds its niche on any global production line. These activities are increasingly under the control of global corporations and institutions, and the state is no longer the most powerful global player. The focus of national economies is outward. The creation of wealth is in the interest of interlocking global institutions and the transnational class rather than local populations. According to R. Mishra, the welfare of the domestic economy, its citizens, or individual nations takes a backseat to the needs of the corporate world.[10]

In addition to this debate, the outcome of this process is under scrutiny: What are the consequences of economic globalization? Where is it taking us? Globalization enthusiasts point to the pace at which wealth is being created at the global level, its potential to increase per capita incomes (trickle-down potential), the speed at which innovations can be used for public good (for example, medical breakthroughs), and the endless benefits of new communication systems. Those who are less than enthusiastic often hold off final judgment and argue that global capitalism itself is neither good nor bad but depends on how global rules and policies are crafted, or on how well communities turn its contradictions into opportunities.[11] Last, there is a growing body of literature showing that, by and large, global capitalism has been devastating for much of the world—including most of Africa. These critics argue that for many, it is an inimical process.[12] According to Taye Assefa and others, globalization is not only "creating new opportunities and benefits but also generating new threats and compounding human suffering." In *Globalization,* S. Sassen turns her attention to the effects of economic globalization on different categories of people. At the international level, its impact depends on a nation's or a region's position within the world's economic order, and in each nation, on a group's (for example, race, gender, class, educational status) social location. She argues that there is, on the one hand, globalization "from above." Those who already have some type of advantage are in a position to be major actors within the budding system. At the international level, such actors are able to build "global institutions," decide on policies, and craft concepts to further their own interests. Also, their lifestyles and working conditions can be sustained only through the extensive consumption of resources, infrastructure, and labor. All this is taken care of as cheaply as possible by others who are scattered in disadvantaged locations around the world (hotel workers, garment makers, tourist workers, domestic workers, and so forth). On the other hand, the latter group experience what Sassen refers to as globalization "from below." These individuals and nations are less likely to benefit from the new technologies and growing global wealth.[13]

Both the policies and the laws formulated within global institutions or by powerful actors and introduced to those below call for the massive restructuring of people's public and private lives. Since the 1980s, the gap between the rich and the poor has generally increased. For Africa specifically, global policies such as the structural adjustment programs (SAPs) developed by the World Bank and the International Monetary Fund (IMF) and new neoliberal trade agreements have resulted in ever escalating crises within African domestic systems. Thus, if both the meaning of globalization and what it portends remain so contentious, one must conclude that the debates outlined above are important. The struggle to name and craft this new process becomes critical to its creation, since accepting the definitions of those who benefit from present trends will, among other things, curtail people's ability to characterize the many laws, policies, and rules that structure economic globalization as, themselves, forms of violence.

The Significance of Defining

As suggested above, success in attempts to name, define, or formulate may in fact help initiate cycles of violence, as when Blacks were defined as three-fifths human in the United States—and could "legitimately" be treated as nonpersons—or when the colonialists defined indigenous African therapeutic systems as immoral. The systems were then neglected both administratively and financially, and in some instances, they were made illegal. These discriminations were initially made on the basis of race. The fact that race is no longer explicitly used to define them does not mean, however, that it has gone away. At the present time, global capitalism is ushering in the delegitimation of various statuses, needs, and expectations across nations. Categories of persons are being constructed as clogs in the wheel of progress or obstacles to a brighter global future. Various groups of workers have become superfluous, and community activists are constructed as impediments to the smooth running of the global system. For instance, workers and their social reproduction have become a "problem" for transnational corporations. Further, the contexts in which local populations now find themselves often lead to choices that make matters worse and result in additional social problems. More attention is usually given to the outcome of these choices than to the *context* in which the choices were made. For example, migrants from the rural areas congregating in the exploding cities of Africa are blamed by national governments for the slums, squatter settlements, and "illegal" economic activities in urban areas rather than the structure of African economies, Africa's relationship to the new global processes, and the corruption of leaders. In many countries (Nigeria, Zambia, Uganda, Mozambique), women and unemployed youth have been rounded up and returned to their villages or deported to work camps.[14] Thus, our understanding of globalization must begin with a review of structured relationships, the construction of "others," and the extent to which new laws, rules, and policies increase existing inequalities and allow more violence in the form of economic hardship or political unrest.

Economic Violence

Laws and policies that affect people's working lives pave the way for economic violence—the economic hardships that materialize. This is perhaps the most talked-about aspect of life on the African continent. After independence, many African countries, like other third world nations, sought funds for development projects or to stem the tide of economic recession. The loans from global institutions came with stringent conditions in a package known as the structural adjustment program. These "one size fits all" policies were handed to African nations beginning in the late 1970s. Structural adjustment required each nation to devalue its currency, reduce spending on (so-called nonproductive) social services, and pay its debts on time. Further, the neoliberal policies emphasized the need to liberalize and open banking systems to global competition, deregulate trade, and allow market fundamentalism to take its course. Alterations in the volume and type of jobs created, as a result of these policies, were one immediate consequence. Public-sector jobs began to disappear as local, state or provincial, and national governments were required to trim budgets. The loss of earnings and benefits had differential impact on categories of workers. Older workers with seniority, the less educated, and female workers have been badly affected. Women, in particular, are under stress, since public-sector work generally comes with important benefits, such as maternal leave, flexibility of hours, and day-care facilities, unlike many private- or informal-sector jobs.[15]

Private businesses within the formal sector also began downsizing. To become more efficient at making profits, transnational corporations seek to lower production costs around the globe by, among other things, reducing the size of the workforce. A study on urban poverty commissioned by the Economic Commission for Africa revealed that by 1999, urban unemployment was very high, reaching 52 percent, 57 percent, 82 percent, and 89 percent in Senegal, Uganda, Tanzania, and Mauritania, respectively.[16] Rising unemployment generates tension, instability, and possible violence, particularly where the pool is largely composed of frustrated youth. Unemployment benefits are meager or nonexistent in many countries. E. Elbadawi and N. Sambanis argue that "the fact that young men in Africa are very poor and not educated substantially increases the risk of civil conflict. Globally, young males are the best recruits for rebellion, and if they have little to lose they are more likely to enlist." Similarly, L. Rappoport supports the argument that "scarcity makes participation in such forms of warfare an attractive alternative for many young men." In addition to this reduction in employment opportunities, corporations are increasing the size of nonstandard forms of employment: the casualization of labor (more part-time or temporary work, greater subcontracting, and home work). For instance, M. Rama reports that between 1984 and 1990, the share of temporary employment in manufacturing in Morocco rose by 20 percent.[17] This resulted in an overall wage reduction of 5 percent. The loss of formal-sector work throws job seekers into the already overcrowded informal sector where government regulations do not protect workers. When husbands lose formal-sector jobs, wives are required to carry greater economic responsibilities, often without formal recognition and at times with growing incidence of spousal abuse.[18] Further, sexual violence is on the increase. Reports from countries such as Nigeria, Ghana, Mozambique, and Zimbabwe reveal that male aggression in schools is condoned, and transactional sex for school fees, food, clothes, and other assets has increased among schoolgirls and women seeking economic survival.[19]

As a result of SAPs, the cost of health care has skyrocketed. Cutting health-care services and applying market principles to health systems translate into user fees, the elimination of subsidies, and reductions in health benefits, as well as the training of fewer health personnel. Nigeria, for example, introduced SAPs in 1986. By 1990, the cost of health care had jumped 400 to 600 percent. Health benefits were reduced for workers and their families. Many avoided or delayed going to the hospital, and others began to increase the use of unskilled or casual health workers (such as volunteer first-aid workers) and itinerant medicine peddlers.[20] By 1995, allegedly 60 percent of the nation's supply of drugs was adulterated.[21] In addition, the supply of medical equipment and materials was grossly inadequate throughout Nigeria. Other countries experienced similar problems, which has resulted in the explosion of preventable diseases like meningitis, tuberculosis, dysentery, and malaria across the continent. Malnutrition is now widespread. The 2005 UN report reveals that in many countries, more than one-third of the entire population is malnourished: Botswana, 30 percent; Kenya, 31 percent; Chad, 33 percent; Malawi, 34 percent; Madagascar, 38 percent; Angola, 38 percent; Tanzania, 44 percent; Zimbabwe, 45 percent; Ethiopia, 46 percent; Zambia, 47 percent; Sierra Leone, 50 percent; and Burundi, 67 percent.[22] It is difficult to believe that such developments would be tolerated in white European countries.

We also need to go beyond the impact that economic policies have on individual nations to analyze some of the regional consequences of global inequalities. These are also set to precipitate new forms of economic violence. The present ideology of unlimited economic growth and endless consumption of (luxury) goods for the rich will, it has been argued, lead to global resource scarcity in the near future, given our finite physical environment.[23] This scarcity is a looming threat not only to the environment but also to resource-rich but economically poor regions and to "excluded" populations in richer regions. While the powerful demand a greater and greater share of global resources to maintain their lifestyles, others will increasingly be unable to obtain the necessary goods for mere survival.[24] According to C. Lewis, "In the late twentieth century, global development leaves 80 percent of the world's population outside the industrialized nations' progress and affluence." By the mid-1990s, the industrialized countries (the G7), with only 26 percent of the world's population, were consuming 81 percent of the world's energy and producing 87 percent of its armaments. Thus, in *The Coming Age of Scarcity,* the basic message is that there is a link between the rise of global capitalism and the growth of global poverty.[25] The fact that these dichotomies are often racialized is further evidence that they cannot be sustained. For a truly civilized world, such disparities must be reduced, and eventually eliminated.

The debt crisis arising from loans that Africa seeks from the richer regions has garnered a lot of attention, since payments rose significantly over the last two decades of the twentieth century and accounted for notable portions of the gross domestic product of many nations. Details of payments made to just one creditor (the International Monetary Fund) show that for 1990, debt servicing was 11.6 percent, 14.2 percent, 19.0 percent, 11.7 percent, and 14.3 percent of the gross domestic product in Tunisia, Algeria, Congo, Nigeria, and Mauritania, respectively.[26] Because each nation has other debts acquired from governments and private organizations, the overall amount used to serve debts had to be much higher. During the 1990s, Africa paid more than twenty billion dollars per annum in debt.[27] Often, more was paid out to service debts than monies received in loans in a given year. Thus, the director of the Fifty Years Is Enough network noted that "in 1996, Africa paid $2.5 billion more in debt servicing than it got in new long-term loans and credits," yet the main reason given for poverty in Africa by the first world is corruption.[28] Because the funds could have been used for economic ventures, there have been persistent calls for debt relief. The United Nations has also weighed in on this debate by stipulating in its Millennium Development Goals agenda that loans and "partnerships" between donors and recipients must henceforth be monitored to stop donor nations from tying financial aid to goods and services produced and supplied by them. This was standard practice in the past and guaranteed that loans were spent in the donor's country, even though the amount borrowed plus accumulated interest were still to be repaid in full. The corrupt activities of the business and political classes in Africa helped to fuel such established practices.

State Violence

I will now turn to another dimension of the cycle of violence: the relationship between the state and its citizenry. The independence decade, which began in the 1960s, was a decade of hope on the continent. National governments were ushered in with the task of improving the economy and social conditions, but the relationship between rulers and the ruled, which had been altered during the colonial period, deteriorated significantly, with state violence becoming a serious problem. Presently, under global capitalism African states are seeking to force the workers to accept SAPs and the neoliberal policies in an attempt to find a niche in the global economic system. In the case of a country such as Rwanda, the Habyarimana regime began using forced labor to cultivate coffee plantations for global production. According to D. N. Smith, "By forcing farmers to specialize in particular crops, the state created a situation of artificial scarcity in which it profited by selling farmers staples it prevented them from producing." Rather than concentrating on food production, SAPs encourage cash-crop production. Flooding the global market with cash crops along with so many other producers certainly does not favor an increase in the price of a nation's crop. It has also led to the neglect of subsistence-food production and the agricultural work of women. Food imports continue to rise, and the forecast for local production remains grim.[29]

Those who dare challenge government policies or programs are dealt with harshly. In Nigeria, successive military governments have attacked protesting university students or minority groups and silenced their leaders, as occurred when Ken Saro Wiwa and other Ogoni leaders were executed for leading protests against oil drilling in their communities, the environmental degradation, and the region's share of revenue from petroleum. The case of South Africa is particularly instructive, since local communities have begun to critique the globalization policies (for instance, GEAR) of the African National Congress. A. Desai reports that the policies of local councils in support of globalization have led to the privatization of many services, the retrenchment of workers, and a rise in the cost of services. The government began cutting off light and water supplies for those too poor to pay. In Soweto, for instance, "some twenty thousand houses had their electricity supplies disconnected every month" in 2001.[30] Electricity rates were higher in Soweto (twenty-eight cents a kilowatt) and rural areas (forty-eight cents a kilowatt) than in rich suburbs (sixteen cents a kilowatt) or for big business (seven cents a kilowatt). People soon began to mobilize not just in terms of demonstrations and coalitions across racial lines (Asians, Coloreds, Blacks) but also in terms of organizing activist committees, such as the Soweto Electricity Crisis Committee, that reconnect the electricity supply disconnected by the government. Desai reports that the type of revolutionary activity developed against the apartheid government is now being resuscitated against the African National Congress. Further, the indigent are resisting the government's attempt to define their communities as irresponsible. Rather, they challenge the legality of the government's activities and target policies that rob them of their ability to pay for services, eat, or go to school—policies they feel attack human dignity and their own conceptions of citizenship rights. Community members are asking not for free services but for affordable rates. The questions now posed by the poor are: Should globalization not be defined in a way that allows them human dignity and economic survival? Does this new process require the marginalization or demise of whole segments of the population?

Workers now complain that the concessions won under the apartheid system are being eroded under the new neoliberal policies of globalization and the government's attempts to attract foreign investment. Foreign investors expect the political class and union leaders in Africa to keep workers in line, even as wages drop and workers are reclassified as part-time, temporary, or casual labor. Food riots, strikes, arrests, and detentions were common over much of Africa in the 1980s and 1990s. A major contradiction is that even though SAPs require states to reduce their size and programs, they are sill expected to remain powerful in order to control the citizenry. Political instability is perceived by both national and international elites as a major deterrent to foreign investment. Similarly, corporations dislike strong unions. As an example of this attitude, Desai recalls the statement of one expatriate general manager: "That refinery is owned by an American corporation. I will not, repeat not, allow some ridiculous South African laws to override my obligation to make money for Exxon and its shareholders."[31]

In looking at the political situation in Africa, many now believe that the new African initiative inaugurated in 2002, the New Partnership for Africa's Development (NEPAD), will play a significant role in solving Africa's problems. Its goals are to keep the reins of a people-centered development in the hands of African states by demanding, in addition to other things, a new partnership with the developed nations of the West. However, as Kunle Amuwo rightly points out, the "authors of the document in question [the NEPAD document] seem to understand neither the system nor the structures with which they are confronted. They have not come to terms with the logic of a system that, vis-à-vis poor countries, often says what it will not do [that is, what it has no intention of doing] and does what it does not say." In other words, there can be no partnership under the present logic of global capitalism. But more important, he then argues that the erosion of state sovereignty as a result of globalization means that states will be unable to deliver "development." African governments will most likely become more repressive in response to protests from frustrated populations. We need to be cognizant of the process by which African states are "permitted to become part of the global system under the regimentation of the West's hegemonic power."[32] There is little room to experience globalization "from above."

Ethnic Conflicts

Until very recently it has been quite acceptable to blame much of Africa's inter-group violence and community rivalry on "ancient" ethnic or religious hostilities. This is particularly true where religious differences overlie ethnic distinctions. Nigeria, for example, is often described as a nation with a North-South split between the warring Muslims of the North and Christians in the South. Not only is reality more complex, given the large pockets of Muslims in the South and Christians in the North, but with more than 250 ethnic demarcations, various minority groups are also discriminated against by majority groups in many of the nation's thirty-six states. The overwhelming attention given to the North-South (or the Hausa-Fulani versus Yoruba-Igbo) split ignores the many other ethnic conflicts that are constantly being manipulated by elites and politicians.

But increasingly, the focus on "tribal" conflicts in Africa is being questioned, and attention is on the impact of economic causes and political constructs. Global warming, famine, and the new neoliberal policies have increased economic rivalry. Communities and ethnic groups clash over dwindling resources, access to land, services, and jobs (as in the Sudan). There are constant calls for a more equitable distribution of resources. In their review of 161 countries around the world between 1960 and 1999, E. Elbadawi and N. Sambanis conclude that "we are able to show that the relatively high prevalence of civil war in Africa is not due to extreme ethno-linguistic fragmentation, but rather to high levels of poverty, heavy dependence on resource-based primary exports and, especially, to failed political institutions."[33] Not only do local communities fight over natural resources such as land and minerals, but these holdings also become easily "lootable" assets for "loot-seeking" rebel movements or convenient resources for sustaining "justice-seeking movements." Further, where there is an abundance of primary resources (diamonds, copper, oil), the government is also able to fund an army and sustain popular support.

In his many books and articles on violence Mahmood Mamdani insists that we not conflate cultural, market-based, and political identities but rather investigate analytically how each is constructed during different historical periods.[34] For Africa, we need to understand how the colonial governments constructed political identities out of cultural groups during the creation of indirect rule. As a legal system, indirect rule divided all colonized subjects into races (Arabs, Asians, Tutsi) or tribes or ethnic groups (Yoruba, Kikuyu, Zulu, Hutu). Each of the latter (tribes) were administered and controlled by local "chiefs" under their "distinct" customary laws within Native Authorities. This structure led to an explosion of corruption, despotism, and abuse, since Native Authorities were accountable to the colonial government and "natives" lost control of their leaders. Equally important was the fact that most social and economic rights (land, marital rights, religious, inheritance, and so on) were dispensed via customary law. Mamdani argues that in most places, this structure was not dismantled after independence. Economic and social rights are still tied to one's ethnic origin. Politically, this means that the larger and wealthier ethnic groups try to marginalize smaller groups within the nation-state in order to control resources. Further, ethnic politics remains important, as politicians fight to capture the government apparatus in order to bring home the bacon to their "tribe." One is never merely a citizen of a nation under such conditions; one is first a member of a cultural group to which one appeals for citizenship benefits.

Intense competition often leads to genocide. The best example is the 1994 genocidal conflict in Rwanda, where, according to Mamdani, the Tutsi had been constructed as a separate and superior "race" by the colonizers and the Hutu as an indigenous ethnic group or tribe. This exacerbated precolonial hierarchies and led to smoldering resentments. After independence, the struggle for hegemony between the two groups led to a series of conflicts in Burundi and Uganda, and finally to the massacre of mostly the Tutsi in Rwanda. About eight hundred thousand people were killed in a little more than three months. Going beyond the usual ethnic analysis, it is clear that at the time of the outbreak, the ruling (Hutu) regime was caught between the economic devastation brought on by SAPs and neoliberal policies, its power tussle with the Tutsi Rwandan Patriots front (in Uganda), and decades of smoldering community politico-economic rivalries.[35] As the government confronted the tensions, it was able to whip up ethnic sentiments to gain popular support from the Hutu masses. Its main goal was to stay in power by any means possible, in order to continue the accumulation of wealth within its ranks. Although the genocide was thus largely engineered by political elites as a calculated risk to hold on to power, it was built on racial and ethnic identities solidified during the colonial era.

Responses to Globalization: Developing Effective Patterns of Resistance

Some scholars argue that the tensions arising from economic globalization and the behavior of national and international elites provide both the impetus and opportunities for the disadvantaged to create solutions.[36] It is hypothesized that both economic turbulence and the weakening of democratic practices will encourage the construction of new approaches that challenge the system. One important development has been the call to think globally. The global perspective is no longer the preserve of global managers, as local actors now realize that their analyses and plans must continuously move between local and international issues. The global *context* in which we now operate must constantly be kept in mind. For instance, it is becoming increasingly clear that much of the work on income generation and microenterprises for informal-sector workers in Africa (particularly among women) is often not as successful as anticipated. As strategies to assist poor women, these projects do not address or alter gender relations in local communities, and therefore leave unresolved many of the obstacles that affect women's ability to generate income. Again, success may be minimal because most of the enterprises are located in the already saturated, resource-poor female-dominated informal sector. Should the informal sector therefore be perceived as the salvation of workers at the very instant that states are withdrawing funds, protection, and benefits from communities? Many groups are working to inform local communities on the global context of their problems, and others are attempting to use the new technologies and contacts to operate at the supranational level.[37]

Briefly stated, there are three major responses to the impact of economic globalization and the various forms of violence in Africa. All three focus on the importance of *organizing*. The three responses are: using international institutions such as the United Nations and its family of agencies, building coalitions and networks of private organizations at the international and regional levels, and creating local grassroots movements.

On the first type of response, the United Nations has developed a set of international conventions and treaties to protect human rights. Under this umbrella each member state is expected to become a signatory and to ratify a wide range of conventions. The aim is to advance and affirm a commitment to the rule of law and fair play. There are hundreds of conventions created to protect various categories of disadvantaged groups. For instance, the 1979 Convention on the Elimination of All Forms of Discrimination against Women (CEDAW) is considered to be women's international bill of rights. There are also conventions on the Rights of Children (1989), Worst Forms of Labor (1999), Protection of the Rights of All Migrant Workers (1990), and To Prevent, Suppress, and Punish Trafficking in Persons (2000). Along the same lines, the Rome Statute of the International Court (1998) established a court (recognized by the UN) with the power to prosecute persons for the most serious crimes against humanity: genocide, war, torture, and aggression. This system of conventions serves as a standard against which individuals and groups can measure the behavior of the state or fellow citizens and appeal for help at the global level. As a result, organizations and nations can monitor the powerful to evaluate the extent to which conventions are being implemented. For instance, the International Advisory Committee, based in Canada, conducted the first CEDAW impact study in 2000.[38] The report stated that among other things, there has been immense government resistance to CEDAW around the world. In Africa in particular, inadequate funding of programs and the marginalization of organizations working for women's rights remain major obstacles. In addition to the "protection" given by this system of conventions, UN organizations such as UNDP, UNESCO, and UNICEF monitor the condition of the world's population, and the results are published each year, as in *The Human Development Report* and *The State of the World's Children*. There are also numerous commissions working on specific programs and projects (for example, violence against women, child health, refugees, and HIV/AIDS). The entire monitoring system provides a base from which citizens and organizations can question or embarrass their governments.

Since the 1980s, interest has grown in the role of nongovernment organizations (NGOs) in building civil society, both at the national and the international levels. At the international level, several of these organizations have special advisory or consultancy status with the United Nations. The NGO movement is attempting to build networks for advocacy, as well as educational and democracy training units. One goal is to help people respond globally to issues. Thus, organizations such as the World Social Forum, the International Campaign to Ban Landmines, and Jubilee 2000 (on third world debt relief) attempt to develop *global* structures that conduct research, lobby effectively, and mobilize public support. They now employ the latest technology, as in using the Internet, to conduct their business. Experienced policy analysts and professionals who are proactive in making specific policy suggestions are more likely to be the ones at the helm of affairs these days. For instance, Jubilee 2000 was able to obtain debt relief for some countries and get the International Monetary Fund to alter some of its policies toward the "heavily indebted poor countries." The group accomplished this goal by lobbying Western governments, who then put pressure on the IMF.[39]

Can such policies be understood as forms of global affirmative action to recompense the worst sufferers for earlier forms of exploitation and resource robbery, grounded in imperialism and race? One outcome of the growth of these networks is that international coverage can often be given to problems facing local or regional NGOs. According to M. Lindenberg and C. Bryant, global NGOs are also attempting to develop "policies on corporate advocacy, defining guidelines for occasions when public criticism is warranted and those when behind-the-scenes discussions and negotiations can be more effective."[40] Organizations are becoming more sophisticated in their strategies: knowing when to pull out of a country for maximum effect, when to base their activities on the work of local NGOs, and when to insist on immediate action (for instance, banning child labor immediately or working to improve working conditions first).

Finally, there are grassroots organizations within every nation. Community organizations working as pressure groups are not new to Africa. From the precolonial through the colonial to the postindependence era, people have organized to address local issues. However, structures and strategies have changed with the times. Today, "traditional" voluntary associations have been influenced by the international NGO movement so that their structures and programs have been overhauled for better effect. A major concern is that African governments often view these organizations as a threat to state authority. To curb threats, governments have refused to register organizations that are critical of their regimes (as in the group Women in Nigeria), or have withdrawn an association's registration license (as occurred in Nigeria, Tanzania, Egypt, Zimbabwe, and Kenya). Imprisoning or harassing leaders and firing sympathizers from their jobs are also common tactics. In Kenya, Tanzania, Nigeria, Uganda, and other countries, laws have been passed to limit the activities of many NGOs. Nonetheless, NGOs have been successful in expanding civil society at the nation level, drawing international attention to their causes, and linking communities to improve grassroots empowerment. For instance, the Grass-root Women Association of Kenya, established in 1997, is an umbrella organization for local associations. The emphasis is on participatory decision making. Two issues being highlighted are violence against women and poverty. Similarly, there are numerous trade unions agitating for reform in the working conditions of workers. Through these organizations, communities are increasingly becoming unaware of their rights, changes in their nation's constitution, or the significance of the UN conventions.

Local NGOs are not merely reacting to change but often seek to initiate changes. A. Desai writes that in South Africa, a growing number of grassroots associations now hold workshops and meetings specifically to educate each other and work on how best to bring about changes that will benefit local communities. Gradually, "large numbers of people in the communities come into contact with each other *in totally new relationships.*"[41]

Grassroots movements appear to be gaining momentum in the struggle against the negative effects of global capitalism. An emergent idea within these movements is that relationships must be fundamentally altered: relationships between governments and global decision-making institutions such as the IMF and the World Trade Organization, on the one hand, and local organizations, on the other. Those at the bottom seek to monitor the activities of those above them and believe that good governance, transparency, and accountability should not apply only to the less powerful. In order to stop the cycle of violence, people feel they must reserve the right to question the activities of those managing affairs at the top. In response to the behavior of the transnational corporations, people within local communities are demanding that they be perceived not only as "workers" in the global market but also as human beings with lives and needs that go beyond the workplace.

Therefore, more and more questions are being raised about this process that seems to reduce everything to the needs of the global market and financial capital. The promise of modernity was that the state would help integrate the various groups into a public with schools, employment, and welfare issues properly addressed. If, as J. Girling points out, this contract is breaking down in Western countries under globalization, where does that leave Africa?[42] The problem goes well beyond the need to attract foreign investment or increase productivity. Rather, the issue is the need to hammer out a new contract—a new way of living together at the national and global levels.

As things stand, globalization enthusiasts argue that the process under way is the panacea for reducing poverty and raising the quality of life in third world regions. However, there are a growing number of voices, many from Africa itself, in opposition to this point of view. The belief is that poverty reduction is not likely to occur under the present regime because economic globalization is not a break from the past. In fact, it builds on earlier global hierarchies. People from the third world, who are largely people of color, still find themselves at the bottom of the economic order. Ongoing economic reforms emphasize wealth accumulation with little attention to global redistribution. For Africa in particular, globalization resembles colonization in a new form, as many have pointed out. In light of this, H. Winant concludes that globalization "is a racialized social structure. It is a system of transnational social stratification under which corporations and states based in the global North dominate the global South."[43]

CHAPTER 3 READING QUESTIONS

1. Koditschek has little to say about the incorporation of large parts of Africa into the British Empire, even though this was happening at the end of the period covered in his work. In a longer piece, he would have considered some of the ways in which Africans and Afro-Caribbeans fit into the evolutionary racial ideologies he discussed. Such ideologies, he would have pointed out, were exceptionally hostile to these particular groups, and offered them few openings to assert their demands for social and political rights. Unable to invoke the Aryan racial heritage, which had been available to the Irish or Indians, they found it extremely difficult to make claims for racial promotion, and were extremely vulnerable to those who would demote them to the lowest rung on the human evolutionary scale. How might these discursive ideological disadvantages, inherited from the colonial period, have contributed to the emergence of the postcolonial realities that Pearce describes?

2. According to Pearce, how do the policies of international capitalist institutions, such as the World Bank and the International Monetary Fund, exacerbate (or even create) the problems of Africa today? Can these policies be characterized as "racist," in the sense that they are based on spoken or unspoken assumptions about the essential nature of Black Africans? How would World Bank or IMF policy makers defend themselves against these charges?

Notes

1. UNDP, *Human Development Report* (New York: Oxford University Press, 2003).

2. UNDP, *Human Development Report* (New York: Oxford University Press, 2002).

3. UNAIDS, "AIDS Epidemic Update, 2006," http://www.unaids.org/en/geographical+area/by+region/sub-saharan+africa.asp, 1.

4. P. Ahluwalia, *Politics and Post-colonial Theory: African Inflections* (London: Routledge, 2001).

5. S. Afonja and T. Pearce, *Social Change in Nigeria* (Essex: Longman, 1986).

6. C. Ake, *Political Economy of Africa* (Harlow: Longman, 1981); F. Fanon, *Studies in a Dying Colonialism* (London: Earthscan, 1989); A. G. Frank, *Sociology of Development and Underdevelopment of Sociology* (London: Pluto, 1971); Mahmood Mamdani, *Citizen and Subject: Contemporary Africa and the Legacy of Late Colonialism* (Princeton: Princeton University Press, 1996); K. Nkrumah, *Neo-colonialism: The Last Stage of Imperialism* (London: Nelson, 1965).

7. A. Escobar, *Encountering Development* (Princeton: Princeton University Press, 1995).

8. A. G. Frank, "Transitional Ideological Modes: Feudalism, Capitalism, Socialism," *Critical Anthropology* 11, no. 2 (1991): 171–88.

9. P. McMichael, *Development and Social Change* (Thousand Oaks, Calif.: Pine Forge Press, 2000); J. Mittelman, "How Does Globalization Really Work?" in *Globalization* (Boulder: Lynne Rienner, 1996): 229–41; F. Piven, "Globalization, American Politics, and Welfare Policy," in *Lost Ground,* edited by R. Albelda and A. Withorn (Cambridge: South End Press, 2002), 27–41.

10. McMichael, *Development and Social Change,* 152; R. Mishra, *Globalization and the Welfare State* (Cheltenham, UK: Edward Elgar, 1999).

11. D. Kellner, "Theorizing Globalization," *Sociological Theory* 20, no. 3 (2002): 286–305; J. Stiglitz, *Globalization and Its Discontents* (New York: W. W. Norton, 2002).

12. Mishra, *Globalization and the Welfare State;* Y. Fall, "Gender and Social Implications of Globalization: An African Experience," in *Gender, Globalization, and Democracy,* edited by M. R. Kelly et al. (Lanham, Md.: Rowman and Littlefield, 2001), 49–74; S. Sassen, *Globalization* (New York: New Press, 1998).

13. Taye Assefa et al., eds., *Globalization, Democracy, and Development in Africa: Challenges and Prospects* (Addis Ababa, Ethiopia: Organization for Social Science Research in Eastern and Southern Africa, 2001), v; Sassen, *Globalization.*

14. D. Green, *Gender Violence in Africa* (New York: St. Martin's, 1999).

15. M. Rama, "Globalization and Workers in Developing Countries," World Bank Policy Research Paper no. 2958 (2003), http://econ.worldbank.org/programs/public_services/library/doc?id=2870, 14.

16. Economic Commission for Africa, *The New Face of Poverty in Africa* (Addis Ababa, Ethiopia: Economic Commission for Africa, 1999).

17. E. Elbadawi and N. Sambanis, "Why Are There So Many Civil Wars in Africa? Understanding and Preventing Violent Conflict," *Journal of African Economies* 9, no. 3 (2000): 244–69; L. Rappoport, "Scarcity, Genocide, and the Postmodern Individual," in *The Coming Age of Scarcity: Preventing Mass Death and Genocide in the 21st Century,* edited by Michael Dobkowski and Isidor Wallimann (Syracuse: Syracuse University Press, 1998), 271; Rama, "Globalization and Workers."

18. G. Emeagwali, ed., *Women Pay the Price* (Trenton, N.J.: African World Press, 1995).

19. F. Leach et al., "An Investigative Study of Abuse of Girls in African Schools," *Department for International Development Educational Publications Despatch,* http://www.dfid.gov.uk/pubs/; R. Manjate et al., "Lovers, Hookers, and Wives: Unbraiding the Social Contradictions of Urban Mozambican Women's Sexual and Economic Lives," in *African Women's Health,* edited by M. Turshen (Trenton, N.J.: African World Press, 2000).

20. M. Arigbede, *Development and Women's Health in Africa* (Lagos, Nigeria: Empowerment and Action Research Centre, 1997); K. Harrison, "Maternal Mortality in Nigeria: The Real Issues," *African Journal of Reproductive Health* 1, no. 1 (1997): 7–13.

21. S. Alubo and F. Vivekanunda, *Beyond the Illusion of Primary Health Care in an African Society* (Stockholm: Bethany Books, 1995).

22. See UNDP, *Human Development Report* (New York: Oxford University Press, 2005).

23. Dobkowski and Wallimann, *Coming Age of Scarcity.*

24. J. Cobb, "The Threat to the Underclass," in ibid., 25–42; T. Trainer, "Our Unsustainable Society," in ibid., 83–100.

25. C. Lewis, "The Paradox of Global Development and the Necessary Collapse of Modern Industrial Civilization," in *Coming Age of Scarcity,* edited by Dobkowski and Wallimann, 44; Escobar, *Encountering Development,* 212; Dobkowski and Wallimann, *Coming Age of Scarcity.*

26. See UNDP, *Human Development Report* (2003), table 16, 292–93.

27. B. C. Chikulo, "Globalization, Debt, and Development in Southern Africa," in *Globalization, Democracy, and Development,* edited by Assefa et al., 154.

28. N. N. Njehu, testimony by the director of Fifty Years Is Enough: U.S. Network for Global Economic Justice to the Africa Subcommittee of the House International Relations Committee hearing "Debt Relief for Africa," April 13, 1999, http://www.50years.org/updates/testimony.html, 2.

29. D. N. Smith, "Postcolonial Genocide," in Coming Age of Scarcity, edited by Dobkowski and Wallimann, 220–44; Economic Commission for Africa, Transforming Africa's Economics (Addis Ababa, Ethiopia: Economic Commission for Africa, 2001).

30. A. Desai, We Are the Poors (New York: Monthly Review Press, 2002), 92.

31. Ibid., 111.

32. Kunle Amuwo, "Globalization, NEPAD, and the Governance Question in Africa," African Studies Quarterly 6, no. 3 (2003), available online at http://web.africa.ufl.edu/asq/vb/v6i3a4.htm; Ahluwalia, Politics and Post-colonial Theory, 70.

33. Elbadawi and Sambanis, "Why Are There So Many Civil Wars?" 245.

34. See Mamdani, Citizen and Subject and "Beyond Settler and Native as Political Identities: Overcoming the Political Legacy of Colonialism," Society for Comparative Study of Society and History 43, no. 4 (2001): 651–64.

35. Mahmood Mamdani, When Victims Become Killers (Princeton: Princeton University Press, 2001); Roger W. Smith, "Scarcity and Genocide," in Coming Age of Scarcity, edited by Dobkowski and Wallimann, 199–219.

36. Kellner, "Theorizing Globalization"; Stiglitz, Globalization and Its Discontents.

37. Ibitola Pearce, "At Work, at Home: African Women Negotiating Global Capitalism," in Black Women in Urban Spaces, edited by G. Tate (New York: St. Martin's Press, in press).

38. M. McPhedran et al., "Overview," in The First CEDAW Impact Study: Final Report (2000), http://www.iwrp.org/CEDAW_Impact_Study.htm.

39. See M. Lindenberg and C. Bryant, Going Global (Bloomfield, Conn.: Kumarian Press, 2001).

40. Ibid., 203.

41. Desai, We Are the Poors, 144 (emphasis added).

42. J. Girling, Social Movements and Symbolic Power: Radicalism, Reform, and the Trial of Democracy in France (New York: Palgrave Macmillan, 2004).

43. H. Winant, The New Politics of Race (Minneapolis: University of Minnesota Press), 131.

4

White without End?

The Abolition of Whiteness; or, The Rearticulation of Race

DAVID ROEDIGER

"Race Over" was the headline for Harvard-based sociologist Orlando Patterson's 2000 soothsayings in the *New Republic*. By 2050, Patterson assured readers, the United States "will have problems aplenty. But no racial problem whatsoever." By then, "the social virus of race will have gone the way of smallpox." Inconsistencies littered the predictions. Blacks in the new raceless United States would use new technologies to change appearances. In the Northeast and Midwest, for example, "murderous racial gang fights" would persist without race. In the Southeast, the "Old Confederacy" race divisions would continue, but would somehow make no difference in the national picture. A far more glaring contradiction obtruded when Patterson added another set of futurological observations in a *New York Times* article that contested the common view of demographers that whites would become a minority in the United States in the twenty-first century. Arguing that "nearly half of the Hispanic population is white in every social sense," Patterson forecast that "the non-Hispanic white population will remain a substantial majority and possibly even grow as a portion of the population." Patterson's point—that the children of non-Hispanic white-Hispanic intermarriages will identify as, and be identified as, "white" is not implausible, but the contrast between the two articles is jarring. Race will vanish, and whiteness will persist.[1]

Patterson is not alone in failing to consider whether and how the virus of whiteness might disappear even as he launches freewheeling discussions of an end to race. To an alarming extent, such discussions echo long-standing assumptions that the identities of people of color (and especially African Americans) are "the problem" when race is considered. Whiteness flies beneath the radar as a norm, not a racial identity. Thus, in the spring of 1997, newsstands sported simultaneously two mass-market magazines featuring an impassioned call for

African Americans, but not whites, to shed their racial identities. In Paul Gilroy's often brilliant *Against Race: Imagining Political Culture beyond the Color Line,* Nazism is the focus of race-thinking past, but Black nationalism and Black cultural production are emphasized when we are told what is keeping us from moving beyond race today. The Web site Interracial Voice, influential in the campaign for multiracial census categories and as a venue for the opinions of anti–affirmative action activist Ward Connerly, consistently blames Black leaders for the persistence of race thinking. Stanley Crouch identifies those same leaders as responsible for mounting a rearguard action, sure to fail, perpetuating the "skin game." More generally, the glorification of "color-blindness" in the United States has specifically exalted *white* (self-proclaimed) color-blindness and has decisively separated the persistence of white identity from the persistence of racism. Whites, it seems, have developed immunities to the virus of race. Even the much vaunted emphasis on multiracial "hybridity," seen as making race unfixed (and not in need of fixing) and obsolete, can fudge on the future of whiteness.[2] To take a particularly dramatic example, the special 1993 issue of *Time* on the "new face of America" morphed into existence Eve, a cover girl for a future America in which the white majority might give way but in which whites were generally imagined to continue to exist even as a "crossbreeding" undermined race. Eve herself was the result of feeding mostly "white" faces into a computer program and, like the similarly generated new multicultural face for advertising icon Betty Crocker, "looked" white.[3]

One noteworthy exception to such failures to consider the possibility of an end to whiteness comes in the recent boom of scholarship and activist writings on the critical study of that identity. Critical studies of whiteness are heir to a particularly rich tradition that has insisted that whiteness is a problem, that it is produced within systems of oppression, and that its production and reproduction must be historically explained. When Amoja Three Rivers recently wrote that "white people have not always been 'white,' nor will they always be 'white.' It is a political alliance. Things will change," she echoed W. E. B. Du Bois's long-ago observation that "personal" whiteness is an identity that has held sway for only a tiny sliver of human history. When Cheryl Harris produced her seminal article on "whiteness as property" a decade ago, she could draw on Du Bois's analysis of the "income-bearing" origins of whiteness. When Alice Walker recently invited white men to explore what they were "other than" white, her remarks resonated with James Baldwin's insistent calling out of white people, encouraging their identification with humanity, not race privilege.[4]

Even so, the outpouring of "whiteness studies" in the recent past has on balance shown how difficult it is to imagine the end of whiteness at least as much as it has charted the possibility of doing so. One great achievement of *Race Traitor,* the journal and anthology that has most fully articulated the case for "abolition" of whiteness, has been to cause even scholarly studies of whiteness to address whether it is possible and desirable to move beyond whiteness. Noel Ignatiev, a coeditor of *Race Traitor* and an important historian of white racial formation, has characterized the split over this question as one between "abolitionists" and "preservationists." However polemical the latter of these two labels may be—Ignatiev's critics would say that they want to improve rather than to simply preserve white identity—it does capture an insistence on the durability of whiteness on the part of many leading writers on the subject. That insistence deserves attention, and criticism, but the "preservationist" critique of "abolitionism" also has some force. Even when it is unpersuasive, that critique taps into the patterns of hegemonic common sense regarding race discussed above. Moreover, at their best, preservationists have raised genuinely difficult questions that abolitionists must address if we are to imagine an end to whiteness and strategies for furthering that end. In reviewing and entering this debate, this chapter argues that its intricacies give us an opportunity to see anew the importance of regarding whiteness as the product of what Eduardo Bonilla-Silva calls a racial system, bound up in property and power relationships, and not simply as a bad or not-so-bad attitude.[5] The preservationist-abolitionist debate, and silences and weaknesses within it, should also cause us to consider, à la Patterson but without following his conclusions, how to think about an end to whiteness in a multiracial context.

The preservationist position is perhaps most ably articulated by sociologist Howard Winant in his "Behind Blue Eyes: Whiteness and Contemporary U.S. Racial Politics." For Winant, skin color marks a reality that apparently cannot be transcended. While praising scholarship historicizing whiteness and locating its origins within "the development and maintenance of capitalist class rule in the United States," Winant wrongly identifies the "New Abolitionist Racial Project" as a white initiative. He does not challenge the abolitionist emphasis on the "vacuity" of white identity or contest the idea that "whiteness may not be a legitimate cultural identity in the sense of having a discrete, 'positive' content" apart from the exercise of privilege. Nonetheless, for Winant, whiteness "is imbedded in a highly articulated social structure and system of significations" and therefore cannot be "repudiated" but rather must be "rearticulated."[6]

Whereas Winant concentrates most of his analysis on the inadequacy of abolitionist strategies and on the rootedness of whiteness, other preservationists are insistent in regarding the *desirability* of shoring up white identities. Two editors of the anthology *White Reign*, for example, seek to intervene in a "white identity crisis" by "conceiving" of "new ways to be white." Another editor, Nelson M. Rodriguez, very usefully defines "solidarity as the opposite of whiteness," but then goes on to proclaim that the "erasure" of whiteness is an "impossible project."[7] Cultural critic Henry Giroux writes of "the recent scholarship on 'whiteness'" as providing an "important theoretical service," but deplores any notion that "'whiteness' is synonymous with domination, oppression and privilege." He rejects as vehemently the political conclusion that we should seek "to abolish 'whiteness' as a racial category and marker of identity." Giroux's call is then to "rearticulate" whiteness as "more than a form of domination" as a "discourse of critique and possibility" rejecting "forms of 'whiteness' structured in dominance and aligned with exploitative interests and oppressive social relations." That such a "progressive whiteness" has at this late date to be "imagined" in classrooms might suggest that the ties of whiteness to oppression are more profound than Giroux allows.[8]

With even cultural critics speaking in terms of identity crises among whites as they counsel us to "rearticulate," "resituate," "redeploy," or "deterritorialize" whiteness, it is perhaps unsurprising that those trained in psychology have greatly influenced the preservationist position. Among the more therapeutically oriented advocates of a refurbished whiteness, race is seldom problematized and only less than fully mature forms of white identity seem to lack positive content. Institutionally, the best expression of this position comes from New Jersey's Center for the Study of White American Culture. The center, whose name carries the subtitle "A Multiracial Organization," distributes "Decentering Whiteness," a provocative position paper coauthored by Jeff Hitchcock and Charley Flint. In arguing that there is a white American culture that can be mined for its progressive elements, the center seeks to sensitize whites to unspoken assumptions regarding the supremacy and centrality of whiteness. It praises the work of Janet E. Helms, a noted psychologist of white racial identity whose ideas are most popularly available in *A Race Is a Nice Thing to Have: A Guide to Being a White Person; or, Understanding the White Persons in Your Life*. Helms's work holds out the desirability of helping an individual to move through various stages of racial hostility, naïveté, and denial to an antiracist identity that "learn[s] to accept Whiteness as an important part of herself or himself and to internalize a realistically positive view of what it means to be white." This position finds echoes in the staged categories of Ruth Frankenberg's brilliant ethnography, *White Women, Race Matters*.[9]

In developing my own position here the aim is not to seek a middle ground. My own abolitionism remains unreconstructed. Following James Baldwin in seeing whiteness as a "lie" that separates its holders not only from the rest of humanity but also from their own humanity, I have no wish to solve its identity crisis. The task of "disillusioning" whites with whiteness, as Franklin Rosemont wonderfully puts it, is far more urgent and appealing. That said, it still seems to me that abolitionists must acknowledge that we have failed to provide a compelling strategy to further the end of whiteness. Calling upon white individuals to opt out of the "club" of whiteness and to subvert the working of the racial system is a part of such a strategy.[10] However, by itself, such a call is open to the charge of being abstract, voluntarist, and individualistic. On those scores abolitionism is not very different from therapeutic versions of preservationism, suggesting perhaps that both "sides" face obdurate contradictions. At this juncture abolitionists would do well to acknowledge the weakest points of our positions, and to debate among ourselves, as a prelude to moving forward. I therefore want to consider several areas in which the force of critiques of abolitionism must be acknowledged even as the preservationist argument does not convince.

A story gives us access to some of the central issues here. A decade ago while I was teaching at the University of Missouri, a student group sought an expanded Black Culture Center. On the day of my guest lecture on race to a peace studies class, the campus newspaper ran the inevitable letters suggesting that "reverse racism" would be triumphant if a new center were built in the absence of a White Culture Center. I began with what seemed to the largely white class an easy question: "What kinds of things would go into the display space in a Black Culture Center?" There were many (perhaps too) ready responses, mostly cataloging music, sports heroes, symbols of oppression, and protest leaders. The second question followed: "What would go in a White Culture Center?" No response was necessarily expected, but the mass squirming in the room suggested that the question should be pursued rather than merely tossed out as food for thought. "Well, what would go in it?" Further squirming and weighty silence. "Take your time." At last a young woman ventured an indirect response: "The whole university is about white studies and white culture. That's what makes a Black Culture Center necessary." Other students gradually began to answer the question directly, hazarding opinions as to artifacts and activities belonging in a center devoted to white culture: Spam, Elvis records, money, Wonder Bread, an aisle from K-Mart, chains and whips from the holding of slaves, pictures of country clubs, a stock exchange, and country music. Students soon asked telling questions about each other's suggestions: Are we saying that white culture is about guilt, emptiness, oppression, and profit? Didn't Elvis make it by recording African American music? What is "white," and what is "American"? How can K-Mart and an exclusive country club (or, to take the first two responses when I later posed the same questions to a legal studies seminar, artifacts from corporate boardrooms and from "ethnic" Fourth of July picnics) be part of a common white culture? If my working-class parents could never dream of joining that country club, are they then less than white? Well into the discussion I asked whether the many comments did not raise the issue of whether there was a "white culture." One student objected, "What can we be if we aren't white?" He added that all "nonwhite" students "got to have" their cultures. Pained silence gave way to a free-for-all of discussion. That discussion continued in the halls long after the class. Some students held that "white" culture's positive content could not be identified because there was no such content. One young white woman, near tears, approached to say she had not been so upset since a teacher made her read Malcolm X's autobiography. Another offered, "Being Jewish, I feel sorry for these white kids." Shortly afterward, and with the class very much in mind, I wrote in introducing *Towards the Abolition of Whiteness*, "It is not merely that whiteness is oppressive and false; it is that whiteness is *nothing but* oppressive and false. . . . It is the empty and therefore terrifying attempt to build an identity based on what one isn't and on whom one can hold back." I argued, "Whiteness in the U.S. is best regarded as an absence of culture."[11]

At least four major objections to such an abolitionist position have been registered. The "White Culture Center" drama helps to explain why such objections can neither be waved away nor simply accepted in what is bound to be a protracted debate containing contradictions resolvable only through political action and over time. The first objection is that the connection of abolitionism with the absence of white culture is "antiwhite" and even, as Annalee Newitz charges, saturated with "hopelessness, brutality, and nihilism" as well as a "contemplative self-destruction." Abolitionist writings, Newitz argues, are akin to "indie" rock's mordant music and especially to Beck's self-descriptive and self-absorbed song "Loser."[12] Certainly, some of Newitz's criticisms found echoes in the peace studies class. The absence of white culture seemed to some students to threaten annihilation—what can we be without white racial identity?

There are compelling answers to the general charge that abolitionist studies are opposed to white people and to the particular charge that "self-hatred" motivates critics of whiteness. Adopting a longer and wider view of critical studies of whiteness is central to framing such answers. The contributions of writers of color, who can hardly be said to be motivated in their critiques of whiteness by self-hatred, have long insisted on a separation between opposing whiteness as a system of privilege and caring for individuals who are called, and call themselves, white. The great African American sociologist Horace Cayton, for example, took great care in describing his 1940s encounter with psychoanalysis. An esteemed university professor, he moved within the "rising, well-to-do Negro class and a group of white intellectuals." However, as he recalled in his 1965 autobiography, *Long Old Road*, all was far from well. In a chapter titled "The Dark Inner Landscape," Cayton recalled his fears that he would never be able to love again. Feigning a desire to be trained in psychoanalysis, but fooling "no one, including myself," he began to frequent the Institute for Psychoanalysis and became a patient of Dr. Helen V. McLean. No African American analysts were available, and Cayton chose McLean in part because he thought that a woman might best understand his problems. Used to doing productive work in integrated settings, Cayton did not much think that race contributed to his deepening anxieties. Even as he related consistent dreams in which terrifying white things and white persons blocked his happiness, Cayton drew no conclusions. McLean gently pursued the matter, asking what all this might mean. At last, Cayton had what he saw as a breakthrough: "I hate white people. I just discovered it. I never realized it before. Not all white people, of course—some I like—but the idea of white people in general."[13]

In separating the personal characteristics of being white from whiteness as power—"The only whitey," Amiri Baraka wrote, "is system and ideology"— scholars and activists of color such as Amoja Three Rivers, Thandeka, Ian Haney Lopez, and James Baldwin clearly identify the "misery" and "spiritual" malaise attendant to whiteness as harmful *to whites*. Baldwin's oft-quoted line, "As long as you think you are white, there's no hope for you," is thus a deeply humanist intervention motivated by anything but hatred, self- or otherwise. One of many regrettable aspects of the recent hyping of the critical study of whiteness as a project of white scholars is that this emphasis on the harm done to whites by whiteness often goes unexplored. For understandable reasons, such scholars have rightly resisted suggesting that those victimized by and those privileged by white supremacy are in anything like equivalent positions. In so doing, however, they have often (mea culpa) had difficulty in showing the extent to which whiteness structures what surrealists have called a "miserabilist" social system, wedding whites to petty privileges not worth having—to property, to management, and to "rigidity."[14]

Of course, any idea of whiteness as a spiritual disease will be threatening to many whites—even to some who would consider race to be a virus and even if a cure is projected. In focusing ire on Malcolm X, the Missouri student who fought back tears picked a figure who himself clearly saw the whiteness he critiqued as a system of power ("white-ism"), not as a biological imperative. Baldwin's observations on the "white man's desire not to be judged by those who are not white" similarly warn us that education regarding the history and the humanism of the critical study of whiteness will not *entirely* blunt the charge that such study is, as a Florida student put it, "down on" white people.[15]

However, the preservationist position does not get us out of the problems raised above. The passion and anxiety with which some of the Missouri students reacted to perceived attacks on whiteness partook of their own doubts regarding the "positive content" of white culture and of their frustrations at not being able to specify such virtues. Again and again ethnographers have pointed to a belief among whites that they lack a white culture. Some writers, such as Ruth Frankenberg and Lorraine Delia Kenny, declare that the contemporary whites they astutely observe only *think* that they lack a white culture and should be reeducated on that point. Other research, such as the remarkably important work on white northern California high schoolers by Pamela Perry, warns that, cheerless as they are, claims by whites to be "cultureless" actually buttress white supremacy as normative and rational.[16] Clearly, such claims are extant, and they cohabit with high anxiety. Thus, to simply be accepting of white culture's "positive content" is also to be at odds with many whites and especially with white youth and to miss their concerns.

A second substantial criticism of abolitionism centers on its reputed difficulty in acknowledging differences among whites who are, as Giroux has it, "positioned across multiple locations of privilege and subordination." On this view, there may not be a "white culture," but there are white workers, white lesbians, white ethnics, white youth, white women, and even "white trash" whose practices and values can be mined in order to "appropriate selective elements of white identity and culture as oppositional." The sense in which the working-class student whose parents could not get in the country club felt estranged from normative, privileged middle-class whiteness illustrates the point. But again the easy-seeming solution, to reach his family as "white workers," begs important questions regarding whether what Thandeka calls the "whited worker" is not separated from meaningful working-class consciousness precisely by whiteness.[17] Similarly, the question cannot simply be whether there are white feminists, blues performers, gay men, trade unionists, and Chicagoans—surely, the variety is there—but whether white identity lets such identities flower more or less fully.

The third objection to abolitionism holds, with very considerable force, that opting out of the white race is not too hard but too easy a move. The asserted nonwhiteness of the Jewish student serves as a handy example, as does the "raceless" way in which I moderated the discussion. In the case of white writers on whiteness, as Ware and Back follow Mike Hill in arguing, a two-ness all too easily develops: a sharp recognition of a system of race privilege coupled with a placing of oneself "outside that system." More broadly, the idea that whites can immediately, voluntarily, and durably become race traitors intersects uncomfortably with long, vexed traditions of blackface minstrel performance and with more recent neoconservative fantasies of "color-blindness." Any easy white assumption that excellent intentions, beats, rhymes, and even politics obviate the need for self-reflection will produce troubling results. Winant writes of whiteness as not being susceptible to "repudiation" via "a mere act of political will." When the "mere act" consists of consuming packaged bits of hip-hop culture, often marketed in highly masculinist and homophobic forms, the idea that renouncing whiteness is too easy gains force. Such is especially the case because, as Robyn Wiegman has shown, the embodied, visible nature of whiteness complicates race treason by making whiteness persist even after its personal renunciation.[18] Thus, near the end of Spike Lee's *Bamboozled,* the white rapper MC Serch participates in full hip-hop gear with an African American crew in a revolutionary (if farcical and tragic) kidnapping. When the cops come, he has to beg to be shot, screaming that he is not white.

Again, the debates here are long established. In 1947 Madison, Wisconsin, preacher Kenneth Patton announced to his congregation that, like the hero

of Sinclair Lewis's postwar novel *Kingsblood Royal,* he had "resigned" from
the white race. Thereafter, he told parishioners, "he would be a colored man."
Joseph Bibb immediately wrote in the *Pittsburgh Courier,* a leading African
American paper, that no white person could "change his race and become a
colored person by merely renouncing white people and moving in with colored
folks." Bibb credited Patton with having done a "noble thing," but he insisted
that Patton would "still think as a white man." The "institutions and systems"
of white supremacy, he concluded, "cannot be eradicated and eliminated by
fortuitous decisions of altruistic white people like Dr. Patton." On the other
hand, the irascible Black journalist George Schuyler immediately replied that,
however "crazy" and "screwy," Patton's idea was worthy of widespread emula-
tion. In a few weeks Reverend Patton himself confessed discouragement with
the experiment, and seemed to agree with Bibb, pronouncing that "action not
words" would eradicate racial discrimination.[19]

Related to the distrust of a facile abandonment of whiteness—with doors
always open to a return—is another large issue that neither abolitionists nor
preservationists have convincingly addressed. That issue is the tendency to
imagine Black and White as the only racial identities germane to discussions
of race treason or race "redeployment." A strong tendency among preservationists and abolitionists is to imagine "becoming Black" as the alternative to white
identity. To the extent that "Black" functions at times as a marker signifying
resistance, abolition's encouragement of a turn of Blackness makes some sense.
But the problems raised by such a stance are many and serious. It leaves the field
open for the sort of extravagant "end of race" preachments from Patterson and
Time on offer at this article's outset, as such prognostications at least enjoy the
advantage of considering the roles of immigration, multiraciality, and hybridity,
however inaptly. The Black-white axis also charts an extremely well-worn terrain
of racial crossings that preservationists sometimes use to argue that whites are
"already" Black in large measure and sometimes ridicule. Abolitionists have at
times blithely dismissed all other "races" as on the way to whiteness. Such an
analysis can make—Blacks being a relatively small U.S. minority—white race
traitors the very motor of history. It liquidates the possibility of a multiracial
assault on white privilege in favor of endless and unresolvable debates about
the authenticity of white kids in hip-hop gear.[20]

A final important preservationist criticism of abolitionism hinges precisely
on its difficulties in detailing just what actions give meaning to race treason. It
is true that, as the abolitionist movement against slavery showed, the fact that
there is not an immediately plausible strategy for reaching a goal does not mean
that the goal itself is suspect, or that such a strategy might not become possible,
dramatically and unexpectedly. Moreover, so long as preservationist thinkers
fail to answer what exactly they mean by the recuperable, "oppositional" element that whiteness contains, they join abolitionists in an airy unwillingness to

specify what is to be done. When strategies are spelled out, both camps tend to emphasize individual transformations. Wiegman's dissection of the tendency of myself and other abolitionists to stress "consciousness as the means to undo the [white] body's social positionality" is thus an acute criticism. She adds that the lonely and voluntary actions urged by "race traitors"—the insistence on the decisive power of a few defectors from the "club" of whiteness—focus typically on masculine heroism and private decisions to confront "official society" physically. Since abolitionists and preservationists, at their best, share an awareness that race thinking is made and remade in systems of structural inequality, the voluntarism of their strategies is especially striking. Clearly, more than just theoretical mistakes are in play, and the weakness of movements for racial justice has broadly impoverished our abilities to imagine social solutions to the white problem. Those of us who speak on whiteness hear the question "Am I doing something wrong?" far more often than "Where do I join?" However, that situation will not continue indefinitely—indeed, mobilizations for immigrant rights and the heating up of African American demands for reparations for slavery may be changing matters now—and the need for thinking through both individual transformation and collective action is pressing.[21]

Like all contemporary opponents of racism, abolitionists must argue both that race is largely a fiction biologically and that race is a pernicious social fact. More specifically, abolitionists must work to identify the workings of white racial privilege while encouraging whites to disidentify with what guarantees those privileges. An emphasis on the misery that whiteness causes whites to accept, in their own lives and in those of others, helps in navigating this terrain. Any successful argument that white racial identity is not a good thing to have must also show that what Alastair Bonnett has called "living without" whiteness leaves *greater* play for identities based on community, class, passionate interests, common struggles, family, gender, ethnicity, region, age, sexuality, and affinities as yet unimagined to develop.[22]

All such appeals will remain abstract if abolitionism divorces itself from the workday struggles against allowing whiteness to pay off as property and privilege. It is one thing to brand the "wages of whiteness" as petty and pitiful when set against broader human happiness. It is quite another to fight for policies that create the sure knowledge that such privileges are on their way out. In the South of a half century ago, for example, the system of segregation left much of the white population immiserated, but the relative advantages of whiteness and the seemingly natural permanence of white supremacy ensured that few would question whether being white was worthwhile. With whites having an average 600 percent more wealth than African Americans and Latinos and with white incarceration rates at less than one-seventh those of African Americans, such a "natural" desire to assert whiteness will persist, even in the wake of post–civil rights gains. If assaults on "whiteness as property" develop alongside integrated class mobilizations for economic justice generally, "disinvestments" in white-ness become far more sustainable. Though less noticed than calls for white individuals to "come out" of the white race, the structural emphasis found in a line of *Race Traitor's* manifesto provides an apt watchword: "The key to solving the social problems of our age is to abolish the white race, that is, to abolish the privileges of the white skin."[23]

CHAPTER 4 READING QUESTIONS

1. Does Roediger's case for the abolition of whiteness have any implications for the abolition or preservation of blackness? Given his position, why might Roediger argue that, although the abolition of whiteness may be a worthy goal for progressive whites, the abolition of blackness can come only as a consequence of the dismantling of the entire race structure itself? Another way of thinking about this question is to consider the relationship between Roediger's argument about whiteness and Helen A. Neville's argument about color-blind racism, which you will encounter in Chapter 5.

2. How does Roediger refute the preservationist argument that it is illegitimate to demand the abolition of whiteness, as this is tantamount to asking white people to give up an important part of their culture and identity?

3. How does Roediger's analysis help us to understand the dangers of viewing race in purely cultural terms, and of ignoring the structures of inequality and oppression that produce it?

Notes

1. Orlando Patterson, "Race Over," *New Republic,* January 10, 2000, 6; Patterson, "Race by the Numbers," *New York Times,* May 8, 2001.

2. Paul Gilroy, *Against Race: Imagining Political Culture beyond the Color Line* (Cambridge, Mass.: Belknap, 2000); "The Interracial Voice," http://www.webcom.com/intvoice/html; Stanley Crouch, "Race Is Over: Black, White, Red, Yellow—Same Difference," *New York Times Magazine,* September 29, 1998, 170–71; Crouch, *The All-American Skin Game; or, The Decoy of Race* (New York: Pantheon, 1996); John A. Powell, "The Colorblind Multiracial Dilemma: Racial Categories Reconsidered," *University of San Francisco Law Review* 31 (1997): 790; Neil Gotanda, "A Critique of 'Our Constitution Is Colorblind,'" *Stanford Law Review* 44 (1991): 2.

3. *Time,* Fall 1993; David R. Roediger, *Colored White: Transcending the Racial Past* (Berkeley and Los Angeles: University of California Press, 2002); Michael Rogin, *Blackface, White Noise: Jewish Immigrants in the Hollywood Melting-Pot* (Berkeley and Los Angeles: University of California Press, 1996), 7–8, 76–79; Lee Svitak Dean, "Recipe for a New Betty Crocker," *Minneapolis Star-Tribune,* March 20, 1996.

4. Amoja Three Rivers, *Cultural Etiquette: A Guide for the Well-Intentioned* (Indian Valley, Va.: Market Wimmin Press, 1991), 8; Cheryl Harris, "Whiteness as Poverty," *Harvard Law Review* 106 (1993): 1710–91; W. E. B. Du Bois, *Dusk of Dawn: An Essay towards the Autobiography of a Race-Concept* (New York: Harcourt, 1940), 129; David Wellman, "Minstrel Shows, Affirmative Action Talk, and Angry White Men: Marking Racial Otherness in the 1990s," in *Displacing Whiteness: Essays in Social and Cultural*

Criticism, edited by Ruth Frankenberg (Durham: Duke University Press, 1997), 328; James Baldwin, *The Price of the Ticket: Collected Nonfiction, 1948–1985* (New York: St. Martin's, 1985); David R. Roediger, ed., *Black on White: Black Writers on What It Means to Be White* (New York: Schocken Books, 1998), 3–26.

5. Noel Ignatiev and John Garvey, eds., *"Race Traitor": Journal of the New Abolitionism* (New York: Routledge, 1998); Ignatiev, "Abolition and 'White Studies,'" http://www.postfun.com/racetraitor/features/whitestudies.html; Eduardo Bonilla-Silva, "Rethinking Racism: Toward a Structural Interpretation," *American Sociological Review* 62 (1997): 465–80.

6. Howard Winant, "Behind Blue Eyes: Whiteness and Contemporary U.S. Racial Politics," in *Off White: Readings and Race Power and Society,* edited by Michelle Fine et al. (New York: Routledge, 1997), 47, 48, 40–53.

7. Joe L. Kincheloe and Shirley R. Steinberg, "Addressing the Crisis of Whiteness," in *White Reign: Deploying Whiteness in America,* edited by Joe L. Kincheloe et al. (New York: St. Martin's, 1998), 10, 14, 5–29; Nelson M. Rodriguez, "Emptying the Content of Whiteness: Toward an Understanding of the Relations between Whiteness and Pedagogy," in ibid., 54, 60. See also Ruth Frankenberg, "Introduction: Local Whitenesses, Localizing Whiteness," in *Off White,* edited by Fine et al., 1–34; and Linda Martin Alcott, "What Should White People Do?" *Hypatia* 13 (1998): 15–17.

8. Henry A. Giroux, "White Squall: Resistance and the Pedagogy of Whiteness," *Cultural Studies* 11 (1997): 385–88; George Yudice, "Neither Impugning nor Disavowing Whiteness Does a Viable Politics Make: The Limits of Identity Politics," in *After Political Correctness,* edited by Christopher Newfield and Ronald Strickland (Boulder: Westview Press, 1995), 276; Peter McLaren, "Decentering Whiteness: In Search of a Revolutionary Multiculturalism," *Multicultural Education* 5 (1997): 4–11.

9. Kincheloe et al., *White Reign,* 3, 60, 196; Janet E. Helms, *A Race Is a Nice Thing to Have: A Guide to Being a White Person; or, Understanding the White Persons in Your Life* (Topeka: Content Communications, 1992); Jeff Hitchcock and Charley Flint, *Decentering Whiteness* (Roselle, N.J.: Center for the Study of White American Culture, 1997); Helms, *Black and White Racial Identity Theory, Research, and Practice* (Westport, Conn.: Greenwood Press, 1990), 55; Ruth Frankenberg, *White Women, Race Matters: The Social Construction of Whiteness* (Minneapolis: University of Minnesota Press, 1993), 194–207, 230–43.

10. Franklin Rosemont, "Notes on Surrealism as a Revolution against Whiteness," *Race Traitor* 9 (1998): 29.

11. David Roediger, *Towards the Abolition of Whiteness: Essays on Race, Politics, and Working Class History* (London: Verso, 1994), 13.

12. Annalee Newitz, "White Savagery and Humiliation; or, A New Racial Consciousness in the Media," in *White Trash: Race and Class in America,* edited by Matt Wray and Annalee Newitz (New York: Stonehill Publishing, 1997), 145–51.

13. Horace Cayton, *Long Old Road* (New York: Trident, 1965), 262, 257–63.

14. Amiri Baraka, *The Leroi Jones/Amiri Baraka Reader,* edited by William Harris (New York: Thunder's Mouth Press, 1999), xiii; Three Rivers, *Cultural Etiquette,* 8; Thandeka, *Learning to Be White: Money, Race, and God in America* (New York: Continuum, 1999),

77–128; Ian Haney Lopez, *White by Law: The Legal Construction of Race* (New York: New York University Press, 1996), 155–95; Baldwin speaking in the 1985 film on his life, *The Price of the Ticket;* Mattias Gardell, *In the Name of Elijah Muhammad: Louis Farrakhan and the Nation of Islam* (Durham: Duke University Press, 1996), 104; Rodriguez, "Emptying the Content of Whiteness," 40.

15. Benjamin Karim, ed., *The End of White World Supremacy: Four Speeches by Malcolm X* (Boston: Arcade, 1971), 130; Baldwin, *Price of the Ticket,* 333; David Roediger, *The Wages of Whiteness: Race and the Making of the American Working Class* (London: Verso, 1999), 187.

16. Frankenberg, *White Women, Race Matters,* 191, 231–42; Lorraine Delia Kenny, *Daughters of Suburbia: Growing Up White, Middle Class, and Female* (New Brunswick: Rutgers University Press, 2000), 159–65; Pamela Perry, "White Means Never Having to Say You're Ethnic: White Youth and the Construction of 'Cultureless' Identities," *Journal of Contemporary Ethnography* 20 (2001): 56–91. See also Charles Gallagher, "White Reconstruction in the University," *Socialist Review* 24 (1995): 165–87; Renato Rosaldo, *Culture and Truth: The Remaking of Social Analysis* (Boston: Beacon, 1989), 198–99; and Thomas K. Nakayama and Robert L. Krizek, "Whiteness: A Strategic Rhetoric," *Quarterly Journal of Speech* 81 (1995): 300.

17. Giroux, "White Squall," 385–87; Ronald E. Chennault, "Giving Whiteness a Black Eye: An Interview with Michael Eric Dyson," in *White Reign,* edited by Kincheloe et al., 317–20; Thandeka, *Learning to Be White,* 39.

18. Vron Ware and Les Back, *Out of Whiteness: Color, Politics, and Culture* (Chicago: University of Chicago Press, 2001), 29; Winant, "Behind Blue Eyes," 48; Robyn Wiegman, "Whiteness Studies and the Paradox of Particularity," in *The Futures of American Studies,* edited by Robyn Wiegman and Donald Pease (Durham: Duke University Press, 2002), 269–304. See also Tim Duggan, "Honky Blues," http://www.salon.magazine.com.

19. "Changing Race," *Race Traitor* 7 (1997): 66–69; Sinclair Lewis, *Kingsblood Royal* (New York: Bantam, 1949).

20. Roediger, *Colored White;* "Abolitionism and the Free Society," *Race Traitor* 12 (2001): 96.

21. Wiegman, "Whiteness Studies," 286; David Roediger, Susan Porter Benson, Fernando E. Gapasin, Ajamu Dillahunt, and Katie Quan, "The End of Whiteness? Reflections on a Demographic Landmark," *New Labor Forum* 8 (2001): 49–63. This article was written before the 2008 elections. For reflections on what they have changed and have left unchanged, see David Roediger, *How Race Survived U.S. History: From Settlement and Slavery to the Obama Phenomenon* (London: Verso Books, 2008), 212–30.

22. W. E. B. Du Bois, *Darkwater* (1920; reprint, New York: Schocken, 1969), 29–30; Alastair Bonnett, *White Identities: Historical and International Perspectives* (Harlow, UK: Longman, 2000), 139.

23. George Lipsitz, *The Possessive Investment in Whiteness: How White People Profit from Identity Politics* (Philadelphia: Temple University Press, 1998), viii, 233; Yochi J. Dreazon, "U.S. Racial Wealth Gap Remains Huge," *Wall Street Journal,* March 14, 2000; Doug Henwood, "Race and Money," *Left Business Observer* 69 (1995): 4–5; Mare Maurer, *Race to Incarcerate* (New York: New Press, 1999); "What We Believe," http://racetraitor .org/.

PART 2

Racial Ideology
and Identity

In Part 1, theories about the political and economic conditions in which race is formed and transformed over time and space were discussed. Each of the four essays provides a context for illuminating the role of shared beliefs about race (ideology), the meaning that individuals attach to race (identity), and the symbols used to represent race (aesthetics) in the (trans)formation process. Part 2 builds on these frameworks and provides an analysis of the dialectic between individuals and systems in structuring racial formations. The authors specifically tackle diverse but interrelated questions centering on the representation and rearticulation of race and racial oppression as expressed in dominant ideologies and racial discourses. All of the chapters focus on critical moments of transformation, when one racial formation was giving way to the next in the United States (see Cha-Jua, Chapter 1). As each author shows, such transitions are moments of potential opportunity, when old racial stereotypes and ideologies are suddenly questioned, and the possibility for more fluid racial identities opens up. Unfortunately, as the chapters demonstrate, the consolidation of a new racial formation often leads merely to new stereotypes and ideologies, which reassert racial privilege and prejudice in an altered form.

This part begins with discussions of contemporary racial ideologies and identities and works back in time from there. The four essays cover a range of racial ideologies and strategies of resistance, from prevailing conservative views to radical positions designed to challenge the racial status quo. It begins with a broad description of color-blind racial ideology, the primary racial ideology that gained importance with the emergence of global capitalism. In this discussion, Helen A. Neville interrogates the racial views of Whites and a range of racialized communities. Next, the push for the establishment of a biracial category to capture the identity of individuals with one Black and one White parent is examined as a way to highlight one type of contemporary identity politics. Also included are two case studies that illuminate the ways in which racial identities are formed and how they are expressed at two separate historical junctures: one case study examines the racial identity formations of Black Power movement activists, and the other is a biographic analysis of Benjamin Brawley, a literary critic, who embraced a conservative Black aesthetic ideology.

In the first chapter, "Rationalizing the Racial Order: Racial Color-Blindness as a Legitimizing Ideology," Neville builds on Cha-Jua's articulation of color-blindness as the dominant ideological process involved in the current (global) period of capitalist accumulation and racial formation. As a psychologist, she places color-blind racial ideology (CBRI) within the social science racism literature. Most psychological theories of racism focus on beliefs of racial superiority or inferiority; thus, many of these theories account for racist attitudes only on individual and group levels. Her conceptualization of CBRI extends this analysis by incorporating the structural foundation of racial beliefs. After outlining core tenets of color-blind racial ideology, she discusses the function of CBRI for Whites and people of color. Drawing on her findings from systematic empirical research in the area as well as events such as the Katrina catastrophe, she builds arguments to support her assertions that for many Whites, CBRI provides a belief system to legitimate their privilege status or inaction in taking measures to confront racial oppression and privilege. For people of color, particularly Black Americans and Latinos, she links CBRI to an extension of false consciousness, arguing that when people of color deny the ideological and structural forms of racism, they are working against their individual and collective group interest.

Whereas Neville provides a sweeping examination of one type of racial ideology, Minkah Makalani's chapter, "Race, Theory, and Scholarship in the Biracial Project," builds on this analysis to explore the ramifications of racial ideology on the identity and politics of Black-biracial individuals. In his analysis, he more directly employs Cha-Jua's Racial Formation and Transformation Theory to investigate the historical limitations, and political implications, of a biracial identity for people with one Black and one White parent as it relates to the Black community. Using a historical analysis of the arguments advocating a biracial identity, he is concerned with the conceptualization of race and racism, the theoretical basis for a biracial identity, and whether a biracial identity will hasten racism's demise. He argues that a biracial identity would in fact have to create a new race, and that this race would necessarily be situated between Blacks and Whites in a reordered, racialized social system. This would not end racism but transform it so as to maintain the racial oppression of Blacks, and make new forms of social control available to the dominate White racial group.

Similar to other essays in this part, Monica M. White examines the ways in which both structure and ideology influence struggle. However, in her essay,

"Sociopsychological Processes in Racial Formation: A Case Study of the Autobiographies of Former Black Panther Party Members," White explores the agency of people in shaping and reshaping racial identity. Grounded in a textual analysis of seven popular autobiographies, White integrates Cha-Jua's racial formation paradigm and psychologist's William Cross's racial identity theory to capture the complex process of racial definition. Findings from her investigation suggest that the activists, and by extension others, received important racial socialization messages through three primary processes: interaction in Black civic institution and kinship circles, exposure to hegemonic racial discourses via private individuals and state control apparatuses (educational system, police, prison), and personal experiences and observations. Individuals have affective responses to these interactions that influence the process in which individuals interpreted and made meaning of these experiences. Racial identity was also found to be influenced by the attributions that individuals credit to racial oppression and race-related incidents. White avoids the pitfall of romanticizing Black life and community; she communicates the complex views that Blacks have about their condition, the class tensions within the Black community, and the choices people make in the development of a (positive) Black identity. As a sociological social psychologist, White is able to convincingly build a case that both objective structures and subjective realities are essential to motivate individuals and collectives to work to challenge and transform oppressive structures.

Whereas White's analysis uncovers the racial formation process of radical, revolutionary Blacks, in the final chapter in Part 2, "Benjamin Brawley and the Aesthetics of Racial Uplift," Jeffrey Williams examines the articulation and implication of a conservative aesthetic ideology on an individual (Brawley) and in a movement (New Negro). This chapter turns from contemporary racial identities and ideologies to examine the case of the African American poet and literary critic Benjamin Brawley (1882–1939). As a product of late-nineteenth-century racial uplift, and a latter-day exponent of Black Victorianism, Brawley was derided and dismissed, during the 1920s, by the leading figures of the Harlem Renaissance (such as James Weldon Johnson and Alain Locke). As a result, Brawley is either forgotten today or remembered as a quaint figure whose Victorian sensibility was out of place when Harlem was in vogue. Williams's aim is to write Brawley back into history, and to promote a better understanding of the strategies of racial uplift and respectability that dominated during the period 1866–1940 (Cha-Jua's plantation economy and apartheid). Black Victorianism, as Williams demonstrates, was a logical and appropriate response to the forms of racism characteristic of this era. Although Brawley's critics grasped the limitations of this strategy (at the end of the period), their own attempt to create a linkage between modernism and primitivism, and their desire to represent Harlem as the antidote to an uptight White civilization, carried formidable dangers of its own.

PART 2 READING QUESTIONS

1. Part 2 is concerned with the making and unmaking of dominant and subordinate racial ideolo-gies. Building on Cha-Jua's and Roediger's analyses in Part 1, the first two chapters tackle the dominance of racial color-blindness in the imagination of individuals and oppressive struc-tures. Is it possible or desirable to usher in a color-blind social order in which race no longer is a salient fixture within the decision-making apparatuses of the United States? If so, what conditions are needed to facilitate the transformation, and what would be the consequences on the political, economic, and racial structures of the country? If not, why?

2. Each of the chapters in this part considers the role of dominant and counterhegemonic racial ideologies at various points over the past century. What are the ways in which these ideolo-gies are expressed in each of the chapters? What are the structural underpinnings of these ideologies?

3. What insights about the link between ideology and structures discussed in these chapters shed light on the nature of struggle, which is the focus of Part 3?

4. In what ways does the content of Part 2 relate to Koditschek's discussion of racial reordering, Cha-Jua's notion of transformation, Roediger's concept of abolitionism, and Pearce's discus-sion of the impact of globalization on strategies of resistance presented in the first part.

Rationalizing the Racial Order

Racial Color-Blindness as a Legitimizing Ideology

HELEN A. NEVILLE

We cannot allow it to be said that the difference between those
who lived and those who died in this great storm and flood of
2005 was nothing more than poverty, age, and skin color.

—Elijah Cummings, former chair the National Congressional
Black Caucus

The storm didn't discriminate, and neither will we in the
recovery effort. . . . When those Coast Guard choppers, many
of who were first on the scene, were pulling people off roofs,
they didn't check the color of a person's skin.

—President George W. Bush

I am hopeless. I am sad. I am angry against my country for
doing nothing when it mattered. . . . My hand shakes with
anger as I write. I, the formerly un-jaundiced human rights
advocate, have finally come to see my country for what it really
is. A monstrous fraud. But what can I do but write about how I
feel. How millions, black like me, must feel at this, the lowest
moment in my country's story.

—Randall Robinson, activist and author

They didn't have the necessary brains and common sense to
get out of the way of a Cat 5 [*sic*] Hurricane and then when it
hit them—stood on the side of the convention Center expiring
while reporters were coming and going.

—Mark Williams, talk show host

The above quotes were taken from the countless interviews, press con-
ferences, and blogs that were completed in the immediate aftermath of Hurricane Katrina. These quotes were selected to represent the range of reactions

people expressed in trying to make sense of the aftermath of Katrina. On August 29, 2005, 145–mile-an-hour winds plummeted the Gulf region of the United States. The winds flattened cities, infrastructures, and human lives. Nearly four years after the storm, experts still do not have an accurate count of how many people perished in the storm and its aftermath, with the death toll ranging from eleven hundred to nearly two thousand. We do know that many residents died because they were unable to evacuate and were thus left with limited food, water, and medical care for up to a week following the storm. About ninety thousand square miles were affected by the hurricane,[1] and many towns and parishes were completely destroyed or remained in ruins weeks after the tragedy. Two days after the category 4 hurricane landed, the levees designed to retain the Mississippi River and Lake Pontchartrain were breached, and New Orleans flooded. Tens of thousands of primarily poor and Black residents were trapped within the confines of the city for almost a week with limited resources and even less assistance from the federal government to evacuate the city and find shelter.

Like many Americans I laid transfixed to the television as the stories and images of the storm and evacuees were broadcasted; I read a variety of news articles on the hurricane and subsequent flood and searched the Internet for alternative views of the unfolding catastrophe. Similar to Randall Robinson, I was overwhelmed, saddened, and outraged by the images and the delayed government response to help the victims of the storm and flood. I was heartened to know that we were not alone in our initial reactions. In the USA Today/CNN Gallup Poll conducted a little more than a week after the hurricane touched, almost all of the Black and White adults polled reported feeling sadness (99 percent and 97 percent, respectively), and the majority of those polled expressed anger (76 percent and 60 percent, respectively). The findings from the Pew Research Center for People and the Press survey conducted within a week of the storm paint a slightly different picture and point to signs of a racial divide early on in terms of emotional responses. About seven out of ten Blacks that were surveyed reported feeling depressed and angry, and more than half of the Whites polled felt depressed (55 percent) and a little less of the Whites polled angry (46 percent).[2] Four years later, I remain angry and saddened about the inability of the government to think creatively in restructuring Katrina, the fact that entire communities have been displaced, and the limited resources provided to survivors as they rebuild their lives.

In this chapter, I argue that the dominant racial ideology of color-blindness is critical in explaining the divide in understanding race-related social phenomena. There was a racial divide in how Blacks and Whites viewed the catastrophe. Although the majority of Black and White citizens immediately following the storm agreed that President Bush could have done more to get the relief efforts moving, the interpretations about the root causes of the delayed response and the human suffering after the storm and flood revealed a racial gulf. In one poll, about six out of ten Black participants believed the slow response was due to the fact that those who were most affected were poor or Black; conversely, only a small percentage of White participants viewed that the delayed response was due to the fact that the victims were primarily poor (21 percent) or Black (12 percent). More revealing is the differences in the perception of whether the consequences of Katrina reflected the persistence of racial inequality; more than seven out of ten Blacks compared to only three out of ten Whites who were polled in about a week of the storm believed that the response to Hurricane Katrina revealed real and sustained racial inequalities in the United States.[3]

It is clear that racial-group membership played a significant role in people's perception of Hurricane Katrina and its consequences. However, understanding the racial ideology (core beliefs about race and racism) of individuals can also help explain the diverging points of view. In this chapter, I am interested in explaining how individuals come to see an incident as racial (or not) and if the expression of color-blind racial ideology has attitudinal and behavioral consequences. I argue that racial color-blindness is a dominant ideology that is used to camouflage racial inequalities in the United States and to justify continued discriminatory practices; these discriminatory practices can manifest themselves in a variety of social and political domains such as the built environment of communities (for example, the placement of low-income primarily Black housing in vulnerable or hazardous neighborhoods such as the flood areas in New Orleans) and in practices to redress wrongdoing (the delayed and inadequate federal response in the days immediately following Katrina or the persistence attacks and undermining of race-based affirmative action in higher education).

Although ideology is often reserved to capture dominant views articulated at the macrolevel and often reiterated at the micro level, as a psychologist I am most concerned with how this dominant ideology manifests itself at the individual and interpersonal levels. I am particularly interested in the adoption, expression, and consequences of color-blind racial ideology. I am thus interested in understanding the process in which President Bush can assert that race had nothing to do with the consequences of Katrina, while someone like Howard Dean (the former chairman of the Democratic Party) can assert that "we must . . . come to terms with the ugly truth that skin color, age and economics played a deadly role in who survived and who did not."[4] Understanding differences of this nature is complex and related to a number of factors, including political beliefs, personality style, pressure from constituencies, political jockeying, and more. However, I proffer that CBRI directly influences individuals' support to maintain the status quo or to disrupt and challenge racially oppressive practices within a system. To address my goals, I first define and identify core premises of color-blind racial ideology. I draw on examples from a variety of research as well as the responses to Hurricane Katrina to highlight critical points. I then describe a series of systematic studies that my colleagues and I have conducted on racial color-blindness among diverse samples. These studies provide empirical support for the link between CBRI and racial attitudes and behaviors.

Defining (Color-Blind) Racial Ideology

Racial ideology is complex, but essentially it can be conceptualized as a global term referring to the dominant views about race within a hierarchal society. According to political scientist Michael Dawson (racial) ideology consists of a "world view readily found in the population, including sets of ideas and values [about race] that cohere, that are used to publicly justify political stances [especially as they relate to racialized matters], and that shape and are shaped by society. . . . Cognitively, ideology serves as a filter of what one 'sees' and responds to [interpersonally and] in the social world."[5] One of the critical features of this definition is the explicit connection between individual beliefs and dominant societal racial beliefs or ideas that are commonly understood and transmitted through a variety of civil society and structural mechanisms. The definition also underscores the function of racial ideology as a method in which individuals encode and interpret racial information and the values they attach to race(ism). In the Katrina incident, those who viewed race as unimportant and racism as a thing of the past were more likely to blame the residents themselves for not evacuating before the storm hit. They construed the delayed response as an unfortunate event. Moreover, they were angered by the allegations of racism. The mere mention of the existence of race and racism can be interpreted by those who adopt a racial color-blind perspective as a serious transgression and may be met with verbal or emotional resistance.

Mark Noonan wrote a blog responding to Randall Robinson's comments that appear at the beginning of this chapter; his comments illustrate the hostile reaction that some have to those who argue that racism continues to be a problem in the United States: "People like Robinson have spent their whole lives spinning a fantasy about 'racist America.' They have their whole careers invested in the premise that America is a gigantic conspiracy of rich, white males to oppress all and sundry. . . . [T]heir default position is to believe anything knaves have to vend about American perfidy."[6]

Individuals respond in a hostile or defensive manner to everyday activities that call attention to race and racism as well. "Tracey," a White college student my colleagues and I interviewed for a larger project examining the racial ideologies of diverse collegiates, also captures the link between ideology and interpretation of racial information in the following quote: "Well . . . Like Jessie Jackson gets on TV and he's just like, 'oh, because we're black we want this or whatever' and then now, like he's a very racist man, against people that aren't black. There's even like Oprah . . . she only wants black people on her show or like she has black people on her show and all of a sudden she turns into like this speaking in kind of Ebonics or whatever." Blacks' challenge of racism and their interactions with other Blacks are perceived by "Tracey" as the embodiment of racism as opposed to a by-product of racial oppression. In this quote, "Tracey's" beliefs about race (that is, race and racism are no longer relevant constructs) play a role in how she construes racial discourse.

Based on the paper-and-pencil survey "Tracey" completed prior to the interview, we identified her as adopting high levels of racial color-blindness. Color-blindness in this context refers to a systematic set of beliefs that serve to deny, distort, and minimize the existence of racism; these individual expressions of beliefs are reflective of a larger set of ideas that serve to justify the racial stratification in the United States. "Tracey's" denial of societal racism led to her interpretation that acknowledging race(ism) is problematic and helps to reinforce racism or what I term the "everything is fine until racial minorities start complaining" argument.

Color-blind racial ideology is also used to serve as a justification system to tolerate injustice. This complex set of beliefs impedes individuals from expressing empathy for groups they may see who are living in racially segregated and impoverished neighborhoods. It is a way of not seeing children who attend underfunded and underresourced schools, people wrongfully sent to prison or sentenced to death partly because of the color of their skin, or, in the case of Katrina, injury to victims of a natural disaster, when those who are most affected are disproportionately poor and Black. In my own work, I have found a relationship between greater endorsement of color-blind racial ideology and increased acceptance of beliefs that we live in a just world both on a personal and a social level: the notion that good things happen to good people and bad things occur for a reason. This type of reasoning also played itself out in how people responded to Katrina. In the words of the Reverend Jesse Jackson, "We have an amazing tolerance for black pain." This sentiment is best captured by former first lady Barbara Bush's comments about the thousands of displaced evacuees seeking shelter in Texas: "What I'm hearing, which is sort of scary, is they all want to stay in Texas. Everyone is so overwhelmed by the hospitality. And so many of the people in the arena here, you know, were underprivileged anyway, so this is working very well for them."[7] Mrs. Bush's comments do not communicate compassion or awareness for the trauma and disruption in the lives of the tens of thousands of evacuees.

Findings from a recent study my colleagues and I conducted examining attributions of Katrina further support the role of racial color-blind ideology in explaining interpretations of the catastrophe. Using a Web-based survey method, we showed White student participants one of three photographs depicting Hurricane Katrina images (Black survivors, White survivors, and neutral or natural disaster with no human images). We then asked them to elaborate on why they thought there was a delayed response to the victims of the storm and flood; we also asked them several questions assessing the degree to which they endorsed structural attributions in understanding the delayed response. White students who adopted higher racial color-blind beliefs and viewed the Black photo stimulus actively rejected social inequality attributions, and lower color-blind participants in the same condition strongly endorsed social inequality attributions. These data help to highlight group differences among Whites. Findings suggest that a general denial of racism worldview is exacerbated when individuals are faced with a racial stimulus.[8]

Drawing on the growing body of literature on racial color-blindness, I contend that color-blind racial ideology is part of the larger legitimizing ideological structure.[9] Legitimizing ideologies are frameworks that serve to justify any form of group-based social inequalities. The focus of this discussion is clearly on race and racial inequalities. I am thus interested in understanding frameworks that are designed to support and legitimize the current racial order. To explain how CBRI works, I will seek to establish four basic premises on which it rests. Then in the remainder of the chapter, I will explain how it can be measured by social science research, and how a critical awareness of its operation can help mental health professionals in dealing with clients.

As the foregoing analysis indicates, my first premise is that *racial inequalities are part of an objective reality;* racial oppression exists! Racism is not merely in the eyes of individuals—present for those who perceive it or more than likely live it and absent for those like "Tracey" or Mark Noonan, whose racially privileged status allows them not to see it. Racism is not subjective. Those who suffer within the current system cannot legitimately ignore or explain away the presence of racism in their personal lives. Scholars from a range of disciplines have documented the persistence of racism as evidenced by the disparities in wealth, housing, education, health, polity, prison, and so on.[10] On nearly every social, political, and economic index, racial and ethnic minority men and women evidence significant inequalities compared to their White counterparts. Certainly, the nature and extent of the injustice depend on gender and race and the intersection of the two.

A complete examination of the nature and extent of the disparities is beyond the scope of the paper; however, a cursory exploration is provided as a way to highlight the type and extent of racial oppression in the United States. This discussion builds on data presented by Sundiata Keita Cha-Jua in Chapter 1 and David Crockett in Chapter 12. Below I briefly underline disparities in economic resources, housing, and health. Although over the past decades the income gap between Whites and racially marginalized groups has declined, a significant disparity still exists between the individual and household incomes of these groups. For example, between 2000 and 2003, the median Black, American Indian, and Latino family household incomes were typically around mid-60 percent to early-70 percent of White family households (approximately $30,000, $32,500, and $34,000 versus $47,000). The income gap increases when one considers the average per capita income.[11] The income gap is complicated by the intersections among race, gender, and family constellation. According to the 2000 census, Black women householders who lived alone had the lowest average earnings, 69 percent and 53 percent of what their Black men and White men counterparts earned, respectively.[12] Since the turn of the new millennium, nearly one-quarter of Blacks and Latinos have consistently lived below the poverty line, and they overwhelmingly reside in racially segregated neighborhoods; these figures are almost three times greater than the poverty rate for Whites; Asian Americans' poverty rate is typically around 1.5 percent greater than Whites.

The sources of these wage inequalities are complex and involve a nuanced consideration of ecological factors such as the political economy of a given place. Another such factor is employment discrimination. Although people would like to assume that racial minorities no longer experience real and sustained discrimination in the job market, findings from empirical studies provide contradictory data. For example, although Asian Americans as a group have per capita and household income that is comparable to that of Whites, similar to Blacks and Latinos they face employment discrimination, as evidenced in the glass ceiling and salary and promotion restrictions. They also do not receive the same returns on their educational and training investments as their White counterparts. Blacks and Latinos also experience discriminations when obtaining low- and high-wage jobs. Sociologists Devah Pager and Bruce Western's study on low-wage discrimination among Black and White job seekers also highlights this point.[13] In a large audit-controlled study, they found that Black male job seekers in New York experienced racial discrimination in their search for entry-level positions. Black male testers had significantly fewer positive responses from potential employers compared to White male testers in general, even when the White male auditor had a criminal record and the Black one did not.

Similar to employment discrimination, income disparities, and differences in rates of poverty, the gap in wealth between racially marginalized groups and Whites in the United States is startling. Across the board, White individuals have greater wealth as evidenced in home ownership and in the enormous difference in net worth. White families' net worth (without home equity) is nearly twenty times that of Black and more than twelve times that of Latino families.[14]

Historically, marginalized racial minorities experienced systematic forms of discrimination in obtaining affordable and safe housing. Although Title VIII of the Civil Rights Act (Fair Housing Act of 1968 and its amendment in 1988) ended de jure housing discrimination based on race, ethnicity, sex, religion, class, family structure, or ability level, there continues to be discrimination in the selling, rental, and financing of housing. In the seminal text *American Apartheid: Segregation and the Making of the Underclass,* sociologists Douglas Massey and Nancy Denton provided a compelling analysis of ecological and structural issues related to housing inequities. Since this important publication in 1993, research has continued to document the multiple ways in which racial minorities are locked out of affordable housing in safe and resource-rich neighborhoods. Findings from the longitudinal Housing Discrimination Study sponsored by the Department of Housing and Urban Development underscore the persistence and pervasiveness of racial injustices in this area. Consistently, Asian Americans, Blacks, Latinos, and Native Americans have experienced systematic discrimination in the housing market, including housing availability (they are more likely to be told that a unit is no longer available to rent), inspection (they are more likely to be denied the opportunity to inspect the housing unit before making a decision to rent), financial assistance, agent encouragement, and residential steering (they are more likely to be encouraged to buy or rent in non-White racially segregated neighborhoods).[15]

A brief exploration of the racial disparities in health also elucidates the influence of multiple levels of oppression on individual and group experiences. Under President Clinton, the Department of Human Services' Office of Minority Health (OMH) identified six major areas of health disparities in the United States: infant mortality, cancer screening and management, heart disease, diabetes, HIV/AIDS, and immunizations. The findings from the OMH's investigation reveal some disturbing racial disparities in health. For example, according to data reported by the OMH, Black infant mortality is more than twice that for Whites, and Black men are two to three times more likely to contract prostate cancer compared to White men. Researchers have built convincing arguments for structural violence as a root cause for the racial disparity for a number of health concerns, especially in the areas of HIV and AIDS.[16]

In some cases, racial minorities have lower or similar incidence of a disease compared to their White counterparts, but because of poor health-care coverage or racialized practices in the medical field, the progression of the disease is different. For example, breast cancer hits women across racial and ethnic lines in the United States, but Black, Latina, and Native American women are more likely to die from the disease compared to their White counterparts. Studies have also indicated that physicians' decision making can be subconsciously influenced by racial and gender biases. Cancer studies have consistently documented these disparities. Two recent studies found that Black patients seeking cancer-related treatments receive less aggressive and potentially lifesaving treatments compared to their White counterparts.[17] In sum, there is a racial hierarchy in the United States in which Whites benefit in terms of access to wealth, better jobs, education, health care, and more. On the other hand, racially marginalized groups have unequal access to power and resources.[18]

My second premise is that the above structural inequalities are masked by a *color-blind racial ideology, the dominant racial ideology in the contemporary period.* In Chapter 1, Cha-Jua cogently describes the development of racial ideologies within the racial transformation process. According to Cha-Jua, color-blind racial ideology captures the dominant racial beliefs in the New Nadir, or the contemporary period of racist formation in the United States over the past 50 years; these beliefs have replaced the older biologic racism that served rationalized racial inequalities and racial oppression in previous eras. My understanding of color-blind racial ideology is consistent with this framework. However, Cha-Jua's examination provides the larger macrolevel analysis, and my interrogation centers on the individual, psychological level. These differences will become more evident in the discussion of my research on the adoption and consequences of color-blind racial beliefs.

It is difficult to substantiate a claim so sweeping as the identification of a dominant racial ideology. Yet other scholars such as Leslie Carr, Eduardo Bonilla-Silva, and Michael K. Brown and colleagues have also argued that racial color-blindness is the dominant racial ideology in the post–civil rights era. In addition to these well-crafted examinations, recent Gallup Poll data provide further documentation of the dominance of color-blind racial ideology. By dominance I mean the prevailing beliefs adopted by those in power and reproduced among the general population, especially those of the dominant race, Whites. In a Gallup Poll News Service report issued in July 2001, the majority of Whites polled expressed views consistent with racial color-blindness. For example, the majority of Whites polled reported they were satisfied with the position of Blacks and other racial minorities in the United States (61 percent), viewed current race relations in the United States as positive (71 percent), and felt as though Blacks and Whites were treated comparably (69 percent), received the same quality of education (86 percent), and had access to affordable housing (83 percent) and in their community (86 percent).[19] In addition, only a handful of Whites polled perceived that Blacks in their community were treated less fairly than Whites in a variety of situations, including public transportation (6 percent), restaurants (10 percent), neighborhood shops (12 percent), on the job (14 percent), and by the police (35 percent).[20] All of these beliefs point to the pervasiveness of the view that racial discrimination is so much on the decline that it is barely recognizable in everyday life. The fact that the majority of Whites rejected the notion that Katrina's aftermath revealed racial inequalities further reflects the dominance of racial color-blindness. And with the election of President Barack

Obama, many now argue that we have actualized the color-blind society Martin Luther King Jr. dreamed about more than forty-five years earlier.

As a psychologist, I am interested in the process in which people extract race and racism from social phenomena—how they can ignore or distort the statistics on the racial gap in education, health, income, and so on. Research, teaching, and practice lead me to speculate that the way in which people define racism plays a significant role in preventing them from actually acknowledging race(ism). Based on individual interviews with racially diverse students and a careful, detailed consensual analysis of the text, my research team members and I identified a number of ways in which racial color-blindness manifested itself in how people described racism. There are multiple definitions we uncovered that helped to serve to limit or distort consideration of structural issues, including defining racism solely as a matter of stereotypes or assumptions (for example, racism is a "a prejudice or stereotype against a different race or the same race" [Black woman]), making race a nonissue by extending the term *racism* to include other forms of discrimination ("racism can be broadened to something more than race" [White male]), and indicating that racism is perpetrated by Whites and racial and ethnic minorities alike ("anyone can be a racist. It's not just Whites" [Latino male]). These definitions are often used to obfuscate structural issues by providing people with a conceptual lens to situate racism as merely a matter of individual or group attitudes. President Bush's response immediately after Hurricane Katrina in which he exclaimed that "the storm didn't discriminate, and neither will we in the recovery effort" underscores the dangers of strictly defining racism as an individual problem. Bush commented rightfully that the Coast Guard did not discriminate when saving residents from flooded areas. However, by defining racism as strictly racial prejudice, he neglected to acknowledge the role that racial stratification played in putting people in harm's way in the first place, and the delayed response to survivors. Definitions of racism also help to minimize the racial social order through the underlying premise that multiple groups experience the same level of discrimination, and that race is nothing new or special in shaping people's experiences.

This latter sentiment is captured in the Academy Award–winning movie *Crash,* directed by Paul Haggis and featuring an all-star cast, with notables such as Don Cheadle, Thandie Newton, Sandra Bullock, Matt Dillon, Brendon Fraser, Terrence Howard, Ryan Phillippe, Larenz Tate, and rapper-turned-actor Chris "Ludacris" Bridges. The movie centers on the intersecting lives of a range of racially and ethnically diverse characters after a White district attorney and his wife are carjacked by two African American males. Although the movie was touted for its unflinching consideration of racism and racial hatred post-9/11, it did little more than reinforce negative racial stereotypes and distort the root causes of racism. Viewers are left with one clear message: that Blacks, Whites,

Asians, and Latinos are all responsible for racial hatred and racism. In the movie, Whites held stereotypical views of Blacks (and for seemingly good reason—the Black characters in the films included criminals who were anti-White, a dirty cop, and a racially insensitive hero); Black characters held anti-White, -Asian, and -Latino sentiments; and the Middle Eastern family was embroiled in anti–racial minority attitudes, leading one of the characters to a violent act. It turns out that the one primary Asian character was involved in the enslavement of Asian immigrants. The clincher, for me, however, was the characterization of the two central White law figures: Sergeant Ryan (Dillon) and Officer Hansen (Phillippe). Ryan, a jaded cop who espouses racist views throughout the movie, is portrayed as compassionate and committed to helping those in need irrespective of race; Hansen adopts an antiracist position but in the end kills a man because of his fears spurred by implicit racist assumptions. *Crash* ultimately points the finger at individuals and each racial group for adopting and acting on racial assumptions; everyone is equally responsible for racial intolerance and for perpetuating racism. Issues related to institutional racism are either omitted or distorted by delimiting the conversation of racism to stereotypes and asserting that racism is everyone's responsibility.

The essence of CBRI, as these survey results and illustrative cases indicate, is to locate racism outside of the structure. By doing this, "solutions" to racial inequalities are made to depend on individual attitudes. The need to challenge or make important changes to institutional practices is downplayed or ignored. For example, in the courses I teach on race and racism, inevitably a few students argue that racism manifests itself in the racial segregation of the campus and thus pose solutions to campus-based racial problems that focus on organizing more interracial activities. Although I am not opposed to developing a space for interracial dialogue and communion, this type of intervention would not help to counter recruitment and retention problems of racially marginalized students and faculty, radically transform the curriculum, or change other aspects of policies and practices that directly impact the racial climate on campus. In sum, a key piece to color-blind racial ideology is not so much the denial of racism, broadly speaking, but rather the limited consideration of institutional racism. The definitions of racism espoused in the media and other information outlets, and adopted on the individual level, are the most common ways in which color-blind racial ideology is (re)produced and remains dominant.

My third premise is that *racial stratification is partially reproduced through the acceptance of the dominant ideology* by those who benefit from and those who are penalized in the system. In this third assumption, both Whites and racial and ethnic minorities must accept the Big Lie that racism does not exist in order to maintain the status quo. Consistent data from qualitative and quantitative sources indicate (not surprisingly) that Whites on average adopt greater levels of racial color-blindness than marginalized racial groups.[21] Whites adopt greater levels of color-blindness, in part, because it is in their individual and group interest to maintain the benefits of Whiteness with minimal psychological and behavioral resistance. Interestingly, though, some level of internalization of the dominant framework is needed to rationalize (and accept) the political, social, and economic dominance of Whites in this society. Although the majority of racial minorities do not accept racial color-blind beliefs, some do. For example, returning to the Gallup Poll results, about four out of ten Blacks polled indicated that Black people were treated about the same as Whites in the communities in which they live and that race relations in the United States were very or somewhat good. About a third indicated that the government should not play a role in improving social and economic conditions of racial minorities, and nearly five out of ten Blacks polled (48 percent) reported that Blacks and Whites have about equal access to affordable housing in their communities.[22]

An interesting paradox arises when racial minorities adopt a "race(ism)-blind" stance. On the one hand, some select individuals may personally benefit from these beliefs, à la Clarence Thomas, Linda Chavez, Richard Rodriguez, and Condoleezza Rice. Select marginalized groups may also benefit from racial color-blindness. The first wave of Cubans in Miami who entered the United States on the eve of the Cuban revolution have profited not only from their anti-Castro, procapitalism positions but also from their denial of racism and racial privilege (their own and that of society).

The model minority myth applied to Asian Americans is also a specific argument that is used to rationalize the racial status quo. Asian Americans may superficially benefit from this positive portrayal. However, the gross overgeneralization of Asian Americans as successful in terms of educational and economic attainment is used to deny racism against other racialized groups. I have heard students and others make comments such as, "If Asians can make it, so can other racial groups if they try hard enough." Legal scholar Frank Wu provides an insightful critique of the model minority myth, arguing that these beliefs also conceal racial discrimination experienced by Asian Americans on jobs and in schools, the government, media, and public spaces, and it feeds anti-Asian sentiments by portraying Asians as a threat. Wu argues that Asian Americans are also victims of racial profiling, as in the case of Wen Ho Lee, a top-clearance scientist at the Los Alamos national laboratories who was falsely accused of being a spy.

When Asian Americans internalize the model minority myth and when other racial minorities adopt a dominant racial color-blind perspective, they may be working against their individual and group interests. So although a few people might benefit professionally or economically for adhering to the dominant racial ideology, the majority of racial minorities ultimately lose out. Drawing on neo-Marxist writings, I argue that "buying into" racial color-blindness by racial minorities reflects psychological false consciousness. Social psychologist

John Jost operationalized false consciousness as consisting of six dimensions: "failure to perceive injustice and disadvantage," or denial of the ways in which groups face inequalities based on their minority status; fatalism, or the belief that even if inequalities exist, there is nothing that can be done to eradicate the disparities; rationalization of the social order or group-based inequalities; blaming minorities for their own oppression; identification with those who are in power, or internalization of oppression; and "resistance to change," or accepting or fighting to maintain the status quo. In my own work, I have found that greater denial of institutional racism among Blacks, Latinos, and Asians is related to increased political conservatism, such as voting for George Bush, less involvement in antiracism activities, and blaming racial minorities themselves for economic and social disparities. By minimizing the importance of race(ism), individuals may support initiatives or practices at work, school, and community that actually harm racial minorities as a group or may inadequately prepare themselves to successfully cope with and challenge potential discrimination they may experience or both.[23]

Although racial color-blindness is a dominant ideology propagated by those in power, *there are counterhegemonic ideologies* primarily adopted by racial minority individuals and civic institutions and to a lesser degree by antiracist Whites.[24] This fourth and last assumption underscores the agency of people to resist and challenge normative beliefs and institutional practices. Color or race consciousness, the primary counterhegemonic ideology, reflects awareness of the racial stratification in society and of the structural dimensions of racism.[25] According to educational sociologist Lee Anne Bell, these are individuals who "tell on" race and "bear witness to social relations that the dominant culture tends to deny or minimize."[26] Telling on race or adopting a race-conscious view may or may not lead to action. Parents of Stratford High School students who actively spoke out against a police "drug" raid that unfairly targeted Black Youth and demanded that the incident be investigated were able to translate their racial and political beliefs into action.

In our study of college students, we also interviewed individuals who not only "told on" race but were engaged in resisting racism. "Ashley," one of the White women we interviewed, talked about growing up in a large metropolitan urban city in an activist family. She relayed numerous accounts of witnessing her Black friends being harassed by the police, feeling helpless as she watched. With her parents she became involved in activism to counter the institutional forms of discrimination in her community that she connected to larger macrolevel systems.

> In my neighborhood, I'm a community activist. . . . It comes from my parents; they are activists—were up until probably like ten years ago. They were full-time activists. Like my mom didn't have a job; she was an organizer. And you know,

we've done lots of things, like we've organized against police brutality by signing petitions, and we tried to implement this thing called the Community and Police Code of Conduct. . . . We've done a lot community policing things, and a lot of youth organizing, to just try to find or just create things to make young people in my neighborhood have other things besides hanging out on the street.

"Ashley" indicated it was harder to become involved with campus activism because of the dominance of White activists. "Here the activists, they're like all these White college students. And I'm not used to that kind of, I'm not used to that kind of crowd. . . . So, I don't do much now, but I talk a lot in class, and I argue. . . . I'll go to a march or something, or I'll go hear a speaker, but I don't really do too much." Although her activism has lain dormant since attending college, she plans to become a teacher in her old neighborhood, which she considers the "biggest activist project of my life."

Correlates and Consequences of CBRI

My colleagues and I have begun to systematically examine individual expressions of CBRI. In this section, I discuss the measurement of CBRI and describe findings from empirical research to better highlight the practice and outcomes of racial color-blindness. Because this is a relatively new research area in the social sciences, I restrict my examination to two outcomes: multicultural counseling competencies and affirmative action beliefs and social action.

MEASURING CBRI

Leslie Carr, one of the first social scientists to quantitatively examine CBRI, assessed racial color-blindness with one item: "Are you color-blind when it comes to race?" In his groundbreaking work, he identified two types of racial color-blindness among White college students: liberal (those who identified themselves as color-blind but supported affirmative action policies) and conservative (those who identified themselves as color-blind and opposed affirmative action policies), both of which were significantly related to increased racial prejudice. My colleagues and I developed the Color-Blind Racial Attitudes Scale (CoBRAS) to address the limitations of assessing color-blindness with only one item.[27] Sample items on the scale include: "Everyone who works hard, no matter what race they are, has an equal chance to become rich" and "Racism may have been a problem in the past, but it is not an important problem today." Emerging data on the CoBRAS have suggested an association between color-blind racial ideology and theoretically relevant constructs. For example, among White college students, higher levels of CoBRAS have been found to be related to higher levels of fear of racial minorities, lower levels of White guilt, and less anger and sadness about the existence of racism,[28] as well as increased racial and gender intolerance and the belief in a just world;[29] among African Americans, the CoBRAS has been found to be related to internalized oppression, antiegalitarian beliefs, and victim-blame ideology.[30]

CBRI AND AFFIRMATIVE ACTION AND SOCIAL ACTION

In addition to linking color-blind racial ideology to racial attitudes, research has also found important relations between CBRI and opposition to race-based affirmative action as well as future participation in antiracist activities. There are at least two studies supporting the association between anti–affirmative action sentiment and CBRI (as measured by the CoBRAS).[31] Germaine Awad and her colleagues surveyed about 375 racially diverse college students about their affirmative action beliefs. Findings from their study suggest that color-blind racial ideology accounted for more variance in anti–affirmative action beliefs, even more so than modern racism attitudes (post–civil right racism attitudes), and after controlling for the effects of racial-group membership and sex. Building on this study, my colleagues and I surveyed more than 600 racially diverse college students. Students were provided an opportunity to elaborate on the reasons for their support for or opposition to race-based affirmative action in higher education. Our findings suggest that greater minimization of institutional racism was related to students' identification of arguments suggesting that "affirmative action does harm" more so than racial-group membership, sex, and personal definitions of racism.

One nagging limitation of self-report attitudes is that it is difficult to determine if they relate to actual behavior. My students and I were interested in examining this very issue. Between five to eight months after we surveyed a large group of racially diverse college students, we examined participants' willingness to partake in a campus-based antiracist activity. We teamed with a campus organization for a semester. The organization is noted for its antiwar activities and its decade-and-a-half-long struggle to depose the university of its racially offensive mascot. Under the guise of the student organization, our research team extended invitations to students who completed the survey the previous semester to participate in the campaign. The campaign encouraged students to write letters or call individual members of the Board of Trustees, encouraging them to vote to remove the mascot. A little more than half (55 percent) of the students who responded to the e-mail request told us that they would not participate in the campaign, about one-quarter (23 percent) indicated that they would write a letter (a few of which even forwarded us a copy), and 22 percent never made a commitment either way, although they indicated that they would "get back to us" with their decision. As expected, students who scored higher on the measure of color-blind racial ideology months earlier were more likely to decline the offer to participate in the letter-writing campaign. Some students were outraged that we contacted them with such a request; a few even wrote lengthy responses detailing their support of the mascot (for example, "STOP EMAILING ME. I am pro [mascot]. There are people around the world who are dying. And you are bitching about the [mascot]. There are worse things around the world; try to change those issues, the important ones.")

CBRI AND MULTICULTURAL COUNSELING COMPETENCIES

A number of psychologists speculated that when counselors ignore the influence of race(ism), they may inadvertently minimize the potential influence of race and ethnocultural factors on the therapeutic process. This, in turn, may serve to isolate racial minorities in seeking or remaining in counseling services. Several studies have assessed the association between racial color-blindness and the therapeutic process, although not always explicitly using this terminology. In a landmark study, psychologist Chalmer Thompson and her student Stephanie Jenal found that when counselors ignored racial issues in a mock counseling session, participants/clients became frustrated and exasperated with counselors; furthermore, the deliberate avoidance of race, even when introduced by the client, disrupted the flow of communication and the counseling process.[32] Also, findings from two recent studies using the CoBRAS suggest that among White psychologists and trainees, minimization of institutional racism is related to decreased ability to contextualize clients' presenting concerns and lower levels of client empathy.[33]

Building on this body of work, my colleagues and I examined the extent to which color-blind racial ideology was related to both self-reported and observed multicultural counseling competencies among practicing psychologists and counselor trainees. As hypothesized, greater endorsement of racial color-blindness accounted for more variance in lower levels of awareness about one's own biases and knowledge about race-related psychological concepts, over and beyond that accounted for by multicultural course work, racial-group membership, and pressure to appear in a socially favorable light. More interestingly, we found that self-reported color-blind racial ideology was related to observed multicultural counseling skills. A critical counseling skill that often guides psychologists' intervention is case conceptualization—or the way in which psychologists understand clients' presenting concern and the strategies they plan to implement in their work with clients.

In our study, a subset of practicing psychologists and trainees completed a case-conceptualization activity prior to completing the CoBRAS and the remaining survey items. Specifically, participants read a brief description of a student seeking services at a predominantly White university counseling center. The mock intake report described Carmen as a nineteen-year-old Latina seeking counseling because of a recent breakup with her boyfriend. She reported signs of depression (such as crying, difficulty concentrating, and suicidal ideation), and experiencing difficulty making new friends. This was the first time Carmen has lived away from her family, and there was no history of mental illness in her family. After reading the intake report, participants wrote a brief (at least three sentences) discussion of what they believed to be the etiology of Carmen's presenting concerns and another brief statement about their treatment strategy if they were to work with Carmen. We then coded the open-ended responses for the level of integration of racial, ethnic, and cultural sensitivity. As expected, we again found that psychologists/trainees who endorsed greater levels of color-blind racial ideology demonstrated lower levels of multicultural case-conceptualization ability on both the etiology and the treatment dimensions, even after controlling for the effects of years of experience and level of multicultural training.

I have included two responses to illustrate the different types of case-conceptualization statements that people who reported high levels of color-blind racial ideology compared to participants who reported a greater level of color consciousness or critical awareness of institutional racism. I selected two extreme and contrasting responses to highlight the different ways in which CBRI may influence one's work with clients. In understanding the hypothetical client's presenting concern and in identifying potential treatment strategies, one participant high on CBRI stated:

> It appears that Carmen is experiencing feelings of depression related to a recent major life event (i.e., breaking up with her boyfriend). . . . It seems that her boyfriend was her primary source of support. Thus, Carmen lost not only her boyfriend, but also her support system. The situation is exacerbated because she finds it difficult developing relationships with her peers. It is possible she has social skills deficits or anxiety related social situations. . . . First, it would be important to understand the significance of the loss of her boyfriend. Next, I would use cognitive-behavioral interventions to help her establish new interpersonal relationships with her peers. These could include challenging cognitive distortions concerning relationships & relatedly doing behavioral experiments to test the validity of certain beliefs.

In this quote, the psychologist/trainee does not mention race, ethnicity, or culture in understanding Carmen's presenting concern. It is not surprising then that his or her suggested treatment plan focused on an individual-level intervention (that is, cognitive-behavioral) to assist Carmen with "cognitive distortions" related to social deficits and anxiety. The quote helps illustrate how ignoring or denying institutional racism can be related to erasing the potential influence of race on individuals' lives and, moreover, lead to culturally insensitive treatment.

The above color-blind response is contrasted with the below counselor, who endorsed low levels of CBRI:

> I would focus on several aspects of etiology of Carmen's difficulties. First, I'd check in with Carmen about her experience as a Latina on a "White" campus (checking on institutional and interpersonal experiences of discrimination). Second, I would check on Carmen's racial/ethnic identity development and its possible effects on C's acculturation. Third, I would ask C about her history and how she sees herself as a person (self-esteem) and family-of-origin relationships with C . . . and her coping strategies through supportive-exploratory therapy. . . . I'd check on C's views of herself as a woman. . . . Lastly, I would focus on empowerment techniques (feminist orientation) to encourage C's strengths as a woman while always focusing on what is culturally and personally appropriate/acceptable to C. If needed, I would also be her advocate.

In contrast to the first quote, this psychologist/trainee places Carmen's presenting concern and treatment plan in a cultural context. Without minimizing or denying individual-level personal issues, the psychologist/trainee identified the potential influence of institutional factors (such as attending a predominantly White campus) and the person-environment fit through the exploration of ethnic identity and acculturation on Carmen's presenting concerns. In addition to suggesting an individual-level intervention (supportive-exploratory therapy), the counselor alluded to intervening on a broader level by indicating that he or she would serve as Carmen's advocate if needed. Thus, it seems like a greater critical understanding of race and racism is connected to an increased ability to provide a cultural context for potential clients' concern and a decrease in overpathologizing potential racial-minority clients.

This lack of awareness of how race(ism) and culture may interface with psychological adjustment is part of a larger trend among mental health workers to assign serious illness or pathology to racial and ethnic minorities. In a *Washington Post* article, reporter Shankar Vedantam highlighted psychiatrists' misdiagnoses of racial minorities.[34] Blacks and Latinos are significantly more likely to be diagnosed with a more serious mental illness like schizophrenia. In one large-scale study, Blacks were four times and Latinos three times more likely to be diagnosed with schizophrenia compared to their White counterparts, even when controlling for wealth and drug use. Part of the problem is that doctors assign greater pathology to symptoms that appear atypical or outside of the norm as more pathological when displayed by racial minorities.

The provision of culturally relevant therapy interventions that acknowledge the influence of race and racism in people's lives is important as we think about assisting Hurricane Katrina survivors in dealing with the aftermath of their ordeal and in rebuilding their lives. Within a month of Katrina, the Association of

Black Psychologists proposed "Guidelines for Providing Culturally Appropriate Services for People of African Ancestry Exposed to the Trauma of Hurricane Katrina." Included in the guidelines were references to race and cultural concepts and how they may influence who seeks assistance and what should be addressed in therapy. Of particular relevance are concepts such as *cultural mistrust* (or distrust individuals may have about White-dominated systems based on a history of racial oppression and exclusion; cultural mistrust may impact who seeks mental health services and one's willingness to share his or her experiences or concerns), *racism-related stress* (therapists should find ways to examine the potential role of racism [and how it intersects with class] on individuals' experiences after the hurricane), and the role of *religiosity or spirituality* in the healing process.[35]

Conclusion

Everyday decisions may be spurred by overarching concerns such as ridding a school of drugs or making a playground safe. However, racial assumptions undergird many "well-intended" actions and policies. The results contribute to a system that perpetuates racial inequalities or in the very least racialized practices such as those that led to the creation of the Hurricane Katrina catastrophe. The crux of contemporary racial ideology centers on excising race and racism from the social equation—to distort or minimize structural racism. In this chapter, I argued for racial color-blindness as a legitimizing belief system that is used to provide ideological support for America's racially stratified social, economic, and political systems; rationalize White privilege and racial disparities; paint inequalities as legitimate; and increase individual and institutional norms that tolerate injustice. I briefly outlined four core premises of color-blind racial ideology: racism is a material reality reflecting institutional discrimination; the denial, distortion, or minimization of structural racism is the crux of color-blind racial ideology; both Whites and to a lesser degree racial minorities accept and perpetuate this ideology; and although CBRI is the dominant racial ideology in the United States at this historical moment, there are counterhegemonic narratives that serve to name and challenge racism.

Social scientists have begun to articulate the nature and consequences of racial color-blindness on individual- and group-level behaviors. My own work as a psychologist has centered on measuring personal minimization of institutional racism (a core aspect of CBRI) and linking these beliefs to a variety of attitudes and behaviors, including racial and gender intolerance, anti–affirmative action beliefs, political conservatism, and lower multicultural counseling skills. There are a number of practical implications of this work for teachers and educators. It appears that a corollary of racial color-blindness is a restricted definition of racism—one that camouflages the structural roots of racial inequalities. The key for antiracist educators is to find ways to stimulate critical awareness of racism for those who benefit from and those who are disadvantaged in the current racial order.

CHAPTER 5 READING QUESTIONS

1. In Chapter 1, Cha-Jua argues that racial ideology serves to support domination, resistance, and transformation. Although Neville builds on this framework, her analysis centers on micro-level expressions of racial ideology. What role does racial ideology play in the reproduction of race relations on the micro- and macrolevels?

2. Neville asserts that the limited awareness of structural racism is the crux of racial color-blindness. In what ways can denial of structural racism serve to rationalize White privilege and racial disparities, paint inequalities as legitimate, and reinforce norms and values that tolerate injustice?

3. Apply the core concepts of racial color-blindness as a legitimizing ideology to your local community (for example, campus community, neighborhood, work environment, and so on).

Notes

1. BBC, "'Desperate SOS' for New Orleans," *BBC News: UK Edition,* September 2, 2005, http://news.bbc.co.uk/1/hi/world/americas/4206620.stm.

2. "News: USA TODAY/CNN Gallup Poll," *USA Today,* September 12, 2005, http://www.usatoday.com/news/polls/2005-09-12–poll-blacks.htm; Pew Research Center for the People and the Press Survey Reports, "Huge Racial Divide over Katrina and Its Consequences," September 8, 2005, http://people-press.org/reports/print .php3?PageID=992.

3. Ibid.

4. Denise Kalette, "Dean: Race Played a Role in Katrina Deaths," September 8, 2005, http://www.pressofatlanticcity.com/life/religion/.

5. Michael Dawson, *Black Visions: The Roots of Contemporary African American Political Ideologies* (Chicago: University of Chicago Press, 2001), 4–5.

6. Mark Noonan, "Katrina and the Race Card," September 15, 2005, http://www .blogsforbush.com/mt/archives/005462.html.

7. Barbara Bush cited in Joseph Kay and Barry Grey, "Laura Bush Takes Umbrage: Racism and the Republican Party," September 10, 2005, http://www.wsws.org/articles/2005/ sep2005/bush-s10.shtml.

8. M. Nicole Coleman, Carla D. Hunter, Brendesha M. Tynes, Helen A. Neville, and Ying-fen Wang, "Legitimacy Ideologies and Attributions Explaining the Aftermath of Hurricane Katrina: An Examination of Racial Color-Blind and Poverty Ideologies," (manuscript under review, 2007).

9. John T. Jost and Brenda Major, eds., *The Psychology of Legitimacy: Emerging Perspectives on Ideology, Justice, and Intergroup Relations* (Cambridge: Cambridge University Press, 2001); Herbert C. Kelman, "Reflections on Social and Psychological Processes of Legitimization and Delegitimization," in ibid., 54–76.

10. Michael K. Brown et al., *Whitewashing Race: The Myth of a Color-Blind Society* (Berkeley and Los Angeles: University of California Press, 2003); J. R. Feagin and H. Vera, *White Racism* (New York: Routledge, 1995); T. M. Shapiro, *The Hidden Cost of Being African American: How Wealth Perpetuates Inequality* (Oxford: Oxford University Press, 2004), 42–59; Frank H. Wu, *Yellow: Race in America beyond Black and White* (New York: Basic Books, 2002).

11. U.S. Census Bureau, *Income of Households by Race and Hispanic Origin Using 2- and 3-Year Averages, 2000-2002* (2002), http://www.census.gov/hhes/www/income/income02/3yr_avg_race.html.

12. U.S. Census Bureau, "The Black Population, 2000" (2001), http://www.census.gov/prod/2001pubs/c2kbr01-5.pdf.

13. Devah Pager and Bruce Western, "Discrimination in Low-Wage Labor Markets: Evidence from an Experimental Audit Study in New York City," http://paa2005.princeton.edu/download.aspx?submissionld=50874.

14. U.S. Census Bureau, "Net Worth and Asset Ownership of Households, 1998 and 2000" (May 2003), http://www.census.gov/prod/2003pubs/p70-88.pdf.

15. U.S. Department of Housing and Urban Development, "Discrimination in Metropolitan Housing Markets: National Results from Phase 1, Phase 2, and Phase 3 of the Housing Discrimination Study (HDS)," http://www.huduse.org/publication/hsgfin/hds.html.

16. See two excellent reviews for a discussion of structural and ecological issues related to the racial disparities in the spread of HIV/AIDS in the United States: Sandra D. Lane et al., "Structural Violence and Racial Disparity in HIV Transmission," *Journal of Health Care for the Poor and Underserved* 15 (2004): 319–35; and V. Mays et al., "HIV Prevention Research: Are We Meeting the Needs of African American Men Who Have Sex with Men?" *Journal of Black Psychology* 30 (2005): 78–105.

17. American Cancer Society, "Breast Cancer Facts and Figures, 2003-2004," http://www.cancer.org/downloads/STT/CAFF2003BrFPWSecured.pdf#search='american%20cancer%20society%20breast%20cancer%20statistics%20by%20race'; American Cancer Society, "Race and Ethnicity Affect Breast Cancer Outcome" (February 2003), http://www.cancer.org/docroot/NWS/content/NWS_1_1x_Race_And_Ethnicity_Affect_Breast_Cancer_Outcome.asp; P. B. Bach et al., "Racial Differences in Treatment of Early-Stage Lung Cancer," *New England Journal of Medicine* 341 (1999): 1198–1205; Steven Zeliadt et al., "Racial Disparity in Primary and Adjuvant Treatment for Nonmetastatic Prostate Cancer: SEER-Medicare Trends, 1991 to 1999," *Urology* 64 (2004): 1171–76.

18. For a more in-depth examination of racial disparities, see Brown et al., *Whitewashing Race;* Feagin and Vera, *White Racism;* Shapiro, *Hidden Cost,* 42–59; and Wu, *Yellow.*

19. Leslie G. Carr, *"Color-Blind" Racism* (Thousand Oaks, Calif.: Sage, 1997); Eduardo Bonilla-Silva, *White Supremacy and Racism in the Post–Civil Rights Era* (Boulder: Lynne Rienner, 2001); Brown et al., *Whitewashing Race;* Darren K. Carlson, "As Blacks Mark History, Satisfaction Gap Persists," February 2004, http://www.gallup.com/poll/content/print.aspx?ci=10627; Gallup Poll News Service, "Black-White Relations in the United States, 2001 Update," http://www.gallup.com/poll/content/print.aspx?ci=9901.

20. Jack Ludwig, "Blacks and Whites Still Perceive Local Treatment of Blacks Differently," May 27, 2003, http://www.gallup.com/poll/8476/Blacks-Whites-Still-Perceive-Treatment-Blacks-Differently.aspx.

21. Helen A. Neville et al., "Construction and Initial Validation of the Color-Blind Racial Attitudes Scale (CoBRAS)," *Journal of Counseling Psychology* 47 (2000): 59–70; Eduardo Bonilla-Silva, *Racism without Racists: Color-Blind Racism and the Persistence of Racial Inequality in the United States* (Boulder: Rowman and Littlefield, 2003); Lee Anne Bell, "Telling Tales: What Stories Can Teach Us about Racism," *Race, Ethnicity, and Education* 6 (2003): 3–28.

22. Gallup Poll News Service, "As Blacks Mark History"; Gallup Poll News Service, "Black-White Relations"; Gallup Poll News Service, "Blacks and Whites Still Perceive."

23. John T. Jost, "Negative Illusions: Conceptual Clarification and Psychological Evidence Concerning False Consciousness," *Political Psychology* 16 (1995): 397; Helen A. Neville et al., "Moving from Racial Color-Blindness to Color-Consciousness: An Examination of Theory, Research, and Practice," three-hour workshop presentation at the Twenty-second Annual Teachers College Winter Roundtable on Cross-Cultural Psychology and Education, New York, February 2005; Helen A. Neville et al., "Linking Racial Ideology to Race-Targeted Attitudes and Social Action," poster session presented at the annual meeting of the American Psychological Association Convention, Toronto, August 2003.

24. The discussion of counterhegemonic racial beliefs is consistent with the tradition of Antonio Gramsci. See his *Selections from the Prison Notebooks* (London: Lawrence and Wishart, 1971).

25. K. Anthony Appiah and Amy Gutmann, *Color-Conscious: The Political Morality of Race* (Princeton: Princeton University Press, 1996).

26. Bell, "Telling Tales," 8.

27. Neville et al., "Construction and Initial Validation," 59–70.

28. Lisa B. Spanierman and Mary J. Heppner, "Psychosocial Costs of Racism to Whites Scale (PCRW): Construction and Initial Validation," *Journal of Counseling Psychology* 51 (2004): 249–62.

29. Neville et al., "Construction and Initial Validation," 59–70.

30. Helen A. Neville and others, "Influence of a Living-Learning Community on Students' Racial Attitudes," poster presented at the annual meeting of the American Psychological Association, Washington, D.C., August 2005.

31. G. Awad, K. Cokley, and M. Ravitch, "Attitudes toward Affirmative Action: A Comparison of Color-Blind versus Modern Racist Attitudes," *Journal of Applied Social Psychology* 35 (2005): 1384–99; Euna Oh et al., "The Belief in Racial Discrimination and Affirmative Action Attitudes: Is There an Association between the Two Perspectives 50 Years after the *Brown* Decision?" (manuscript under review).

32. A. W. Burkard and S. Knox, "Effect of Therapist Color-Blindness on Empathy and Attributions in Cross-Cultural Counseling," *Journal of Counseling Psychology* 51 (2004): 387–97; Helen A. Neville, R. L. Worthington, and L. B. Spanierman, "Race, Power, and Multicultural Counseling Psychology: Understanding White Privilege and Color-Blind Racial Attitudes," in *Handbook of Multicultural Counseling*, edited by J. G.

Ponterotto et al., 2d ed. (Newbury Park, Calif.: Sage, 2001), 257–88; Chalmer E. Thompson and Stephanie T. Jenal, "Interracial and Intraracial Quasi-Counseling Interactions When Counselors Avoid Discussing Race," *Journal of Counseling Psychology* 41 (1994): 484–91.

33. George V. Gushue, "Race, Color-Blind Racial Attitudes, and Judgments about Mental Health: A Shifting Standards Perspective," *Journal of Counseling Psychology* 51 (2004): 398–407; Burkard and Knox, "Effect of Therapist Color-Blindness," 387–97.

34. Shankar Vedantam, "Racial Disparities Found in Pinpointing Mental Illness," *Washington Post,* June 28, 2005, http://www.washingtonpost.com/wp-dyn/content/article/2005/06/27/AR2005062701496_pf.html.

35. Association of Black Psychologists, "Guidelines for Providing Culturally Appropriate Services for People of African Ancestry Exposed to the Trauma of Hurricane Katrina," September 2005, http://www.abpsi.org/special/hurricane-info1.htm.

6

Race, Theory, and Scholarship in the Biracial Project

MINKAH MAKALANI

Since the early 1990s, there has emerged in the United States a push to racially reclassify persons with one black and one white parent as biracial. A central feature of what I am calling the biracial project is a cohort of scholars, themselves biracial identity advocates, who argue that such an identity is more appropriate for people of mixed parentage (PMP) than a black one.[1] These scholars maintain that when PMP identify as biracial, they gain a more mentally healthy racial identity, have fewer experiences of alienation, and are able to express their racial and cultural distinction from African Americans. In addition to the presumed personal benefits of such an identity, these scholars suggest that a biracial identity is a positive step in moving society beyond race and toward a color-blind society. What remains troubling about this scholarship, though, is a tendency to conceptualize PMP as a distinct racial group, and the inattention to the potentially negative political impact such a reclassification would have on African Americans.

Historically and currently, white supremacy in the United States has hinged on the oppression of people of African descent. The position of African Americans in the political economy has served as the basis for developing a racialized social system, restructuring that system at different historical moments, and incorporating new social groups into the racial hierarchy as races. Asserting a new racial group premised on a claim to an inherent (biological) whiteness and a rejection of blackness taps into the intricacies, logics, and values of that very system. It is therefore important to remember that the push for a biracial racial category arose and made its greatest strides amid predictions that by the year 2050 whites will be a numerical minority. More than a question of self-identity, the push for a biracial identity concerns substantiating the existence of a new race to be positioned as an intermediary between blacks and whites in a reordered racialized social system. Indeed, in the United States there have always been multiple racial groups situated below whites in the racial hierarchy. Sociologist Eduardo Bonilla-Silva has recently argued that, increasingly, different groups are beginning to hold a position of "honorary whiteness" within that hierarchy. Taking into account the structures of race in Latin America and the Caribbean, I remain unconvinced that an honorary white racial status in the United States would include PMP, as Bonilla-Silva suggests, though I agree with his claim that various racialized groups that were previously denied the privileges of whiteness increasingly enjoy advantages, privileges, and access to centers of power that continue to be denied black people and those whom Bonilla-Silva calls the "collective black." Far from helping to erase existing color lines or challenging the new racial formations described by Sundiata Keita Cha-Jua and Bonilla-Silva, it would draw yet another color line. And unlike certain Asian and Latino groups, a new biracial race stakes its claim, quite literally, on possessing whiteness.[2]

The biracial project approaches racial identity as racial identification, or the assertion of a racial category. Using identity as a synonym for race has also entailed inadequate attention to the complexities of identity. Consequently, these works rarely engage the psychological scholarship on black identity formation, not to mention the historical, sociological, and cultural interrogations of blackness that have appeared in Black Studies over the past century.[3] Most troubling is the inattention, if not utter aversion, to the history of PMP considering themselves black and struggling over the meanings of blackness.[4]

It is hardly coincidental that these scholars presume certain antiracist attributes to inhere in a biracial identity. In asserting the subversive character of a biracial identity, Maria P. P. Root maintains that it "may force us to reexamine our construction of race and the hierarchical social order it supports." Naomi Zack and G. Reginald Daniel more plainly argue that a biracial identity hastens the end of racial categories altogether by challenging popular notions of race. For Zack in particular, a biracial identity serves as the basis for "ultimately disabus[ing] Americans of their false beliefs in the biological reality of race," thus leading society away from racial classifications and hastening racism's demise.[5] Still, the progressive qualities of a biracial identity are more apparent than real, largely asserted with little research substantiating the claims of its proponents.

The presence of a biracial race would certainly disrupt popular ideas about race, but as scholars supporting biracial identity root it in biological notions of race "mixture," it seems unlikely that such a disruption would result in the end of racial classifications. Work on race in the Caribbean and Latin America shows that a racially mixed identity is entirely consistent with a racialized social system. Moreover, recent work interrogating-color blindness has shown that this is the current dominant racial ideology, suggesting that a color-blind society as a goal is more likely to ensure the persistence of racism than its decline. I therefore find especially troubling the claims by Naomi Zack, G. Reginald Daniel, Kathleen Odell Korgen, Paul R. Spickard, Maria P. P. Root, and others discussed below, that the biracial project represents a progressive social movement.[6] In my view, based both on the popular push for such a reclassification and the scholarship discussed here, this project is less concerned with ending racism than with responding to the racialization of all people of African descent in the United States as black.

Situating the discussion of biracial identity in the context of race and racial oppression as structural relationships, I provide a detailed review of the theoretical and prescriptive literature advocating a biracial identity.[7] Specifically, I am concerned with this racial project's theoretical basis for a biracial identity, how it conceptualizes race and racism, the place of the one-drop rule in this conceptualization, and the defense of biracial identity as an antiracist tool.

Conceptualization of Race and Racism

People with one black and one white parent have always been present in the black community. Following 1967, when antimiscegenation laws were declared unconstitutional, black-white interracial couples in the United States gave birth to more than 1 million people. In the 1990s alone, these births (more than 300,000) were 1.4 percent of total U.S. births, 8.9 percent of all births with at least one black parent, and 43 percent of all births with parents from two different racial groups.[8] Yet on the 2000 Census, only 784,764 persons (0.6 percent of the U.S. population) marked black and white as their racial designation, even though an estimated 75 percent of African Americans have white or American Indian ancestry or both.[9] Although scholarly and lay advocates of biracial identity point to the census as evidence of a growing biracial race, these returns (the varied problems with census figures and data culled from them notwithstanding) account for less than half of all people with one black and one white parent.[10]

Census returns themselves hold less significance than the meaning given to them by biracial identity scholars. Drawing on a social constructionist view of race to substantiate their claim that a biracial group does exist, these scholars argue that the fulcrum of racism is the "one-drop rule." The "rule" assumes the biological and primordial differences between races, and thus any black ancestry, however distant or imperceptible, marks one as racially black. A black identity is therefore an oppressive identity because, the argument goes, it trades in the same belief in biological races that defines anyone with African ancestry as black. In turn, it is oppressive to classify PMP as black because to do so prohibits them from identifying with their white racial heritage (an identification that would necessarily challenge the idea of biological race). The biracial project also contends that PMP are marginalized from the black community, which creates identity issues that can be resolved only through a new racial identity. This has produced an uncritical acceptance of the claims by PMP that they are marginalized from and ridiculed by the black community, leading many to claim that African Americans are incapable of battling racism, and that a biracial identity's inherent challenge to biological notions of race stands alone as the last weapon against racial oppression. Curiously, what emerges from these labyrinthine arguments is a subtle inversion of the one-drop rule that defines a person with parents from two different racial groups as necessarily biracial.

The One-Drop Rule and Biracial Identity

The race as a social construction argument has had powerful and politically important effects, especially in its emphasis on the social contingency of race rather than its natural (biological) reality. I want to argue instead that races— certainly social constructions, like the family, courts, winking, and honking a horn—represent a particular set of historical processes whereby disparate social groups were transformed (and continue to be transformed) into racial groups. These processes involve what are taken as common physical characteristics, but also, and more important, political economy, relationships of domination, national formation, citizenship, and colonialism—in short, the privileging of certain groups over others within a given social order (which may be national or global or both). Races are therefore better understood as historical political groupings rather than social constructions, as this emphasizes the positioning of social groups within a certain set of power relationships, focusing attention on the self-activity of racialized groups in that context. As this suggests, I find problematic the use of a social constructionist framework to argue the one-drop rule as fundamental to black identity and continuance of white supremacy.

In overstating the role of the one-drop rule in white supremacy and black racial identity, these scholars tend to overlook critical aspects of racial oppression, and the specific function of that "rule" itself.[11] The belief in superior and inferior races hardly depends on either an ethical, moral, or popular notion that one would call the "one-drop rule." Such a rule neither creates social inequalities of race nor singularly and solely perpetuates systems of racial oppression, but rather is a function of racial ideology. Too great an emphasis on this "rule" understands race narrowly in the U.S. historical context, and is of little value when examining those societies (for example, South Africa, the Dominican Republic, and Brazil) where the rule does not exist.[12] As an ideological function or a racial discourse, I am generally perplexed that the opposition to this rule has focused largely on how it defines blacks as anyone with African ancestry, while missing its more important point: defining whites as those who have only European ancestry. Some whites may indeed view PMP as biracial or nonblack, but generally not as white. This recognition is important in light of counseling psychologist Lynda D. Field's claim of a correlation between a white Reference Group orientation in PMP and a poor self-concept. Field argues that communities of color "offer youths standards of beauty, emotional expressiveness, interpersonal distance, degree of extraversion, and comfort with physical intimacy that is often quite different from the white norm" and can give an adolescent a sense of affirmation, a claim that departs sharply from much of the biracial identity literature characterizing a black identity as mentally unhealthy.[13]

The "one-drop rule" view of race describes black racial identity as a passive internalization of racism. With minimal (if any) attention to group historical experience, community dynamics, cultural activities, and political struggles, arguments for a biracial identity tend to distill into attacks on the validity of blackness. Consider historian Paul R. Spickard's highly suggestive observation that understanding a racial group requires one to consider that group through their interaction with other racial groups in order to fully grasp the contours of their identity. Despite echoes of an outdated race-relations paradigm, Spickard at least gestures at the dynamics of social relationships in understanding racial-group formation and identity. Yet in discussing black racial identity, he fails to carry this through, and offers the vacuous claim that "what went unnoticed" in scholarly and popular discussion of African-descended people passing as white is that "the majority of mixed people were denying their heritage in a different way: they were passing for Black." Among the multiple problems with the claim, primarily and most obviously it ignores the power dynamics in which passing (whether temporary and situational or as a lifelong and psychologically exacting choice) became a strategic response to racial oppression. Sociologist F. James Davis echoes Spickard when he suggests, in what is the most blatantly biologically determinist argument in this body of literature, that "it would make as much sense from a genetic standpoint to say that the child with a black and a white parent is white as to say it is black." Lest one assume this a rhetorical ploy to make a point, Davis goes on the assert, "More logically, the child is racially mixed, and predominantly white unless one parent is unmixed African."[14] Such disregard for the histories of racialization in the United States depends on a view of race as a basic human attribute, or alternatively, and not without some contradiction, as a personal choice. We would do well to heed legal scholar john powell's point that, though everyone is an individual, we are not defined in isolation.[15]

Philosopher Naomi Zack is less concerned with an individual identity than with using biracial identity to challenge popular notions of race. Her deployment of the "one-drop rule" maintains that any racial designation (as in black or white) is always essentialist and lacks a scientific basis and historical support, and is therefore necessarily racist. She too challenges the social constructionist view of race, but she does so in order to insist that races are always and simplistically remnants of nineteenth-century racial theories that asserted the purity of a white race over an inferior black one. Yet one notices some confusion in her argument, as she later claims that the main problem with black and white racial designations is not the biological purity supposedly invested in them but their failure to "permit the identification of individuals . . . as mixed race, [therefore making it] impossible for [those individuals] to have mixed-race identities." And because an individual racially classified as black is not accorded the same rights and privileges as one classified as white, Zack finds the "concept of a black American race . . . coercive" and suggests that "perhaps the time has come to reject that concept." Biracial identity therefore possesses the greatest potential to challenge racism. "If it is possible for people to be of mixed race, based on their genetic endowment alone," Zack argues, "then race is not an essential or even an important division between human beings, either naturally or culturally." A biracial identity therefore becomes "a way of resisting the racism inherent in American racial designations" because it would create "a new person racially" who possesses the "option of racelessness," and to be "raceless in contemporary racial and racist society is, in effect, to be anti-race." Zack goes on to insist that a black racial identity is morally unfounded and inherently racist and, with little sense of the tragic irony of her argument, concludes that black people ignore "reason" and are instead guided by "passion" in their racial self-identification. The problem with her approach, as Black Studies scholar Rhett Jones points out, is its assumption that to fight racial oppression from the subject position of blackness perpetuates ideas of racial purity and, by extension, racism. In short, Zack blames black people for the persistence of racism, and charges them with oppressing PMP by forcing them to identify as black and thereby denying their complete racial background.[16]

Zack's philosophical tautology is riddled with theoretical pitfalls and contradictions. Foremost, her argument misses the point that the subordination of African-descended peoples is not contingent on their being classified as black. In addition, it negates any social basis for racial identities among subordinate groups and imparts too much control in their racialization to whites. Thus, when Zack views a black racial identity as embracing essentialism, she ultimately attempts to negate black people's historical agency and reality. It bears pointing out what should be obvious: that she undermines her own antirace, antiessentialist argument with a biologically determined biracial identity. If races are scientifically unreal, then there is no basis for identifying a "mixed-race" person. Ultimately, such an identity presumes, at whatever level, the existence of black and white racial groups that ultimately produce "mixed-race" progeny. Zack also fails to explain how, if black and white racial designations are oppressive and inherently racist, a biracial designation would be any less so. I doubt that a biracial identity is the only "effective intellectual weapon against American racial classification, which is to say, against the core of American racism," when it in fact needs those very classifications.[17]

Defending Biracial Identity as an Antiracist Tool

Despite criticisms that a biracial identity would create a new race and therefore reinforce racism, biracial identity scholars insist that a biracial identity (and by extension, biracial people) will move society beyond racial differences, and therefore beyond racism. One strain of this argument is that a biracial identity neither creates a new race nor rejects blackness but embraces whiteness. Another strain views PMP as cosmopolitan or marginal people possessed of the requisite worldview to move society beyond race and racism and usher in a color-blind social order. Both arguments dismiss the suggestion that a biracial identity would negatively affect African Americans.

G. Reginald Daniel regards the task confronting people with a biracial identity as developing strategies where they assert their ties to, and membership in, the white community without negatively affecting their relationship with the African American community. In this way, a biracial identity is a unique, multidimensional identity set apart and against a "one-dimensional" black identity. Rebecca Chiyoko King and Kimberly McClain DaCosta echo Daniel's argument by considering the push for a biracial identity as seeking to redefine race: "*The task for mixed-race African Americans in redefining race is to broaden prevailing notions of what it means to be African American, so that identifying with one's nonblack heritage does not preclude identification with one's black heritage. The* task is not to be recognized as a separate and distinct group, but to be recognized as both/all, with access to all sides of one's heritage."[18]

King and DaCosta depart from Daniel, though they argue that PMP are squarely within the African American community and merely seek to expand its boundaries, not create a separate identity or community.[19] Although acknowledging that PMP always already existed within the black community, they nonetheless romanticize the push for a biracial identity by ignoring the persistent calls by advocates not to classify PMP as black, for the establishment of a separate racial group, and the antiblack racism of much of the popular literature. And in light of the scholarship over the past decade discussing the economic, social, political, and philosophical problems of whiteness, it is troubling that they never interrogate the "white" that is supposedly identified with. Indeed, studies demonstrating the centrality of whiteness to social relationships of power—where nonwhites are subordinated for their lack of whiteness—suggest the need for a more critical approach to any effort claiming to embrace whiteness.[20]

Underlying both Daniel and King and DaCosta is the assumption that an African American identity precludes embracing or fails to acknowledge non-African ancestry. They find the 1960s and the Black Power movement pivotal in this regard, as they maintain that black pride made black a racial identity that denied nonblack ancestry. Daniel even argues that a black identity is premised on an antiwhite stance. What this misses, however, is that African-descended peoples have struggled over what it means to be black since the 1700s,[21] and that the Black Power movement was merely one period in this intragroup struggle. At issue in the 1960s was a new direction for the Black Freedom Movement; integration was a finite political goal, and black control over community institutions became a primary objective in the late 1960s, as many identified a link between racism in the United States and imperialism in Africa. Equally important was the cultural revolution that emphasized African aesthetic values, de-emphasized white ancestry as important in the black community, and raised dark skin and Africanoid features as standards of beauty. Obviously, this over-simplifies an extremely complex history, but the point is, as Jon Michael Spencer notes, African Americans are familiar with the negative effects an emphasis on white ancestry can have in the black community. According to Verna M. Keith and Cedric Herring, Richard Seltzer and Robert C. Smith, and Mark E. Hill, not only is there still a light-skin standard of beauty among African Americans, but skin color continues to influence the social stratification of the black community, affecting educational levels, income, and housing. Thus, what has been judged a narrow, antiwhite black identity is more appropriately understood as an attempt to mitigate against whiteness being valued over blackness in important ways among black people.[22]

Equally problematic is Daniel's and King and DaCosta's misleading portrayal of whites as increasingly liberal and blacks as increasingly conservative on questions of race. First, both overlook the continued segregation of African Americans, the poorer educational systems they must endure, lower median incomes for black families, and higher incarceration rates for blacks than whites; in short, they disregard the persistence of white racism. Second, as Eduardo Bonilla-Silva and Amanda Lewis point out, "There is fairly strong evidence that whites underreport their 'racism,'" and when studies have "probed more deeply into whites' racial attitudes [they] have shown that whites still believe many of the stereotypes about blacks and harbor hostility toward them." They also found that whites show general support for the principles of integration, equal opportunity, and affirmative action but are resistant to policies that would guarantee racial equality. This raises serious doubts about the claim that whites now accept interracial marriages and the children born from interracial relationships. These relationships and their progeny are certainly more readily accepted now than before the 1960s, but this is a relative statement, with little actual evidence to suggest a widespread pattern.[23] Greater attention is also necessary to the belief among many African Americans that a biracial identity is an attempt to gain political, economic, and social benefits from the official acknowledgment of white ancestry.

Daniel exhibits this contradiction in biracial identity scholarship when, in a single essay, he contradicts himself about whether a biracial identity would keep PMP connected to a black identity:

> *The carriers of the new multiracial consciousness . . . are not, therefore, seeking special privileges that would be precluded by identifying as Black.* Whether they call themselves "mixed," "biracial," "interracial," or "multiracial," these individuals represent, rather, the next logical step in the progression of civil rights, the expansion of our notion of affirmative action to include strategies not only for achieving socioeconomic equity, but also for affirming a nonhierarchical identity that embraces a "holocentric" racial self.[24]

A biracial identity is presented as bringing about an egalitarian society that allows people to embrace all their racial and ethnic backgrounds in a nonhierarchical manner. Daniel therefore views as extreme those claims that such an identity would create a racial structure like what exists in South Africa. Yet only a few pages later, he writes:

> What should be pointed out in this matter . . . is that the mere recognition of multiracial identity is not in itself inherently problematic. The critical question is whether the dynamics of race relations . . . are to operate horizontally (that is, in an egalitarian manner in which equal value is attached to differences) or vertically (that is, in an inegalitarian manner, in which differences serve as the basis for perpetuating inequalities). *Being multiracial in a hierarchical system simply means being just a little less Black and thus a little less subordinate, but does not assure equality with Whites.*[25]

Despite insisting that a biracial identity will not impart special privileges based on being nonblack to those who would be defined as biracial, he nonetheless claims that because they are not black, they will be a little less oppressed. This is a semantic sleight of hand, as there is no real difference between receiving "special privileges" and being "a little less subordinate." More important, this reflects a value system where being white is primary and being nonblack secondary.[26]

More important than being "less black" is the affirmative claim of being biracial. A biracial race, according to Daniel, would be able to eventually move blacks and whites "beyond their separate and hostile worlds, by insuring that wealth, power, privilege, and prestige are more equitably distributed among Anglo America's varied citizenry." Essentially, this paraphrases Zack's contention that the problem with the Black Freedom Movement is its acceptance of the one-drop rule.[27] More revealing is its framing of progress in terms of attaining power and privilege based on an Anglo-America citizenship framework, a frame that has perpetually depended on an other—non-Anglo-American, noncitizen. What remains out of focus is the ability of racism to function without racial categories or a color-conscious racial ideology. Moreover, in a period when serious attention to the interconnectedness of class, race, and gender has illuminated the complexities of racial domination, such an argument is alarming—one wonders where Mexican immigrant workers and Middle Eastern or South Asian Muslims would fit into the new distribution of power and privilege.

A more nuanced argument for biracial identity hastening racism's demise is the marginal-man theory. This theory claims a cosmopolitanism among PMP because of their ambiguous position in the racial hierarchy. Because the marginal person hails from, but is not part of, the black and the white communities, he or she has a "keener intelligence" and a unique, broader, even more "rational" worldview than nonmarginal people. Sociologist Kathleen Odell Korgen has taken great pains to ground this theory in a historical context by identifying two key elements of marginality: PMP feel unable to fit in, and they have a more objective, or "cosmopolitan," view of society. Although she claims these characteristics are rarely found among PMP born before 1965, she suggests they are readily apparent in those born after 1965. Part of the reason those born after 1965 resemble the marginal person is that they supposedly have fewer experiences where black people accept them as black. But as with much of Korgen's study, this argument suffers from poor methodology. First, she uncritically accepts her respondents' reporting of their experiences, rather than viewing them as data for analysis. For instance, the most common example of rejection offered is some form of the dozens. Individuals recall being ridiculed by their peers for having a fair complexion, a fine grade of hair, or a white parent, which made them feel unwanted in the black community. Given that the dozens also target those who are poor or overweight or have a dark complexion, broad nose, or kinky hair (in other words, any manner of physical attribute or life circumstance is subject to ridicule), one wonders how her respondents replied to these taunts.[28] In addition, black middle-class youths typically have their "blackness" called into question by working-class and poor black youths and are taunted for "talking white" or "thinking" they are "better" than their poorer kith. In these cases, questions of authenticity, such as cultural affectations, speech, dress, mannerisms, fashion, hairstyle, or residence, mask class antagonisms—an experience working-class and poor blacks certainly endure in black middle-class settings. Clearly, the dozens is a problematic, complex cultural practice that at once betrays a degree of internalized racism while simultaneously strengthening the ties that bind black people together. Still, it is hardly a clear indication of social rejection. We must take seriously the experiences of PMP, but these experiences should be engaged critically, with attention to how class, gender, and personal choice inform these exchanges. Moreover, they must be weighed against the fact that not all PMP recount experiences of rejection or feel alienated from the black community.

Korgen avoids treating alienation as a complex, multilayered, and problematic experience by emphasizing that PMP born after 1965 have consciously chosen to live apart from the black community. "They actively attempt to straddle the racial divide," she explains, and "in doing so, they are prime candidates for the role and experience of marginal persons." Unintentionally, she brings the agency of this cohort into question, allowing for class and personal choice to be considered as factors in evaluating reported experiences of rejection. Several empirical studies demonstrate that most people who *identify* as biracial are middle class, reared in predominantly white social environments, and had minimal interaction with African Americans.[29] Korgen goes even further to suggest that because of their economic status, they have few if any black role models, that their black parent "implicitly promotes interacting with white persons," and that because they "have little, if anything, in common with poor black Americans, it is no wonder young biracial persons recognize their white heritage." Beyond her unfounded assumption that PMP are rarely poor, Korgen implies that black people and a black identity are inextricably tied to poverty, and that the higher economic status of PMP precludes their interacting with black peers or having black role models. The black middle class is large enough, and black suburban communities are in such quantities, that middle-class PMP could reasonably interact with black peers and have black role models of a similar class standing. Class differences among African Americans also mean that a black identity is dynamic, not "one-dimensional," as African Americans are a heterogeneous group. Moreover, a more pressing concern is that middle-class parents of PMP largely involve their children in white social and cultural practices and institutions, reside in predominantly white communities, and rarely involve their children in black sociocultural settings, thereby implicitly endorsing interaction with whites as preferable to interaction with blacks. As a result, these individuals are likely to be culturally illiterate in black social settings and are therefore more susceptible to ridicule. It is not, then, that recognizing one's white ancestry is a logical result of one's marginalization—the black middle class, especially the older black elite, has traditionally recognized its white ancestry. The increasing sociopolitical distance between PMP and African Americans is structured into their socialization into adulthood.[30]

Too often, studies of biracial identity miss the fact that African Americans are a heterogeneous social group with important class, gender, and regional differences (to name just a few) that should caution against arguments for a monolithic black community. Too often these works assume blackness as solely working class and poor, which involves an attendant supposition of an authentically black person as racially pure. But as legal scholar Tonya Hernández notes, to view race as culturally based is to "mistakenly essentialize the concept of race" and miss that "race is a group-based experience of social differentiation that is not diminished by a diverse ancestral heritage." The question of rejection and acceptance, then, is more complex than biracial identity scholars suggest. To be sure, there are instances where PMP are rejected by black people, but these experiences hardly represent rejection by the entire black community. As Kerry Ann Rockquemore shows, a new social setting or a different phase in life can often produce drastically different experiences. One of Rockquemore's respondents reported feeling rejected and ostracized from her black peers when she attended a public high school that was 50 percent black. When this woman transferred in her sophomore year to a Catholic high school with only a handful of black students, she felt accepted as black, which she reported continued upon entering a midwestern Catholic university.[31]

Discussions of rejection and acceptance often also obscure experiences that PMP have with white racism. France Winddance Twine conducted a study of sixteen women of mixed parentage who had acquired a white or racially neutral identity during adolescence but later acquired either a black or a biracial identity. Twine's respondents were raised in predominantly white middle-class environments and had minimal contact with African Americans. They grew up viewing themselves as white or racially neutral, in part because their mothers had not given them a racialized identity and their peers did not identify them as racially distinct. Once these women entered puberty and started dating, they faced rejection by white male peers, which caused cognitive dissonance regarding their racial identity. Their identities began to change once they entered the University of California at Berkeley and encountered its politicized racial communities; eventually, they all developed stable racial identities. In each case, they encountered rejection by the white community they had grown up in and identified with. Indeed, this suggests that PMP will be just as alienated from white people and white society as are other people of color.[32]

With all these possibilities, it is doubtful that the "marginal person" is naturally imbued with objectivity, rationality, and a keener intelligence that would allow him or her to assume the vanguard of U.S. race relations. Korgen, basing her argument on a statistically limited sample, maintains, "Those who claim a biracial identity view race and our race-based society in general in a markedly different manner than the average monoracial American." Though entirely possible, this does not necessarily mean that such a view is broader or more objective than that of people who are not "marginal." The most obvious problem is Korgen's failure to analyze her respondents' statements. Rather than demonstrate their broader worldview, she merely accepts their claims to possess such a worldview. There is, however, a more serious theoretical problem: Korgen's failure to critique, modify, or bring into the current historical era Robert Park's seventy-two-year-old idea of the marginal man. As she accepts Park's essential-ist, racialist, and masculinist premise, it is hardly surprising that she exemplifies what Michael Spencer identifies as a tendency to view PMP as intellectually superior to "unmixed" blacks, a reformulation of the antebellum "mulatto hy-pothesis" that hopelessly dovetails into biological determinism. Korgen would make PMP race seers, purveyors of a new racial order based solely on their mixed parentage and date of birth—which presumably signals their distance from blacks and proximity to whites. Unfortunately, her examples rarely sup-port her claim. Her respondents reveal an ambiguous understanding of race and racism and at times a negative valuation of black people, Africanoid fea-tures, and African American culture, something that Rockquemore also found in her research. When taken into consideration with other empirical studies and personal narratives, what has been identified as a broader outlook on race is actually a color-blind racial ideology that slights the continued salience of race and racism in U.S. society and typically evidences some form of antiblack racism. Given that race theorists have recognized color-blindness as the current dominant racial ideology, one could reasonably conclude that the cosmopolitan worldview may threaten a more detrimental than beneficial social order. This lends support to Spencer's claim that a biracial race in the United States would likely stay on the nonblack side of the color line rather than reach across it in significant numbers to intermingle with black people.[33]

A few scholars have confronted the shortcomings and contradictions in the arguments for a biracial identity. Nearly all the biracial identity scholars agree that race is a social construction, but their arguments for a biracial identity are undergirded by biological determinism. There is a persistent claim that PMP are not seeking a special status, though some scholars have reluctantly recog-nized that such an identity would necessarily racialize PMP, and still others have openly proclaimed that this new race would be given more privileges than African Americans. This undermines the already weak assumption that such an identity would hasten the end of racism. Aside from implying a special quality for PMP, it wants to be antirace while simultaneously contributing to a new racial formation through the creation of a new race.

Michael C. Thornton, Kerry Ann Rockquemore, Lynda D. Field, and France Winddance Twine are harbingers of new approaches to biracial identity. Thorn-ton is critical of the idea that PMP are a distinct group and that a biracial identity will hasten the end of racism, though he fully supports a biracial identity on a personal level. Rockquemore identifies multiple meanings for a biracial identity that makes obsolete the monolithic one assumed by many scholars. Field has directed critical attention to the problems of a white Reference Group Orienta-tion for PMP, pointing out that it may lead to developmental and self-esteem problems. Twine has also presented evidence that, contrary to popular belief, the white community has not (color) blindly opened its arms to PMP.[34] It also bears noting that these scholars are willing to engage Black Studies scholarship or present their work in venues that engage Black Studies scholars. This is important because, despite the protests of some white parents of children of mixed parentage, these are issues with which the black community must grapple.

Unfortunately, none of these scholars has offered a sustained critique of the push for a biracial identity or the scholarship supporting that push.[35] Very little critical debate exists among biracial identity scholars, and the critical works of Jon Michael Spencer, Lewis R. Gordon, Rhett S. Jones, Christine B. Hickman, Tonya Katerí Hernández, and john powell have gone largely unnoted. More important, though, is the intellectual plunder of the black activist-intellectual tradition promoted by biracial identity scholars that, oddly enough, coincides with an attack on that very tradition. Zack advocates constructing a "mixed-race" history by removing historical actors of mixed parentage (or lineage) from black historical texts, an enterprise that would indict those historical actors as having failed to truly understand their "racial" reality while simultaneously denying African Americans the agency to define themselves. She has mounted a spurious attack on the black activist-intellectual tradition by claiming that African Americans' criticisms of white people and racial oppression are instances of morally based extrinsic racism.[36] And when we consider Zack's argument that maintaining a black identity is based on "passion," not "reason," along with the fact that not a single biracial identity scholar has criticized her on this point, we discover an insolence toward African Americans that is only less grave than the contempt that prompted the argument itself.[37] Indeed, the lack of debate among biracial identity scholars has produced a body of scholarship more concerned with citing colleagues than correcting intellectual and political errors or seriously engaging scholarly criticism.

Conclusion

The decision by PMP to assert a biracial identity is a personal choice, but such a choice does not occur in a vacuum. It occurs in a society where class exploitation, racism, and sexism remain important fissures affecting the organization of society. Racial identity, therefore, has real consequences for the organization of the institutional infrastructure and social relationships of power between groups. The choice of a biracial identity is no different, as it cannot be divorced from the push for a biracial identity that seeks to separate PMP as a distinct racial group. This would require a restructuring of the racialized social system so that PMP would not be treated as black and would receive some of the psychological and material "wages of whiteness." Psychologically, this would mean that several PMP would achieve what Gordon identifies as the imperative of being anything but black. Materially, the likelihood is that they would have higher median incomes than blacks; receive home loans at a higher frequency and at lower interest rates; create residential, cultural, and institutional distance between themselves and African Americans; experience more amicable interactions with the state than African Americans; further weaken already fragile black congressional districts; and situate themselves as a new model minority. These are not all inherently negative, but they are collectively premised on the continued oppression of blacks. Moreover, the underlying color-blind racial ideology would make it even more difficult to document and struggle against racial discrimination, segregation, racial profiling, and racial terrorism; it would also render affirmative action and equal opportunity employment unnecessary as politically progressive social programs. In short, a new airbrushed color line would be drawn, with a biracial race on the nonblack side and with new forms of social control helping the dominant social groups maintain the exploitation of subordinate groups.

Works addressing PMP and biracial identity must keep in focus the structural character of race and racial oppression. Most germane to this question is the persistent historical correlation between skin color and social stratification within the black community. If color continues to impact educational attainment, occupation, income levels, and spousal selection irrespective of background and sociodemographic characteristics, then the biracial project's embrace of whiteness threatens to exacerbate those correlations and transform them into racial distinctions.[38]

The question of a biracial identity will continue to be an issue for PMP in the foreseeable future, if for no other reason than the agitation of their white parents. Biracial identity scholars have overlooked the antiblack racism of the popular movement and have themselves forwarded unsophisticated arguments that reproduce those sentiments. Black Studies scholarship on biracial identity must therefore address the historical nature of social relationships, institutional infrastructures, and ideologies that have oppressed, and continue to oppress, African Americans and consider what a biracial identity would mean in light of that history. It is therefore necessary to have a sound theory of race and racism that avoids idealistic postulations that would support the biologically determined arguments for a biracial race. And though a *black biracial* identity is less problematic, it has the potential to exacerbate differences among black people that raise questions about its social value. In the end, a biracial identity is a political question that renders personal identity and choice relevant questions in theorizing the structures of racial oppression.

CHAPTER 6 READING QUESTIONS

1. According to Makalani, in what ways are biracialists manipulating the racial discourse and what are the dangers and limitations of the emerging discourse?

2. Makalani exposes a tension between personal and political racial identities. According to Makalani, what undergirds this tension?

3. Makalani's exploration centers on contextualizing, summarizing, and analyzing the scholarship behind the biracial project. Extending Makalani's analysis, what structural changes in the United States have allowed for the emergence of and push for a biracial identity?

Notes

I would like to thank Helen A. Neville and Sika Dagbovie for their careful reading and comments on an earlier draft of this paper.

1. "People of mixed parentage" refers to people with one black and one white parent. Though cumbersome, the term does not have the political implication of "biracial," which, given the current discourse, implies a new racial group. Also, unless in a direct quote, *biracial* is substituted for terms such as *multiracial, mixed race,* and so on.

2. On the biracial project's claim to whiteness, see Minkah Makalani, "Rejecting Blackness and Claiming Whiteness: Antiblack Whiteness in the Biracial Project," in *White Out: The Continuing Significance of Racism,* edited by Ashley W. Doane and Eduardo Bonilla-Silva (New York: Routledge, 2003), 81–94.

3. For work on black identity formation, see William E. Cross Jr., *Shades of Black: Diversity and African-American Identity* (Philadelphia: Temple University Press, 1991); William E. Cross Jr., Thomas Parham, and Janet Helms, "The Stages of Black Identity Development: Nigrescence Models," in *Black Psychology,* edited by Reginald Jones (Berkeley: Cobb and Henry Publishers, 1991), 319–38; Beverly Vandiver, William E. Cross Jr., Frank Worrell, and Peony Fhagen-Smith, "Validating the Cross Racial Identity Scale," *Journal of Counseling Psychology* 49, no. 1 (January 2002): 71–85; and Frank Worrell, William E. Cross Jr., and Beverly Vandiver, "Nigrescence Theory: Current Status and Challenges for the Future," *Journal of Multicultural Counseling and Development* 29, no. 3 (July 2001): 201–13. For the earliest psychological studies advocating biracial identity, see C. Kerwin, J. G. Ponterotto, B. L. Jackson, and A. Harris, "Racial Identity in Biracial Children: A Qualitative Investigation," *Journal of Counseling Psychology* 40, no. 2 (1993): 221–31; C. Kerwin and J. G. Ponterotto, "Biracial Identity Development: Theory and Research," in *Handbook of Multicultural Counseling,* edited by J. G. Ponterotto, J. M. Cases, L. A. Suzuki, and C. M. Alexander (Newbury Park, Calif.: Sage Publications, 1995), 199–217; and W. S. Carlos Poston, "The Biracial Identity Development Model: A Needed Addition," *Journal of Counseling and Development* 69 (November–December 1990): 152–55.

4. Joel Williamson, *New People: Miscegenation and Mulattos in the United States* (New York: New York University Press, 1984). For a discussion of the historiographical problems in Williamson's work, see Minkah Makalani, "A Biracial Identity or a New Race? The Historical Limitations and Political Implications of a Biracial Identity," *Souls* 3, no. 4 (Fall 2001): 78–84.

5. Maria P. P. Root, introduction to *Radically Mixed People in America,* edited by Maria P. P. Root (Newbury Park, Calif.: Sage Publications, 1992), 3; G. Reginald Daniel, "Beyond Black and White: The New Multiracial Consciousness," in ibid., 340; Reginald Daniel, "Black and White Identity in the New Millennium: Unsevering the Ties That Bind," in *The Multiracial Experience: Racial Borders as the New Frontier,* edited by Maria P. P. Root (Thousand Oaks, Calif.: Sage Publications, 1996), 124–35; Naomi Zack, *Race and Mixed Race* (Philadelphia: Temple University Press, 1993), 143; Naomi Zack, "American Mixed Race: The U.S. 2000 Census and Related Issues," *Harvard BlackLetter Law Journal* 17 (2001): 34; Bijan Gilanshah, "Multiracial Minorities: Erasing the Color Line," *Law and Inequality* 12 (1993): 183–204; Paul Spickard, "The Subject Is Mixed Race: The Boom in Biracial Biography," in *Rethinking "Mixed Race,"* edited by David Parker and Miri Song (London: Pluto Press, 2001).

6. David Parker and Miri Song, "Introduction: Rethinking 'Mixed Race,'" in *Rethinking "Mixed Race,"* edited by Parker and Song, 1–22; Albert Mosley, "Are Racial Categories Racist?" *Research in African Literatures* 28 (1997): 101–11; Leslie G. Carr, *"Color-Blind" Racism* (Thousand Oaks, Calif.: Sage Publications, 1997); Helen A. Neville, Roderick L. Lilly, Richard M. Lee, Georgia Duran, and Lavonne Browne, "Construction and Initial Validation of the Color-Blind Racial Attitudes Scale (CoBRAS)," *Journal of Counseling Psychology* 47 (2000): 59–70; john a. powell, "The Colorblind Multiracial Dilemma: Racial Categories Reconsidered," *University of San Francisco Law Review* 31 (1997): 197–212; Eduardo Bonilla-Silva, *White Supremacy and Racism in the Post–Civil Rights Era* (Boulder: Lynne Rienner, 2001).

7. In the time since this essay was originally written, in 2003, and its publication, the body of work advocating a biracial identity has grown considerably, and has become more nuanced in its arguments. I have chosen to forgo incorporating a critique of this new scholarship, largely because it has become quite unwieldy, but more important because it has offered little that would alter my central argument.

8. Peggy Pascoe, "Miscegenation Law, Court Cases, and Ideologies of 'Race' in Twentieth-Century America," *Journal of American History* 83, no. 1 (1996): 44–69; U.S. Department of Health and Human Services, *Vital Statistics of the United States, 1990. Part 1, Natality* (Washington, D.C.: U.S. Government Printing Office, 1994), table 1-34; U.S. Department of Health and Human Services, *Vital Statistics of the United States, 1991. Part 1, Natality* (Washington, D.C.: U.S. Government Printing Office, 1995), table 1-34; U.S. Department of Health and Human Services, *Vital Statistics of the United States, 1992. Part 1, Natality* (Washington, D.C.: U.S. Government Printing Office, 1996), table 1-34; U.S. Department of Health and Human Services, *Vital Statistics of the United States, 1993. Part 1, Natality* (Washington, D.C.: U.S. Government Printing Office, 1999), table 1-34; U.S. Department of Health and Human Services, *Vital Statistics of the United States, 1997. Part 1, Natality,* April 24, 2000, available online, at http://www.cdc.gov/nchs/data/tlx1197.pdf (accessed May 14, 2000), table 1-11. At this writing, statistics were available only for the years 1990, 1991, 1992, 1993, and 1997.

9. U.S. Census Bureau, "Overview of Race and Hispanic Origin: Census 2000 Brief," March 2001, http://www.census.gov/prod/2001pubs/cenbr01-1.pdf (accessed May 14, 2001), 8.

10. Several biracial identity scholars contend such a race already exists. See Michelle M. Motoyoshi, "The Experience of Mixed-Race People: Some Thoughts and Theories," *Journal of Ethnic Studies* 18, no. 2 (1990): 89; Christine Iijima Hall, "2001: A Race Odyssey," in *Multiracial Experience,* edited by Root, 395–410; and Jan R. Weisman, "An 'Other' Way of Life: The Empowerment of Alterity in the Interracial Individual," in *Multiracial Experience,* edited by Root, 152–64. However, some biracial identity scholars question this assertion and challenge the idea of separating PMP from blacks. See Michael C. Thornton, "Is Multiracial Status Unique? The Personal and Social Experience," in *Radically Mixed People,* edited by Root, 324; Rebecca Chiyoko King and Kimberly McClain DaCosta, "Changing Face, Changing Race: The Remarking of Race in the Japanese American and African American Communities," in *Multiracial Experience,* edited by Root, 239; Lynda D. Field, "Piecing Together the Puzzle: Self-Concept and Group Identity in Biracial Black/White Youth," in ibid.; Deborah Johnson, "Developmental Pathways: Towards an Ecological Theoretical Formulation of Race Identity in Black-White Biracial Children," in *Radically Mixed People,* edited by Root, 44.

11. See Christine B. Hickman, "The Devil and the One Drop Rule: Racial Categories, African Americans, and the U.S. Census," *Michigan Law Review* 95 (1997): 1163–1265, for an argument that the one-drop rule holds political strategic value for black people.

12. G. Reginald Daniel, "Passers and Pluralists: Subverting the Racial Divide," in *Racially Mixed People,* edited by Root, 91; F. James Davis, *Who Is Black? One Nation's Definition* (University Park: Pennsylvania State University Press, 1991), 5, 42, 63; Paul R. Spickard, "The Illogic of American Racial Categories," in *Radically Mixed People,* edited by Root, 12–23; Zack, *Race and Mixed Race,* 75–76; Theodore W. Allen, *The Invention of the White Race,* vol. 1, *Racial Oppression and Social Control* (New York: Verso Press, 1994); Eduardo Bonilla-Silva, "Rethinking Racism: Toward a Structural Interpretation," *American Sociological Review* 62, no. 3 (1996); Charles W. Mills, *Blackness Visible: Essays on Philosophy and Race* (Ithaca: Cornell University Press, 1998); Sundiata Keita Cha-Jua, "Racial Formation and Transformation: Toward a Theory of Black Racial Oppression," *Souls* 3, no. 1 (Winter 2001).

13. Field, "Piecing Together the Puzzle," 225.

14. Paul R. Spickard, *Mixed Blood: Intermarriage and Ethnic Identity in Twentieth-Century America* (Madison: University of Wisconsin Press, 1989), 10, 12–14, 17; Spickard, "Mapping Race: Multiracial People and Racial Category Construction in the United States and Britain," *Immigrants and Minorities* 15, no. 2 (1996): 107–19; Davis, *Who Is Black?* 15, 125, 178. See also Kenan Malik, "The Mirror of Race: Postmodernism and the Celebration of Difference," in *In Defense of History: Marxism and the Postmodern Agenda,* edited by E. Meiksins Wood and J. Bellamy (New York: Monthly Review Press, 1997), 112–33; and Cheryl I. Harris, "Whiteness as Property," *Harvard Law Review* 106 (1993): 1735.

15. powell, "Colorblind Multiracial Dilemma," 799.

16. Zack, *Race and Mixed Race,* 3–5, 97, 157–58, 164, 165; Rhett S. Jones, "The End of Africanity: The Bi-racial Assault on Blackness," *Western Journal of Black Studies* 18, no. 4 (1994): 202.

17. Zack, *Race and Mixed Race,* 164.

18. Daniel, "Black and White Identity," 129, 138; King and DaCosta, "Changing Face, Changing Race," 239 (emphasis in the original).

19. For other works that explore how PMP express a biracial identity as part of a black identity, see Kerry Ann Rockquemore, "Between Black and White: Exploring the 'Biracial' Experience," *Race and Society* 1, no. 2 (1998); and Sika Alaine Dagbovie, "Black Biracial Crossings: Mixed Race Identity in Modern American Literature and Culture" (Ph.D. diss., University of Illinois, 2004).

20. For work on whiteness as a power relationship of domination, see Harris, "Whiteness as Property"; Tonya Katerí Hernández, "'Multiracial' Discourse: Racial Classifications in an Era of Color-Blind Jurisprudence," *Maryland Law Review* 97 (1998); Charles Mills, *The Racial Contract* (Ithaca: Cornell University Press, 1997); David Roediger, *Towards the Abolition of Whiteness: Essays on Race, Politics, and Working Class History* (New York: Verso Press, 1994).

21. See Sterling Stuckey, *Slave Culture: Nationalist Theory and the Foundations of Black America* (New York: Oxford University Press, 1987), chap. 5.

22. Jon Michael Spencer, *The New Colored People: The Mixed-Race Movement in America* (New York: New York University Press, 1997), 53–55; Verna M. Keith and Cedric Herring, "Skin Tone and Stratification in the Black Community," *American Journal of Sociology* 97, no. 3 (1991); Richard Seltzer and Robert C. Smith, "Color Differences in the Afro-American Community and the Differences They Make," *Journal of Black Studies* 21, no. 3 (1991); Mark E. Hill, "Color Differences in the Socioeconomic Status of African American Men: Results of a Longitudinal Study," *Social Forces* 78, no. 4 (2000): 1437–60.

23. Daniel, "Black and White Identity," 132, 238; Eduardo Bonilla-Silva and Amanda Lewis, "The New Racism: Racial Structure in the United States, 1960s–1990s," in *Race, Ethnicity, and Nationality in the United States: Toward the Twenty-first Century,* edited by Paul Wong (Boulder: Westview Press, 1999), 69; Kathleen Odell Korgen, *From Black to Biracial: Transforming Racial Identity among Americans* (Westport, Conn.: Praeger, 1998), 21. That 40 percent of Alabama's voters in 2000 sought to keep a state ban on interracial marriages suggests that Korgen's assertion is misguided.

24. Daniel, "Beyond Black and White," 334 (emphasis in the original).

25. Ibid., 339–40 (emphasis added).

26. Lewis R. Gordon, "Critical 'Mixed Race'?" *Social Identities* 1, no. 2 (1995): 386, 391–92.

27. Daniel, "Black and White Identity," 139; Zack, *Race and Mixed Race.*

28. Korgen, *From Black to Biracial,* 52, 69–70; William D. Pease, *Playing the Dozens* (New York: Viking, 1990).

29. To my knowledge, no study exists that shows a majority of PMP are middle class or live in predominantly white communities.

30. Korgen, *From Black to Biracial,* 55, 79. Korgen's survey sample consisted of forty respondents, the majority of whom were college students in New England. This replicates the problems found in earlier psychological studies of biracial identity. See, for example, Kerwin et al., "Racial Identity in Biracial Children"; Kerwin and Ponterotto, "Biracial Identity Development"; and Poston, "Biracial Identity Development Model."

31. Hernández, "'Multiracial' Discourse"; Rockquemore, "Between Black and White," 204–5.

32. France Winddance Twine, "Brown Skinned White Girls: Class, Culture, and the Construction of White Identity in Suburban Communities," *Gender, Place, and Culture* 3, no. 2 (1996): 205–24. Twine's sample included women whose fathers were African American and mothers were either white or Asian. Also see Twine, "A White Side of Black Britain: The Concept of Racial Literacy," *Ethnic and Racial Studies* 27, no. 6 (November 2003): 878–907, which examines the ways that white parents in Britain encourage their mixed-race children to assume a black identity as an antiracist tool.

33. Korgen, *From Black to Biracial,* 79; Rockquemore, "Race and Identity: Exploring the Biracial Experience" (Ph.D. diss., University of Notre Dame, 1999); Bonilla-Silva and Lewis, "New Racism," 55–101; Carr, *"Color-Blind" Racism;* Neville et al., "Construction and Initial Validation," 59–70; Spencer, *New Colored People,* 155.

34. Also see Lise Funderburg, *Black, White, Other: Biracial Americans Talk about Race and Identity* (New York: William Morrow, 1994), for examples of persons of mixed parentage (even those born after 1965) experiencing white racism.

35. The most sustained critiques have been of Zack's philosophical arguments in *Race and Mixed Race.* See Jones, "End of Africanity"; Gordon, "Critical 'Mixed Race'?"; and Lewis R. Gordon, *Existentia Africana: Understanding Africana Existential Thought* (New York: Routledge, 2000), 96–117.

36. See Kwame Anthony Appiah, *In My Father's House: Africa in the Philosophy of Culture* (New York: Oxford University Press, 1993), 13–17, for a discussion of intrinsic and extrinsic racism.

37. Zack, *Race and Mixed Race,* 157, 165.

38. See also Claude Anderson and Rue L. Cromwell, "'Black Is Beautiful' and the Color Preferences of Afro-American Youth," *Journal of Negro Education* 46, no. 4 (1977): 76–88; Hill, "Color Differences," 1437–60; Michael Hughes and Bradley R. Hertel, "The Significance of Color Remains: A Study of Life Chances, Mate Selection, and Ethnic Consciousness among Black Americans," *Social Forces* 69, no. 1 (1990): 1105–20; and Tracy L. Robinson and Janie V. Ward, "African American Adolescents and Skin Color," *Journal of Black Psychology* 21, no. 3 (1995): 256–74.

7

Sociopsychological Processes
in Racial Formation
A Case Study of the Autobiographies of
Former Black Panther Party Members

MONICA M. WHITE

Social scientists who study race have identified a number of theories that describe how individuals relate to and understand their social location and the implications of that location for their identities and opportunities. Often called *racial formation,* different disciplines have contributed specific areas of emphasis to an understanding of the nature of this racial identity and awareness. Michael Omi and Howard Winant define racial formation as the "sociohistorical process by which racial categories are created, inhabited, transformed, and destroyed" and suggest that "everybody learns some combination, some version, of the rules of racial classification, and of her own racial identity, often without obvious teaching or conscious inculcation." As the process through which individuals are divided into racial categories, racial formation suggests that race becomes meaningful "as a descriptor of group or individual identity, social issues, and experience."[1]

Psychology, with its emphasis on mental processes and the emotional and behavioral characteristics of individuals, offers an understanding of the psychological processes involved in racial formation. Representative of these psychological theories is William Cross's theories of Nigrescence or the "psychology of becoming Black." In his earlier and revised theory, he emphasizes the transformation of the psychological development of the individual by situations and the process through which individuals begin to see themselves from a different racialized perspective. Cross suggests a metamorphosis or a set of stages through which African Americans who experience self-hate can move from "self-hating to a self-healing and culturally affirming self-concept." As a result of their progression through these various stages, individuals experience a different self-orientation and an "emergent or new identity."[2] Cross's work suggests that the sociohistorical environment serves as the source that stimulates psychological self-transformation.

The discipline of sociology tends to focus on structural aspects of the process of racial formation. Two representative structural theories of racial formation are Omi and Winant's and Eduardo Bonilla-Silva's theory of racialized social systems. Omi and Winant argue that conceptual definitions of racial categories become institutionalized, whereupon they influence conceptions of race. This process of racial formation is created ideologically and is implemented by racial etiquette, "a set of interpretive codes and racial meanings which operate in the interactions of daily life." They assert that this racialization process becomes second nature as a result of its focus on "learning of combinations of rules for racial classification and of their own racial identity." Bonilla-Silva's theory of racialized social systems also addresses the structural conditions of race and racism and suggests that "after a society becomes racialized, racialization develops a life of its own." His emphasis is on how race influences social relations, thereby becoming an influential "criterion for vertical hierarchy in society." Racialized social systems, defined as "societies in which economic, political, social and ideological levels are partially structured by the placement of actors in racial categories or races," are historically contextual, hegemonic, hierarchically patterned, acquire autonomy, and produce independent social effects.[3]

Historical perspectives of racial formation offer yet another vantage point on structural dimension of racial formation. In one such example, Sundiata Keita Cha-Jua articulates a model of Black Racial Formation and Transformation.[4] An extension of Harold Baron's historical theory of racial formation, this model is an analysis of the historical conditions of African Americans placing emphasis on political economy and Black racial oppression. Although it uses the Black experience as an example, this theoretical perspective is also applicable to the racial identities of other minorities. It proposes a structural theory of racial formation that includes a periodization of material conditions, collective ideology, collective struggle, and other structural factors such as "demographic patterns, socioeconomic structures, historical processes, institutional arrangements, social movements, material and expressive culture, and psychological attitudes."[5]

Psychological explanations of racial formation that emphasize individual and subjective realities and sociological approaches, which concentrate on structural and objective aspects, fall short in understanding how individuals make sense of their racialized experiences in ways that propel them to participate in movements designed to ameliorate conditions of injustice concerning race. Neither approach alone can explain the dynamic interplay among historical situations, collective ideological interpretations, and individual explanation and analysis. Both objective structures and individual subjective feelings must be considered to understand the complex process of racial formation. This chapter posits an approach that combines the strengths of each discipline into a single analysis. By using the autobiographies of former Black Panther members, I provide a sociopsychological analysis of movement participants' interpretations of the cultural messages that were crucial in the development of their racial identities. Their life stories show both the influences of stages of individual psychological development and the ideological frameworks that provide the structural influences that contributed to the creation of their racial identities.

Autobiographies: Interpretation of the Lives of Activists

As the data for this study, I selected for analysis the autobiographies of seven former Black Panther members who were affiliated with the organization during the late 1960s through the early 1970s. The autobiographies used for this analysis are Angela Davis, *Angela Davis: An Autobiography*; Assata Shakur, *Assata Shakur: An Autobiography*; Elaine Brown, *A Taste of Power: A Black Woman's Story*; Huey Newton, *Revolutionary Suicide*; Bobby Seale, *A Lonely Rage*; Eldridge Cleaver, *Soul on Fire*; and William Lee Brent, *Long Time Gone: A Black Panther's True-Life Story of His Hijacking and Twenty-five Years in Cuba.*[6]

Through the activists' recollection of events through their autobiographies, they interpret significant events in their lives as social, ideological, or psychological determinants that led to their participation in organizations for social justice. I chose to study members of the Black Panther Party (BPP) because of their participation in an influential revolutionary and radical political organization. Although the Black Panthers were often criticized, they were also successful in redistributing resources to African Americans in aligning with other groups advocating socialist revolution. The BPP also promoted self-defense and encouraged a liberatory political education for community members as ways to foster social, political, and economic liberation. At various stages of the BPP's existence, its ideology progressed from Black nationalist, where the emphasis was on racial dignity, self-pride, and self-reliance, to Newton's more socialist concept of "intercommunal nationalism," an ideology he argues emphasizes the international unification of other economically oppressed individuals.

Membership in the BPP, then, suggests that the individuals whose works I analyze constructed their autobiographies to feature race. The Panther narratives are "comprehensive autobiographies," which according to Bruce Berg "span the life of the individual from his or her earliest recall to the time of the writing of the work and includes descriptions of the life experiences, personal insights, and anecdotal reminiscences."[7] Moreover, they offer data about the sociological, ideological, and psychological determinants of movement involvement as a result of racial formation. Admittedly, use of autobiographies as data requires caution.

Autobiographers often have their own agendas; in terms of self-presentation, political activists are often influenced by their political ideology at the time of writing. In addition, these writings must be analyzed in light of research on memory, understanding that retrospective recollections are not always accurate. What the authors present may not provide an accurate picture of an event, a situation, or even their own perspectives at the time. Despite these shortcomings, life stories do provide important information on authors' reflection of the significant personal and social events that led to their social activism. The kinds of messages they received and the ways in which they chose to interpret those messages—reflections contained in the autobiographies—provide valuable information regarding their rationalization of their racialized experiences.

An Overview of the Seven Black Power Movement Activists

A brief explanation of each of the activists-autobiographers provides a sense of the rich data they provide for this study. Angela Davis was raised in Birmingham, Alabama, by both parents, who were educators; her mother was a primary school teacher who spent summers working on a master's degree in education, and her father taught history at a local high school but eventually left the classroom to purchase and run a gas station in the predominantly African American section of Birmingham. Davis was a student of Herbert Marcuse and earned a doctorate in philosophy. She was active in the Student Nonviolent Coordinating Committee and participated in the BPP of Northern California, which was an organization founded by Roy Ballard and Kenny Freeman (formerly members of CORE, the Congress of Racial Equality) based in San Francisco. With no affiliation with Newton's BPP for Self-Defense, the Northern California Panthers' primary goal was to "develop the theoretical analyses of the Black movement, as well as to build structures within the existing movement."[8] Later, Davis was also a member of the American Communist Party. Through her work in these organizations, she began to work on behalf of political prisoners.

Elaine Brown was raised in Philadelphia by her mother, whom she identified as an "industrial and working-class rock."[9] She worked at a clothing factory and faced economic hardships, but she was committed to Brown's education, enrolling her in experimental private schools for her K–12 education. Brown began her activism as a member of the Black Congress, a conglomeration of Black organizations in the Los Angeles area whose aim was to serve the needs of Black people. She worked for the Black Congress newspaper *Harambee* and, during her tenure with the BPP, edited the *Black Panther Newspaper*. Within the party, she also held the positions of deputy minister of information, chairperson and minister of defense, and party chief. Brown was active in the survival programs of the organization, such as the free-breakfast program, free legal and medical clinics, and the Oakland Community Learning Center, helping to expand services to the community. She eventually ran unsuccessfully for political office and was a delegate to the California Democratic Convention in 1976.

Assata Shakur was raised in Wilmington, North Carolina, by her maternal grandparents. Her grandparents owned their home and opened a business called Freeman Beach on the property that provided African Americans with amenities such as a restaurant, restrooms, and a club for dancing and listening to music. Before the third grade, Shakur returned to Jamaica, New York, to live with her mother, where she attended public schools. Some of her most vivid childhood experiences were due to the influence of her aunt Evelyn, whom she describes as "the heroine of my childhood."[10] As a lawyer, Evelyn helped cultivate an appreciation for cultural and artistic experiences, strongly encouraging Shakur to read, listen to music, and experience public museums. Shakur was an activist in the student rights' movement, especially active in the Oceanhill-Brownsville community uprising for public control of schools. She became a member of the BPP and later joined the Black Liberation Army (BLA). She was active in the anti-Vietnam movement, the struggle for welfare recipients' rights, free-breakfast programs in poor Black neighborhoods, and campaigns on behalf of prisoners' rights. Arrested and convicted of charges stemming from an incident on the New Jersey Turnpike that left a state trooper and a fellow BLA member dead, she escaped from prison in 1979. She now lives in Cuba, where she was granted political asylum.

Huey Newton was born in Monroe, Louisiana, the last of seven children. The family moved frequently, finally settling in Oakland, California. His mother worked in the home; his father was a minister and held various manual-labor jobs to sustain the family. Newton describes his upbringing as "poor," yet in spite of the family's economic conditions, Newton notes that he "never felt deprived."[11] Newton was a cofounder of the BPP and served in various leadership positions in the organization when he was not incarcerated as a political prisoner. He started the organization in reaction to the police brutality he both witnessed and experienced within the Black community. As a law student, Newton believed that with a combination of revolutionary action and education, Black people would be able to mobilize to bring an end to their oppression and liberate themselves.

Bobby Seale, also a cofounder of the BPP, was born in Texas and moved with his family to Oakland, California, at the age of eight. His father was a carpenter who built the family's first house. As a student at Merritt College, Seale participated in several nationalist organizations, seeking a way to explain and understand the oppression he had seen in his own life. During the 1968 Democratic National Convention in Chicago, Seale became part of the Chicago 8, accused of inciting a riot with members from other organizations such as the Students for a Democratic Society and the Youth International Party. As the BPP diminished in influence and began to move toward more institutionalized political participation, Seale ran for mayor of Oakland in 1973. Though he did not win, he did place second to an incumbent and was proud to demonstrate the power of the Black vote.

Eldridge Cleaver was born in Arkansas, the third son of six. His father was a Pullman porter on the railroad and a pianist, and his mother was a teacher. Although he enjoyed school, Cleaver argues that much of his education came from criminal justice institutions: "fourteen years in jails; reform schools; adjustment, classification and detention centers; and state prisons."[12] Cleaver served as the BPP's minister of information. He served several years in prison for assault with intent to commit murder and was heavily influenced by the Nation of Islam. While incarcerated, Cleaver wrote his first memoir, *Soul on Ice,* which became mandatory movement reading for its description of the rage among Black men in the United States. Upon his release, he served as editor and a featured writer of *Ramparts,* a radical Left newspaper in the Oakland area and also served as the editor of the *Black Panther Newspaper.*

William Lee Brent was born and raised in Franklin, Louisiana, by his mother, who did "day work." Brent, a sister, and his mother lived for extended periods with family members who would take them in during financial difficulties. He describes his family as "dirt poor and nearly illiterate" and often remarks about his difficulties with authority in the classroom and in the military.[13] Brent was considered one of the "seasoned" members of the Panthers because he was thirty-seven years old when he joined, and he rose through the ranks of the BPP to become Eldridge Cleaver's chief of security. His participation with the Panthers was short-lived. After being arrested for a shootout with the San Francisco police, Brent hijacked an airplane to avoid charges and, like Shakur, is currently living in exile in Cuba.

Making Meaning: Analysis of the Autobiographies

Using textual analysis consistent with grounded theory, I analyzed these autobiographies of former Panther members focusing on their descriptions of social and psychological determinants of their racial identity development.[14] This method focuses on theory generation rather than on theory verification. The researcher does not undertake the research task with hypotheses in mind that are to be either verified or rejected. Rather, the undertaking is focused on the systematic view of data that will result in the development of propositions or hypotheses about them. The researcher provides evidence for the existence of these propositions but does not endeavor to test them empirically at this stage.

The theoretical underpinnings of the grounded method of theory generation come from several sources. The primary epistemological assumptions are those of the phenomenologist rather than the positivist. Phenomenologists attempt to suspend presuppositions about the phenomenon under review and seek to describe the essence of experiences that are intuitively apprehended by the subjects. Positivists, on the other hand, search for facts or causes of social phenomena outside the individual and are less concerned with the subjective states of individuals. The grounded-theory process is also rooted in the comparative analytic method, which has both anthropological and sociological sources. In sociology, both Max Weber and Emile Durkheim used the comparative method to generate theory. In anthropology, the comparative method has been used to arrive at an understanding of societies; the study of the Iroquois by Lewis Henry Morgan is cited as an early and influential use of the method.[15] A third source for this method is fieldwork, which found its greatest development in the field of anthropology. A major quality of fieldwork methodology is that it is emergent rather than preplanned in nature. As the researcher proceeds with the study, the unfolding of the information points to the direction of further research.

Because my interest in this study is in discovering how the activists identified social and psychological determinants of racial identity, I coded my data by identifying passages in the autobiographies in which the authors explicitly mentioned race. I then compared and contrasted these passages in an inductive process, sorting them into major variables relevant to the process of racial identity formation.

CORE THEMES

Three variables emerged as important in this process: sources of knowledge about race, attribution of cause for a problem in which race was central, and the author's emotional reaction to particular racialized experiences. Sources of knowledge are the locations from which individuals receive messages about race; they are collective and community-based influences and thus represent the social dynamic. Attribution of cause for a problem in which race is central is the writer's identification of the source of difficulty or the defect in the situation to which he or she responds; the cause identified is either individual or structural, so this variable can be either psychological or social. Emotion is the way individuals feel as a result of a particular interpretation of a racial experience; thus, it is a psychological factor.

I then compared and contrasted the excerpts pertaining to each of the three major categories or constructs concerning the formation of racial identity to develop propositions concerning the nature and function of each of the major categories. I compared and sorted the data within the three categories until no further conceptual variables were generated and sufficient support had emerged for the existence of particular propositions that described the qualities and functions of those variables.

This process revealed that source of knowledge is critical in the process of racial identity formation. Attribution for a racial experience and emotion—the two other primary constructs—appear to be dependent on source of knowledge. My analysis thus focuses on the three sources of racial knowledge that emerged from the data: kinship networks, hegemonic influences, and direct experience. These varying sources of knowledge are described by the autobiographers as providing differing kinds of information that contributed to each author's development of a Black racial identity. They differ with regard to the specific messages to which the social activists responded, the sources of the interpretation of the situation, and the emotions that accompanied the specific situation.

Kinship Network as a Source of Knowledge

As a source of knowledge, the kinship network and Black civil society consists of family, friends, and the intraracial group of the Black community. Largely responsible for providing messages for individuals to explain their early experiences of race, the kinship network assisted the individuals in understanding their social conditions. Black civil society, a concept developed by Georg Hegel, argues that between the state and the individual, civil society serves as an extension of familial relations and bridges social institutions to the individual. Through the mechanism of Black civil society, "the wants of the individual are supplied by each individual's pursuit of his own particular interests."[16] The kinship network and its larger social networks of Black civil society provided messages that were largely reinforcing to the positive self-development of the autobiographers and instilled resources for resistance against the racist system. In cases where the social structure and its institutions were disparaging or destructive, the messages of the kinship network often provided guidance by which the individual would be encouraged to seek alternate routes for survival and success. The messages about race from the kinship network taught that racial identity lay in individual qualities.

The authors reported several cases in which the importance of individual resistance was conveyed to them through storytelling or re-created tales. Often featuring a family member as the protagonist, these stories told how individuals had been protected from the aggression of white authorities by their resolution and strength. For example, Shakur described an encounter between her grandmother and a white truck driver who, "in an arrogant tone of voice, ordered my grandmother to open the gate so that he could turn his car around." In an attempt to convince her to change her mind, the truck driver said, "Come on now, auntie, I got a mammy in my house," to which she replied, "I don't care if you've got a hundred mammies in your house. . . . I want you off of my property now! Right now!" Because of her defiance, not only was he unable to turn around, but he was forced to back up for more than a quarter of a mile. Shakur remembered her and her grandmother "laughing so hard the tears fell from our eyes." This experience instilled a sense of respect for her grandmother's acts of resistance, to which she credits her own strength.[17]

Newton described how his father's resistance involved an acceptance of a label. Through his father's stories, Newton argued that the moniker of "crazy" was one that provided a sense of protection for the family because no one was willing to engage the family in conflict because of his father's assumed refusal to adhere to the contemporary racial social norms. Although the activists often characterized these stories as entertaining, they also saw them as attempts to discuss how the family resolved hostile and racist situations.

Although not always positive, kinship networks and Black civil society taught significant lessons about the importance and value of struggle, dignity, and self-respect. Shakur recalled several incidences where her mother and grandmother refused to adhere to the submissive position expected of Blacks. In one situation, her mother was able to purchase tickets to an amusement park that Blacks were not allowed to enter by telling the park managers that she was from a "Spanish country and that if he didn't let us in she would call the embassy and the United Nations." In yet another situation, though it was commonly accepted that white store owners often sold inferior goods to people in the Black community, Shakur's grandmother demanded that she go back to the store in such instances: "'You tell them that you don't want any garbage, and you'd better not come back with any.' . . . If the store owner sold me something that my grandmother didn't like, I would have to return to the store and get the thing changed or get my money back. 'You speak up loud and clear. Don't let me have to go down to that store.' Scared to death of the fuss my grandmother would make if she had to go to the store herself, I would hurry back to the store, prepared to raise almighty hell." In other instances, Shakur was told by her kinship network, "You show those white people that you are just as good as they are."[18]

Other members of the kinship network were the teachers in the preintegration period. Shakur mentioned the commitment that was evident by her Black teachers: "The teachers took more of an interest in our lives because they lived in our world, in the same neighborhoods. . . . [T]hey tried to protect us as much as they could." Davis also remembered a teacher who was fired because he refused to allow a white administrator to refer to him by his first name. Not only did she respect this teacher for demonstrating resistance, but she also recalled feeling "appalled" that the Black community stood by in virtual silence.[19]

The messages received from kinship networks and Black civil society featured the activists' individual capabilities and unique qualities. Often, in these situations, kinship networks suggest positive messages with regard to the individual but in some cases negative messages referencing the African American collective. One form such messages took, particularly in their childhoods, was a comparison between the activists themselves and other African Americans. This occurred in the form of a command to associate only with particular groups of African Americans, distinguishing between the qualities they were told they had and that others did not. For example, Shakur, who was middle class as a child, recalled her grandparents telling her to play with "decent children" and not to associate with "alley rats," positing an economic distinction between those who were considered more well off versus those who were poor and working class. For others, distinctions were made on the basis of not economics but appearance. Brown noted how her mother reinforced the idea that she was "better" than the other Black children in her neighborhood: "She would always tell me how beautiful I was, 'the most beautiful girl in the world.' I was not like the other colored girls in our neighborhood, she told me. They had skin that was too dark and facial features that were too African and hair that was not 'good' like mine."[20] These examples of kinship network as a source of knowledge featured explanations of racial identity rooted in individuality and uniqueness. Even though these comparisons seem negative on the surface because they separate and divide African Americans from one another, these messages have a positive intent: to make children feel confident about their capacities.

The focus on individual qualities and capabilities featured in messages about race from family members does not mean that racial identity was constructed apart from an awareness of collectivity. In some cases, the activists themselves chose to affiliate with those against whom they were compared, embracing a collective perspective. Shakur, for example, openly defied her grandmother's warnings and engaged deliberately in "alley rat playing," and she expressed feelings of solidarity with those with whom she was forbidden to interact. She stated, "My grandmother had a little alley rat right under her roof and she didn't even know it." Davis also expressed her realization of class distinctions between herself and her classmates, along with her sense of social responsibility for those of lower classes: "I had a definite advantage: my parents would see to it that I attended college, and would help me survive until I could make it on my own. This was not something that could be said for the vast majority of my schoolmates." Instead of accepting this as a reality, in an act of resistance, she often stole money from the bag of coins her father brought back from the service station nightly. "The next day I gave the money to my hungry friends. . . . I would just have to suffer the knowledge that I had stolen my father's money."[21] These activists turned messages that constructed race as an individual construct, then, into a collective one that featured their solidarity with others.

Many of the social activists, including Newton and Shakur, expressed positive emotions when discussing racial experiences that featured the kinship network as a source of knowledge. As they described their interpretations of these experiences, they often described desire for survival, dignity, pride, a sense of connectedness, self-worth, stability, and friendship as emotions they felt. While Newton described his father's resistance as a means to maintain dignity and pride, these emotions were transferred to him and his brothers merely in the recounting of these liberatory moments. As Newton explained, "I heard these stories and others like them over and over again until in a way his experiences became my own."[22]

Kinship messages that featured some act of struggle often were used to generate positive emotions. In situations where activists resisted or refused to accept negative messages, they identified resistance as a way to preserve dignity. One of Newton's moments of resistance in the classroom yielded respect from his classmates. Preparing to return to class from recess, Newton was removing sand from his shoes when his teacher accused him of delaying his return to class. As punishment, she "slapped me across the ear with a book." Newton's response was to throw his shoes at her as an act of defiance: "I received a great deal of respect from the other children for that act; they backed me for resisting unjust authority. In our working- and lower-class community we valued the person who successfully bucked authority. Group prestige and acceptance were won through defiance and physical strength, and both of them led to racial and class conflict between the authorities and the students."[23]

Shakur also described her mother's creative resistance in her demand to be allowed to purchase tickets to an amusement park, including the emotions she and her mother felt as a result: "I couldn't believe it. All at once we were laughing and giggling and riding the rides. All the white people were staring at us, but we didn't care. We were busy having a ball. . . . I was in my glory. . . . We sang and laughed all the way home."[24] Positive emotions, then, were experienced as the activists responded to the messages of race from kinship messages.

Hegemonic Representatives as a Source of Knowledge

Hegemonic influences as a source of knowledge regarding racial identity and racial formation are those that come from outside of the Black community. Hegemonic influences are the racist messages from mainstream institutions and come from sources such as educators and police officers. The messages from these hegemonic sources are attributed to structural, as opposed to individual, explanations, and the emotions that are associated with them are largely negative.

The educational environment provides most of the examples of hegemonic factors as sources of knowledge. When the activists discussed attending racially segregated schools with Black teachers, they considered the teachers to be extensions of the Black community. These teachers demonstrated a genuine concern for the students' success and helped to contribute to a positive racial identity. However, the activists provided many more examples where they encountered white educators in racially integrated schools who harbored racist attitudes and attempted to impart a negative racial identity to the Black children. In most of these cases, the activists interpreted their encounters as due to individual distrust on the part of the educators, and they explained their experiences as part of a racialized and classed social structure that benefited from the oppression of Black and working-class people.

Newton provided an example of such a hegemonic source of knowledge as he described his experiences with reading. The racial messages that he described while reading stories such as "Sleeping Beauty," "Little Black Sambo," and "Briar Rabbit" are largely structural and negative: "Our image of ourselves was defined for us by textbooks and teachers." He explained that not only did he individually identify with the negative representations of Blackness as demonstrated in the stories, but he saw these stories as impacting the racial identity of other Black students in his classes. Brent's description of his educational experiences largely agreed with Newton's, but instead of books, he described interactions with a specific teacher. He recalled that the teacher "despised her black-skinned, nappy-headed charges and never missed a chance to belittle and humiliate us." Brent noted how this educational experience was related to the larger structural conditions of African Americans when he explained that "school was only a dress rehearsal for the roles we would play as we grew up in a world where poverty, physical abuse, and senseless violence prevailed." Shakur reinforced these sentiments when she described a situation where she encountered a teacher who tried to get students to appreciate classical music. Although she admitted that many students loved music, they hated music class: "The teacher talked to us as though we were inferior savages, incapable of appreciating the finer things in life. . . . [S]he would scream at us and call us names like hooligans and ignoramuses. And we returned her insults."[25]

Demonstrating hegemonic influences as a source of knowledge, the examples obtained from the autobiographies illustrate the ways in which educational institutions, teachers, and administrators relayed largely negative information regarding racial identity. Teachers were often mentioned as exhibiting abusive behavior toward the activists often based on racist stereotypes. Conversely, these activists often described their reaction to these situations as an early form of resistance either in the form of verbal or physical self-defense.

Encounters with members of law enforcement were another example of institutional representatives of the hegemony. Brent described a situation where he and some friends went to a picnic in a park that was designated as "white" by segregationist laws. They were attacked by a group of white neighborhood boys who began shooting at them with rifles. An altercation ensued, and Brent and his friends were arrested and charged "with everything from trespassing to unprovoked assault." The whites were released without charge and were asked to testify against Brent and his friends, who were eventually convicted. Brent's message from this incident is illustrated in a comment he credited to his cousin: "Always remember the laws are made to protect white folks, not niggers." Through this experience, his sense of racial identity was based on the idea that Blackness insinuated guilt and "only heightened my resentment of authority and laws in general."[26]

In a similar situation, while shining shoes, Cleaver and his friends were approached by law enforcement. He described the police offers as "five big burly white cops" and explained being arrested and intimidated for not using the "police sponsored" shine boxes. Once released and again shining shoes, Cleaver was approached by his father. His dad tossed the shoe-shine fee for using the police-owned box into the street and said, "If they wanted it they could get down on their knees and pick it up." He continued, "Ain't no son of mine gonna shine no damn shoes!"[27] This example illustrates his father's influence on the formation of his racial identity by helping him understand and challenge the police officers' racial and economic exploitation.

The emotions that were associated with these hegemonic influences of racial formation varied. Under those situations where the activists either acquiesced or accepted the opinions of those in positions of authority, they described negative feelings such as anger, shame, confusion, and disengagement. Brent's reflection of the social role of education is representative; he saw that "the underlying goal was not to educate us so that we'd be able to compete in society. It was to instill fear and obedience to authority. To make us understand our place in the world and accept it without question." Newton described his attendance in the remedial class, which he referred to as the "dumb class," as generating a feeling of being "constantly uncomfortable and ashamed of being Black." He suggested that Blacks who struggle for success through education often get "nowhere."[28]

Shakur described a similar racial experience in which she felt negative emotion. When one of her white coworkers asked her feelings regarding the race riots of the mid-1960s, she explained, "The only thing i can remember thinking was that i wanted to see the rioters win." When an office secretary cornered her in the restroom and asked her about her feelings about "those people" who "were so stupid and dumb for rioting because they were just tearing up their own neighborhoods and burning down their own houses," this secretary asked Shakur, "Isn't that a shame? Isn't it?" Her reply was "Yes." This moment of acquiescence and refusal to reveal her true beliefs left her feeling that she had betrayed the struggle of other Black folks: "I was disgusted with myself." Eventually, she reversed her reaction and planned a speech she had ready in response to the question regarding her support for the rioters. This moment of resistance, as she planned it, would allow her to clear her conscience by telling what she really felt: "What do you mean, they're burning down their houses? They don't own those houses. They don't own those stores. I'm glad they burned down those stores because those stores were robbing them in the first place!" Ultimately, this response precipitated her being fired, yet her reaction to this was, "When I was finally fired, I was relieved."[29]

Davis agreed that resistance was a way to maintain dignity. After hearing about the Black families who were integrating a previously all-white neighborhood, resistance for her and a few friends was a way to "defen[d] our egos. Our weapon was the word. We would gather on my front lawn, wait for a car of white people to pass by and shout the worst epithets for white people we knew. . . . Then we would laugh hysterically at the startled expressions on their faces. I hid this pastime from my parents. They could not know how important it was for me, and for all of us who had just discovered racism, to find ways of maintaining our dignity."[30]

Activists' descriptions of hegemonic racial messages suggest that they sought to degrade Black people and adversely impact Black racial identity development. Although many of these experiences were negative and evoked a defensive reaction on the part of the social activists, their interpretation of these racialized incidences suggests that the reverse happened and these experiences facilitated the activists' learning of a positive racial identity. Moreover, the activists' responses to these incidences offered solace in that they provided proof of their abilities, even as children, to resist an institutional oppressor.

The sources of knowledge on which the activists drew were not always discrete and clearly separated between kinship and the hegemony. In some cases, these two sources of knowledge were conflated for the activists, particularly when family members and friends delivered hegemonic messages intended to affirm and support. For example, Brown presented a description of some childhood games and rhymes that provided negative conceptions of Blackness: "If you white, you right; if you yellow, you mellow; if you brown, stick around; if you black, git back; Way Back!" Shakur also discussed such games at length, recalling the names of those whose features were more "African" than American: "We would call each other 'jungle bunnies' and 'bush boogies.' We would talk about each other's ugly, big lips and flat noses. We would call each other pickaninnies and nappy-haired so-and-so's."[31]

In their use of derogatory names as insults, the activists distinguished among one another, seeing individual features as the cause for racial difficulties. Davis reminisced about how her playmates and childhood friends "were learning how to call each other 'nigger,' or what . . . was just as bad in those days, 'Black' or 'African,'" both of which were considered synonymous with "savage." Yet she found most disturbing comments concerning her light complexion: "I used to secretly resent my parents for giving me light skin instead of dark, and wavy instead of kinky hair."[32]

Brown provided another example when she saw in herself all the ways that she was "better" than her neighborhood playmates and much more like her white wealthy classmates. Based on her participation in ballet and classical piano and her vocal intonation, which she identified as her "ultimate disguise . . . I listened to them, paid attention to their grammar, their syntax, their cadence. I learned to speak exactly like white people." She asserted, "I was really becoming white." She stated that this sentiment was echoed by her classmates and teachers: "'You know Elaine, you're not like the other coloreds. You're different.'" Based on a desire to accept this "honorary" whiteness, she "grew to hate to leave school."[33]

Direct Experience

A third source of knowledge about racial identity for the activists was direct experience. Instead of a message that is given to them by friends and family or the dominant culture, this source of knowledge involves the individuals directly in racial incidents. With direct experience as a source of knowledge, they are not being told stories that model appropriate action by their families, and they are not receiving cultural messages of negative stereotyping about their race in general. Instead, they themselves are confronted with a racial situation that involves them specifically, and they must decide how to respond. How they choose to respond becomes, of course, a source of knowledge for them for future such encounters.

Direct experience as a source of knowledge takes place both in the moment of an encounter and in the reflection on the encounter after the fact. More important, however, it involves a dynamic interplay between the two other sources of knowledge the activists identify—kinship networks and hegemonic factors. In these situations, individuals bring with them the knowledge they have gained about race from these two sources—one largely positive, where the cause of the racial unease is seen largely as individual and spawns positive emotions (messages from friends and family), and one largely negative, hegemonic factors in which the explanation for the race-related problem is also seen largely as structural and generates largely negative emotions in response. At the moment of a racialized experience, individuals must choose which messages to privilege in deciding how to respond. They stand poised between the two sources of knowledge and are able to choose whether to align with one or the other or to create a response that synthesizes them. Racial identity formation, then, with this step, becomes a process of choice in response to the sources of knowledge about race to which they previously have been exposed.

Attributions of Race-Related Incidents

The data from the autobiographies do not suggest a clear pattern in terms of the attributions of the explanations for these incidents in which the activists are directly and personally involved. Although there are some instances in which they attributed the cause of a racial experience to individuals, there are an equal number of instances where the activists saw structure as responsible for the situation. The autobiographies contain many structural attributions as explanations of the cause of racial experiences—where the activists saw the cause in social conditions. Brown provided such an example in her discussion of her decision to break off a relationship with her white lover, Jay Kennedy. Early in their relationship, he attempted to encourage a positive sense of identity by complimenting her on her "African" features, but she came to see his comments as "not as a compliment to me. I resented his aside. I thought of it as an uncomfortable reminder that I was a Negro, or black." Brown decided to break off the relationship and explained how she felt at the time in this way: "My pain is not unique. Others, like me, are suffering. There is only one, ultimate source of our suffering—the white man and his greed. The white man has stolen everything from us."[34] By this description of events, she explained her decision to leave by citing a structural cause. The cause of their failed relationship was the fact that he represented "the man."

Brown also provided an illustration of an example of structural attributions when she described a situation where a fellow classmate, an African American student, had been overlooked in the award ceremony during commencement: "When she was passed over for the awards . . . I became perturbed. . . . I started to become angry, watching white girls in white dresses get out of their seats; watching white girls in the front row . . . accept their prizes with boring little speeches; watching white girls sit down. . . . [I]t was an outrageous display of racial prejudice—a concept, a reality that was so profound it was not missed even by me, who wanted to be white."[35] This situation reveals the ambiguity in terms of causal attributions the activists felt in response to racial knowledge derived from direct experience. They were willing to locate in structural causes aspects of racial identity but, at the same time, clung to psychological desires that contradicted those analyses—the desire to be white or to be with a white man, for example, as Brown described.

Seale described a situation of individual attribution, where he internally identified his responsibility for behavior, explaining his internal resentment while in the military. While waiting in line, he was bumped by "another white boy." He hit the man, providing first a structural explanation but, upon further analysis, then an individual explanation. "I felt rotten, knowing I had really hit that boy for nothing. . . . I had to face the fact that somehow it was wrong for me to beat on the white boy just because I felt like it." Seale chose here not to see the man who had bumped him as a generalized white enemy, representing a racial social structure.[36]

Yet another example of individual attribution occurred when Seale practiced avoidance as resistance: "I had quit my job because an old white worker made reference to me as being the 'only nigger' and me trying to know too damn much. Instead of letting myself get worked up to a desire to kick his ass, I calmly terminated my employment there, believing that there were plenty more jobs where that one came from."[37] In this case, he chose to attribute the racial comments to a misguided individual and focused on his own abilities that would allow him to find another job.

The numerous examples of the emotions that accompany these racial incidents are varied, as are the causal explanations the activists provided. Those who experienced positive emotions often did so when they observed or participated in practices of collective struggle or independent resistance. Davis described positive emotions while listening to Malcolm X, for example: "I was fascinated by his description of the way black people had internalized the racial inferiority thrust upon us by a white supremacist society."[38] She went on to say that although she had difficulty accepting his religious doctrine, she was "mesmerized" by his willingness to speak directly to a mostly white crowd and place at their feet a strong sense of responsibility for the social conditions of African Americans.

Brent described positive emotions felt when he encountered the BPP. He stated, "The audacity of these young blacks excited me and stirred emotions I thought had died years ago. I was proud that they had armed themselves and faced the enemy on his own ground." Concomitant with these positive emotions were negative feelings associated with his own inactivity: "I felt cowardly and ashamed because I was just sitting around bitching or pretending indifference about the shit going down in our communities while these young people were making history."[39]

There were other times when the activists felt and expressed negative emotions. Davis provided such an example as a result of a series of racialized events that were occurring in her hometown while she was studying in New York. On the one hand, her emotions were mostly connected to the sense of not being active in the struggle. For example, she stated, "Although I was involved in the movement . . . I felt cheated: precisely at the moment I had decided to leave the South, a movement was mushrooming at home." She described her desire to withdraw from school in order to join the liberation struggle, but her parents attempted to convince her that she should stay and complete her final year of studies. The result was frustration: "I was too distressed and frustrated to keep my mind on my school work." Davis revealed a set of negative emotions in her search for other students of color who understood her emotional reactions to the struggle: "I lived with this alienation and began to cultivate it in a romantic sort of way. If I felt alone, I refused to feel sorry for myself and refused to fight it by actively seeking friends; I would be alone, aloof, and would appear to enjoy it." Newton's expression of negative emotions was largely connected to the structural conditions he experienced. He stated, "We were getting back at the people who made us feel small and insignificant at a time when we needed to feel important and hopeful. We struck out at those who trampled our dreams."[40]

These findings suggest that there is variance in terms of the attributions of cause for racialized experiences and the activists' emotional responses to them. The activists, then, were making choices from among those offered them by the two primary sources of knowledge on which they had to draw—kinship and hegemonic factors. They tended not to follow either the lead of the kinship networks and Black civil society or the hegemonic messages exclusively in deciding how to act in racialized situations. Attributions of cause were both individual and structural, suggesting they were creating attributions different from the ones in the messages they had received. This undoubtedly is a natural response as individuals begin to see that structural explanations cannot always be applied to individuals' behaviors. It also undoubtedly reflects their desire to feel pride in Blackness and to act to proclaim that pride and the remnants of desire they felt earlier to be white and to fit into the white hegemony. In choosing both positive and negative emotions, the activists were choosing from the largely positive emotions generated in messages about race from the kinship networks and Black civil society and from the largely negative emotions generated by the hegemonic influences.

Conclusion

I began this study seeking to discover the degree to which BPP activists' interpretations of their racialized experiences were rooted in social or psychological causes and explanations or both. I discovered that kinship networks and hegemonic influences are two sources of knowledge that provide differing information regarding racial identity, therefore providing varied perspectives for the formation of the racial identity of these social activists. Both psychological and social determinants of racial formation were present when they described their direct experiences, and they felt both negative and positive emotions associated with these interpretations.

In contrast to Omi and Winant's theory of racial formation, and Bonilla-Silva's theory of racialized social structures, these findings suggest that to describe the process of racialization without including both psychological and social factors that contribute to individuals' understanding of their racial identity is difficult. This work thus provides a new understanding of the process because it ultimately suggests that people are drawing on both kinds of factors to develop their identities around race. For instance, they rely on both kinship networks and hegemonic influences as sources of information about race and are given largely individual explanations through kinship sources and structural causal explanations for race through hegemonic sources. They are taught to feel both positive and negative emotions in response to their race as a result.

Theoretically, these findings are largely consistent and align with both Cross's theory of Nigrescence, which privileges individual identity, and Cha-Jua's Black Racial Formation Theory, which focuses on structural sources of racial development. Nigrescence theory explains black self-concept—both individual and collective, identity socialization, and identity resocialization. With its focus on social factors, this theory emphasizes individual identity development and the transformation of these identities based on the collective black experience. Cha-Jua's theory of Black Racial Formation emphasizes the structural factors of political economy, black racial oppression, and the collective black experience in both ideology and struggle. The findings presented in this chapter provide insight into the process through which collective experiences become translated via various sources of information into an understanding of racial identity.

This study brings to the fore the significance of a factor largely undertheorized in the literature on racial formation—the source from which racial identity formation is derived. Although much of the previous work on racial formation references received information, little work seeks to explore the precise nature and sources of this information. Source of information for the construction of racial identity, then, deserves more attention than it has previously been given. The autobiographies analyzed for this study suggest that the activists paid a great deal of attention to the worldviews of kinship and the hegemony and that interpretation of their racial experiences and racial identity was dependent, to some degree, on the activists' use of these sources.

The third contribution this study makes to an understanding of racial formation is the significance of the element of choice in this process. These findings suggest that choice plays a greater role in the formation of racial identity than has been understood or demonstrated. This element of choice influences how activists make use of the messages they are given to create identity, the cause they cite for racialized experiences, and the emotions they feel in response to such experiences. When they are directly involved in experiences where race is featured, their choices multiply. In these cases, they must choose which source of information to privilege, whether to synthesize those messages or to create a response not modeled by either source. They make choices about how to act in such situations.

The critical role that choice plays in the formation of racial identity that I have identified here raises myriad questions. The most obvious and probably most important one is how individuals who see themselves as marginalized and oppressed come to understand the choices that are available to them. These individuals are receiving contradictory messages from home and hegemonic white institutions—one set of messages tells them that they are capable and are able to successfully resist racism, while the other set suggests that they cannot. When they are confronted with racism directly, they then must pull from these conflicting frameworks to develop their own responses. This study can only point to this question; it cannot answer it because these autobiographies are *post facto* reflections on their actions and do not allow insights into the factors that went into their choice-making processes at the time of the activists' responses.

A second question raised by the findings of this study is how social activists describe structural conditions in ways that make them appear solid and factual and thus obstacles either to be resisted or to be acquiesced to. Equally important is how these descriptions can be undermined to provide choices that are more liberatory in nature. More attention to the kinds of messages that individuals receive from kinship networks may provide one answer to this question because they often appear to be messages that do not define structural conditions as immutable and insurmountable.

I acknowledge that my analysis produces some surprising findings. I did not expect the autobiographies of former Black Panther members to suggest that racial formation is not given, a somewhat formulaic process in which structural conditions play a primary role. Even these individuals, though, who have constructed their lives in resistance to racism, point to ways in which racial formation operates in liberatory rather than constraining ways and suggest that they make choices as part of that process. I hope that my tentative effort here to map out this alternative perspective on racial formation will encourage others to contribute to our understanding of the factors that affect choice in the process of racial formation and its use in efforts to achieve liberation.

CHAPTER 7 READING QUESTIONS

1. Through the textual analysis of seven autobiographies of former Black Panther Party members, White uncovers three sources of racial knowledge: kinship influences, hegemonic influences, and direct experiences. In your own life story, what are the sources that have influenced your understanding of race, what have been some of your emotional reactions to this type of socialization, and how have these experiences shaped your identity?

2. White's study highlights the role of individual agency and choice in the formation of racial identity. What are the processes in which individuals who view themselves as marginalized and oppressed come to understand the choices that are available to them?

Notes

1. Michael Omi and Howard Winant, *Racial Formation in the United States: From the 1960s to the 1990s*, 2d ed. (New York: Routledge, 1994), 55, 60; Howard Winant, "Racism Today: Continuity and Change in the Post–Civil Rights Era," *Ethnic and Racial Studies* 21 (1998): 756.

2. William Cross, "The Psychology of Nigrescence: Revisiting the Cross Model," in *Handbook of Multicultural Counseling*, edited by Joseph Ponterotto et al. (Thousand Oaks, Calif.: Sage Publications, 1995), 96.

3. Omi and Winant, *Racial Formation*, 62; Eduardo Bonilla-Silva, "Rethinking Racism: Towards a Structural Interpretation," *American Sociological Review* 62, no. 3 (June 1997): 475, 469.

4. See Chapter 1.

5. Sundiata Keita Cha-Jua, 15.

6. Angela Davis, *Angela Davis: An Autobiography* (New York: Random House, 1974); Assata Shakur, *Assata Shakur: An Autobiography* (Westport, Conn.: Lawrence Hill, 1987); Elaine Brown, *A Taste of Power: A Black Woman's Story* (New York: Pantheon

Books, 1994); Huey Newton, *Revolutionary Suicide* (New York: Harcourt Brace, 1973); Bobby Seale, *A Lonely Rage* (New York: Times Books, 1977); Eldridge Cleaver, *Soul on Fire* (Waco: World Books, 1978); William Lee Brent, *Long Time Gone: A Black Panther's True-Life Story of His Hijacking and Twenty-five Years in Cuba* (New York: Times Books, 1996).

7. Bruce Berg, *Qualitative Research Methods for the Social Sciences,* 5th ed. (Boston: Allyn and Bacon, 2003), 200.

8. Davis, *An Autobiography,* 160.

9. Brown, *Taste of Power,* 47.

10. Shakur, *An Autobiography,* 37.

11. Newton, *Revolutionary Suicide,* 16.

12. Cleaver, *Soul on Fire,* 14.

13. Brent, *Long Time Gone,* 68.

14. Barney Glaser and Anselm Strauss, *The Discovery of Grounded Theory: Strategies for Qualitative Research* (New York: Aldine, 1967).

15. Max Weber, *Economy and Society* (1921; reprint, Totowa, N.J.: Bedminster Press, 1968); Emile Durkheim, *Suicide: A Study in Sociology,* translated by George Simpson and John A. Spaulding (New York: Free Press, 1951); Lewis Henry Morgan, *League of the Haudenosaunee, or Iroquois* (New York: Dodd, Mead, 1901).

16. *Dictionary of History of Ideas,* s.v. "civil society."

17. Shakur, *An Autobiography,* 27.

18. Ibid., 28, 20, 36.

19. Ibid., 29; Davis, *An Autobiography,* 94. .

20. Shakur, *An Autobiography,* 21; Brown, *Taste of Power,* 21.

21. Shakur, *An Autobiography,* 21; Davis, *An Autobiography,* 93, 89.

22. Newton, *Revolutionary Suicide,* 32.

23. Ibid., 21.

24. Shakur, *An Autobiography,* 28.

25. Newton, *Revolutionary Suicide,* 20, 22; Brent, *Long Time Gone,* 23; Shakur, *An Autobiography,* 136.

26. Brent, *Long Time Gone,* 42.

27. Cleaver, *Soul on Fire,* 46, 47.

28. Brent, *Long Time Gone,* 22; Newton, *Revolutionary Suicide,* 42.

29. Shakur, *An Autobiography,* 149–50.

30. Davis, *An Autobiography,* 80.

31. Brown, *Taste of Power,* 32; Shakur, *An Autobiography,* 30.

32. Davis, *An Autobiography,* 96.

33. Brown, *Taste of Power,* 27–33.

34. Ibid., 93, 103.

35. Ibid., 65.

36. Seale, *A Lonely Rage,* 81.

37. Ibid., 111.

38. Davis, *An Autobiography,* 126.

39. Brent, *Long Time Gone,* 87.

40. Davis, *An Autobiography,* 112, 118; Newton, *Revolutionary Suicide,* 28.

Benjamin Brawley and the Aesthetics of Racial Uplift

JEFFREY WILLIAMS

In May 1939, the *Crisis,* the organ of the NAACP, published a tribute to the late Benjamin Griffith Brawley (1882–1939), an inspired teacher at the Negro colleges. Written in the fashion of the day by a former student, John W. Parker, the article is hagiographic in its praise. As a result of Brawley's passing, Parker laments, "something has gone out of the life of every lover of truth, beauty, and culture." In the short span of a half century, Brawley distinguished himself as a minister, teacher, scholar, and author, displaying "three great gifts—vitality, intelligence, and a superior artistic sense." Parker highlights the Victorian sensibility that placed Brawley on a collision course with younger artists and intellectuals of the Harlem Renaissance: "His was the idea that good literature must rest on a sound artistic basis; it must teach and its teachings must fall within the pale of traditional moral standards." Despite a lengthy list of books "brought out by our most noted publishers and adopted as standard texts in many of our leading American colleges," he continues, Brawley's "unwavering devotion to cultural correctness" placed him at odds with trends of the day. "Steeped in the classic Harvard tradition," he was "often out of step and out of sympathy with the so-called new literary genre."[1]

Parker's homage underscores the paradox of Brawley's considerable contributions in the daunting task of racial uplift. As a poet, historian, literary critic, professor of English, and administrator at various black colleges, Brawley's multifaceted participation in African American civil society reflected the ambitious and often ambivalent aims of uplift ideology—to foster collective racial progress through the development of individual character, to rehabilitate the image of the race by demonstrating its capacity for civilization and culture, and to underscore racial progress by emphasizing class distinctions within the race. At institutions like Morehouse College and Howard University, Brawley worked to prepare his students for participation in a larger American experience. In literary and social histories such as *A Social History of the American Negro* (1921), *The Negro in Literature and Art in the United States* (1921), *Early Negro American Writers* (1935), *The Negro Genius* (1937), *and Negro Builders and Heroes* (1937), he chronicled and critiqued black contributions to American civilization. As part of a larger tradition that traces it origins to the early part of the nineteenth century, Brawley worked with notables such as W. E. B. Du Bois, Alain Locke, James Weldon Johnson, Francis Grimke, Carter G. Woodson, Sterling Brown, Ira De A. Reid, and John Hope. Within the African American educational and scholarly community, he was an important presence. At the time of his death, many considered him Morehouse College's most distinguished son in scholarship. The author of countless books, articles, pamphlets, book reviews, editorials, shorts stories, poems, and songs, Brawley belongs to a list of well-published and highly intellectual African American scholars and leaders who have been almost completely overlooked in historical and literary scholarship. Despite attestations of his acumen in the classroom by former students, and general acknowledgment by scholars of the period, Brawley remains, as Parker described him, "out of step and out of sympathy" with those who view Harlem as the mecca of black modernism. Indeed, one scholar has aptly noted that Brawley's life "cries out for a biographer."[2]

Parker is not alone in his assessment of Brawley's significance. In "Criticism at Mid-century," Ulysses Lee labels Brawley one of the "dominant critics of the thirties and forties," along with Sterling Brown and Alain Locke.[3] Their aesthetic ideologies, Lee argues, were linked by a shared concern with racial progress and a desire to delineate the race's distinctive genius. Nonetheless, Parker's encomium might well have been an elegy for the man and his critical legacy. With rare exception, Brawley's role in African American letters has been buried by the passage of time, or dismissed by scholars impatient with his rigid conception of literature as a "handmaiden of progress."[4] Despite his considerable efforts to foster and chronicle black achievement, Brawley is virtually ignored in contemporary scholarship. When not ignored, he is isolated from other critics who regarded art as an instrument of social change. For the most part, Brawley is dimly remembered as a quaint figure whose Victorian sensibility was quite out of place when Harlem was in vogue.[5]

Despite denunciation of his Victorian values, little, if any, attempt has been made to understand their influence on Brawley's aesthetic ideology or their relation to the larger traditions of racial uplift. Rooted in the Victorian values of racial uplift, Brawley believed that art should improve the material and moral circumstances of African American life. These values led Brawley to conflate the realms of literary and social criticism and to reject what he regarded as the "ghetto realism" of the Harlem movement. He preferred instead writing that documented the black man's potential for "culture," or, put differently, for manners and morals. The task of literature, he believed, was to rehabilitate the image of the race and to promote Christian civilization. In articles appearing in the *Southern Workman,* the organ of Hampton Institute, and in works like *The Negro Genius,* Brawley objected to the nature and quality of the literary works produced by artists associated with the Harlem movement. Rooted in the mandates of respectability and racial uplift, he valued the formalities of the Western high-art tradition, particularly an elegance of expression that offered new evidence of advancement and achievement, of "the Negro's" coming of age. Along with other New Negro intellectuals, he believed that a positive self-image, forged in such achievement, would be the starting point for a better chance in the American experience.

In a letter to James Weldon Johnson, Brawley stated, "We have a tremendous opportunity to boost the NAACP, letters, and art, and anything else that calls attention to our development along higher lines." Consistent with these aims, his purpose in works like *The Negro Genius* was to delineate the race's distinctive contributions in the realms of art and culture. While committed to the aims of the New Negro historical project, his uneasiness with the artistic direction of the "so-called Renaissance" eclipsed his early appreciation of the movement's possibilities. As early as 1927 he objected to the movement's focus on low culture, particularly jazz and the blues. In a *Southern Workman* article titled "The Negro Literary Renaissance," Brawley lamented the movement's corrupting influence on black romanticism: "His greatest gift," an innate love of song and dance, "had become his greatest downfall" in Harlem. Asserting that the romantic temper of the period had cultivated a mood "that was the very essence of hedonism and paganism," he derided jazz as "a perverted form of music originating in Negro slums," and the blues as "a new form of so-called art."[6] Appalled by an emphasis on free verse, he criticized artistic impulses that annihilated form. Brawley would repeat these charges in various articles over the years and in *The Negro Genius* ten years later. Despite the passage of time, he maintained his attack on the artistic failings of Harlem's younger writers, whom he dubbed "the New Realists."

Brawley's misgivings with the artists of this period illustrate one of the more significant shortcomings of the Victorian values of racial uplift and respectability that influenced both the form and the content of black texts from the post-Reconstruction era up through the Harlem era. Rooted in the mandates of black Victorianism, African American writers, even those famous for their skill with Negro dialect, like Charles Chesnutt, Frances Harper, and Paul Laurence Dunbar, believed that positive images of black life would help to demolish racial barriers. Rather than an unconditional claim for black humanity, these writers sought to highlight "class distinctions, indeed, the very existence of a 'better class' of blacks, as evidence of race progress."[7] Even as they insisted on the obligation of creative artists to highlight racial progress, black Victorians often employed the very images of black degradation that they sought to combat. In works such as *The Marrow of Tradition, Iola Leroy,* and *The Sport of the Gods,* these writers depicted lower-class black people as primitive and in need of "uplift." Enmeshed in this ambiguity, black Victorians were often uneasy with depictions of the common man as the emblem of black authenticity. Implicit in their conception of culture was a qualified claim for both citizenship and humanity. Concerned with demonstrating achievement to a doubting and skeptical world, they regarded Harlem as a cultural stage for a genteel performance that would prove that certain blacks, if not all, were ready for the responsibilities and rewards of citizenship.

Little, if any, attempt has been made to examine Benjamin Brawley's link to larger traditions of racial uplift that trace their origins to the efforts of free blacks to gain respectability in the antebellum era. By situating Brawley in the ambivalence of Victorian culture, we gain insight into the complex modes of social action and cultural expression through which black elites sought to counter oppression and empower themselves as agents of uplift. Sustained reflection on his life and thought helps to understand the social and psychic tensions engendered by the contradictory position of black elites as a social class that aspired for greater inclusion in the American Dream and as a racially subordinated caste. A review of racial uplift ideology and how it gave rise to an "ambivalent art" also helps to understand the conflict between these black Victorians and the younger artists and intellectuals of the Harlem era who found the race's distinctive contributions to American life in the culture of the common man.

The Ideology of Racial Uplift

In the late nineteenth and early twentieth centuries, most whites viewed African Americans as a "homogenous mass of degraded people."[8] Whites perceived the African presence as a national liability in the imagined community, a "body of death" chained to the larger body politic. Despite the inability of whites to think in terms of a stratified black society, by the late nineteenth century, a small but growing African American middle class regarded its own existence as prima facie evidence of racial progress. An African American elite, whose culture and style of living often more closely resembled that of the better class of whites, shouldered the burden of "uplifting the race" during the period that historian Rayford W. Logan has labeled "the Nadir" (1880–1915). During this turbulent era, the voting and civil rights gains of Reconstruction (1864–1876) were systematically dismantled. Confronting violence and extralegal terrorism of often barbaric intensity and a virulent racial discourse in which science and the rhetoric of lynching converged, these black elites sought to rehabilitate the image of the race by embodying "respectability" and an ethos of service to the masses. Believing that improvement of their material and moral condition through self-help would diminish white racism, African American elites emphasized education, achievement, and propriety as marks of personal distinction that would refute racial distinctions and establish a basis for positive black identities. Confronting the deep-rooted prejudice of the period, black leaders insisted on the responsibility of each individual to uplift all by "striving to embrace piety, practice thrift and temperance, comport one's self with well-mannered dignity, and seek all advantages that education offered." African American leaders of the period sought to demonstrate cultural parity with whites of the highest attainment, to challenge judgments of black capacity based on the behavior of a "degenerate few," and to assert African American manhood and citizenship.[9] Respectability connoted possession of the intellectual and literary skills necessary for African Americans to contribute their own authoritative voices as equals to the nation's ongoing civic discussions.

The evolving ideological formations and social relations of this period help to understand the race relations of the era in which Benjamin Brawley came of age. Efforts by African Americans during Brawley's life to uplift themselves into conditions of respectability provoked violent resistance from the vast majority of whites, particularly in an unreconstructed South. The intrusion of the black body into white social space led to mythic discourses and mob violence. In response to perceived horrors of "black Reconstruction," and its efforts to assimilate newly emancipated bondsmen into the body politic, white southerners enacted a response that led to a low point in American race relations. As Logan notes, "Southern state laws, railway regulations, and customs began to fix the pattern of segregation which was to become even more rigid until the middle of the twentieth century."[10] Perhaps more important, a decline in political and civil rights brought with it an upsurge in racial violence against African Americans. The lynch mob was commonplace in a campaign of violence and intimidation intended to disfranchise African Americans politically and socially. This occurred against the backdrop of pseudoscientific theories of racism, eugenics, and social Darwinism. In the rhetoric of lynching and in novels of national reconciliation, Africans Americans were depicted as a biologically inferior and immoral race that would never achieve parity with white Americans. As in earlier periods, white Americans imagined a community in which black Americans were figured as "the other."

As in earlier periods, the themes and tensions of racial uplift ideology were conceived in response to a pervasive racial discourse. Kevin Gaines notes that black elites, concerned with improving the collective social fortunes of the race, placed emphasis on "self-help, racial solidarity, temperance, thrift, chastity, social purity, patriarchal authority, and the accumulation of wealth." Due to the network of institutions for group elevation within antebellum free-black communities, and to the efforts of early leaders to uplift themselves to conditions of respectability, racial uplift ideology had indeed stressed deference from "the lowest orders."[11] Despite such emphasis, racial uplift was initially conceived in collectivist terms. This connotation of racial uplift persisted in the wake of Emancipation, when a view of education as the key to liberation shaped the efforts of black Victorians.

In the post-Reconstruction era, however, racial uplift ideology was transformed by Jim Crow terror, New South economic development, and the imperatives of a transatlantic Victorian culture. In this context, racial uplift became an ideology of self-help articulated mainly in middle-class specific terms rather than a broader egalitarian social context. Consistent with the late Victorian emphasis on autonomous individualism and personal achievement, black elites opposed racism by pointing to class distinctions within the race as evidence of evolutionary progress. Retreating from natural-rights arguments, they regarded freedom as a reward for upright, cultured behavior. An unconscious internalized racism fostered an ambivalent relationship with the black masses. "Amidst legal and extralegal repression," Gaines argues, "many black elites sought status, moral authority, and recognition of their humanity by distinguishing themselves, as bourgeois agents of civilization, from the presumably undeveloped black majority; hence the phrase, so purposeful and earnest, yet so often of ambiguous significance, 'uplifting the race.'"[12]

A distinctive feature of black Victorians committed to racial uplift in the late nineteenth and early twentieth centuries was the quest for gentility. African American elites argued their capacity for assimilation into the larger society by displaying external evidence of culture, refinement, and character. Guided by the rules of the "genteel performance," they regarded manners and morals, rather than material possessions, as the true measures of success and social class. Gentility forbade loud talking and laughing in public, or any behavior considered vulgar, annoying, or crude. Self-restraint, the prime attribute of gentility, important in all matters from emotion and expression to dress, was the basis of collective racial improvement. Further, black gentility dictated that "race men" rationalize personal success in terms of the collective advancement of the race.[13]

The quest for black gentility went beyond a simple emphasis on proper conduct. African American elites sought to fulfill the majority society's normative gender conventions and to adopt its sexual attitudes. Educated African Americans regarded the family and patriarchal gender norms as crucial markers of respectability and racial progress. Seeking to counter the charge of sexual immorality directed at black females, the black women's club movement adopted the motto "lifting as we climb," reflecting its efforts to elevate the race by teaching women the importance of home and woman's moral influence within it. In their paeans to patriarchal family life, black elites explicitly celebrated Victorian standards of genteel courtship and premarital chastity.

The quest for black gentility, in all of its dimensions, fostered aspirations of a stratified African American society, successive classes with higher and higher sexual morals. Defining themselves in relation to the masses, black Victorians posited that the two groups were in different phases of development. "Contrasting their own adherence to the genteel performance with the crude behavior with which they credited the lower classes," writes Williard B. Gatewood, these elites "often assumed the role of instructing the lower classes in the essentials of the genteel performance." Others, replicating the racial fictions used to justify segregation even as they contested them, believed that little could be done to improve the collective fortunes of the race. In their minds, the measure of gentility was the distance between themselves and the masses. The tensions of racial uplift ideology are visible in Gatewood's assertion that "some aristocrats of color alternated between the uplift approach and the stratagem of placing distance between themselves and the ill-mannered masses. Or, on occasion, they attempted both approaches simultaneously."[14]

These black Victorians created a network of religious, educational, and social institutions to prepare black Americans for participation as American citizens. Albert G. Miller has described the results of their efforts as a "civil society," composed of "churches, the Free African Society, the Prince Hall Masons, literary societies, schools, and newspapers, provid[ing] a social space of discussion of public concerns.[15] Created as buffers from white society and as tools of liberation, these entities formed an institutional base for African American leaders who surpassed the often hollow, abstract rhetoric of racial uplift with practical service to the race. Their techniques of persuasion and instruction, of self-improvement and improvement of others, were manifestations of black Victorianism.

Benjamin Brawley and the Ideology of Racial Uplift

Benjamin Brawley's link to the traditions of racial uplift ideology began with his father, Charleston-bred Edward McKnight Brawley, a free-born black of considerable attainments. After attending the Institute for Colored Youth, a Philadelphia school noted for its emphasis on "character building," Edward Brawley earned a degree from Bucknell University in 1875 and a master's degree from the same institution in 1878. In 1885, when Benjamin was three, Edward Brawley became president of the newly created university for blacks at Selma, Alabama. Later he would return to South Carolina as the president of Morris College, which he helped to found. From 1912 to 1920, Edward Brawley pastored White Rock Baptist Church in Durham, North Carolina. He spent the last years of his life as a professor of theology at Shaw University in Raleigh, North Carolina.[16]

Due to Edward's ministerial career, young Benjamin never lived in Charleston. Comments found in "A Southern Boyhood," however, suggest the importance of his father's origins in the formation of his class-conscious identity: "I regret that there is nothing romantic about my story. I was not born in a log cabin, and never slept under a pavement. I was not even brought up on a farm. My father was from Charleston; his people had been free as far back as they could remember."[17]

Edward's origins among Charleston's free antebellum elite, his pursuit of education, and his subsequent achievements had tremendous implications in his son's life. Despite the challenges of the Nadir, black Victorians sought status by reference to achievement, personal culture, and family background. Denied opportunity in other areas of endeavor, they often forged successful careers in education and in the ministry. Guided by his father's example, Benjamin's life-long pursuit of education and culture was in many ways an "errand of tradition" rooted in the Victorian imperatives of racial uplift ideology.

Benjamin's upbringing illustrates black Victorians' regard of the home as the earliest and most import locus for the transmission of culture. Confronting the horrors of "the Nadir," Edward and Margaret Brawley appropriated Victorian gentility as an approximation of racial equality. Accordingly, the Brawley home was an orderly and secure place in which Benjamin and his siblings were properly indoctrinated before being sent into a rapidly changing world that threatened not only their genteel values but their very humanity. Benjamin's later exaltations of domestic virtue, symbolized by home, family, chastity, and respectability, and an ethic of religious piety were scripted responses to stereotyped representations of black Americans as irremediably trapped in a primitive stage of development. During the so-called Progressive Era, minstrelsy, literature, science, and the rhetoric of lynching were linked by a denial of black simultaneity. Benjamin's lifelong practice of "humanistic self-cultivation, Protestant self-denial, and bourgeois self-control," cultivated in the bosom of black gentility, was a deliberate rejection of a narrowly racialized identity. Raised in the American South during a period characterized by violence and degradation against black bodies, Brawley's life and career reflected the bourgeois optimism characteristic of black Victorianism.

Despite the frequent moves required by Edward's ministerial duties, Benjamin received the kind of education given only to well-to-do Americans at the turn of the century. A precocious learner, he was nurtured in a household that valued moral instruction and classical learning as the chief ingredients of social mobility. Margaret provided early instruction and Bible study; his father introduced him to the study of Greek. Crediting both parents with his success,

Brawley describes the domestic ideal: "While my father was my chief mentor and critic, it was my mother who gave me my love for the beautiful and who urged me to produce things worthy of criticism."[18] Operating within her sphere of influence as the guardian of moral, religious, and other cultural values, Margaret Brawley conceded to her husband's "superiority" in the more important domain of reason. As the maternal "Angel in the House" atop the domestic pedestal, Margaret managed simultaneously to be a submissive helpmate and a repository of moral and cultural authority. The Brawley household was the epitome of domestic harmony.

If the Brawley household seemed to be a domestic model of social harmony, it nonetheless gave rise to a tremendous spirit of competition. Conforming to the contradictory expectations of the domestic ideal, the Brawley home served as a refuge from the marketplace while simultaneously socializing Benjamin to succeed in the competitive realm. Consistent with his faith in autonomous individualism, Benjamin was noted for an enterprising and competitive spirit. Entering school in Nashville, Tennessee, he was placed in the third grade. An account of his youth, found in "A Southern Boyhood," offers further evidence of Brawley's early faith in autonomous selfhood. Characteristic of the period's success literature, it celebrates his youthful habits of efficiency and time thrift. After spending an industrious summer engaged in study for the oncoming year, he passed the examinations and was advanced to the next class.

Subsequent experiences illustrate his life and aims as superego for the race. Entering Atlanta Baptist College (Morehouse College) at thirteen, he discovered his life's purpose when he realized "that not everyone had read Shakespeare and Hugo at home." Older students frequently brought their assignments for his approval before submitting them to their teachers. Outside the classroom, Brawley was a quarterback on an early football team, manager of the baseball team, foreman of the college printing office, and along with another student, Timothy Williams, founder of the student journal, the *Athenaeum,* which ultimately became the *Maroon Tiger.* Active in various literary societies, he published an early poem, titled "A Prayer," in response to a lynching.[19] Surrounded by the Christian influences of his early upbringing, Brawley followed in his father's footsteps as a civilizing missionary. Graduating with honors in 1901 as one of the institution's youngest graduates, he embodied the attributes of the ideal Victorian gentleman. Moments after accepting his first teaching assignment in Georgetown, Florida, he received a better offer from the superintendent of schools in Deland. Declining the offer, he stated, "I decided not to begin my career as a teacher by breaking a contract."[20]

Much like his father, Brawley's subsequent career reflected a commitment to the Victorian strategies of racial uplift. In 1902, he returned to Morehouse College as an instructor of English. In 1906, after receiving a bachelor of arts from Chicago, Brawley was promoted to professor of English at Morehouse. After receiving a master's degree from Harvard in 1908, he served from 1910 to 1912 at Howard University as a professor of English. In 1912, he returned to Morehouse College as its first dean. Later, in 1920, Brawley journeyed to Liberia to do an educational survey of the country. From 1923 to 1931 Brawley served as a professor of English at Shaw University in Raleigh, North Carolina. In 1931, he accepted a professorship at Howard University, where he remained until his death in 1939. Brawley's career as a teacher continued the ethos of self-help and service to the race that had characterized his father's endeavors.

Brawley's pursuit of educational excellence combined Victorian imperative with racial wisdom: "I soon saw that for a Negro to win recognition in any field he would need to hold before him an unusual standard of excellence. Where discount had to be made for prejudice, he had often to do a task even better than anybody else." The shortcomings of other teachers led him to strive for self-improvement in a manner consistent with the values of his upbringing. His comments reveal a unique sensibility, one that combined study of the classics with the goal of creating modern workers: "I regretted accordingly to see that many teachers put forth little real effort for self-improvement, that they had no reserve power, and that in writing they were often guilty of the most flagrant errors. I resolved forthwith to learn with the utmost detail any subject that I approached. Somehow I had the feeling that if a man made himself the most efficient electrician or dentist in a community, he would not have to wait long before people turned to him for help."[21]

Brawley's career as an educator and administrator at the Negro colleges helps to understand his role as superego for the race. Working with John Hope at Morehouse College as the institution's first academic dean, Brawley maintained a strict New England code of conduct intended to eradicate any tendencies toward frivolous or immoral conduct. Students were suspended or expelled for cursing, smoking, misbehaving in class, playing cards, or comparable infractions. Subsequent to his death, Nathaniel Tillman, a former student, described Brawley's legacy as the first dean of the college: "In the latter position he standardized the curriculum and courses, integrated the academy and college work, re-wrote and enlarged the catalogue, and in the main exerted such influence upon the College that traces of his work may be seen today in spite of the fact that since his departure in 1920 the College has passed through nineteen years of the most rapid and revolutionary changes in its history."[22]

As dean and registrar of each student in the academy and the college, Tillman says, Brawley often gave oral and qualifying exams to new students. He taught a full schedule, coached dramatics and debating, and trained speakers for the weekly rhetoricals. Despite a heavy program of work, Tillman notes, "Dr. Brawley established a reputation for promptness and thoroughness." Ever vigilant in his role as superego for the race, he missed "only one day from his office in the course of five years." Serving the institution for another eight years, he was also credited during this time "with increasing the efficiency of classroom work" and "with building a well-rounded course of study."[23]

Teaching by precept and by example, "he worked hard and demanded hard work from his students." Ira De A. Reid, who would achieve considerable stature as a scholar himself, remembered Brawley as "the picture of a gentleman, correct, precise and mannered in every move." De A. Reid believed that "Brawley more than any one else, gave Morehouse efficiency, power of expression, and habits of study." He describes Brawley's famous response when students in his English IV failed to complete a homework assignment. "Dr. Brawley politely stepped to the door, opened it, and said, 'Gentlemen, that is all.'" His students left the session feeling sufficiently chided. Commenting on Brawley's prowess in the classroom, he states, "English poets and essayists from Chaucer and Milton to Brooke and Meredith lived with you after you had studied them with Brawley." Perhaps more important, De A. Reid remembers a "penchant for correctness" consistent with Brawley's role as superego for the race: "Then Brawley gave us exemplary teaching in other things—manners. I err, I should say gentility. There were certain hall marks of a gentleman—his attire, his speech, his presence, his manners, his learning, and these we should learn, observing them well in all things. Many of them were fast-lagging ways in a world already beginning to feel the social disturbances of a world war, but they were correct according to Dean Brawley, and we never saw him slip."[24]

Ever concerned with uplifting the race, Dean Brawley considered it his racial duty to teach students lessons "not in the textbook." Perhaps he knew of Edward S. Green's *National Capital Code of Etiquette,* one of the "scores of etiquette books" read by members of the black elite. Published in 1920, "it provided detailed rules on correct dress and table manners, proper conduct in public, the staging of dinners, dances, and weddings; the art of conversation, visiting cards and mourning." In a 1925 essay in the *Southern Workman* titled "Not in the Textbook," Brawley lamented the decline of gentility, particularly among black students who seemed to believe "the thought that worth consist not in what one *is* but in what one *has.*" Consistent with Green's assertion that good manners should rest on "a foundation of human kindness, honesty, and character," Brawley argued that character could be shaped by "careful development of habit." Just as Green emphasized the need for "self-control through careful practice, so that restraint and polite behavior came naturally," Brawley detailed the responsibility of teachers to capitalize on each "unusual opportunity for development in self-control." The basis for collective racial progress was the disciplined autonomous self, nurtured by "home training" and the moral instruction of Christian teachers.[25]

The Negro Genius and the Aesthetics of Racial Uplift

The Victorian values of racial uplift influenced both the aesthetic mandates and the themes of African American expression from the post-Reconstruction era up through the New Negro movement of the 1920s. Because they shared in and lived life according to the Victorian values of the larger society, a crucial force in black expression of the period was the interaction of racism and the middle-class character of black writers. Reflecting the tensions and ambiguities of racial uplift, ambivalence was a key structural element of African American expression. Even those writers known for their celebrations of black folk culture viewed art as an instrument of social change. Their attempts to gain "civil rights by copyrights" reflected their faith that literary endeavor would challenge white beliefs in black inferiority. Protest and gentility, the development of inner virtue through cultivation of proper thoughts and feelings, were key characteristics during a period of literary assimilation.[26] While striving for assimilation into the larger white society, however, black Victorians worried that the race would lose its distinctive identity in the process. As a result, many were committed, simultaneously and paradoxically, to the "racial ideal," that is, a belief that blacks exhibited a clear racial particularity and therefore had a distinctive message for humanity. The resultant tensions—between the desire to put the best foot forward and the desire to celebrate the black folk tradition—shaped the aesthetic ideology of Benjamin Brawley and other black Victorians.

Trained at elite institutions by white scholars with little regard for vernacular expression, Brawley clearly favored the formalism of the genteel tradition. Like many black Victorians, he found value in the black folk tradition only as a starting point for the race genius who would create black classical traditions. Consistent with his emphasis on discipline and self-restraint in the classroom, Brawley's conception of culture had more to do with polite manners, respect for traditional learning, appreciation of the fine arts, and, most important, a devotion to classical traditions. Like the Victorian poet Matthew Arnold, Brawley believed that culture should be the source of morality and inspiration. He conceived of literature as criticism of life, as an instrument of the best kind of education. Brawley's literary critiques were ultimately social and political judgments. Even discussions of style were essentially about society. The task of literature, he believed, was to promote civilization by making men more reasonable, social, spiritually enlightened, morally sensitive, and clear thinking. The literary scholars who trained him had been Anglophiles who hoped to reproduce all that was good in English civilization. In similar fashion he dedicated his own life to the study and teaching of perfection, believing that he was preparing an educated black elite to assume leadership of society, and to act as a civilizing force.[27]

Brawley's aesthetic ideology grew from the antebellum efforts of black elites to gain respectability through the pursuit of "literary character." Black writers rooted in this tradition mingled notions of refinement and morality with those of racial improvement to form what might be termed an aesthetics of racial uplift.[28] These black arbiters of culture hoped that by imitating the aesthetic values of the larger white society, African American artists would aid in the larger cause of raising the race. By demonstrating that they could be coworkers in the kingdom of culture, black Victorians hoped to earn a berth in modern civilization. Art was seen as a progressive force and as exerting a moral influence.

In the postbellum period, black writers wedded to the mandates of respectability employed the themes of racial uplift in didactic fashion. In novels like Frances Harper's *Iola Leroy* one finds clear acceptance of the need for literacy and cultural production as prerequisites for civilization. A white man who loves a black woman articulates the role of black expression: "Out of the race must come its own defenders. With them the pen must be mightier than the sword. It is the method of civilization, and they must use it in their own defense."[29]

From origins in the antebellum literary societies through the post-Reconstruction fiction of Charles Chesnutt, Paul Laurence Dunbar, and Frances Harper, this belief persisted through the Nadir, surfacing in the aesthetic ideologies of older race leaders associated with the Harlem movement. By the 1920s this conception of literature was a "received idea," a gauntlet thrown to black artists and intellectuals increasingly conscious of their second-class citizenship. Artistic endeavor, particularly the creation of a literary tradition, was an accepted barometer of the race's progress toward civilization.

Along with others, Benjamin Brawley accepted this equation. Brawley's preference, revealed in works such as *The Negro Genius,* was for Europeanized art that would promote racial acceptance and integration. Brawley routinely criticized younger artists for their insufficient mastery of Western techniques as well as their focus on lower-class black life, particularly in the urban landscape. Condemning art for art's sake as decadent, Brawley argued the moral function of art. In "Art Is Not Enough," an article published in the *Southern Workman,* Brawley drew parallels between the fin de siècle aestheticism of the decadent movement in England and artistic developments in Harlem. In Brawley's estimate, the "hedonism and paganism" of the Harlem movement were products of an "art for art's sake" heresy that could be traced from origins in the "paganism" of Keats and the "sensuousness" of Rossetti and the other pre-Raphaelites to Edgar Allan Poe, whom he particularly blamed for contending that "Art had nothing to do with Science, the search for truth, on one hand, or with Religion, the basis of conduct on the other." This "divorce of art and morality," Brawley argued, had been the "secret of many of the wasted lives strewn like wrecks over the reign of Victoria."[30] He regarded artistic developments in Harlem in a similar light.[31]

192 · JEFFREY WILLIAMS

Brawley and other black Victorians envisioned a literature that would appeal to the consciences of white readers, deploring the constraints that restricted blacks, even those of admirable attainments, from meaningful roles in society. Consistent with the mandates of racial uplift, black Victorians sought recognition of their humanity by ranking themselves at the top of an evolutionary hierarchy within the race based on bourgeois morality. Ironically, this desire to "live fully," along with the demands of the marketplace, led these black writers to employ images of the so-called primitive, morally deficient lower classes to underscore their own class superiority. From Charles Chesnutt and Frances Harper in the post-Reconstruction era to Booker T. Washington and James Weldon Johnson in the early twentieth century, representations of culturally backward, morally suspect blacks are commonplace in the literature of uplift. Furthermore, black elites were hostile to writers who questioned the values of bourgeois culture by celebrating the virtues of the black masses. Despite their desire to explicate a distinctive black genius, strict moral mandates led critics like W. E. B. Du Bois to condemn writers who flaunted the conventions of genteel protest with sympathetic representations of urban culture. After reading Claude McKay's *Home to Harlem,* Du Bois remarked that he felt "distinctly like taking a bath." Similar sentiments led Brawley to condemn Langston Hughes's *Fine Clothes to the Jew* for its "sheer coarseness and vulgarity."[32] Du Bois and Brawley were concerned that favorable depictions of low-down folks, the "debauched tenth," would impede integration. The proper medium of expression was Europeanized art that pled for admission into American social space while demonstrating the black man's moral sensibility as well as his proficiency in Western techniques and practices.

Judged from the perspectives of the present day, their aims seem overly optimistic, particularly to those who dismiss the aesthetic as a tool of hegemony and thus inherently opposed to progressive politics. But this Promethean optimism was fully in accord with the thinking of many black and white intellectuals during the Progressive Era. These men and women were convinced that racial problems were social aberrations due to moral corruption, fear, or ignorance. Literary endeavor was only part of a program of propaganda and persuasion that would earn for the black man, or at least a certain segment of black America, the respect of high-minded men of the white race. Black and white could meet on "the common ground of shared artistic passion."[33] The older critics of the Harlem movement did not dwell in this haven of aesthetic idealism alone. Despite their differences, both those artists and intellectuals associated with the Old Guard, and those younger artists with whom they quarreled, were convinced that civil rights could be gained by copyrights.

The tensions inherent in racial uplift ideology were manifest in other ways as well. The desire to impose universal discipline on black Americans visible in Brawley's efforts as teacher and administrator points to an internal dialectic within the black Victorian sensibility, between the competing influences of Enlightenment rationalism and romantic nationalism. Along with other black Victorians seeking to explicate the Negro genius, Brawley was torn between a conception of progress that exulted in cultural development and a romanticized view of the black masses, between the desire for assimilation and a belief in black distinctiveness. Like Du Bois and other black Victorians, Brawley viewed black people as a mystical or metaphysical entity. His lifelong efforts to tame and routinize the folk spirit rising from the soul of the black masses, so apparent in his labors as a teacher and critic, would paradoxically destroy the very "Negro genius" that he extolled.

Black and Victorian: Benjamin Brawley and the Negro Genius

The Negro Genius reveals the competing influences of the two cultural perspectives at the heart of black Victorianism—romantic nationalism and cultural evolution. Black Victorians looked to the agrarian past and to simple, premodern people for the key to racial identity and progress. Writers such as Alexander Crummell, Anna Julia Cooper, and W. E. B. Du Bois imagined a glorious past in the preindustrialized age, where the "soul" of the race had its roots. Intellectually indebted to German nationalism, chiefly the social thought of Johann Gottfried van Herder, black Victorians believed that the highest cultural values traced their roots to the so-called vulgar and lowest levels of society. These sentiments are apparent in the introductory essay, where Brawley locates "the Negro genius" in the traditions of the past, and in the language, customs, and art of the poorer and rural people. Running counter to such sentiments, however, was a belief in cultural evolution that meshed with the progress narratives of the day. Consistent with an Enlightenment worldview, black Victorians believed that cultures progressed in stages from barbarism to civilization. Accordingly, *The Negro Genius* reflects Brawley's concerns with confirming black progress. Often apparent in cultural evolution was, if not condescension toward traditions outside the realm of urban industrial life, an ambivalence toward tradition-based rural culture. Because they believed that civilization reflected inevitable progress and the common destiny of mankind, black Victorians generally viewed industrialized Western culture as the peak of civilization.

Reflecting the tensions between romantic nationalism and cultural evolution, the notion of a distinctive black contribution to progress is a salient theme in the writings of black Victorians. Alexander Crummell believed that each race had its distinctive genius and a singular contribution to world civilization. Mindful of the contributions of the Jews, the Greeks, and the Romans to the progress of mankind, Crummell spent twenty years cultivating Africa's contribution to world civilization. He was never quite clear just what the distinct contribution of Africa was, nor did he believe contributions remained the permanent, exclusive property of any race. Because he viewed the process of civilization as one of mutual exchange, he believed that Africans had to earn the respect warranted by civilized people. Crummell called for an elite leadership to lead a collective effort to contribute to the world's cultural wealth in a way that could be described as definitely "Negro."[34] His views would find later expression in Du Bois's writings regarding the role of the Talented Tenth.

Influenced by the racial discourse of the dominant society, Crummell's views of the race were not always positive. In contrast with Herderian expressions extolling the virtues of the premodern African, he often expressed the view that Africans were universally lacking in "civilization," which they would have to acquire in order to avoid the fate of other indigenous peoples. In 1897 he founded the American Negro Academy for the purpose of undertaking the "civilization of the Negro race in the United States, by the scientific processes of literature, art, and philosophy." His preference for rational order led him to view black people as "children of the sun" in need of hardier studies and more tasking scholarship to counterbalance a "permanent tropical element."[35] A view of blacks as an aesthetically gifted people who possessed enthusiasm, but no discipline, led him to emphasize the need for character building, the elevation of moral life, and intellectual rigor. His ambivalence regarding racial character—rooted in the competing values of romantic nationalism and cultural evolution—would become a common characteristic of racial uplift ideology.

In *A Voice from the South,* published in 1892, Anna Julia Cooper argued for the preservation of the racial spirit as an instrument of progress. "Each race has its badge, its exponent, its message, branded in its forehead by the great Master's hand which is its own peculiar keynote, and its contribution to the harmony of nations." Cooper believed that equilibrium among the races, rather than racial repression, was "the condition of natural harmony, of permanent progress, and of universal freedom." To achieve balance in the body politic, the "tropical warmth and spontaneous emotionalism" of the Negro was needed to offset the "cold and calculating" qualities of the Anglo-Saxon. Thus, America's "Race Problem" was, in her view, a "guaranty of the perpetuity and progress of her institutions." A shared mistrust of the mob linked Cooper with Crummell, a young Du Bois, and later Brawley. Revealing the concern for rational order that characterized black Victorian thought, she argued that the black man's "instinct for law and order, his inborn respect for authority, his inaptitude for rioting and anarchy, his gentleness and cheerfulness as a laborer, and his deep-rooted faith in God will prove indispensable and invaluable elements in a nation menaced as America is by anarchy, socialism, communism, and skepticism poured in with the jail birds from the continents of Europe." Conscious of her gendered exclusion from the American Negro Academy, she nonetheless praised its efforts to promote intellectual work and higher education among African Americans: "I believe with our own Dr. Crummell that the Almighty does not preserve, rescue, and build up a lowly people merely for ignoble ends."[36]

Perhaps the earliest expression of Du Bois's Victorian beliefs regarding inherent group temperament or ideals is found in his initial address to the American Negro Academy, "The Conservation of Races." Promoting a cultural celebration based on both general racial pride and a particular group sensibility, he believed that "the race idea, the race spirit, the race ideal" were instruments of progress. He argued for the preservation of the racial spirit as "the vastest and most ingenious invention for human progress." The significance of race was not in "mere physical distinctions." Instead, the deeper differences were "spiritual, physical, differences—undoubtedly based on the physical, but infinitely transcending them." Each race possessed some distinct spiritual and physical differences: "The English nation stood for constitutional liberty and commercial freedom; the German nation for science and philosophy, the Romance nations stood for literature and art." Some of the "great races of today," Du Bois continued, "have not as yet given to civilization the full spiritual message which they are capable of giving." To the question of how this message might be delivered, Du Bois proclaimed: "For the development of Negro genius, of Negro literature and art, of Negro spirit, only Negroes bound and welded together, Negroes inspired by one vast ideal, can work out in its fullness the great message we have for humanity." If the Negro was to place "among the gaily-colored banners that deck the broad ramparts of civilization" one that was "uncompromisingly black," the answer lay not in "absorption by the white Americans" but in cultivation of a distinct racial identity.[37] Despite Du Bois's early and ongoing admiration of European culture, his references to black folklife emphasized what he considered its primitive aspects. Contrasting the sensuous, tropical love of life of black people with the cool and cautious New England reason of whites, he proclaimed in *The Gift of Black Folk* that "the Negro is primarily an artist."[38]

Brawley's conception of "the Negro genius" is a less radical formulation of ideas often attributed to Du Bois.[39] Brawley took up the gauntlet thrown by Du Bois regarding a distinct black contribution to progress. In "The Conservation of Races," Du Bois asked, "How shall this message be delivered; how shall these ideals be realized?" Brawley's attempts to explicate "the soul of the race" reflect the competing influences of cultural evolution and romantic nationalism implicit in Du Bois's question. Although his larger aim was to dismantle racial barriers, Brawley's assertion of an exotic black particularity, a racial *Volkgeist*, was quite similar to Du Bois's paeans to the premodern folk. Like Du Bois, Brawley too felt the need to hold on to some claim of distinctive black character. Without a distinct Negro character, there could be no Negro genius. If the Anglo-Saxon was preeminently gifted in the "domain of pure intellect" and the Jews showed greatest strength in areas having to do with the will, especially with morality, then the Negro race was "the race of feeling." Joining Du Bois and others in a cultural celebration of black particularity, he located the "peculiar genius" of the race in the artistic realm. Consistent with Du Bois's assertion that "we are that people whose subtle sense of song has given America its only American music," Brawley proclaimed that all major achievements by black people up to his own time had been in the arts. "Let *us* not be misunderstood," he stated. "In *our* emphasis on achievement in the arts," he continued, "*we* do not mean to say that the Negro can not rise to distinction in any other sphere." After noting his "notable advance in scholarship," he said, "*We* do suggest, however, that every race has its peculiar genius and that, as far as *we* can at present judge, the Negro, with all his manual labor is destined to reach his greatest heights in the field of the artistic. On every hand *we* have proof of this tendency."[40] Despite such pronouncements, Brawley was not able to find value in the artistic endeavor of Harlem's younger artists. The tensions of racial uplift ideology help to understand Brawley's conflict with younger artists of the era, most notably Langston Hughes. In large part, Brawley has been defined by this conflict.

Benjamin Brawley and Langston Hughes

Historicizing Benjamin Brawley's presence as the Victorian voice of racial uplift helps us to understand not only his place in a critical continuum but also his relationship with Harlem's younger artists in a larger compass of culture. The range of critical responses to sympathetic representations of the black masses illustrates the tensions inherent in elite conceptions of uplift; challenges to its fixed traditions by younger artists reflect a larger contestation of meaning. Artists like Langston Hughes, Claude McKay, and Zora Neale Hurston clearly rejected the Victorian values inherent in the hegemonic beliefs of older race leaders. By allowing the subpoetic black masses to speak through their art, these artists advanced a more modern conception of uplift, one favoring a broader vision of collective social aspiration, advancement, and struggle.

The conflict between Benjamin Brawley and Langston Hughes was a symbolic battle for the image and future of the race reflecting opposing views of racial uplift. Returning from his adventures abroad, Hughes and his mother lived briefly with prosperous cousins in Washington, D.C. This experience led him, in *The Big Sea*, to criticize the class and color snobbery of black elites. It also led to significant changes in his aesthetic ideology:

> To me it did not seem good, for the "better class" Washington colored people, as they called themselves, drew rigid class and color lines within the race against

Negroes who worked with their hands, or who were dark in complexion and had no degrees from colleges. These upper class colored people consisted largely of government workers, professors and teachers, doctors, lawyers, and resident politicians. They were on the whole as unbearable and snobbish a group of people as I have ever come in contact with anywhere. They lived in comfortable homes, had fine cars, played bridge, drank Scotch, gave exclusive "formal" parties, and dressed well, but seemed to me altogether lacking in real culture, kindness, or good common sense.[41]

The pretensions of the "best colored society" drove Hughes to seek relief on Washington's Seventh Street, "the long dirty street where the ordinary Negroes hang out, folks with practically no family tree at all, folks who draw no color line between mulattos and deep dark browns, folks who work hard for a living with their hands." Such people played the blues, ate watermelon, barbecue, and fish sandwiches, shot pool, told tall tales, looked at the dome of the Capitol and laughed out loud." To black elites, these "low-down folks" were the source of the minstrel images they sought to combat. Rejecting snobbish relatives, Hughes embraced the culture of his newly discovered racial family. Hughes says, "I tried to write poems like the songs they sang on Seventh Street—gay songs, because you had to be gay or die; sad songs, because you couldn't help being sad sometimes."[42]

Much of what we know about Benjamin Brawley has been shaped by his response to the literary insurrection that began at this moment, challenging Victorian conceptions of culture. From his perch as an academic critic, Brawley led an indignant response to Hughes's *Fine Clothes to the Jew.* To Brawley's chagrin, this work captured what Richard Barksdale describes as the "bluesy exuberance of black life found in the big city."[43] In *The Negro Genius,* Brawley fumed:

> About Langston Hughes the only thing to observe is that here we have the sad case of a young man of ability who has gone off the wrong track altogether. We are sure that he can get on the right track, but it will take a strong wrench to put him there, also a little time. When Mr. Hughes came under the influence of Mr. Carl Van Vechten and the "Weary Blues" was given to the world, the public was given to understand that a new and genuine poet had appeared on the horizon. It mattered not that the thing contributed had been done before by Vachel Lindsay; the book was full of jazz, and that was enough for the public. After all, however, it is not an author's first book that determines his quality, but the second, for the first book may be an accident. "Fine Clothes to the Jew" hardly stands the test. In fact, one would have to go a long way to find more of the sheer coarseness and vulgarity than are to be found between the covers of this little book. We forbear quotation. We are sorry Mr. Hughes wrote it, and we hope that he will never write another like it.[44]

In *The Big Sea*, Hughes responded with veiled irony: "Benjamin Brawley, our most respectable critic, wrote: it would have been just as well, perhaps better, if the book had never been published. No other ever issued more fully reflects the abandon and vulgarity of its age."[45] Hughes's polite dismissal influenced scholarly perception of Brawley. Brawley and others like him are identified as an "Old Guard," class consciousness distinguished from the "New Guard" by a different aesthetic. This bifurcated perception of the movement, influenced by Du Bois's famous formulation of the cultural ambivalence of African American intellectuals, forms the dominant metaphor of the period. From Nathan Huggins to George Hutchinson, the movement is most often described in terms of duality, as a Manichaean binary of old and new, rich and poor, black and white, primitive and civilized, gay and straight. Accordingly, Brawley and Hughes are seen as representatives of opposing traditions.

Rejecting the mandate of older race leaders that whatever literature the black man produced must not only protest racial conditions but also promote racial integration, Hughes chose instead to celebrate black life for its own sake, to uplift the race by humanizing the common man. To the chagrin of black critics, he fashioned an aesthetic rooted in secular folk material, orature forged in the heat of slavery and the injustice of postslavery racial oppression. The subsequent publication of *Fine Clothes to the Jew*, in 1927, shocked and startled black cultural monitors, leading them to denounce Hughes as the "poet-lowrate of Harlem."[46]

In an interview with the *Chicago Defender*, he explained his desire to humanize the common man, to "catch the hurt of their lives, the monotony of their jobs, and the veiled weariness of their songs." The poem "Elevator Boy" emerged from this effort:

> I got a job now
> Runnin' an elevator
> In the Dennison Hotel in Jersey.
>> Job ain't no good though. No money around.
>> Jobs are just like chances
> Like everything else.
>> Maybe a little luck now.
>> Maybe not. Maybe a good job sometimes;
> Step out o' the barrel, boy. Two new suits an'
> A woman to sleep with.
>> Maybe no luck for a long time. Only the elevators
> Goin' up an' down,
> Up an' down,
> Or somebody else's shoes
> To shine

Or greasy pots in a dirty kitchen. I been runnin' this
Elevator too long.
      Guess I'll quit now.[47]

Like much of his work during this period, this poem dramatizes the response of urban workers to racism and economic exploitation. Gradually recognizing that the industrial North was not the promised land initially envisioned, newly arrived southern migrants and other urban dwellers were less than enthusiastic about their prospects in the emerging economic order. Implicit in the "elevator boy's" bluesy monologue is a rejection of the bourgeois virtues considered necessary by black elites for entry into American social space.

Rather than putting the best foot forward by highlighting the lives of black elites, Hughes attempted to humanize the people lowest in the social order. Enmeshed in an elite conception of racial uplift, Brawley did not view these humanizing techniques favorably. His response to "Elevator Boy" helps us to understand the ambivalent antimodernism that characterized both the Harlem Renaissance and the Southern Renascence, as well as the conflation of literary and social criticism found in both movements. In an essay titled "The Negro Literary Renaissance," published in the *Southern Workman* in April 1927, Brawley criticized the modern temper for its "lack of regard for any accepted standards," for its "preference for sordid, unpleasant or forbidden themes," and for "turning away from anything that looked like good honest work in order to loaf and to call oneself an artist": this is the "very latest thing" in English prose as cultivated by Negro "artists."[48]

> On the main point, however, that about unwillingness to work, we may note in Mr. Langston Hughes some lines entitled "Elevator Boy," which will hardly do for quoting in this magazine but which end thus:
>
> > I been runnin' this Elevator too long.
> > Guess I'll quit now.
>
> As to all of which we submit simply that the running of an elevator is perfectly honorable employment and that no one with such a job should leave it until he is reasonably sure of getting something better.[49]

Brawley's response to "Elevator Boy" illustrates the tensions that tormented black Victorians well into the twentieth century, the conflict between an antimodern sensibility and the desire to depict emerging modernity as a narrative of black progress. Influenced by the cult of science and technical rationality that accompanied American industrial development, Brawley accepted the need for the rationalization of human endeavor. Consistent with the systematic organization of economic life for optimum productivity, one's individual life had to be ordered for maximum personal achievement. However, Brawley also believed that the urban industrial landscape undermined the moral and cultural authority that fostered these values. Looking at black life through the lens of southern racial discourse, he believed that the common black man needed the constraints of rural life to curtail innate and unhealthy impulses. Brawley's objection to the elevator boy's indolence emanates from a similar agrarian sensibility as exhibited by Booker T. Washington in *Up from Slavery.*

Although he accepted the role of art in re-creating a racial narrative consistent with the spirit of progress in the larger society, Brawley's southern sensibilities attenuated the sense of modern doubt that plagued black Victorians, leaving him unable to envision Harlem as the symbol of racial advancement. Even as James Weldon Johnson bravely extolled Harlem's virtues as the race capital in *Black Manhattan,* Brawley saw poems like "Elevator Boy" as evidence of a growing urban pathology. Adhering to conservative notions of uplift, Brawley insisted that art demonstrate the spiritual, social, and intellectual condition of the better class of blacks.

Conclusion

As the embodiment of antimodern ambivalence, Benjamin Brawley has the dubious distinction of being a neglected figure in two literary movements, the Harlem Renaissance and the Southern Renascence. As part of a critical continuum formed with other black Victorians, Brawley believed that "a critical mass of exemplary talent could make things better."[50] As a black agrarian he questioned, like his southern counterparts, the marriage of material and spiritual progress in the Zion of modern industrial society and brought a stern republican moralism to the aesthetic endeavor of the Harlem movement. Although it is customary to discuss the agrarian movement as a rejection of modern culture, few have peered beneath the Promethean optimism of the New Negro to examine the social and psychic tensions that plagued black Victorians. Despite the official optimism of racial improvement efforts, many black elites were uneasy with the leveling influences of prosperous mechanization and the loss of cultural authority in an increasingly secular society.

CHAPTER 8 READING QUESTIONS

1. Compare and contrast the class distinctions made within the black community in Williams's account of black Victorians and White's description of the messages activists from the Black Power movement received growing up.

2. What internal and external factors helped shape the ideology of racial uplift in the Black community?

3. Williams provides a detailed analysis of the diverging views of the aesthetic ideology among participants of the Harlem Renaissance. In what ways do racial ideology and attributions of race-related phenomena (as described by White) account for the wide-ranging positions from people such as Langston Hughes, on one end of the continuum, and Benjamin Brawley, on the other?

Notes

1. John Parker, "Benjamin Brawley," *Crisis* 46 (May 1939): 144.

2. Jeffrey P. Green attributes the lack of scholarship on Brawley to his status as a southerner. "Educator, scholar, author, poet, literary critic and historian, Benjamin Brawley had a Southern upbringing and worked in Southern colleges, in Atlanta; Washington, and Raleigh, N.C. His presence in the South may have been the reason why historians have virtually ignored him, although his writings, such as *Negro Genius, A Social History of the American Negro,* and *A Short History of the American Negro,* appear in bibliographies." Green asserts, "Black historiography has concentrated on the Northern states in the 1910s and 1920s, at the cost of ignoring Brawley." Green argues that "black history in those decades might take on a fresh perspective if the emphasis on Northern urban life was changed" ("Four Letters from Benjamin Brawley," *Journal of Negro History* 68 [1983]: 309).

3. Whereas Sterling Brown and Alain Locke are revered figures in African American cultural and intellectual history, Brawley, an equally prolific scholar, critic, and writer of the period, is neglected in contemporary scholarship. Ulysses Lee discusses the three as part of a "well formed way of looking a the Negro literary artist and at the Negro in American literature." As "teachers and missionaries," Lee says, black critics rarely had time to examine the form and substance of black literature, but were instead concerned with black art as "new evidence of advanced and achievement, to be shared and gloried in all members of the race" ("Criticism at Mid-century," *Phylon* [1950]: 329).

4. Lee argues that black criticism has generally been a "handmaiden of progress, illuminating not the work themselves but the wonder that they exist, analyzing not the problems and methods of the authors but their effect, actual and probable, upon their audiences always remembered as comprising both Negro and whites" (ibid., 328). Lee's argument is consistent with my assertion of an "aesthetics of racial uplift."

5. Hughes scholars and scholars of the Harlem Renaissance are dismissive in their treatment of Brawley. Richard Barksdale decries Brawley's "rigidly Victorian approach to life and literature" (*Langston Hughes: The Poet and His Critics* [Chicago: American Library Association, 1977], 30). David Levering Lewis labels Brawley as "fatuous" and "the dean of Afro-American bluenoses" (*When Harlem Was in Vogue* [New York: Oxford University Press, 1981], 189, 192). Arnold Rampersad's tour de force, *The Life of Langston Hughes: I, Too, Sing America,* vol. 1, *1902–1941* (New York: Oxford University Press, 1986), makes only fleeting reference to Brawley as "hidebound." Nathan Huggins, in *Harlem Renaissance* (London: Oxford University Press, 1971), fails to mention Brawley, as does Cheryl Walls, in *Black Women of the Harlem Renaissance* (Bloomington: Indiana University Press, 1995).

6. Parker, "Benjamin Brawley," 144; Benjamin Brawley, "The Negro Literary Renaissance," *Southern Workman* 56 (April 1927): 178.

7. Kevin Gaines, *Uplifting the Race: Black Leadership, Politics, and Culture in the Twentieth Century* (Chapel Hill: University of North Carolina Press, 1996), xiv.

8. Williard B. Gatewood, *Aristocrats of Color: The Black Elite, 1880–1920* (Bloomington: Indiana University Press, 1990), 7.

9. Gaines, *Uplifting the Race,* 69, 68.

10. Rayford W. Logan, *The Negro in American Life and Thought: The Nadir, 1877–1901*

(New York: Dial Press, 1954), 40. Logan, one of Brawley's colleagues at Howard, used the term *nadir* to describe the late-nineteenth- and early-twentieth-century period in which blacks saw a significant erosion of civic and social equality. In recent years, black scholars have attacked the use of this term, purportedly because it suggests black passivity during these turbulent times. Other scholars see this period as the first true "renaissance" in black literary expression. Sandra Gunning examines this period as an "intersection of several historical and cultural events: an unprecedented rise in the number of lynchings, an outpouring of distinctive narratives concerned with white supremacy and alleged black degeneration in the wake of Reconstruction; the continuing expansion of the movement for Woman Suffrage and a growing demand among various groups of white women for higher education and an increased level of sexual and social freedom; the flowering of a small but active postslavery generation of African American male and female writers intent upon making their political and artistic mark on the American literary scene" (*Race, Rape, Lynching* [Oxford: Oxford University Press, 1996], 4). Gunning is one of the growing list of scholars who examine the responses of black writers to the mythic discourse of race.

11. Gaines, *Uplifting the Race*, 2; James Brewer Stewart, "Modernizing 'Difference': The Political Meanings of Color in the Free States, 1776–1840," *Journal of the Early Republic* 19 (Winter 1999): 691–712.

12. Gaines, *Uplifting the Race*, 2.

13. Gatewood, "The Genteel Performance," chap. 7 in *Aristocrats of Color*, 182–209.

14. Ibid., 186–88.

15. Albert G. Miller, *Elevating the Race: Theophilus G. Steward, Black Theology, and the Making of an African American Civil Society, 1865–1924* (Knoxville: University of Tennessee Press, 2003).

16. For details of Edward Brawley's early life, see William J. Simmons, *Men of Mark* (New York: Arno Press, 1968), 908–18. The details of his later life can be found in the *Crisis* 21 (December 1920): 75; and 26 (May 1923). Dividing his time between teaching and preaching, the traditional occupations of the black elite, Edward Brawley also found time to write. Known as an "energetic and exceedingly fine speaker and writer," he authored *Sin and Salvation,* a textbook on evangelism, and edited both the *Baptist Tribune,* a weekly denominational organ, and the *Evangel,* a monthly pamphlet. He is best known, however, for *The Negro Baptist Pulpit* (Freeport: Books for Libraries Press, 1971), an edited collection of sermons and papers. His lead article, "Contending for the Faith," demonstrates the concern with uplift that guided the thinking of black elites in his day. While commending white missionaries for their efforts to help blacks become "American Christians," Brawley reveals his pride in the collective advances of the race.

17. Benjamin Brawley, "A Southern Boyhood," *Reviewer* 10 (1927): 70.

18. John W. Parker, "*Phylon* Profile, XIX: Benjamin Brawley, Teacher and Scholar," *Phylon* 10 (1949): 15.

19. Ibid., 16. See also Parker's "Benjamin Brawley and the American Cultural Tradition," *Phylon* 14 (1955): 185.

20. Benjamin Brawley, "The Lower Rungs of the Ladder," in *The Negro Caravan,* edited by Sterling A. Brown, Arthur P. Davis, and Ulysses Lee (New York: Arno Press, 1969), 758.

21. Ibid., 761.

22. His former student and later chairman of the English Department at Morehouse Nathaniel P. Tillman wrote, "Benjamin Griffith Brawley, '01" in the *Bulletin of Morehouse College* 8 (May 1939): 2, 11. When Brawley died in 1939, he was a professor of English at Howard University, his second time as a member of its faculty. He spent the bulk of his career, however, as a teacher and administrator at Morehouse College, which he attended as a student and was reputedly its youngest graduate. As part of the Archer-Brawley-Hope triumvirate, he helped to establish Morehouse as a reputable center for the education of young black men and wrote the first history of the institution. At the time of his death, "Dean Brawley" was considered the most accomplished son of the college in scholarship. Reflecting the considerable irony surrounding his scholarly legacy, a recent Web site listing one hundred of the institution's most illustrious graduates does not include Brawley.

23. Ibid.

24. Ira De A. Reid, "Three Negro Teachers," *Phylon* (Second Quarter 1941): 142.

25. Gatewood, *Aristocrats of Color,* 183–84; Benjamin Brawley, "Not in the Textbook," *Southern Workman* 53 (December 1926): 320.

26. See Dickson Bruce, *Black American Writing from the Nadir: The Evolution of a Literary Tradition, 1877–1915* (Baton Rouge: Louisiana State University Press, 1989), for a description of literary assimilation and the black quest for gentility. Bruce relates this quest to the Victorian values of the larger culture (19–20).

27. Henry May, *The End of American Innocence: A Study of the First Years of Our Own Time, 1912–1917* (New York: Alfred A. Knopf, 1959). May helps to understand the emergence of elite traditions in American life.

28. Wilson Moses, in *The Golden Age of Black Nationalism, 1850–1925* (New York: Oxford University Press, 1978), and Kevin Gaines, in *Uplifting the Race,* argue that ambivalence regarding the role of culture and civilization had an impact on the efforts of black elites at racial and social uplift. In *Black American Writing from the Nadir,* Dickson Bruce views these tensions as the central interpretative focus of his book. My aim is to situate Brawley in the ambivalent ideology developed by black elites as a response to violent racism in order to describe the "aesthetics of uplift" that led to the ambivalent art of the day.

29. Williams Andrews, ed., *The African American Novel in the Age of Reaction* (New York: Mentor, 1992), ix.

30. Benjamin Brawley, "Art Is Not Enough," *Southern Workman* 61 (December 1932): 489.

31. Brawley, "The Negro Literary Renaissance," 177.

32. W. E. B. Du Bois, "The Browsing Reader: 'Home to Harlem,'" *Crisis* 35 (1928): 202; Brawley, "The Negro Literary Renaissance," 183.

33. Nathan Huggins, *Harlem Renaissance* (London: Oxford University Press, 1971), 5.

34. Moses, *Golden Age,* 77.

35. Ibid., 59, 73, 75.

36. Anna Julia Cooper, *A Voice from the South* (New York: Oxford University Press, 1988), 152, 160, 173.

37. W. E. B. Du Bois, "The Conservation of Races," in *W. E. B. Du Bois: A Reader,* edited by David Levering Lewis (New York: Henry Holt, 1995), 21, 22, 23. Du Bois's

famous address to the American Negro Academy is an important document in the black Victorian tradition.

38. W. E. B. Du Bois, *The Gift of Black Folk* (Millwood, N.Y.: Kraus-Thomson Organization, 1975), 287.

39. Bruce, *Black American Writing from the Nadir.* Bruce discusses the relationship between the ideas of Du Bois and Brawley.

40. Du Bois, "The Conservation of Races," 23; Benjamin Brawley, *The Negro Genius: A New Appraisal of the Achievement of the American Negro in Literature and the Fine Arts* (New York: Dodd, Mead, 1937), 9 (emphasis added).

41. Langston Hughes, *The Big Sea* (New York: Hill and Wang, 1940), 207.

42. Ibid., 209.

43. Barksdale, *Langston Hughes,* 4.

44. Brawley, "The Negro Literary Renaissance," 182–83.

45. Hughes, *The Big Sea,* 266.

46. Barksdale, *Langston Hughes,* 25.

47. See Sterling Brown, "Book Reviews," *Opportunity* 15 (September 1937): 28.

48. Brawley, "The Negro Literary Renaissance," 178.

49. Ibid., 179.

50. Lewis, *When Harlem Was in Vogue,* xvi.

PART 3

Struggle

Our third and final part, "Struggle," is the logical culmination of the first two parts. "Racial Structures" and "Racial Ideology and Identity." Part 1 explored the origins and development of racial structures, U.S. Black racial formations (Cha-Jua, Chapter 1), the initial reconstruction of racial ideology within the British Empire (Koditschek, Chapter 2), and the impact of global capitalist mandated structural adjustment on Africa and African resistance to its destructive policies (Pearce, Chapter 3) and challenged the feasibility of rehabilitating and thus preserving whiteness, arguing that not only is it a product of racial oppression but it also derives its meanings from racial oppression, from white supremacy (Roediger, Chapter 4). Part 2 explored the relationship between ideology, identity construction, and representation. Specifically, it examined the usage of a color-blind racial ideology as the new racial ideology justifying the new Black formation, the New Nadir (Neville, Chapter 5). A related essay (Makalani, Chapter 6) critiqued the movement to construct a new biracial census category, arguing that it represented an anti-Black move designed to distinguish "biracials" from Blacks, thereby elevating their status above that of Blacks in a new racial hierarchy reminiscent of Latin American racial structures. The last two essays in that part explored the identity development and radicalization of Black activists during the 1960s via psychologist William Cross's Nigrescence model (White, Chapter 7), whereas the last chapter (Williams, Chapter 8) exposed the shortcomings of racial uplift ideology via a recovery and interrogation of Benjamin Brawley, an early-twentieth-century literary critic and amateur historian who expounded a conservative ideology and aesthetic theory that the author characterized as "black Victorianism."

Part 3 builds on the insights developed in the essays in the previous two parts. In Part 3, the authors put theory into practice and demonstrate the transformative possibilities when ideology becomes a material force shaping the consciousness of individuals and communities organized to fight for interests and against disparities that their *racialized* identities serve to mark.

The activists chronicled here barely resemble the "universal subject" Marx envisioned, and they certainly do not reflect the "historical agent" imagined by Marxists, particularly U.S. Marxists. Nevertheless, African Americans and other oppressed racialized people have led, composed, or participated in the most transformative social movements in the history of the United States. C. L. R. James's prescient thesis comes to mind. During the 1930s, James argued that the African American freedom struggle was central to socialist revolution. James's axiom serves to remind us that the historical agency of the descendants of that "precious cargo" forcibly brought to this country is not inconceivable within a reconstituted race-conscious Marxism constructed around an acknowledgment that history admits to plural and partial agents all chipping away at the structures and ideologies of global racial capitalism.

We end this book with four essays, each of which excavates neglected instances of agency by largely working-class individuals, organizations, and impoverished communities of color. These movements occurred at different historical moments and in different regions across the United States. Each essay chronicles and analyzes the variegated strategies and multifaceted tactics deployed by activists determined to eliminate the systems of racial oppression they faced. Each essay is a study in courage, as the participants of each narrative bravely challenge apparently hegemonic structures bolstered by corresponding ideologies that declared them and their constituencies less than, if not completely sub-, human. Collectively, the essays cover most of the twentieth century and wind their way into the new millennium.

The stories told by this group of scholar-activists are narratives of crushing defeats, partial victories, and, most important, enduring determination. Few of the victories were long lasting, and most led to incorporation in the system rather than fundamental transformation of racial capitalism. Yet these authors recover heroic struggles and recount the lives, ambitions, and visions of courageous and creative men and women who fought the state (mainly the local state), avaricious corporations, and arrogant college and university administrations from New York to Los Angeles, from the 1930s to the early years of the twenty-first century. All of their long-term projects were, as W. E. B. Du Bois said of Reconstruction, "splendid failures." Nevertheless, despite their inability to transform the U.S. state, abolish racial oppression, and end economic exploitation, each of the activists chronicled in our third part left a valiant legacy whose story can inspire future generations to summon the resolve to dedicate their lives to the destruction of capitalism, racial oppression, and its allied oppressions.

In Chapter 9, "Organizing from the Margins: Japanese American Communists in Los Angeles during the Great Depression," Scott Kurashige challenges the "model minority" myth by recovering the laudable legacy of working-class Japanese immigrants' Depression-era trade union radicalism. Much of "Organizing from the Margins" chronicles the intriguing possibilities Los Angeles provided multiracial activists for organizing all people on the dark side of the color line. Specifically, Kurashige reconstructs the interconnection among Japanese, African American, and Mexican radicals. Today we call the combination of multiethnic support activities, coalitions, and alliances rainbow activism, but in the 1930s, it was understood as part of the "internationalist" strategy of the Communist Party, USA (CPUSA), though it involved organizing by citizens and immigrants within the spatial confines of the United States.

The concept of "margins" is central to Kurashige's analysis. In L.A., the small Japanese immigrant population was additionally marginalized by racial oppression. To be a Japanese radical in Depression-era L.A. required a particular heartiness and dedication to the anticapitalist cause. Japanese radicals were triply marginalized. They were marginalized within the Japanese community, stigmatized with the anticommunist slur "aka," were a target of L.A.'s infamous and excessively brutal "Red" squad, and suffered racial discrimination within the CPUSA.

By the beginning of the 1940s, with the Pacific war looming, Japanese radicals saw their project stall. Shunned by moderate Japanese, abandoned by former allies from behind the veil, and betrayed by their white working-class allies in the CPUSA, Japanese radicals ended "the red decade" isolated and targeted for political repression. Kurashige concludes that after nearly a decade of valiant struggle against racial oppression and economic exploitation, "Race, class, and national oppression had conspired to make every road a dead end for Japanese Americans."

In Chapter 10, "Between Civil Rights, Black Power, and the Mason-Dixon Line: A Case Study of Black Freedom Movement Militancy in the Gateway City," Clarence Lang analyzes the struggles of ACTION, a militant Black-led interracial organization in St. Louis, Missouri. Between 1965 and 1984, the Action Committee to Improve Opportunities for Negroes (ACTION) created a strategy that involved the confluence of Black nationalist posturing and militant rhetoric and tactics with largely traditional civil rights goals and objectives. In this sense ACTION was similar to other offshoots of the Congress of Racial Equality. However, few of these "in-between" groups were as successful or survived as long. As Lang demonstrates, ACTION was always focused on more than "civil rights," if by civil rights one means the desegregation of public accommodations. According to Lang, ACTION was organized to fight for expanded job opportunities in the city's utility companies and aircraft industry. ACTION was not composed of traditional theorists—rhetoricians—but consisted of men and women of action, whose strategies and tactics came not from formally derived doctrines but from engagement, the give-and-take of struggle. ACTION's activities reflected an organic ideology that combined racial, class, and gender identities into a social movement based on hard-hitting guerrilla tactics. In this project Lang links ACTION's emergence in St. Louis to the city's physical and social location in a border state whose racial control system had attributes of both the North and the South. Lang seeks to explain why ACTION emerged in the mid-1960s, and why that moment helps us understand why it came to reflect both the politics of civil rights and Black Power. Lang maintains that an organization like ACTION suggests that no clear line of demarcation existed between the strategies, tactics, and goals often attributed separately to either the civil rights or the Black Power movement. He argues that this "in-betweenness" was not at all contradictory. For him, civil rights and Black Power were not the same, but neither were they sharply distinct. Rather, he views them as phases of a much larger Black Freedom Movement. In its broad themes, this project contributes to a revisionist labor and working-class historiography on the intersections of race, class, and gender. It explores the activity of Black working people not only at the point of production but also in community space. Moreover, this chapter contributes to literature addressing the intersection between the civil rights movement, on the one hand, and Black working-class agency, on the other. Finally, Lang uses ACTION and St. Louis as prisms to debate questions of continuity and discontinuity, and the distinctions between civil rights and Black Power.

Pedro Cabán in Chapter 11, "Common Legacies, Similar Futures: African American and Latino Studies," investigates the radical origins and subsequent development of African American and Latino studies (Chicano and Puerto Rican). In doing so, Cabán not only uncovers the similar origins, mutual goals, and related conceptual frameworks of these parallel intellectual projects but also persuasively argues that they have equivalent futures.

According to Cabán, in their struggle to democratize the university, Black, Chicano, and Puerto Rican studies posed four fundamental challenges to the Euro-American academy. Students and scholars from racialized communities sought to redirect the resources of historically white universities toward communities of color and to produce new research about those communities. Second, Black, Chicano, and Puerto Rican scholars exposed universities' complicity in re-creating the social order, especially dominant racial formations. Third, scholars from these communities not only produced scholarship on their communities but, more important, also generated scholarship that was, in the idiom of the day, "relevant." That is, the new generation of dark intellectuals produced scholarship that was imbued with the liberatory politics of the social movements that spawned them. Fourth, intellectual activists of color produced work that challenged the rigid disciplinary barriers prevailing in mainstream scholarship. They called for and worked toward the production of "collective and collaborative interdisciplinary research."

Cabán concludes that these insurgent intellectual projects were at best only partially successful. Perhaps the greatest success was simply surviving. Over the past forty years, as younger scholars divorced from the racialized academic communities' formative battles have entered the units, the emphasis on radical critiques of U.S. society and community engagement has given way to a corporatized professionalization. To revitalize the racialized communities' disciplines, Cabán proposes that they launch a large-scale comparative project that explores their linkages, commonalities, differences, and conflicts. For Cabán, a cooperative comparative project of this sort is not only central to reenergizing racialized community studies but also an important part of building a radical multiracial social movement.

In our final chapter, "'Livin' Just Enough for the City': An Essay on the Politics of Acquiring Food, Shelter, and Health in Urban America," David Crockett examines the effects of racial oppression in shaping the experiences of African American consumers in the food, housing, and health markets. Providing an analysis of his twenty-two informants, Crockett unravels the web of urban racism that connects place, mobility, and consumption into an interlocking system of racial and class oppression. He is also interested in exploring intraracial class differences as well as interracial differences in the market for basic goods and services. Additionally, he is particularly attuned to the multiple ways in which African Americans, especially the Black working class, negotiate and deploy microstrategies of resistance to racialized capitalism.

Milwaukee, Crockett's site of study, is a highly segregated city, scoring .826 (1.0 is the highest possible score) on the Index of Dissimilarity, which measures residential segregation. What Douglas Massey and Nancy Denton have termed *hypersegregation* provides the context for and structures the environment in which Black consumers encounter not only the housing market but the retail food and health care industries as well. For instance, he discovered that only one of twenty-two large supermarkets was located in the Black and Latino/a communities, and that food cost 24 percent more in the small stores proliferating in those communities. Additionally, Crockett charts the vast differences between working- and middle-class Blacks' access to quality health care and the racialized challenges each class confronts. The distinction between home owners and renters, according to Crockett's informants, is one site in which the construction of class-based identities is fracturing the African American community.

Crockett concludes his study with a set of brief policy recommendations. He calls for closing the loopholes in fair-housing legislation, greater regulation of lending institutions, reparations, and strategies that will bring Blacks trapped in ghettos access to healthy and affordable food. In this regard Crockett's concluding study turns full circle back toward the kind of work racial community studies scholars advocated during the formative years of Black and ethnic studies.

PART 3 READING QUESTIONS

1. It is often difficult to measure a social movement's success. What activities and campaigns do you consider successful for the social movements discussed in this part? Beyond specific campaign victories, how else might you consider the activists and organizations examined in this section as successful?

2. Discuss the similarities and differences between the movements discussed by Kurashige, Lang, Cabán, and Crockett. Three of the essays focus on specific cities, Milwaukee, St. Louis, and Los Angeles. How did the political economy, spatial structure, and demography of each city condition the kinds of issues that each social movement confronted?

3. The activities studied by each author not only occurred in different regions but also took place in different time periods. Place each local movement in its national and worldwide sociohistorical contexts. For instance, what was the impact of the cold war on Asian American organizing in Los Angeles or the rise of global capitalism on the possibilities for activists in Milwaukee? Lang and Cabán focus on the actions of two different social classes or strata within classes, workers and students. In what ways did the class position of these two groups matter, in terms of their goals, objectives, ideology, strategy and tactics, and discourses? Were the possibilities for large-scale militant organizing better in the 1930s–1940s, the 1960s, or the turn to the twenty-first century?

9

Organizing from the Margins

Japanese American Communists in Los Angeles during the Great Depression

SCOTT KURASHIGE

In the early 1930s, Japanese American activists in Los Angeles produced and distributed bilingual English-Japanese flyers declaring "Scottsboro Boys Must Be Freed." Their flyer detailed how nine African American youth had been jailed (and eight sentenced to death) for dubious rape charges in the racially biased Alabama case. More specifically, the activists were outreaching for a forum featuring Angelo Herndon, the African American activist from Georgia whose recent arrest for political activities had moved the International Labor Defense (ILD) to champion his cause. The campaign to build Japanese American solidarity with the Scottsboro Boys was the work of the Japanese American branch of the ILD and the "Japanese section" of the Communist Party, USA. The CPUSA's Japanese section also published the *Rodo Shimbun* out of its San Francisco headquarters. The newspaper's March 3, 1934, "Japan Nite" program proved to be one of the era's most interesting examples of cultural exchange and international solidarity. These events typically served as vehicles for recruiting members, raising funds, and showcasing the cultural work of Communist-led arts collectives. But this one had an added dimension. In addition to jujitsu performances, theater, dancing and a chop suey dinner, it featured Langston Hughes speaking on the subject of "the Japanese and Darker Races."[1]

Campaigns to support the Scottsboro defendants, Angelo Herndon, and the African American freedom struggle were part of a range of activities undertaken by Japanese American radicals under the banner of internationalism during the Depression. Such activism drew considerable attention in its time. In close contact with many activists of color, writer and social critic Carey McWilliams once wrote that Japanese Americans had a "long record of incipient trade-union activity."[2] For Asian American historians, the story of Japanese immigrant radicalism is required reading. However, among the general public and the wider body of academics, little is known about the long history of Japanese American resistance to exploitation and efforts to build working-class solidarity. More commonly, Japanese Americans, like other Asians, are thought to be a "model minority"—politically passive and averse to relating to other communities of color. The ideological value of racial stereotypes can, of course, exert a powerful impact, especially on those who wish to believe that the "positive" stereotype of their own group is true. By recovering counternarratives, however, historical research possesses the ability to challenge assumptions about the "essence" of racial groups, both past and present. By freeing ourselves of fixed conceptions about particular communities of color, we become more receptive to the possibilities for collaborative scholarly and activist work.

Such displays of black and Japanese solidarity were anything but ordinary in the 1930s. It is precisely because the concepts of full racial equality and interracial unity were considered so marginal to mainstream American society that they were most likely to find a home in the CPUSA. Anticommunism in Japan combined with domestic racism and class oppression to push Japanese immigrant workers and radicals to the margins of society. It was here, however, that they joined with other radicals to embrace an internationalist vision of communism as an alternative to the capitalist order. The CPUSA was far from perfect, and its advocacy often proved less than effective. Nonetheless, in Depression-era Los Angeles, it was the closest thing to a consistent voice against racism, as it affected not only African Americans but Asian and Mexican Americans as well. To appreciate its impact on these communities, Robin D. G. Kelley's "bottom-up" history of African American Communists in Alabama during the Depression is instructive. In *Hammer and Hoe,* Kelley notes that the "local cadre tried their best to apply the then current political line to the tasks at hand." However, "because neither Joe Stalin, Earl Browder, nor William Z. Foster spoke directly to them or to their daily problems," Alabama Communists were forced to generate their own strategies and tactics at the grassroots level.[3] The CPUSA provided a space where radical activists of color could develop and espouse oppositional ideas and visions that were repressed not only by the dominant society but also by the ethnic institutions controlled by elites of color.

During the Depression, Japanese American radicals seized the opportunity provided by the changing structure of the Los Angeles labor movement, which moved from a position of total exclusion of Japanese Americans to one of inclusion on a special basis. In doing so, radicals sought to stem the division between race-nationality and class that was promoted by the craft unionism of labor leaders, on the one hand, and the paternalism of ethnic business leaders, on the other. For its part, organized labor was willing to accept Japanese Americans only on its own terms. The democratizing influence of the Congress of Industrial

Organizations had yet to be felt in the city, and the American Federation of Labor (AFL) unions adopted a business unionism approach that made it complicit in the racial oppression endured by Japanese American workers. In Los Angeles, the connection of issues of race and class occurred mainly in Communist-led unions. However, as the U.S. Supreme Court and America's political leaders had extinguished any hope that Japanese immigrants had of becoming naturalized citizens, working in Communist fronts subjected immigrant radicals to greater state repression.

In the end, the gargantuan task of overcoming chauvinism within the labor movement, paternalism within the Japanese American community, and red-baiting within both proved too much for the Japanese American radicals to overcome. The chapter that follows is thus not a story of triumph. Rather, it draws attention to problems inherent in radical organizing from the margins. Drawing on the history of Japanese American radicalism in Los Angeles as a case study, my goal is to provide an example that shows how and why we must think about the intersection of race, class, and nation when analyzing the construction and destruction of social movements.

Race and International Solidarity

At the outset of the 1930s, the Communist Party had yet to take off in Los Angeles. The local organization was composed mainly of Jewish workers from Boyle Heights, perhaps reflecting that community's direct relationship to Russia. By the end of the decade, however, the CPUSA in Los Angeles would grow to nearly 3,000 members and include significant numbers of Asian, Mexican, and African Americans. Although radicals never represented a hegemonic bloc within the Japanese American community, their history is significant in that they exerted a weight upon the community far greater than their numbers would suggest— particularly in the eyes of the state, which commandeered immense resources to combat them. Furthermore, compared to the population at large, radicals constituted a relatively high proportion of the Japanese American community. Consider the fact that during the Depression there were nearly 200 Japanese American members of the CPUSA plus 1,000 more "fellow travelers." In the early 1930s, while roughly one out of every 5,000 persons in the U.S. population was a member of the CPUSA, one Communist could be found for every 650 persons in the Japanese American community. This is even more astounding when one considers that the entire membership of the Japanese Communist Party never reached 1,000 prior to the war.[4]

Japanese Americans were drawn to the CPUSA for two principal reasons. First, whereas mainstream politicians and organizations repeatedly used Japanese Americans as convenient scapegoats, the CPUSA stood out as an organized force that was willing to embrace the struggles of the most alienated and disenfranchised. The Depression began with the worldwide Communist International (Comintern) having resolved to combat the liberals and social democrats whose reformism they judged to be the primary impediment to the revolutionary upsurge of the workers. Although this "Third Period" of Communist organizing has been criticized for its "ultra-Left" orientation, the politics of the period actually favored greater participation of people of color in the CPUSA.[5] The line of combating "Right opportunists" in the labor movement and seeking unity only "from below" led the CPUSA to promote vehicles of worker organizing that were independent of the AFL. Because the AFL had a history of excluding people of color, these initiatives of the Left provided a new opening for activists of color. Furthermore, the CPUSA's embrace of the "Negro nation" thesis—positing that the Black Belt South constituted an oppressed nation of African Americans with the right to secede from the United States—promoted the idea that special attention should be given to work on African American issues throughout the nation. Through organizing campaigns like those supporting Angelo Herndon and the Scottsboro defendants, the Communists positioned themselves as the political party willing to take stands that mainstream organizations would not touch.

Second, the party's participation in the Comintern and subscription to its line on internationalism made it the most attractive vehicle for Japanese immigrants seeking to support the Japanese Communist Party. For Issei Communists, the Japanese state and its fascist ideology were the primary enemy, and the United States, considered a bourgeois democracy, was a place of relative sanctuary. In this context, an ideology rooted in "internationalism"—rather than nationalism per se—formed the root identity of Japanese American Communists. As historian Robert Scalapino writes, "Japanese Communists were unable to capture and use nationalism, but instead were forced to fight it because it was a deadly weapon in the hands of their opponents." Communism was branded illegal in Japan, and state repression combined with internal factionalism brought the party to the brink of extinction during the 1930s. Thus, just as Lenin did most of his prerevolution writings outside of Russia, the work of the Japanese Communist Party came to depend heavily on those living in exile.[6] In this regard, the CPUSA became a temporary home for stateless people. The ideology of internationalism served to bridge the struggle of Japanese Americans with the class struggle in Japan, for it was the worldwide advance of the working-class movement that provided hope to balance the tremendous setbacks suffered by the party in Japan.

Although radicals of various ideological persuasions were among the earliest immigrants from Japan, the organization of Japanese Communists in Los Angeles began to congeal around 1926 and 1927, when a series of study groups, political associations, and publications were formed. Following the proverbial splits of these early leftist groups, Communists established the *Rodo Shimbun* newspaper and the Japanese Workers Association *(Rafu Nihonjin Rodo Kyokai)*, which officially became the CPUSA's "Japanese section" in 1928. The Japanese Workers Association recruited "gardeners, farmhands, domestics, and day workers along with a few students," but also fell victim to the sectarianism of the "Left" Third Period. Its program pledged to work with "all anti-capitalist groups" but refused to cooperate with "pacifists, reformists, and the like." To celebrate the tenth anniversary of the Russian Revolution, Los Angeles members marched down the streets of Little Tokyo waving the hammer and sickle, shouting communist slogans, and unsettling the Japanese community's residents. Japanese American Communists protested speaking tours by "social democrats" from Japan, denounced the imminent prospects of global warfare, and held fundraisers for the Japanese Communist Party.[7] The "Protest Resolution against Japanese Imperialism," circulated in 1932, captured the essence of the internationalist position. The resolution demanded the release of all political prisoners in Japan, an end to the Japanese invasion of Manchuria, and a halt of "the planned Japanese attack on the Soviet Union." In closing, it expressed solidarity with the people of China and the Soviet Union, Japanese workers, peasants, and anti-imperialists.[8]

Internationalism was more than a pragmatic device designed to take advantage of Soviet aid. The universalist notions of human equality inherent within the ideal of internationalism provided Japanese American Communists with a means to develop a radical critique of the conditions prevalent in their community. When Karl Yoneda ran for the California Assembly on the Communist ticket, he stressed that the "COMMUNIST PARTY sincerely fights for complete equality of all races." In a handbill titled "Why the Japanese Should Vote Communist," Yoneda condemned the "California bosses" for their decades-long "race hatred campaign against Orientals," as well as the "labor fakers" who supported such campaigns by "constantly [fighting] the 'yellow peril' instead of the 'capitalist peril.'" Contrary to both the Democrats and the Republicans, he contended that the Communists were the only party to address the "Japanese question" within its platform and to fight "for the interest of the Japanese and other Oriental people."[9]

More directly, the ideology of internationalism served as a theoretical basis for linking the struggles of Japanese Americans with those of other communities of color and progressive white activists. In the late 1920s, Japanese American Communists established their own branches of the International Red Aid and International Labor Defense. For instance, through the ILD branches in Los Angeles and San Francisco, Japanese Americans organized support for labor activist Tom Mooney in addition to the Scottsboro defendants. Mooney had been imprisoned since 1916 for a San Francisco bombing incident that killed several people. Labor activists insisted he was innocent, and their continued pressure led to a pardon by Democratic governor Culbert Olson in January 1939. In these instances, Japanese American radicals (not all members of the ILD were CPUSA members) worked with larger campaigns of the ILD and the CPUSA, seeking to build support among their community for these causes and using the high-profile campaigns to attract their more ideologically inclined brethren.[10]

In the late 1920s and early 1930s, Japanese American labor radicals allied with the Communist-led Trade Union Unity League (TUUL), which CPUSA leader William Z. Foster described as a "broad, independent, united front movement of Communists and progressives." Consistent with the line of the "Third Period," TUUL challenged the "class collaborationism" of the AFL. It promoted "Class against Class" struggle through the construction of independent industrial unions and explicitly listed "social equality for the Negro people" as a plank of its platform.[11] Workers of color were especially crucial to the efforts of TUUL, as the CPUSA sought to build an independent base that would contest for power against the established trade unions and political parties. For instance, in 1933, the Cannery and Agricultural Workers Industrial Union of TUUL led twenty-four of California's thirty-seven agricultural strikes, the majority of which centered on Mexican American workers. The main Southern California formation of the Agricultural Workers Industrial Union developed out of a multiethnic strawberry workers' strike involving Japanese, Mexican, and Filipino Americans in the spring of 1933 near Stanton. Delegates to the founding conference on April 9, 1933, included twenty-eight Japanese American workers from ten different camps.[12]

Japanese American radicals promoted multiethnic solidarity to overcome the old management tactic of pitting different ethnic groups against each other. For instance, in 1903, when fourteen hundred Mexican workers went on strike from Pacific Electric, Henry Huntington replaced them with African American and Japanese American scabs, who were accompanied by state troopers wherever they worked. Ethnic divisions were central not only to the strategy of the bourgeoisie but to the craft-union orientation of the AFL as well. As Tomás Almaguer has noted, after the Japanese-Mexican Labor Alliance of farmworkers defeated antagonistic growers in the historic Oxnard strike of 1903, Samuel Gompers sought to divide the workers by admitting the Mexicans and rejecting the Japanese for membership into the AFL. By the time Depression-era migrants came looking for agricultural work in California, Japanese Americans had risen to be among the ranks of the growers. In response to the growers' appeal to Japanese American workers to stand with them on the basis of ethnicity, Japanese American radicals circulated many handbills among the workers of their nationality that read simply, "DO NOT SCAB!"[13] Such work appears to have had a significant impact on the Stanton strawberry workers' strike. The growers association sought to break the 1933 strike by offering a raise to only the Japanese workers. The *Western Worker* lauded the workers' response: "This move to split the growing unity of Japanese, Mexican and Filipino workers, temporarily weakening the front, has not fooled the Japanese, particularly in view of the opinion expressed by some camp bosses of not hiring them any longer as 'the Japanese are too expensive.' Realizing it was their unity with all the other pickers which won the concessions they gained, they are now strongly of the sentiment for all sticking together when the next crop is due."[14]

As Issei truck farmers became the target of increasingly militant labor action, the entire Japanese American community became engulfed by the debate over workers' rights. The large El Monte berry strike of June 1933 spread to onion and celery growers in the Westside and covered five to seven thousand workers. On one side stood a workforce that included whites and Asians but was mostly Mexican. On the other side stood growers who were predominantly Japanese. The impact of the strike reached Mexico, where the national federation of unions threatened a boycott of all Japanese goods. This spurred action from the Japanese consulate, which joined with the Mexican consulate to negotiate a strike settlement among multiple parties.[15]

The intervention of community activists loomed especially large in the Venice celery strike of 1936, which inspired what was probably the largest organizing campaign of Japanese radicals in Southern California agriculture during the Depression. Demanding a raise in the hourly wage and collective-bargaining recognition, more than one thousand Mexicans, Japanese, and Filipinos from the Federation of Farm Workers of America and the California Japanese Agricultural Workers Union (CJAWU) went on strike against Japanese growers on April 17, 1936. The CJAWU had formed in June 1935 and was headed by socialist president Saisho Tokijiro and secretary Mike Deguchi, a Kibei CPUSA member. During the course of events, both were jailed for strike agitation. With the Southern California Farm Federation of eight hundred Japanese farmers backing the celery growers, labor organizers sought Japanese American community support for a broad boycott of crops grown by the growers' association. Though technically petty capitalists, Japanese immigrant gardeners stood in the main with the strikers. The strike came to an end when the Japanese American farm federation cut a deal this time with just the Mexican majority of workers. The eight hundred members of the CJAWU were further rebuffed when the AFL denied their request for affiliation. Despite their incomplete success, the agricultural organizing drives had at minimum exposed the potential for an innovative social movement that was both interethnic and fueled by the united effort of community-based organizing and action at the point of production.[16]

Beyond taking up particular campaigns for improving social conditions or relations between the races, Japanese Americans challenged the ontology of race through their work. Commenting on the activist upsurge during the Depression, Douglas Monroy writes in his book on Mexican Americans in Los Angeles, "The radicals of all ethnic and political persuasions, social democrats, and New Dealers all affirmed that the way things were regarding the distribution of wealth and power had to do with the actions and constructions of human beings."[17] Consistent with new anthropological notions of culture emerging in this era, such thinking contested the idea that a natural order underlay social inequality. In this manner, universalist ideas of humanity espoused by Communists were also an implicit critique of biologically based notions of race. This was especially crucial for Japanese American radicals who sought to struggle not only against racism in the United States but also against a Japanese state that justified its imperialist aims by highlighting the unique qualities of the so-called Japanese race.

Class Conflict in the Japanese American Community

Although exclusionary policies ranging from the Gentlemen's Agreement of 1908 to the Immigration Act of 1924 especially sought to bar Japanese laborers, they still constituted the largest sector of the Japanese American community in Los Angeles during the Depression years. While discriminatory practices in the primary labor market led to an overrepresentation of Japanese Americans in small business, the majority (54.6 percent) of males in the community worked jobs whose classification by the 1940 census generally implied blue-collar or low-wage service work. Such classifications encompassed craftsmen and foremen, operatives, domestics, service workers, farm labor and foremen, laborers, and the unemployed. An additional 21.2 percent of the workforce was located in the heterogeneous "clerical, sales, and kindred" where "fruit stand boys" would be located. Although an even greater proportion (62.9 percent) of Japanese American women fell into these same blue-collar and low-wage service-work categories, many worked as domestics for white households or in other occupations overlooked by labor organizing centered on male organizers and workers.[18] Given the prevalence of ethnic small businesses, a large percentage of the male workforce was employed by other Japanese Americans. Thus, the challenge for Japanese American workers was overcoming *both* the white supremacist societal order *and* the class hierarchy within the ethnic community. Many of those seeking to link these struggles turned to the Left.

Communists played the leading role in organizing Japanese American workers in Los Angeles throughout much of the Depression for three reasons (beyond the obvious point that communist ideology identified the proletariat as the agent of revolutionary change). First, the racism of the AFL pushed Japanese American worker organizing beyond the pale of the mainstream trade union. Second, the Japanese American community leaders of the entrepreneurial class pushed Japanese American worker organizing beyond the pale of the mainstream ethnic organizations and promoted the formation of ethnicity-based "company unions." Third, the Japanese American Communists represented the grouping most organized, most dedicated, and most willing to risk personal sacrifice for the sake of building class struggle in the community.

Building from the community's origins in agriculture, entrepreneurship in wholesale and retail produce proved critical to Japanese American urban economic strategies. As with other organizing campaigns of the early 1930s, Japanese American radicals began their efforts to organize produce workers by establishing independent workers' organizations linked to Communist-led trade union activity. Issei Communist Ohkaneku Tokujiro led the first such effort, publishing the *Fruit Stand Worker* newsletter under the alias George Higashi.[19] Reflecting the necessity to reach the American-born Japanese—many of whom had limited or no Japanese reading ability—as well as non-Japanese in the industry, radicals began to print more materials in English. An English version of the *Fruit Stand Worker* distributed in January 1933 sought to empower produce workers to wage a class struggle by pointing out that each boss was "only one representative of a small capitalist class while we are many representatives of a large working class." It listed four demands that it called for workers to adopt: a minimum wage of eighteen dollars per week, an eight-hour day and six-day workweek, no layoffs, and immediate payment of back pay.[20]

The newsletter also provided step-by-step advice for workers to get organized. First, it advised them to discuss the four demands with other workers during "lunch hour or on the way home" and also "with your intimate friends and casual acquaintances." After gaining support for the demands from a majority of the workforce, the organizers were directed to "choose a few men to put them before the boss," backed by the "determined support" of the rest. Finally, the newsletter encouraged the workers to stand strong and militant: "The boss may shed tears and pretend that he can't afford the demands. He may attempt to frighten the workers by shouting 'get out.' But do not quit your job because that won't help anything. Instead, you must stick together against discharge. We must put up a struggle and, if necessary, a strike."[21]

Radicals sought to connect their produce-industry organizing to related areas of work through the Food Workers Industrial Union (FWIU) of TUUL. Another newsletter released in 1933 under the auspices of the FWIU (and most likely written by the same forces behind *Fruit Stand Worker*) was the *Jungyoin* (Bulletin). The bulletin targeted wholesale and retail produce workers in "Los Angeles, Pasadena, Glendale, Hollywood, Santa Monica, and elsewhere" and called for an end to "miserable wages and slave-like conditions." Its main function was agitational, as the following quote from a wholesale worker identified only as "Harry" will attest: "ACTION! ACTION! Immediate ACTION is what we need right now!" Longer workdays in the wholesale-produce industry were in part the result of increased competition between the downtown markets, as attempts to draw patrons led to market opening times that inched closer to midnight than dawn. One handbill circulated by radicals claimed that many in the industry were forced to work eleven-hour days and some fourteen and fifteen hours. A retail worker named Henry Tahara wrote, "Let me tell you something about the condition in our shop. We work from seven in the morning till 9:30 at night. Seven of us used to work but now only five of us are working. So you see how hard we have to work. And mind you that our wages are only $40.00 per month." Tahara also condemned the insincere efforts of Japanese American merchants to promote ethnic solidarity to quell intraethnic class tensions. He said that his boss "gave us a dope that there is no boss in our shop because, we work like one family." However, when workers raised the demand listed in the bulletin, they were told, "You don't like it here then get out!" Tahara concluded, "We work like one family. OH-YEH!"[22]

Yet these early efforts of Depression-era radicals to organize the produce industry do not appear to have been very fruitful. Although the agitational materials of the early 1930s produce-industry organizing provide an important documentation of worker sentiments and radical visions, they perhaps best serve to recount the organizers' frustrations. As one bilingual handbill from May 1934 remarked, "Many attempts to organize the fruit-stand workers throughout the city have been made so far without much success due to the fact that it lacked 100% cooperation among the workers." The flyer posed the question, "Are we all satisfied with the present wages and time of work?" followed by its own response, "Deeply in our heart, IT IS NO." Labor radicals recognized the effectiveness of ethnic solidarity as an entrepreneurial strategy judging by the handbill's conclusion. "The fruit-stand owners have their organization to defend their own interests. WHY SHOULDN'T WE HAVE OUR OWN?"[23]

Red-baiting and antiunion activity hampered organizing efforts. One flyer aimed at the "Fellow Workers of Fruit Stand of L.A." appealed to the rank and file to take a stand against such repression: "The sole purpose of this black listing is to oppress and to discharge the militant workers of the fruit stands who are fighting for a better working conditions such as higher wages and shorter hours, if we cannot stop their black listing system what will be the result? More intensified exploitation such as cheaper wages and longer hours."[24] Another major setback occurred when George Higashi was arrested in January 1934 for publishing *Fruit Stand Worker*. In July 1934, he took a "voluntary" deportation to Peru.[25]

While produce workers proved particularly challenging to organize, another attempt by Japanese American radicals to build an urban base of workers addressed restaurant workers. The restaurant workers' conditions of work reflected the marginal status of ethnic enterprises whose market competitiveness relied on underpricing the competition. The cafés occupied a niche left by the mainstream restaurant industry by concentrating in less desirable sections of the city. To attract customers in the midst of the Depression, Fred Tayama's U.S. Cafés built their reputation on a menu offering a full-course meal for ten cents. Yet these rock-bottom-priced meals were made possible only by the intense exploitation of the workforce. In effect, it was hardship and adversity that trickled down best to the workers. Japanese American radicals particularly criticized Tayama for pledging "to better the welfare and status of Japanese-Americans" and "bring to them good living, opportunity for development, racial and social equality" as a prominent leader of the Japanese American Citizens League while treating workers under his own purview harshly.[26] They formed the Japanese Restaurant Employment Union and worked in alliance with the Food Workers Industrial Union of TUUL to organize the multiethnic workforce in the cafés. The largest upsurge in the campaign occurred when workers at Tayama's four-restaurant chain went on strike in March 1934. The Japanese, Filipino, and white strikers demanded an eight-hour day, a six-day week, and a fifteen-dollar weekly minimum. Management responded by ordering three of the "ringleaders" arrested and firing more than twenty workers. Within a few days, Tayama agreed to terms that allowed the union to declare victory. However, this appears simply to have been a tactic employed by management to quell the disruptions, as the paper agreement proved difficult for the workers to enforce.[27]

Despite the uneven results of the strike, the threat of unionization was at least enough of a concern to restaurant owners that they were the prime supporters of a conservative ethnic employees' association that formed in 1935. The mission statement of the Japanese Workers Association of Southern California stated in no uncertain terms that "the new organization is not in any way connected with the radical Communistic groups and is purely a non-profit welfare body seeking to be a central office for the vast number of laborers among the Japanese and nisei." Its purpose was to promote not class warfare but the "general welfare, comfort and convenience and economical accommodation of Japanese workers."[28]

The continuing struggle of restaurant workers during the Depression took an interesting turn in the summer of 1937, when the AFL granted a charter to the Los Angeles Oriental Restaurant and Hotel Employees' Union no. 646. The grouping of two hundred workers that constituted Local 646 grew out of the earlier efforts at U.S. Cafés. Kentaro Abe, an Issei Communist who organized the U.S. Café strike, served as the secretary-treasurer of the new union. Despite the organizing gains, conditions were still miserable. Workers at the O.K. Café, one of three restaurants where Local 646 members struck in August 1938, were forced to work every day of the month with no days off. Fred Tayama was acting in sync, if not in concert, with the white business owners of the Southern

California Restaurant Association's secret "Group A" that was set up during the Depression to destroy unions by providing strikebreakers with guards and maintaining blacklists. He successfully appealed to the courts in May 1938 for an antipicketing injunction designed to stop Local 646's organizing drive.[29]

In effect, it was the wretched conditions of work in the ethnic economy that forced the AFL to reconsider its practice of racial exclusion, if only slightly. The newspaper of the Los Angeles Central Labor Council noted that the Local 646's charter gave it "jurisdiction over all Oriental-owned establishments in Los Angeles" and commented that this specific attempt to organize Asians was "the first of its kind issued by our international."[30] Since the cafés catered heavily to non-Japanese customers, the low-priced meals and wages of the Japanese American cafés threatened to undercut prices and wages at white-owned establishments. The AFL's resolution of the "Oriental problem" was patterned after its treatment of African American workers, which allowed for the unionization of minority workers but failed to grant them equal status as white workers in the house of labor. The pattern had emerged around the turn of the century. As Alexander Saxton writes, "Gompers and his AFL colleagues—still advocating unity of all workingmen—gave their approval to special segregated locals which controlled the competition of blacks and collected their dues money while denying them any effective voice in union policy."[31] Local 646's arrangement represented a contradictory development. Japanese Americans finally gained membership in the AFL, but they were decidedly marked as inferior and relegated to at best second-class citizenship in the brotherhood of labor.

Repression of Immigrant Radicalism

Communist-inspired "independent" organizing attracted those seeking radical alternatives to life under American capitalism. However, those who organize around the sharpest social contradictions dividing the haves and have-nots always run the risk that they will bear the sharpest brunt of political repression when the social order is threatened. In Los Angeles, the attack on radical dissent was led by Capt. William F. "Red" Hynes of the notorious Los Angeles Police Department (LAPD) Red Squad. In conjunction with conservative business interests and civic boosters, the Red Squad served to maintain the city's "open shop" town reputation, which stretched from the 1911 defeat of a Socialist candidate for mayor to the mid-1930s. Persistent assaults by the Red Squad had helped squash the Wobblies in the years following World War I. In one of the most infamous events in the city's history, more than seven hundred strikers and defenders of civil liberties were arrested at "Liberty Hill" in a crackdown on the Great San Pedro Strike led by the International Workers of the World in the spring of 1923. With the Communists now the central target of a broad-based repression of dissent, the Red Squad was emboldened by the 1929 election of former Klansman John Porter to mayor of Los Angeles. Police Commissioner Mark Pierce declared that "Communists have no constitutional rights and I won't listen to anyone who defends them." As one of the appointees responsible for police oversight, Pierce added, "The more the police beat them up and wreck their headquarters, the better."[32] Immigrants proved especially vulnerable. The agricultural industry, which did not appreciate losing workers to the Mexican repatriation, began to push for strict measures against those who remained. In 1935, the growers successfully lobbied the state to force immigrant laborers off relief.[33]

As "aliens ineligible for citizenship," Japanese immigrants were particularly susceptible to state repression in the United States. Japanese immigrant radicals, who expressed international solidarity through the ILD's campaigns to free jailed radical Tom Mooney and the Scottsboro defendants, quickly found themselves among the ranks of those most in need of defense. Issei community leaders were not likely to rush to their aid. For instance, the Japanese vernacular press elicited scant sympathy for the plight of radicals. Togo Tanaka, a Nisei journalist for the *Rafu Shimpo* in the 1930s, noted that the staff of the city's three Japanese American newspapers "generally acknowledged that to become tainted with the label 'Aka' or Communist was a cardinal sin." Moreover, *aka,* which literally translates to "red," was a stigma applied not only to CPUSA members but to any advocate of workers' rights or critic of Japanese militarism.[34] Furthermore, because they were outspoken opponents of the emperor in Japan, the cost of being deported—certainly imprisonment, possibly execution—was especially high for Japanese American radicals. These special conditions simultaneously brought out the most heroic notions of humanity and idealism alongside confusion, fear, and betrayal. A small number of Japanese American informers aided the efforts of both the American and the Japanese anti-Communists by infiltrating radical organizations. Repressive campaigns dealt crippling blows to the movement, contributing eventually to the virtual extinction of the organized Japanese American Left.

Two years after the high-profile execution of radicals Sacco and Vanzetti sent shock waves throughout America, one of the first Issei Communists to be arrested and deported was Kenmotsu Sadaichi. Having recently moved from Los Angeles to San Francisco to lead the Japanese section of the CPUSA and edit the *Rodo Shimbun,* Kenmotsu was central to leftist circles. In what would establish a pattern of repression, activist support, and deportation, he was arrested in San Francisco for being a member of the CPUSA on December 15, 1929. Although the ILD rallied to his defense, they were unable to prevent his conviction, imprisonment, or deportation. However, they did prevent his being deported to Japan by raising money for his "voluntary" relocation to the Soviet

Union. On December 16, 1931, the day of his departure from Angel Island to the Soviet Union, which he considered "Our Fatherland," Kenmotsu expressed sentiments of gratitude and solidarity in a letter to the ILD: "I was saved by the I.L.D. from the deportation to Japan, the fascist country. I realize by this that I am in the hands of you, namely, I belong to you—to the revolutionary movement. I pledge here to continue the revolutionary movement up to the end. This is the only [way] to answer for your comradely support against deportation to Japan." Despite his deportation, Kenmotsu remained optimistic that he would continue his work in exile and that the workers' advance would continue. He concluded, "U.S. Government succeeded to deport me due to the reason that I belong to our Communist Party. But the government is unable to 'deport' our party and its movement which has the historical necessity and importance."[35]

Attempts to organize both rural and urban workers were dogged by state repression. Because concentrations of Japanese American workers remained in agriculture, Communists sought to reach them through the Agricultural Workers Industrial Union. Party cadre Horiuchi Tetsuji ventured out from Los Angeles to agitate workers in the Imperial Valley. Horiuchi was in the midst of leading a farmworkers' strike when authorities nabbed him in January 1930. The ILD worked to aid him and nine other union organizers, all of whom were given lengthy sentences. After serving two and a half years in Folsom Prison, Horiuchi took a "voluntary" deportation to the Soviet Union and left from San Pedro in August 1932.[36]

As Communists mobilized the scores of jobless during Hoover's term, Japanese Americans sought to organize their brethren and form a Japanese branch of the Los Angeles Unemployed Council. In the course of this work, Yamaguchi Einosuke, a day laborer, was arrested in March 1931 at a demonstration against unemployment. Yamaguchi, whose June 1929 order of deportation had been stayed, was deported based on a reopening of the same order in March 1932. He, too, took a "voluntary" deportation to the Soviet Union with the aid of the ILD. Like Yamaguchi, a number of other deportees of the early 1930s were drawn from the ranks of laborers rather than intellectuals. For example, those arrested for political activity in Los Angeles included gardeners Tani Noboru and Nishimura Soichi. Most were younger men in their twenties and thirties. Kenmotsu, Horiuchi, and Yamaguchi were all pivotal members of the party who had been involved in the earliest efforts to organize a Japanese American collective of Communists in Los Angeles. Their arrests set the stage for an even bigger blow to the party.[37]

Just before dawn on January 16, 1932, snow began descending on Los Angeles for the first time in more than fifty years. Issei Communists thus stood less than a snowball's chance of surviving in Los Angeles. The LAPD Red Squad and local authorities raided a meeting of Communists at a hall in Long Beach and captured 120 party members. Among those arrested were nine Japanese immigrants along with one Greek and one Asian Indian, who were set for deportation. In response, Japanese American radicals in the ILD moved to defend their comrades. One bilingual flyer urging supporters to attend the February 2 trial of those arrested read: "AS PART of the bosses' program of hunger and unemployment a new reign of terror has been launched against workers who DARE TO PROTEST against the misery of their conditions! In an effort to still the militant voices of workers who refuse to calmly watch their families suffer the pangs of starvation, the bosses send their uniformed and plain-clothes thugs to break up workers' meetings, raid their homes, arrest them and beat them up!"[38] Unable to stop the deportation, the ILD then worked to raise funds for more "voluntary" deportations to the Soviet Union.[39]

Although ILD organizing generated new interest in the CPUSA and its work, the endless activity in response to state repression of immigrants must certainly have slowed down Communist campaigns to build a mass base of Japanese American workers (that is, of course, after the "chilling effects" of the repression itself took effect). Raising money, staging rallies, defending comrades in court, and negotiating with immigration officials all consumed time and resources. For instance, as the case of Taira Renji demonstrates, the ILD needed to raise in the neighborhood of $500 in the midst of the Depression for each "voluntary" deportee. In January 1933, Taira was arrested in Los Angeles for union activism. He was then found to have violated the Immigration Act of 1924 and ordered deported. The ILD cited a need of $300 for his fare and board to the Soviet Union, plus an additional $1.01 per day to pay to keep Taira at Angel Island until passage could be arranged. Taira eventually left for Moscow on July 30, 1933.[40] The Long Beach raid was particularly crippling given the immediate loss of cadre. Not only did the incident mark the occasion for the most Issei radicals ever seized and deported, but it also devastated the party-building efforts of Issei in Los Angeles.

Soon enough, even "Japan Nights" became targets of Red Squad repression. On February 11, 1933, the Puroretaria Geijutsu Kai (Japanese Proletarian Art Club), *Rodo Shimbun,* and the Japanese branch of the Los Angeles ILD (named after Horiuchi Tetsuji) sponsored a night of culture at the John Reed Club in Hollywood. A handbill produced by the Japanese Branch of the International Labor Defense and the Young Communist League (YCL) claimed that "450 workers of all races and nationalities" were in attendance. The art club had just completed its play *The Dawn of Manchuria,* and the audience was moving into the auditorium for dancing when "Red" Hynes and his squad crashed the party. The Red Squad then shut down the event, cleared out the building, and arrested Karl Yoneda.[41]

The Red Squad publicized the raid as an attack on Japanese militarist elements. The Japanese American ILD and YCL countered that such stories in the "capitalist press" were pure fabrication: "What is the truth? All the so-called weapons were material rented from a theatrical costume house for the play. These newspapers purposely used this story and wrote it so that it would increase the war-mindedness of the American workers against the Japanese workers."[42] Privately, the authorities moved to intimidate the Japanese American Communists and their sympathizers by vandalizing the John Reed Club. Although they inflicted serious economic damage, they seemed to have been especially disturbed by a mural painted by the Japanese Proletarian Art Club symbolizing cross-racial solidarity. Underneath a bilingual English-Japanese banner reading "Workers of the World Unite" was a large painting of the Scottsboro Boys. The Red Squad fired bullets through the foreheads of each of the nine defendants depicted in the mural.[43]

The symbolic violence of the Red Squad demonstrated the danger that internationalism posed to the state, which faced its greatest crisis of legitimacy since the Civil War. Though Japanese Americans were united with African Americans by racial oppression, their nationality ultimately cut them off from multiracial organizing. Those who were officially "aliens" were caught in the web of deportations, but even American-born Japanese were stripped of their freedom of mobility and their constitutional rights by the federal government's exclusion and internment orders during World War II. In addition, class conflict augmented the contradictions of oppression. The radicals' efforts to organize Japanese American–owned establishments were thwarted by the employers' calls for their workers to stick with them as members of an embattled and embittered minority. Although suffering frequent setbacks, Japanese Communists remained indefatigable during the Depression. In response to the John Reed Club disruption, they vowed, "we will carry on our work; for the interests of the workers of all countries. We appeal to you to stay with us in the fight, against police terrorism, and for the right of the workers to organize."[44]

But with the Pacific war on the horizon, things would get far worse before they bottomed out. The radical idealism of the Depression would quickly be replaced by pragmatic concerns about war and survival. Even the CPUSA would suspend the membership of Japanese Americans solely on the basis of ethnicity. Having set out to unite the masses of Japanese Americans into a multiracial movement against discrimination and exploitation, Japanese American radicals wound up tailing the leadership of the assimilationist Japanese American Citizens League and dissolving as an organized presence after the war. Sadly, their expatriate comrades paid an even bigger price for their idealism. The struggle for "voluntary" deportation to the Soviet Union earned at least five Japanese immigrants imprisonment and execution as "infiltrators" during the Stalinist purges.[45] Race, class, and national oppression had conspired to make every road a dead end for Japanese Americans.

CHAPTER 9 READING QUESTIONS

1. Kurashige relates that during the Great Depression, 1 out of every 5,000 persons in the United States was a member of the Communist Party, USA, but among Japanese Americans, 1 out of every 650 was a member. How do we account for such a high proportion of radicals within such a small population and one that has generally been considered a "model minority"?

2. Scholars and activists often attribute defeats to both internal dissension and external repression. In the case of Japanese immigrant radicals in Los Angeles during the 1930s, to what extent does Kurashige attribute their failure to achieve their organizing objectives to political repression?

3. Why and in what ways was internationalism a threat to the state? Although Japanese immigrant radicals organized around internationalism, ultimately their nationality was used to divide them from their "American" counterparts. In your opinion, did racial and national identity facilitate or impede struggle against capitalism in the United States in the 1930s?

Notes

1. International Labor Defense, "Scottsboro Boys Must Be Freed," Folder 2, Box 1, Karl Yoneda Papers (hereafter cited as KYP), Collection 1592, Special Collections, Young Research Library, University of California, Los Angeles; "Langston Hughes at Japan Nite," March 3, 1934, Folder 5, Box 1, ibid.

2. Carey McWilliams, *Prejudice, Japanese-Americans: Symbol of Racial Intolerance* (Boston: Little, Brown, 1944), 93.

3. Robin D. G. Kelley, *Hammer and Hoe: Alabama Communists during the Great Depression* (Chapel Hill: University of North Carolina Press, 1990): xiii–xiv.

4. Dorothy Ray Healey and Maurice Isserman, *California Red: A Life in the American Communist Party* (Urbana: University of Illinois Press, 1993), 40–41; Karl G. Yoneda, "U.S. Japanese Socialists-Communists in the 1930s and 1940s," unpublished manuscript dated January 11, 1977, Folder 1, Box 13, KYP; William Z. Foster, *History of the Communist Party of the United States* (New York: International Publishers, 1952), 261, 292, 307, 380; Robert A. Scalapino, *The Japanese Communist Movement, 1920–1966* (Berkeley and Los Angeles: University of California Press, 1967), 45.

5. The line adopted at the Sixth Comintern Congress (1928) was based on an analysis of the period (dubbed third for its succession of two previous periodizations) as one of heightened contradictions. It called for an attack on the "right-wing elements" within Communist Parties and on Social Democrats, who were labeled "social fascists" for policies the Comintern believed were objectively aiding the ruling class. See Foster, *Communist Party of the United States,* 265–66.

6. Scalapino, *Japanese Communist Movement,* 34–45 (quote on 44).

7. The first organized grouping in Los Angeles involving Japanese American Communists was the Reimeikai. Founded in 1926, the group began as a "social issues study group" *(shakai mondai kenkyukai),* congregating around the collectively owned Owl Restaurant in the Little Tokyo area. Although it initially involved both workers and intellectuals from diverse tendencies, the Communist members began to exert greater leadership over the small group. Ideological differences led to a dissolution of the Reimeikai and its reconstitution in 1927 as the Kaikyusensha (Class Struggle Society)

without three non-Communist dissenters. The new organization moved into an office on Second and Weller and published its own journal, *Kaikyusen* (Class Struggle), aimed at "overtly Communist propaganda." See "Miyagi Yotoku's Notes," Folder 4, Box 13, KYP; and Karl Yoneda, *Ganbatte: Sixty-Year Struggle of a Kibei Worker* (Los Angeles: UCLA Asian American Studies Center, 1982), 16–19.

8. "Protest Resolution against Japanese Imperialism," December 1932, Folder 2, Box 13, KYP.

9. "Why the Japanese Should Vote Communist," August 15, 1934, Folder 5, Box 1, KYP.

10. Louis B. Perry and Richard S. Perry, *A History of the Los Angeles Labor Movement, 1911–1941* (Berkeley and Los Angeles: University of California Press, 1963), 493; Vivian McGuckin Raineri, *The Red Angel: The Life and Times of Elaine Black Yoneda* (New York: International Publishers, 1991), 21–34.

11. Foster, *Communist Party of the United States,* 257.

12. Douglas Monroy, *Rebirth: Mexican Los Angeles from the Great Migration to the Great Depression* (Berkeley and Los Angeles: University of California Press, 1999), 226; "Strawberry Fields Organize for Strike," *Western Worker,* clipping dated April 16, 1933, Folder 10, Box 2, KYP.

13. David Clark, *Los Angeles: A City Apart* (Woodland Hills, Calif.: Windsor Publications, 1981), 20; Uchikoshi Arao, "A Town That Used to Be Lil' Tokio," *Kashu Mainichi,* April 11, 1937; Tomás Almaguer, *Racial Fault Lines: The Historical Origins of White Supremacy in California* (Berkeley and Los Angeles: University of California Press, 1994), 183–204; Alexander Saxton, *Rise and Fall of the White Republic* (London: Verso, 1990), 293–319; miscellaneous handbills from TUUL, Agricultural Workers Industrial Union work in 1933, Folder 2, Box 1, KYP; a strike of lettuce workers for a decent wage in Imperial Valley is referenced in Downtown Sub-section Communist Party, "Strike! Don't Scab! Protest!" February 16, 1935, Folder 3, Box 1, ibid.

14. "'Build Union!' Is Cry as 2nd Crop of Strawberries Due," *Western Worker,* clipping dated May 1, 1933, Folder 10, Box 2, KYP.

15. Monroy, *Rebirth,* 225–30.

16. Yoneda, "U.S. Japanese Socialists-Communists"; Program of the Inaugural Meeting of the California Japanese Agricultural Workers Union, Union Church, Los Angeles, June 8, 1935, Folder 3, Box 1, KYP; "JAWU-Venice Strike," May 2, 1936, ibid.; "ILD—Defend Arrested Workers," June 1936, ibid.; Nobuya Tsuchida, "Japanese Gardeners in Southern California, 1900–1941," in *Labor Immigration under Capitalism: Asian Workers in the United States before World War II,* edited by Lucie Cheng and Edna Bonacich (Berkeley and Los Angeles: University of California Press, 1984), 458–66; Foster, *Communist Party of the United States,* 303–4.

17. Monroy, *Rebirth,* 256.

18. Leonard Bloom and Ruth Riemer, *Removal and Return: The Socio-economic Effects of the War on Japanese Americans* (Berkeley and Los Angeles: University of California Press, 1949), 2.

19. Karl G. Yoneda to Dmitry Muravyev, November 9, 1964, Folder 2, Box 13, KYP; James Oda, *Heroic Struggles of Japanese Americans: Partisan Fighters from America's Concentration Camps,* 3d ed. (North Hollywood: James Oda, 1982), 240.

20. *Fruit Stand Worker,* January 15, 1933 (hand-dated), Folder 2, Box 5, KYP.

21. Ibid.

22. "Fruit-Stand Sales-Boys! at Grand Central Market. Organize for Better Condition! Join the Food Workers Industrial Union" [ca. December 1933], Folder 2, Box 1, KYP; Food Workers Industrial Union, "Let's Have a Mass Meeting," April 20, 1934, ibid.; Food Workers Industrial Union, *Jungyoin* [Bulletin], 1933, Folder 2, Box 5, ibid.

23. "We Must Organize," Grand Central Market Initiative Groups, May 19, 1934, Folder 2, Box 1, KYP.

24. "Fruit Stand Workers!" Folder 2, Box 1, KYP.

25. Yoneda to Muravyev, November 9, 1964; Oda, *Heroic Struggles*, 240.

26. Shuji Fujii, "Fred Tayama: Hypocrite?" *Doho*, March 1, 1939.

27. "Cafe Workers in Walkout at Three in Jail," *Rafu Shimpo*, March 19, 1934; Food Workers Industrial Union, "Support U.S. Restaurant Workers for Better Conditions," March 15, 1934, Folder 2, Box 1, KYP. See also multiple handbills from the Japanese Restaurant and Food Workers Industrial Union dated December 13, 1933, January 13, March 21, 25, April 7, and May 14, 1934, ibid.

28. Program of the Japanese Workers Association of Southern California's "Modern Little Tokyo" event, June 19, 1935, Folder 4, Box 2, KYP.

29. Bill Barrett, "Really a Unique Organization," *Los Angeles Citizen*, August 27, 1937; Yoneda, "U.S. Japanese Socialists-Communists"; "Restaurant 'Sweat Shops' among Japanese Exposed," *Doho*, July 1, 1939; "Oriental Culinary Workers on Strike: Three Cafes Unfair," *Los Angeles Citizen*, August 5, 1938; Perry and Perry, *Los Angeles Labor Movement*, 459–60; "Ban Union Pickets as Court Backs Tayama to Quell Disturbance," *Rafu Shimpo*, May 14, 1938.

30. Barrett, "Really a Unique Organization." It should be pointed out that the local was "segregated" to the degree that it effectively grouped all Japanese American workers into one local. In fact, it may have included some whites employed by Japanese cafés.

31. Alexander Saxton, *The Indispensable Enemy: Labor and the Anti-Chinese Movement in California* (Berkeley and Los Angeles: University of California Press, 1971), 272.

32. Clark, *Los Angeles*, 132; Robert Gottlieb and Irene Wolt, *Thinking Big: The Story of the "Los Angeles Times," Its Publishers, and Their Influence on Southern California* (New York: Putnam, 1977), 187–89, 193–96, 203 (Pierce quote).

33. George J. Sanchez, *Becoming Mexican American: Ethnicity, Culture, and Identity in Chicano Los Angeles, 1900–1945* (Oxford: Oxford University Press, 1993), 224.

34. Togo Tanaka, "The Vernacular Newspapers," p. 8, reel 106, Japanese American Evacuation and Resettlement Records, Bancroft Library, University of California at Berkeley.

35. Karl Yoneda to Elizabeth Gurley Flynn, July 27, 1964, Folder 2, Box 13, KYP; "Miyagi Yotoku's Notes"; Sadaichi Kenmotsu to Frank Specter, December 16, 1931, Folder 9, Box 2, ibid.

36. International Labor Defense, "Mass Meeting—April 14 [1931]," Folder 2, Box 13, KYP; Yoneda to Muravyev, November 9, 1964; Raymond F. Farrell to George E. Brown Jr., March 26, 1973, ibid.

37. Yoneda to Muravyev, November 9, 1964; Farrell to Brown, March 26, 1973; "Appeal to Unemployed Japanese in Los Angeles Area! Meeting on November 22, 1931," Folder 1, Box 1, KYP; Yoneda to Flynn, July 27, 1964.

38. International Labor Defense, "Fight! Against Police Brutality! Demonstrate against Starvation," Folder 2, Box 1, KYP.

39. "Workers to Be Deported, $300 Needed by End of November 1932," January 15, 1932, Folder 2, Box 13, KYP.

40. Yoneda to Muravyev, November 9, 1964; Farrell to Brown, March 26, 1973; "$500 Needed for Deportation Fund!" March 18, 1933, Folder 2, Box 13, KYP; "Help Raise Funds for Voluntary Departure," May 25, 1933, ibid.

41. Japanese Branch of the International Labor Defense and the Young Communist League, "Terror against Japanese!" Folder 9, Box 2, KYP; "Reed Club Denied Hynes Indictment for Recent Raid," *Illustrated Daily News,* February 15, 1993.

42. Japanese Branch of the International Labor Defense and the Young Communist League, "Terror against Japanese!"

43. Raineri, *Red Angel,* 44–45.

44. Letter to members and sympathizers of the John Reed Club of Hollywood from the chairman of the Japanese Press Conference, 1933, Folder 9, Box 2, KYP.

45. My awareness of the five known executed under Stalin stems from fall 1991 conversations with Yuji Ichioka about Japanese media reports.

10

Between Civil Rights, Black Power, and the Mason-Dixon Line

A Case Study of Black Freedom Movement Militancy in the Gateway City

CLARENCE LANG

When construction began on the federally assisted Gateway Arch project in the early 1960s, St. Louis, Missouri's civic elite viewed it as a means to revitalize the blighted downtown riverfront area. Located near the banks of the Mississippi River, the Arch would be the centerpiece of the Jefferson National Expansion Memorial, symbolizing St. Louis's importance as the Gateway City to the American West.[1] Many local Civil Rights activists, however, saw in the Arch project a continuation of racial discrimination.[2] African Americans worked as laborers at the site, but none were employed in the skilled building trades. In the midsummer of 1964, the Congress of Racial Equality (CORE) picketed the Old Courthouse, where the construction project's downtown offices were located. On July 14, while construction workers lunched, Percy Green and Richard Daly climbed 125 feet up the unfinished structure, using a partially enclosed steel surface ladder. The two CORE members refused orders by authorities to disembark until Black workers received at least 10 percent of the jobs at the site.[3] Green and Daly's defiance was part of a wave of similar insurgencies that had occurred at construction sites in New York City, Philadelphia, Newark, and Cleveland, Ohio. In St. Louis, the protest became part of a chain of events that led the U.S. Justice Department to file a "pattern or practice of discrimination" suit against the St. Louis AFL-CIO Building and Construction Trades Council under Title VII, which governed equal employment opportunity in the newly implemented 1964 Civil Rights Act.[4]

The demonstration at the Arch occurred under the auspices of St. Louis CORE, but it marked the beginnings of the Action Committee to Improve Opportunities for Negroes (ACTION). Active between 1964 and 1984, the organization offers entry into several tributaries of Black social history. Foremost, this work augments new historical interpretations asserting that Civil Rights and Black Power were not dichotomous political projects, as historians claimed in the past. No impenetrable line of demarcation existed between the forms of activism attributed separately to either "Civil Rights" or "Black Power." ACTION's program and membership exhibited qualities one could ascribe generically to either liberal integrationism or Black nationalism, yet the organization did not fit neatly in either category. Instead, it straddled a blurred line between the two, illustrating both the unities and the ruptures between the strategies, tactics, and goals of these two historical moments of African American insurgency. Second, ACTION's locality in St. Louis, a border-state metropolis, demonstrates that "Civil Rights" was not simply a southern movement, and that "Black Power" was not merely a northern aberration. As scholars have recently explored, both stages of protest enveloped the Northeast, Midwest, West Coast, and South, as well as the border cities in between.[5]

This chapter argues that ACTION's symbolically "in-between" character was not at all contradictory. This calls into question efforts to mythologize Civil Rights and vilify Black Power in the popular memory, or reduce the former to a southern phenomenon and the latter to the North. But while they are not sharply discontinuous, neither are Civil Rights and Black Power collapsible historical constructs. Ideologically, liberal integrationism formed the dominant discourses of Civil Rights, whereas Black Power reflected the hegemony of African American nationalist thought. Although Civil Rights strategies may have emanated from Black institutional and communal bases, the strategies of Black Power were, by comparison, purposefully geared toward advancing the interests of Black economic and political "community control," and asserting African American cultural integrity, identity, and consciousness in the realms of fashion, art, and music. Full participation in U.S. society grounded the demands of Civil Rights activism. The goals of Black Power, though not exclusive of this aim, were more open-endedly concerned with "Black self-determination," which could mean inclusion in the United States or, in some expressions, complete territorial separation.

Similarly, Civil Rights and Black Power mirrored tactical differences. Both nonviolent resistance and defensive violence were indicative of each, yet Black Power also endorsed, at least rhetorically, the legitimacy of open rebellion and revolution. These ideological, strategic, and tactical divergences characterized the written and spoken words of leading Civil Rights and Black Power figures. In fact, the contrasts were most striking among those Black Power proponents who had been Civil Rights workers. Civil Rights and Black Power were also distinctive in the constituencies each attracted. At a basic level, both were cross-class in composition, but Black Power spoke most directly to a rising new mass constituency: young urban castaways of deindustrialization, urban renewal, and "hard-core unemployment" buttressed by an escalating war in Vietnam. Further, if Civil Rights conjures images of a southern-focused struggle, it is not simply because journalists and historians contrived this depiction. As many activists themselves recognized, Black racial oppression was most starkly expressed in the South (where Reconstruction had been violently aborted and legal segregation established) than in the North (where African Americans objectively had greater social and political space). By the same token, the association between Black Power and the North is not merely arbitrary. After the passage of the Voting Rights Act in 1965, many veterans from the southern theater of battle did reorient their organizational efforts to northern sites. Moreover, federal War on Poverty programs, in linking the national state with disproportionately midwestern and northeastern city governments, provided an actual institutional, programmatic footing for would-be Black Power organizers.

Completely obliterating the distinguishing traits between "Civil Rights" and "Black Power" ignores the profound ideological, strategic, and tactical transformations they represented, and philosophically removes the Black experience from the fluid patterns of continuity and change that ground historical inquiry. Using ACTION as an illustration, this chapter contends that Civil Rights and Black Power drew adherents from similar, overlapping memberships. Yet Civil Rights and Black Power were identifiable *phases* of what historian Clayborne Carson describes as a "Black Freedom Struggle" (or Black Freedom Movement) evolving over time.[6] Likewise, freeing "Civil Rights" and "Black Power" from their regional straitjackets is no basis for arguing that racism, and Black social movements, in the South were indistinguishable from their expressions in the North. I maintain that the Mason-Dixon line matters to the historiography of the modern Black Freedom Movement every bit as much as ideological, political, and organizational evolutions embodied in the transition from the slogan "Freedom Now" to "Black Power."

This chapter locates ACTION within the changing character and membership of CORE, and the contradictions of the Civil Rights struggle of the early 1960s. Second, it discusses ACTION's own development, rank-and-file membership, strategies, tactics, ideological orientation, and overall political program. This work then describes ACTION's major organizational campaigns and interactions with crosscurrents of Black Power in St. Louis during the late 1960s, and discusses its gradual decline. My contention is that the current thrust in Civil Rights and Black Power Studies, by uprooting the history of the Black Freedom Movement from considerations of periodization and place, ultimately leaves us with timeless and spaceless narratives of protest and resistance. This effectively undermines historians' ability to analyze and interpret the African American experience.

Black Life in St. Louis

St. Louis is deservedly known as the "Gateway City." It was a key center of riverboat commerce, and a midcontinental railroad link between eastern capital and the frontier west of the Mississippi. On a vertical axis, the city embodied a "mutual checkmating of Northern and Southern influences." Missouri entered the union as a slaveholding state in 1820, driving a wedge between the free states of the Old Northwest and the far western hinterlands. During the Civil War, St. Louisans split between pro-Confederate and pro-Union sympathies; Missourians, like citizens in Kentucky and Maryland, avoided secession. After the war, St. Louis, like its midwestern neighbors, became a heavily industrialized urban center and, unlike its southern neighbors, heavily unionized. Unlike the South, too, St. Louis attracted a diverse European immigration, though the city's more numerous German and Irish populations were culturally dominant. Whereas the South was heavily Protestant, Catholicism formed the cornerstone of St. Louis's religious life. Moreover, in contrast to the South, where all formal politics after 1910 fell under the aegis of the lily-white Democracy, St. Louis retained a two-party structure.[7]

The city remained an uneven site of convergence of both formally articulated segregation and de facto practices of racial control, which gave Black life a duality that paralleled African American experiences in other border cities such as Baltimore, Louisville, and Cincinnati. Missouri law forbade interracial marriage and integrated schooling, though open seating prevailed on public conveyances. Black children in the city had separate, and fewer, public recreational facilities. Theaters, municipal swimming pools, and restaurants were also segregated, but public libraries were not. Because Black St. Louisans could vote, they held political office early on, and used their strength in district elections to gain lower-level patronage jobs and services. Consequently, local political regimes tended to shy away from the overt brutality used in other cities to preserve Jim Crow. Yet the suppression of racial tension served the interest of racial control, not racial justice. Similarly, the franchise did not translate into equal participation at the bargaining table, where white political and business leaders made the major decisions affecting Black communities.[8]

Most Black St. Louisans earned their livelihoods as personal servants, and as unskilled and common laborers in the steel, packing, tobacco, food processing, brick, and railroad industries. Of the two thousand African Americans employed in local steel production in 1920, more than eighteen hundred were common laborers. Black women, especially, were overrepresented in domestic work. Most skilled trade unions, particularly the building trades, barred Black workers altogether. African Americans earned an average of fifty-seven cents an hour, half the average for white workers. Jim Crow was also manifest in the city's housing patterns. Following the example of citizens in Baltimore and Louisville, white voters in St. Louis passed a residential segregation ordinance in 1916. Efforts by the local branch of the National Association for the Advancement of Colored People (NAACP), and a U.S. Supreme Court ruling, overturned the law, but real estate agents and home owners' groups used private restrictive covenants to contain St. Louis's swelling Black population (until 1948, when a U.S Supreme Court ruling, *Shelley v. Kraemer*, rendered them unenforceable). Most African Americans occupied the crowded northern fringes of the downtown business district and the three wards nearest the central riverfront. Mill Creek Valley, located in this area, was a maze of cheap tenements and hotels, pawnshops, churches, and factory-lined streetcar tracks. West of the downtown-midtown area, Elleardsville, known as the "Ville," similarly became an African American enclave, and the center of Black St. Louis's dense social, cultural, and educational institutions.[9]

St. Louis CORE and the Postwar Black Revolt, 1948–1964

ACTION had its most immediate origins in the St. Louis Committee of Racial Equality. Established in 1942, CORE was an outgrowth of the Fellowship of Reconciliation, a small Christian pacifist group. Rooted in Gandhian thought and interracialism, the committee sought to apply the philosophy of nonviolence directly to racial problems. Formed in 1947–1948, St. Louis CORE participated in a broad interracial campaign to desegregate St. Louis's public swimming pools, but during its first six years the committee's main focus was on desegregating lunch counters at downtown department stores, drugstores, and dime stores. The committee achieved some success by the late 1950s, when even the major department stores began opening their eating accommodations to Black St. Louisans. The city's downtown movie houses, theaters, and hotels also began to slowly, unevenly, desegregate. Historians have overemphasized the 1954 *Brown v. Board of Education of Topeka* decision, and other Supreme Court decisions that chiseled away the edifices of legal racism, to the detriment of mass direct action. But this was also a period in which bus boycotts in Baton Rouge (1953–1954) and Montgomery (1955–1956) propelled Black rights to the forefront of the national agenda. This set the stage for a mass-based challenge to segregation rooted in the nonviolent resistance methods the Fellowship of Reconciliation and CORE had pioneered.[10]

The "Freedom Rides," begun in May 1961 to test the integration of interstate terminals, catapulted CORE to national prominence. In the three-year period that followed, CORE assumed a larger role in southern voter registration. Although Civil Rights struggles unfolded in cities around the nation, the movement's epicenter was the South, for it was there that conditions of Black political disfranchisement and economic subordination were most sharply articulated.

However, job discrimination in northern and border states became CORE's central organizational emphasis. The mass nature of these campaigns allowed CORE to enlist, for the first time, substantial numbers of working-class Black people. Circa 1960, an estimated 214,337 African Americans lived in St. Louis, many of them recently migrated from Mississippi, Tennessee, Arkansas, and Alabama. With the explosion of mass direct action, many of these St. Louisans aligned themselves directly with protest organizations. Among those who joined St. Louis CORE during this period were Percy Green, a skilled radio and electrical mechanic at the McDonnell Aircraft Company.[11]

Green joined the organization a scant six months before St. Louis CORE launched a massive 1963–1964 boycott against the Jefferson Bank and Trust Company, one of several financial institutions that employed no Black St. Louisans in clerical work. Nine high-profile demonstrators were arrested, and several more arrests followed. Regular CORE meetings skyrocketed from ten people to a staggering three hundred—most of whom were new grassroots participants unaffiliated with the organization. With much of the experienced leadership behind bars, Green assumed responsibility for coordinating picket lines at the bank, and soon became chairman of CORE's employment committee. The local Urban League and NAACP, initially supportive of the boycotters' aims, turned against the protests when insurgents continued to defy a court injunction prohibiting disruptions at the bank. But many working-class African Americans like Green who joined CORE during this period were skeptical of the tactics of polite noncooperation. As this new constituency became more engaged, CORE's thrust became both more creative and militant.[12]

Thus, the Jefferson Bank boycott reflected the many changes occurring in CORE nationally. A tension existed between tactics of economic coercion and social disruption and the organization's philosophical commitment to pacifism. Other conflicts involved a tug-of-war between those who counseled gradualism and others who questioned the organization's "tea and donuts" civility. The growing working-class, Black, and mass character of CORE's activities also were increasing demands for African American leadership. When the boycott ended with the placement of Black bank tellers in early 1964, members of St. Louis CORE split over what some considered the protest's limited gains. Nationally, the strategic successes and failures of the 1961–1964 period led many members of CORE, as well as the Student Nonviolent Coordinating Committee (SNCC), to search for new organizational visions. Passage of the Civil Rights Act of 1964, and the 1965 Voting Rights Act, further undermined the shaky consensus they had shared with moderate organizations like the NAACP and the Southern Christian Leadership Conference (SCLC).[13]

The landscape of Black political activity and consciousness also was shifting in response to several economic and social processes at work since the late 1940s.

New industries in electronics, chemicals, and aerospace defense prospered in the St. Louis area, but manufacturing in the city declined overall, as did retail trade. This degeneration in St. Louis's industrial vitality and downtown commerce reinforced a growing joblessness among the local Black population. St. Louis mayor Joseph Darst, and his successor, Raymond Tucker, typified city officials across the nation who faced the uncertain urban-industrial future by fashioning progrowth alliances to strengthen downtown, build expressways, and remove urban "obsolescence." Tucker helped consolidate Civic Progress, Inc., a consortium of the city's top business and civic figures. Created in 1952, this loose coalition heavily promoted civic improvement bond issues to underwrite new urban development and resuscitate the central business district. This progrowth orientation, coupled with the effects of federal highway and housing acts, only contributed to the Gateway City's continuing woes. Highway construction eviscerated St. Louis's central-city areas, and facilitated an ongoing white suburban and business exodus west of downtown. Private banks, and the federal housing and veterans' administrations, favored home-owner loans to single-family dwellings in the new "homogenous" neighborhoods at the western periphery, and redlined older areas of the city. Simultaneously, federally assisted slum clearance expedited Black residential displacement and new forms of ghettoization. Mill Creek Valley became the major target of local urban-renewal initiatives. Beginning in 1959, demolition of the area dislocated an estimated twenty thousand Black people, 10 percent of St. Louis's African American population.[14]

Many of the "Mill Creek exiles" beelined to Carr Square Village, the Pruitt-Igoe homes, Darst-Webbe, and other low-rent federal housing projects on the city's near North and near South sides, both directly adjacent to the urban-renewal area. The neighborhoods north of Delmar Avenue also became solidly Black, as white St. Louisans quit their homes in the city for residences at the suburban fringe. In 1960, the St. Louis Urban League reported, 70 percent of the city's 214,337 African Americans lived in or near deteriorating housing stock, much of it built prior to 1939. Through the 1948 *Shelley v. Kraemer* Supreme Court ruling, and the efforts of the Greater St. Louis Committee for Freedom of Residence, many Black families of means relocated to nearby St. Louis County suburbs. But continuing employment discrimination affected workers' ability to secure lives outside the deteriorating urban core. At the zenith of the Civil Rights struggle, two St. Louis metropolises were coming into form: a central hub abutting the river, mainly Black and poor, and a suburban crescent, largely white and more affluent.

This growing racialized poverty undermined the promises of the Civil Rights and Voting Rights Acts, further disintegrated a volatile Civil Rights consensus, and as in other urban centers seeded the soil for a revivified Black nationalist upsurge. By 1966, both SNCC and CORE nationally had endorsed interpretations of a slogan, "Black Power," geared toward inner-city community organizing. Hence, ACTION emerged from the economic travails of Black working-class life, tensions within CORE around the militancy of its new grassroots membership, and the overall schisms altering the Civil Rights struggle.

"More and Better Paying Jobs for Black Men": ACTION's Program and Strategic Thrust

The Action Committee to Improve Opportunities for Negroes began in January 1964, when the denouement of the Jefferson Bank boycott split the ranks of St. Louis CORE. Direct-action dissidents began consolidating a separate infrastructure, though as the Gateway Arch demonstrations illustrated, they continued to organize protests in CORE's name. In December 1964, the dissidents stepped fully into view. ACTION established headquarters at 2906 Union Boulevard, in the Ville area. The newborn group's name evoked conflicting images. The use of the term *Negro* suggested an Old Guard Civil Rights organization, given that younger activists were rapidly adopting the nomenclature of "Blackness." But the group's acronym—"ACTION"—implied a militancy that set it apart from existing Civil Rights groups. Its twenty-five initial members, though diverse in composition, mainly reflected the more grassroots and action-oriented forces that had gravitated toward CORE's employment committee.[15]

The rank and file, which expanded to about one hundred people, combined a cross-section of three constituencies. The first were petty elites, who hailed from established ecumenical, pacifist, and radical backgrounds. Some, like Robert Curtis, were Black professionals. Sister Cecilia Goldman, who chaired ACTION's religious committee, was a Maryknoll nun. The Reverend William Matheus, another member, was rector at St. Stephen's Episcopal Church, a bulwark for progressive social causes. The second constituency was a larger number of Black working-class people. Green, Ivory Perry, and Doris Gammon, a young wife and mother, were among those who fitted this description. This segment had been CORE's most vital, giving the organization its mass base. In particular, Luther Mitchell, a World War II veteran from Chicago, brought to ACTION an interest in Black history that would prove vital in enlarging the group's base. The third, and most numerous, ACTION membership was an emerging cohort of Black youth between the ages of twenty and thirty. Facing diminished job opportunities, dislocated by urban renewal, and isolated by postwar ghettoization, this wing was most receptive to the appeals of Black Power.

ACTION focused on securing more and better employment opportunities for Black St. Louisans, specifically good working-class jobs with ample benefits. Unemployment among African Americans in St. Louis was nearly three times greater than among whites, and Black workers' wages lagged. In 1959, Black St. Louis families brought home an annual income of $3,718, as opposed to $6,300 for white families, or 59 percent. In 1960, some 11 percent of all Black families in the city of St. Louis had annual incomes of less than $1,000. "One of every three Negroes that are employed works either in private households or as service workers," the St. Louis Urban League summarized.[16] While superficially demanding greater job opportunities for African American women, ACTION organizers mainly regarded Black women as the extensions of male wage earners within two-parent households. Early organizational leaflets rallied members and potential supporters around the slogan "More and Better Paying Jobs for Black Men": "ACTION is spearheading a project to obtain good-paying jobs for Negro men, both unskilled and skilled—with main emphasis on those jobs requiring little or no formal education and little or no previous experience. Good paying jobs of this type are found in Big Business, who can afford ON-THE-JOB TRAINING for their employees."[17] The reasoning for this focus on Black male employment stemmed from a belief that improving their conditions would ultimately "rescue" Black women from the vagaries of wage labor and economic deprivation. This emphasis also followed a related, though contradictory, folk assumption that employers hired African American women in prestigious positions to preempt the meaningful employment of Black men. Although it was demonstrably true that Black male employment was especially acute in St. Louis, the male-centered dimension to ACTION's working-class program nonetheless overlooked how racism constrained Black women's economic chances. Granted, many local phone companies employed a select number of educated Black women as telephone operators. Most Black women in St. Louis, however, remained in domestic-oriented work, subject to low wages and irregular hours. Arguments privileging Black manhood also shared the same discursive space as "War on Poverty" arguments blaming "matriarchy" for the poverty and cultural dysfunction in African American communities. Such points of view fed a conviction that Black women acted, through no fault of their own perhaps, as a barrier to Black men assuming their rightful place as the heads of households and communities. On the one hand, then, the organization's credo responded to African Americans' limited job opportunities as workers. At the same time, it reflected how race, gender, and the dominant ideas of the period shaped the grievances and agendas of dissidents even as they challenged the status quo.

To fight for this ideal of the Black wage-earning "family breadwinner," members targeted several major local employers—McDonnell Aircraft (which became McDonnell Douglas Corporation in 1967), Southwestern Bell Telephone Company, Laclede Gas Company, and Union Electric Company. Overall, ACTION's leaders were mindful that many labor unions colluded with management in discriminating against Black workers, yet they understood that outside the building trades, where craft unions wielded influence through apprenticeships, employers held the reins of hiring and promotions. Employment at the utility companies was a vital theater of Black struggle because the local manufacturing base, though important to the city's economy, did not compare to Chicago or Detroit, where more opportunities existed for work in heavy industry. Since they enjoyed franchises granted by the city also, the utilities bore a special obligation to practice fair employment. Yet figures painted a pattern of discrimination. A 1958 study of the phone company had revealed that out of a workforce of 7,000, African Americans constituted only 121 employees, and 92 percent of these were in custodial positions. By July 1963, the company had 9,000 employees, 123 of whom were Black. Consistent with the earlier numbers, 84 of them were custodians. Drawing on experiences from the Jefferson Bank boycott, activists reasoned that only by exploiting these firms' fear of negative publicity could they wrest meaningful concessions to St. Louis's Black working class.[18]

Major Organizational Campaigns, 1965–1967

ACTION first exploded in a flurry of motion in the spring and summer of 1965, when activists targeted the downtown offices of the utility companies in a series of disruptive demonstrations. In a concurrent thread of activity, the organization fought the formidable McDonnell Aircraft Company over its noncompliance with the 1964 Civil Rights Act. The aircraft giant had a poor image among many Black St. Louisans, who referred to the company as "Daddy Mac"—both an acknowledgment and a derision of its paternal image as the St. Louis area's largest industrial employer. Green's own troubles with the company extended back to August 28, 1964, when the firm fired him. Coming a month and a half after his televised exploits on the beams of the Gateway Arch, he had reason to believe his dismissal stemmed from his known Civil Rights involvement. Protesting his dismissal, and McDonnell's hiring and upgrading procedures, Green and a group of activists had staged an automobile "stall-in" in October 1964, tying up employees' cars near the plant. In July 1965, civil rights workers hit McDonnell with a "lock-in" at the company's downtown offices. The organization had, that same day, filed charges of employment discrimination with the new Equal Employment Opportunity Commission, alleging that of the 500 African Americans employed among McDonnell's 35,000 workers, 90 percent did menial and janitorial labor. The charges also claimed that personnel administrators discouraged Black workers at the company from participating in on-the-job training programs and other vehicles of promotion.[19]

The campaigns against these major businesses converged in ACTION's sustained protest of the city's annual Veiled Prophet parade and ball, an affair melding city boosterism, secret society ritual, Mardi Gras carnival, and debutante soiree. Both the public parade and the exclusively private ball revolved around the masked, enigmatic Veiled Prophet of Khorassan, selected from St. Louis's business elite. The Mystic Order of the Veiled Prophet of the Enchanted Realm, the organization coordinating the events, further consolidated the already dense relations among the city's Brahmin class, most of whom already worked together in Civic Progress and shared membership on the same corporate boards of directors.[20] To militant Civil Rights workers, historian Thomas Spencer maintains, "the Veiled Prophet celebration symbolized racism and white control of St. Louis's economy," especially because this exclusive whites-only organization held its gala ball at the Kiel Auditorium, a public tax-supported institution.[21]

"Integrationist" Strategy, "Black Power" Adaptations

On a plane parallel to its sorties against the utilities, McDonnell, and the Veiled Prophet, ACTION interfaced with an emergent Black nationalist groundswell. A renaissance occurred with the transformation of SNCC and CORE, and the development of new organizations such as the Revolutionary Action Movement, US Organization, and the Black Panther Party (for Self-Defense). Similar sentiments supported the formation of militant Black union caucuses, and propelled demands for Black Studies curricula on college campuses and universities. The northern base of these organizations and activities reflected how the movement's center had shifted to the urban Midwest, Northeast, and West Coast; many veterans of southern campaigns sought to develop programs that matched conditions in northern ghettoes. Inspired by protracted anticolonial movements abroad, and taking their theoretical cues from Algerian revolutionary Frantz Fanon, an emerging cohort of movement workers viewed violence, turned against one's oppressors, as a necessary catharsis for the oppressed. This became a feature of the Black Power militancy in both rhetoric and practice.[22]

St. Louis was part of a national "riot cluster" that exploded in the late summer of 1964 in Harlem, North Philadelphia, and Paterson, New Jersey. In early July 1964, what began as a sick call to police on St. Louis's near North Side snowballed into civil disorder when officers attempted to break up a domestic disturbance. During an hourlong confrontation, a large group of mostly Black teens and young adults lobbed rocks and bottles at a gathering force of forty policemen and twenty-five cruisers. The skirmish ended when police scattered the crowd with tear-gas grenades.[23]

Threats of Black Power insurrection hovered, too, at the edges of many nonviolent demonstrations. Following an ACTION protest against the Veiled Prophet parade in October 1965, some one hundred Black youth took to Delmar Avenue, smashing automobile and store windows. During another incident, in May 1967, activists protested the lack of trash removal from a neighborhood near Compton Avenue, an area of Black residence south of downtown. Twenty-five ACTION workers raked debris from a vacant lot into the street, partially obstructing traffic. When police responded to motorists' complaints about the blockage, residents pilloried them, and passing cars, with bottles and brickbats. In September 1967, more serious rebellions occurred in neighboring East St. Louis, Illinois, following an appearance by SNCC chairman H. Rap Brown and the police shooting death of a Black youth. Even many of ACTION's own protest tactics revealed how thin the line was between nonviolent militant protest and urban rebellion. A little more than a month after the clash on Compton Avenue, police arrested Green and three other ACTION members after two Wonder Bread delivery men reported the tires of their trucks deflated. Neither could identify any of the four Civil Rights workers as the vandals, and the men were released. Yet ACTION members at the time had been distributing leaflets urging supporters to let the air out of the tires of Wonder Bread, Southwestern Bell, Laclede Gas, and Union Electric vehicles.[24]

To the extent these episodes manifested the new Black nationalism, such politics amounted to more than unharnessed rage. Downtown growth schemes, the "subsurvival" living conditions of many African Americans, and the Lyndon Johnson administration's declared War on Poverty were all part of the framework in which Black Power was articulated. Between 1967 and 1969, the administration of Mayor Alfonso J. Cervantes declared as blighted five city blocks downtown, making the area ripe for redevelopment. The soaring, 630–foot Gateway Arch opened to the public in 1967–1968, and the vaunted riverfront renaissance proceeded with several other massive construction projects. But by 1968, St. Louis also had one of the highest-concentrated ghettoes among the major northern and border cities, and the nation's highest infant mortality rate. The Gateway City was one of the few major cities that had not experienced serious rioting, though on the basis of statistics, observers noted, it could yet become the nation's most riot-scarred city. Because of their intent on clearing blighted property for high-priced renewal, officials were lax in enforcing building codes, creating an underreported problem of lead poisoning among Black children who often ate flecks of peeling plaster and paint. The metropolitan area also had one of the nation's worst cases of Black "hard-core joblessness," with sixty thousand African Americans fitting this description. The low rates of job placement by the Human Development Corporation, the city's main antipoverty agency, also dashed expectations of a comprehensive remedy to their problems. Public assistance benefits, moreover, ranked among the lowest in the country, while inner-city residents paid 6 percent more for groceries than suburbanites at the same chain supermarkets. St. Louis's Freedom of Residence Committee and the Open Housing Act of 1968 may have broken barriers to fair housing, but a growing number of Black St. Louisans literally could not afford to take advantage of the new opportunities, which intensified urban grievances.[25]

Great Society–linked organizations like St. Louis's Mid-City Community Congress and the West End Community Conference gave many Black Power advocates an institutional foothold beyond mere rhetoric. Younger activists addressed varied issues of chronic unemployment, inadequate housing, Black electoral power, and economic development. The city's Black-owned Gateway National Bank opened in 1965, while the Supreme Court ordered a reapportionment of Missouri's congressional districts. The ruling boosted North St. Louis's electoral power, creating the conditions for William L. Clay—a former alderman, Jefferson Bank boycotter, and ward committeeman—to become the state's first Black U.S. congressman in 1968. All of these developments embodied the nationalist self-assertion of the period.

Because ACTION was born at the pregnant moment when "Freedom Now" was giving way to "Black Power," its members were informed by the movement's political and cultural trajectory. From the outset, the organization kept its headquarters in St. Louis's solidly Black Ville area, and its agenda revolved around building the community's own internal reserves. As the decade proceeded, many ACTION workers also cultivated a stylistic presence more akin to Black Power than Civil Rights. Many Black male members wore dark berets, army field jackets, denim jeans, work boots, African-print vests, and dark sunglasses popular among the young urban Black nationalists influenced by revolutionary guerrillas abroad. Reflecting these influences, the organization developed a youth auxiliary, whose membership sported dark T-shirts emblazoned with the words "A.C.T.I.O.N. Guerrilla Force."

Culturally, the organization also sponsored a Black Veiled Prophet Ball, and while it was conceived as a lampoon of the regular Veiled Prophet soiree, it nonetheless served as an affirmation of Black culture. First held in 1966, the ball reflected a new "Black Is Beautiful" ethos that rejected European-American standards of fashion and physical loveliness. Further, Mitchell's knowledge of Black history became the basis for forming an ACTION history department, which he chaired. The committee distributed weekly questionnaires on African American history, delivering them primarily in Black neighborhoods. This interaction along with Mitchell's prior involvement with Chicago's Southside Community Art Center were geneses for a community-driven mural project to bring art and history to the public. He coordinated the painting of a "Wall of Respect" mural at the intersection of Leffingwell and Franklin avenues, near the site of the July 1964 disturbance. Modeled after Chicago's own famous "Wall of Respect," the mural featured a collage of sixteen famous faces, including W. E. B. Du Bois, Muhammad Ali, Ray Charles, Martin Luther King Jr., and Malcolm X. Marcus Garvey's famous quote, "Up You Mighty Race," underscored the images. Begun in the summer of 1968, the Wall of Respect became, after its completion, a potent cultural symbol and a popular meeting place for young Black artists and political organizers.[26]

ACTION's organizational rhetoric evinced a similar fusion of certain liberal integrationist and Black nationalist influences. The masculinist leadership style of many Black Power proponents, and their keenly felt need to "reassert" Black manhood, meshed with ACTION leaders' own liberal-derived convictions that African American men had been emasculated, making their communities vulnerable to a culture of poverty. It bears reminding that Civil Rights organizations like the SCLC had a male-centered culture in which women's roles were circumscribed and their leadership suppressed. SCLC president Martin Luther King Jr., for instance, was generally uneasy around politically assertive women. Even during the planning of the 1963 March on Washington, organizers had to be pressured to simply give women a token presence on the rostrum. Clearly, African American male chauvinism was not the exclusive province of Black nationalists. Further, although they did not eschew a "Civil Rights" label, ACTION members defined the group in much broader terms as a "human rights protest organization" seeking to elevate economic justice above business concerns. ACTION's stance on "armed self-help" was similarly ambiguous. While SNCC and CORE publicly endorsed activists' right to self-defense in 1966, ACTION members remained committed to their nonviolent roots. Yet members periodically participated in survival training. Green commented at the time, "I don't belittle those who talk violence. I don't condemn or condone them. But the way to deal with them is by rectifying the system." Consistent with many ACTION founders' earlier involvement in CORE, adherence to nonviolence was strategic, not philosophical.[27]

The presence of whites, who were 40 percent of ACTION's membership, also confused those who saw, at first glance, a Black nationalist group. At a time when white members resigned from CORE and SNCC amid internal strife, ACTION remained stridently interracial. This position was not without controversy among some Black members, who viewed the strategy as outdated. But while rebuffing the racial insularity of many younger Black militants, ACTION's leadership served notice to white members that they would participate in ACTION on terms defined by African Americans. Drawing from experiences in CORE, Green concluded, "If there was going to be mutual respect, whites would have to submit to black leadership, in contrast to what had happened in the NAACP and CORE, where many top ranking officials were white, and the rank-and-file was largely black."[28] Black activists occupied top positions of leadership in the organization.

St. Louis's Black Liberation Front

This approach to interracialism was consistent with ACTION's participation in the nationalist Black United Front (later renamed the Black Liberation Front). A loose coalition formed around 1968, it included CORE, ACTION, and several local Black Power organizations: the Mid-City Community Congress, the Zulu 1200s, and the Black Liberators. Against the backdrop of a massive St. Louis public-housing rent strike, the abandonment of the War on Poverty, and the "benign neglect" of the new Richard M. Nixon administration, the Black Liberation Front adopted a militant new program of grassroots struggle.[29]

James Forman, SNCC's former executive secretary, garnered national attention in May 1969 when he interrupted services at New York City's Riverside Church to present a "Black Manifesto." Published by the Detroit-based Black Economic Development Conference (BEDC), the document called for white religious organizations to render five hundred million dollars in reparations for the funding of a Black southern land bank, business cooperatives, and other ventures. The BEDC steering committee called for a widespread campaign of civil disobedience that would expose organized Christianity as a source of Black oppression, and as an institution that owed a debt.[30]

Beginning in the summer of 1969, ACTION and the Black Liberation Front launched separate series of disruptions at St. Louis's major churches. Performed during weekly services, these "Black Sunday" demonstrations were similarly geared toward exacting millions of dollars in reparations from wealthy Christian institutions. Protesters distributed copies of the "Black Manifesto," castigated white clergy and their congregants for turning a blind eye to urban poverty, and directly implicated the churches in the ownership of slum properties. ACTION workers called on the Missouri Episcopal Diocese and the St. Louis Catholic Archdiocese to, among other things, publicly list all their property holdings and end any investments in Laclede Gas, Union Electric, Southwestern Bell, and McDonnell Douglas. Ultimately, neither the local nor the national reparations campaign fully realized its goal. Yet activity in St. Louis and elsewhere was successful in the much more significant goal of bringing the issue of reparations to a national audience in the early 1970s. ACTION's work with the Black Liberation Front demonstrated the organization's broad programmatic scope. Specifically, the group's reformist goal—improving employment opportunities vis-à-vis the '64 Civil Rights Act—provided a foundation for a deepening commitment to confronting concentrations of power held by a local elite.[31]

The Decline of Black Insurgency and ACTION's Dissolution

Obstinate efforts against McDonnell Douglas also continued. ACTION had issued a four-page report in July 1969 detailing the extent of racial discrimination practiced by the corporation. Drawing on his own federal statistics, Congressman Clay wrote the firm's president, James S. McDonnell, urging reform. Edward Kennedy, the prominent U.S. senator from Massachusetts, called for a review of a $7.7 billion fighter contract the U.S. Department of Defense had recently awarded the company. In January 1970, while his own lawsuit against McDonnell Douglas moved through the courts, Green testified before the U.S. Commission on Civil Rights. He used the opportunity not only to air many Black workers' grievances with the corporation but also to blast the Defense Department for giving the firm lucrative contracts: "How in the world could a company that has had as many complaints levied against it along racial lines, a company who has yet to have 10 percent black employment," receive 90 percent of its work from the federal government? "This only indicates that the Government itself aids white racism to be practiced upon black people here in St. Louis."[32]

ACTION's campaign against the Veiled Prophet also reached an apotheosis. During the December 1972 ball, Gena Scott, "disguised" in full evening dress, used a spotlight cable to slide from the balcony rafters and land near the masked icon. Despite injuring herself, she managed to rush the figure and remove both his veil and his crown before being ushered away and arrested. Maintaining their deference, most local media withheld the name of the exposed prophet, though the St. Louis Journalism Review revealed his identity as Tom K. Smith, a vice president at the Monsanto Chemical Company and a Civic Progress alumnus.[33]

If ACTION did not accomplish all of its members' aims, the organization nevertheless accomplished more than its critics admitted. The 1964 Gateway Arch demonstration helped spur the creation of minority apprenticeship and outreach programs in construction, which became a template for similar plans in Philadelphia, Cleveland, and the San Francisco Bay area. In 1967, the Justice Department dropped its charges against St. Louis's Building and Construction Trades Council and two of its unions. A judge dismissed the remaining charges a year later. Nevertheless, new affirmative action mandates helped Black construction workers win greater access to skilled trades jobs (though, as Thomas J. Sugrue argues, building trades unions undermined these mandates by adopting antidiscrimination agreements that avoided concrete results).[34]

ACTION also helped secure the hiring of more African Americans in meter reading and telephone installation jobs. The combined pressure of ACTION-led work shutdowns, and an Equal Employment Opportunity Commission suit, forced Laclede Gas to announce, in August 1976, a plan for hiring minorities for 40 percent of new job openings. In challenging a federal contract to McDonnell Douglas, the organization's efforts helped pressure the corporation into changing its hiring and upgrading policies. Through a series of appeals, Green's suit also made its way before the U.S. Supreme Court. In *Green v. McDonnell Douglas Corporation* (1973), the Court ruled that plaintiffs in a racial discrimination suit need only establish "minimum proof" that they were denied employment, or discharged, due to racism; the burden of proof then fell on employers. Like the Arch controversy, the *Green* case became the model for subsequent employment discrimination suits. In harassing the Veiled Prophet Organization, moreover, ACTION attacked a hegemonic symbol of financial, governmental, and corporate influence over the city's affairs. In masterminding the Veiled Prophet's exposure, the organization stripped the icon of its symbolic power and mystique. On the heels of a successful class-action suit instigated by ACTION, the Veiled Prophet Organization was also forced to relocate its annual ball to a private venue in 1974.[35]

At the same time, the wave of mass-based ferment, which had buoyed movement organizations like ACTION, was ebbing. Johnson's War on Poverty—which rested on an assumption of Black cultural pathology, and never received the funding commensurate to its ambitious goals—succumbed first to war in Vietnam, then reaction at home. Political repression by local, state, and federal authorities also fed the movement's decline. Like a number of organizations, ACTION became a target of the Federal Bureau of Investigation's Counterintelligence Program, which director J. Edgar Hoover launched to subvert Civil Rights, Black Power, and antiwar activity. An FBI memorandum from the St. Louis special agent in charge, dated September 2, 1969, informed the D.C. headquarters that "ACTION, a local Black activist group whose membership includes both Negroes and whites, is at the present time the only Black group of any significance other than the NOI [Nation of Islam]" in St. Louis. The memo continued: "This Division is considering the best way to exploit differences among the membership with a view toward decreasing the group's effectiveness." In early 1970, FBI agents mailed a phony letter to the husband of Jane Sauer, a white ACTION worker. Anonymously signed "A Soul Sister," the letter intimated that Sauer was having assignations with Black men in the organization. The ruse revealed not only the FBI's derisively caricatured view of Black vernacular but also agents' own latent fears that Black social movements were a prelude to sex between white women and African American men. The attempted sabotage did not curtail Sauer's political activities, as bureau agents had anticipated, but she and her husband consequently separated.[36]

Nixon's electoral triumphs in 1968–1972 signaled an overall shift to the right in American social and urban policy. Prowar riots waged by construction workers against antiwar demonstrators in St. Louis and New York City were emblematic of a rising "silent majority" steeped in white grassroots resentment. The success of the Black revolt also contributed to the movement's very demobilization. A new Black middle class, molded in the crucible of Civil Rights and Black Power, emerged in the professions, the corporate elite, and electoral politics. As early as 1970, the local St. Louis press gave favorable publicity to the private business ventures of militant-talking Black entrepreneurs, and even President Nixon could endorse a "Black Power" construed as private business development.[37]

Opposition to federally mandated affirmative action contract letting and employment policies grew amid declining economic conditions and inflation.

The ensuing "Reagan Revolution" of the 1980s inaugurated a full-scale assault on the progressive legacies of the previous two decades. Even the *Green* ruling was reversed: in 1989, the U.S. Supreme Court ruled in *Atonio v. Wards Cove Packing Company* that the burden of proof fell on alleged victims of racism and sexism to prove employer discrimination—and to demonstrate that such practices did not serve "legitimate business goals." When ACTION's leadership chose to disband in the early '80s, the resolution reflected both a dispersion of members and a reassessment of its effectiveness in the changed conditions of the post-1975 period. Margaret Phillips, a former white member, attributed ACTION's end to an inability to develop a program beyond "jobs." Thus, although the organization helped expand employment opportunities for Black working people, its leadership never formulated a sustainable response to central-city decline, which eviscerated many of the breadwinner jobs advocated by Black Freedom Movement activists.[38]

As in other old urban centers, unemployment and means-tested welfare programs placed greater demands on St. Louis's budget. At the same time, industrial-commercial flight and tax abatements granted to downtown developers by Cervantes and subsequent mayors shrank the city's tax base and constricted vital social services. By 1975, the Pruitt-Igoe complex was destroyed, the first high-rise public housing project in the nation to face the wrecking ball. While new corporate headquarters scraped the downtown sky, City Hall shut Homer G. Phillips Hospital, which had been a source of pride and identity among Black St. Louisans. At decade's end, African Americans constituted 46 percent of St. Louis's 453,000 inhabitants, and many inhabitants of the surrounding St. Louis County had come to regard the city as dangerous and dysfunctional. In 1980, two urban sociologists ranked the Gateway City the nation's second most depressed city, on the basis of housing stock, per capita income, and degree of population decline. By then, the African American working class that fueled the Civil Rights and Black Power struggles had become a "subproletariat" consigned to menial service jobs at the margins of a new postindustrial urban economy oriented toward recreation and corporate services.[39]

Just as ACTION had continued previous threads of social insurgency, other protest organizations followed in its wake. In 1980, a group of Black Power veterans formed the Organization of Black Struggle, and invited Green to sit on its advisory committee. Although the organization worked most directly around the issue of police brutality, its members were part of a progressive coalition committed to electing the city's first Black mayor. These grassroots efforts paid off in 1993, when St. Louisans elected Freeman Bosley Jr. Green accepted an appointment as the head of the city's minority-participation program, charged with monitoring and enforcing racial minority and female access to city contracts. Although Bosley's election and Green's position demonstrated the progress achieved by the Black revolt, most Black St. Louisans remained mired in deteriorating conditions that neither an African American mayor nor the fair vetting of business contracts could ameliorate. By 2001, St. Louis ranked as the nation's ninth most segregated city, riven by high Black unemployment and low household income. The building trades remained as segregated as ever: in 2002, only 5.5 percent of all construction workers were Black.[40]

Civil Rights, Black Power, and the Mason-Dixon Line: A Conclusion

An assessment of ACTION's origins, its own independent development, and its participation in Black Power politics reveals that differences among periods of Black social ferment, though certainly real, are not as clear as previously assumed.[41] Younger historians' turn away from "discontinuity" and "spontaneity" as overriding themes in African American popular movements augurs well for studies of the Black Freedom Movement. Among other benefits, the new emphasis on "continuity" offers a better view of the complex traditions of Black political and intellectual thought that formed the scaffolding of modern Civil Rights and Black Power struggles.

One supposed difference between Civil Rights and Black Power is that the latter was interested in broader issues than the former. In this depiction, Civil Rights was concerned primarily with the (middle) "classes" and Black Power with the "masses." But the racial-class concerns of working people were not unfamiliar territory to Civil Rights workers. Activists in St. Louis, and elsewhere, were raising questions about institutional racism, working-class employment, and poverty well before the late 1960s. "Civil Rights" clearly constituted more than middle-class Blacks' efforts to ingratiate themselves to whites.

Another purported difference between Civil Rights and Black Power was that the first was nonviolent, whereas the second advocated forms of violence. As evinced in ACTION's approach, most Civil Rights protesters regarded nonviolent direct action as a tactic, not a philosophy—just as most Black nationalists viewed the right to self-defense in contingent terms. In many locales, Civil Rights workers resorted to arms to protect themselves from white vigilantes, while many Black Power activists pursued nonviolent methods toward their political goals. Then, too, "Civil Rights" has been used to evoke the imagery of God-fearing, morally fastidious Black southerners, whereas "Black Power" is identified with northern ghetto pathology. These stereotypes ignore the Civil Rights struggles that occurred north of the Mason-Dixon, including border cities like St. Louis, and overlook their secular groundings among people who did not attend Sunday school. In the inverse, clichés about Black Power being strictly of the North disregard its core precepts formulated in the South. When SNCC workers called for "Black Power" in 1966, it was not from a rooftop in Harlem but rather in the wake of a SNCC campaign to gain Black political control in Lowndes County, Alabama. Moreover, the participation of biracial clergy in the "Black Sunday" demonstrations in St. Louis and other cities showed that Black nationalist programs could, and did, interface with Christian doctrines and institutions—in contrast to the reigning assumptions about Black Power's profane quality.

A final, overarching assumption about the two periods is that Civil Rights was interracial, and therefore "integrationist," whereas Black Power was anti-white and "separatist." This loses the fact that Civil Rights struggles often flowed from the collective resources of African American communities and institutions, which supported movement programs and, in ACTION's case, provided the space where movement organizations were headquartered. Civil Rights militants like Green were committed to interracial politics only insofar as they strategically advanced the fight for Black equality. And although it is true that some Black nationalist organizations actively opposed coalitions with whites, others—notably the Black Panthers—helped build multiracial alliances. "Black Power" was not a unified ideology but rather an umbrella covering diverse, often contradictory, nationalist tendencies. The integrationist-separatist dichotomy also confuses the meanings of *integration* and *assimilation*. Although used interchangeably, they are in fact different terms. *Assimilation* evokes a cultural negation, in this case of Black institutions and identity. *Integration,* on the other hand, can best be understood as the abolition of legal and structural barriers to Black citizenship in the United States. This does not preclude the building of separate Black institutions.

ACTION embodies a conjuncture of these many factors. First, because the group was based in a border-state metropolis—neither the Mississippi Delta nor entirely the Midwest—it symbolizes the broad geographical scope of Civil Rights and Black Power movements across the North and South. Second, the organization's interracial membership was not contradictory to a Black leadership, or an interest in promoting a Black cultural and political identity. Similarly, although the organization's name included an antiquated term, *Negro,* ACTION participated in Black Power organizations and programs. Third, in their campaigns, members employed tactics of nonviolent direct action, but these methods served strategic, rather than ideological, purposes. Fourth, ACTION's goal of expanding Black working-class employment and economic opportunities was consistent with mainline Civil Rights activism, as well as certain trends of Black Power. In this vein, attacking racial discrimination was not contradictory to the goal of Black institution building. In fact, the latter has often required the former as a precondition. Fifth, while its reputation was that of a "Civil Rights" group fighting to implement equal opportunity provisions of federal law, ACTION's members also viewed themselves as a "human rights" organization attempting to uproot institutional racism and economic inequality. One can view ACTION's reparations campaign, and its battle against the Veiled Prophet, in this light.

Likewise, the organization drew its personnel from a variety of demographics: white clergy, peace activists, and university liberals; Black skilled professionals; Black working-class activists who had gained their formative political experiences during the Jefferson Bank boycott; and Black youth steeped in the popular idioms of Black nationalism. Grappling with ACTION's history helps make the case for why a dichotomous view of Civil Rights and Black Power obscures more than it illuminates. Ultimately, it reduces Black political culture to a secession of strategic and tactical opposites—"integrationism" versus "separatism," "nonviolence" versus "self-defense," or "peaceful" versus "militant." Drawing such contrasts confirms popular fables about a nonthreatening Civil Rights movement that united Blacks and whites around a color-blind dream of individual opportunity and an atavistic Black Power movement that drove them apart through unfair demands for Black group rights. An approach singularly focused on strategies also evades any real engagement with the substance of Black political and intellectual thought, which has informed any number of seemingly contradictory strategies and tactics.

In understanding "Civil Rights" and "Black Power" as unstable categories, however, scholars must resist the temptation to collapse them into the same entity. Some, like Clayborne Carson, Charles M. Payne, and Timothy B. Tyson, have attempted to transcend the notion of "Civil Rights" altogether, protesting that it says too little about the longer movement for political, social, and economic justice. They would use in its place Carson's "Black Freedom Struggle," arguing that this framework casts the popular struggles of the 1950s, '60s, and '70s in terms broader than legislative reforms, and places its origins before *Brown*. Others, like Tyson and Peniel E. Joseph, favor "Black Power" as a concept enveloping the decades both before and after World War II.[42]

Such perspectives have powerful appeal and open vital avenues of investigation. Yet the tendency to disintegrate "Civil Rights" and "Black Power" dispenses with historical periodization, and the sense of the motion and change central to comparing and contrasting different moments in time. Without periodization, scholars of the Black Freedom Movement blind themselves to developments that are "new," as well as "old," and efface the *evolving* nature of social movements, their dynamic internal processes, and their transformative effects on movement participants. Ignoring considerations of change re-creates the same error that social historians have made in the past about Black popular movements, but this time in reverse: continuity replaces discontinuity as the central reality of African American struggle. Granted, African Americans have fought conditions of racial degradation across time, but those conditions have not been the same over the span of U.S. history. Similarly, Black responses to racial oppression and discrimination, while sharing commonalities, have been specific to a given historical moment. And although the ideologies that have informed these movements have certain consistencies, ideas are nonetheless shaped against the needs of a given period.[43]

Scholars have been equally hasty in dissipating distinctions of place between southern and northern expressions of white racism and Black resistance. It is not shocking that many of the same scholars denying historical periodization in Civil Rights and Black Power Studies are also among those seeking to dismantle the Mason-Dixon Line from this historiography. The declining regionalism of the South in national politics since 1965 has likely influenced this trend, lulling historians into reading the present backward. Historians' recent turn toward globalization, and a resulting de-emphasis on the politics of the nation-state and region, perhaps are other factors in the current trend of muting southern particularism.[44] Certainly, caricatures of the U.S. South have scapegoated the region as the fountainhead of Black racial oppression. In one vein, then, the argument for doing away with the North-South dichotomy rests on the reasonable premise that racism has permeated the whole of the United States. (If anything, the recent rehabilitation of the South as a center of economic opportunity for Black professionals has subtly reversed regional stereotypes, casting Dixie as a new "Promised Land.") Scholars are also right to challenge "static and bifurcated regional images" equating the southern movement with racial integration and nonviolence and northern activity with self-destructive Black "separatism." Likewise, they are correct to reject a master narrative in which Black northern protest is rendered "ancillary and subsequent to the 'real' movement in the South," as Evelyn Brooks Higginbotham admonishes.[45]

However, these broad truths are no basis for doing away with the significance of place in movement narratives, no more than the continuities between "Civil Rights" and "Black Power" justify erasing historical periodization. In arguing for North-South continuity, the new Civil Rights–Black Power thrust avoids important considerations of political economy, and does away with an expansive literature on southern history. The South is by far the nation's most historically distinct region; scholars differ only over the *extent* of this distinctiveness. It was the only region in the United States to develop a slave economy rooted in plantation agriculture. Well into the twentieth century, it remained not only the most agricultural but also the least urbanized and industrialized—and the poorest, with minimal taxation and public expenditure. Politically, the South cohered around a vigorous sectional defense of the "peculiar institution" via discourses of states' rights and a strict constructionist interpretation of the U.S. Constitution.[46]

Experiences of secession, military defeat, occupation, Reconstruction, and white supremacist "redemption" also formed the taproot of southern distinctiveness. So, too, did the South's postwar reincorporation, which transformed the region into an outpost of northern industrial capital and low-wage labor. Moreover, its ethnically homogenous white population (stemming from a lack of diverse European immigration) and its disproportionate Black population (tied to the labor demands of a plantation slave system) made the South the most racially dualistic in character. This lent itself to an intense preoccupation with African American subordination and social control, particularly in those areas where Black people were most numerous. Granted, race relations were neither equitable nor serene in the North, yet conditions in the South provided the firmament for the legal institutionalization of Black disfranchisement and racial segregation after the demise of Reconstruction. These elaborately codi-fied means of racial domination in the South gave rise to a one-party order based in a Herrenvolk Democratic solidarity, and buttressed by the advent of all-white primaries. Further, the absence of two-party politics begat a southern demagogic tradition that relied on individual flamboyance, white supremacy, xenophobia, and rhetorical excess. African American oppression in this "Solid South" not only formed the cornerstone of the region's general poverty but also stimulated a corresponding politics of racial mediation and accommodation, as exemplified by the "Tuskegee Machine" of Booker T. Washington.[47]

Of course, one must guard against reifying myths of a monolithic South. Yet this does not mean that the South did not have its own specific deeply ingrained legacies. This is not to suggest that the South was more "backward" than the North. Respecting the regional distinctiveness of the North and South need not result in a depiction of the South as "bad" or the North as "good." Neither is it the case that those who distinguish between the two regions automatically harbor biases against northern protest under the faulty impression that the North was more racially "enlightened." The regional differences at issue are not *normative* but rather *historical* in the broad sense of being social, economic, and political. To the extent that regionalism provides a conceptual tool for analyzing a na-tional context, border communities like St. Louis are remarkable for providing insight to historical unities and discrepancies between the North and the South (in the same way that a group like ACTION provides a means of identifying the strategic, tactical, and ideological continuities and disjunctures between Civil Rights and Black Power).

The point is that the Mason-Dixon Line and the distinctions between the de jure and de facto forms of racial oppression it personified were not simply ephemera, no more than were the contrasts between "Freedom Now" and "Black Power." In the 1955–1965 period, when de jure racism existed, its elimination became critical to achieving political, social, and economic parity. The Black movement's predominant strategy became nonviolent mass direct action aimed at the edifices of U.S. racial apartheid and disfranchisement. This activity took the form of demands for desegregation, with liberalism as the dominant ideological paradigm. Black radical political tendencies existed at this time, but their existence was "underground," or they were actively silenced.[48]

The 1965–1975 period developed in a qualitatively different context. The locus of movement activity shifted from South to North. This had material, historical groundings in the legal demise of formal racial discrimination in the South and the Black migration to the urban Northeast and Midwest that continued into the mid-'60s. By this period, profound economic realignments, under way since the 1950s, began to register socially, spawning both federal War on Poverty programs and a wave of Black urban revolts. Insurgents confronted a historical moment in which their efforts had outlawed legal racism, yet joblessness and underemployment, police abuse, and similar structures of de facto racial oppression persisted. Activists explored strategies that were more self-consciously nationalist and radical in ideology, form, and content. It was hardly coincidental that the widespread adoption of a "Black" identity, as opposed to "Negro," occurred during this particular historical moment. Not only did many grassroots Black movement workers see themselves as engaged in revolutionary struggle in the United States, but they also viewed this as a constituent part of the anticolonial and anti-imperialist movements being fought at the time by other third world peoples. In this context, once "subterranean" trends fully surfaced aboveground as Black nationalist ideas reached the broad audiences they had lacked during the previous period.

Between 1955 and 1975, then, African Americans confronted dramatically different typologies of racial subjugation, and they employed different ideological, strategic, and tactical means to fashion their dominant responses. Still, Civil Rights and Black Power are best understood not as distinctly separate entities, nor even as the same entity, but rather as *phases* within a broader Black Freedom Movement covering the sweep of African American history.

It is encouraging that revisionist historians are complicating depictions of "Civil Rights" and "Black Power," the relationship between the two, and their regional dynamics. More than just historiographical issues are at stake in reassessing the history of Civil Rights and Black Power struggles. A revised, critical scholarship offers a yardstick against which to measure contemporary Black politics and a signpost of how contemporary activists have either continued or sublimated previous transcripts of struggle. Exactly thirty-five years after Percy Green and Richard Daly dramatized the demand for Black skilled construction jobs at the Gateway Arch, nine hundred people converged at Goodfellow Boulevard in North St. Louis, near the ramps leading to and from Interstate Highway 70. A contingent of three hundred marched onto the highway and fanned across I-70's five lanes. Chanting "No justice, no peace!" and sitting on the highway, the throng of mostly Black protesters stopped rush-hour traffic for an hour. The coalition that organized the demonstration was broad-based in character, but its guiding nucleus was a consortium of Black-owned firms whose dispute with the Missouri Department of Transportation stemmed from the lack of state highway construction contracts to minority businesses. The contrast between the demand for better-paying jobs in 1964 and business contracts in 1999 speaks to the shifting meanings of economic justice, parity, and opportunity for African Americans in the post–Civil Rights and Black Power periods—in the North, South, and all points between.[49]

CHAPTER 10 READING QUESTIONS

1. The term *in-betweenness* is central to Clarence Lang's discussion of St. Louis and ACTION. Discuss the various attributes he assigns to this concept. He uses it synonymously with the concept "Gateway City." Using these concepts in concert examine the historical development of racial oppression in St. Louis. Elaborate on how this history of regional and racial "in-betweenness" shaped the development of ACTION and African American politics in the early 1960s.

2. Discuss St. Louis's changing political economy between 1948 and 1984. How did the downturn in industrial employment and eventual deindustrialization and transformation to a service-based economy affect African Americans, in terms of immigration, neighborhood residence, employment and occupation, and incorporation into the city's political infrastructure?

3. Assess ACTION's decision to focus on the "family breadwinner," or Black male employment, in industrial jobs as its strategy for African American upward mobility. How do you evaluate this decision? Was it sexist, based on myths that Black women's employment was designed to emasculate Black men and that they were better paid than Black men, or was it a realistic evaluation of the structural sexism that limited women to gendered occupations that paid them less than men?

4. Trace the development of the Black Freedom Movement in St. Louis from the World War II–era protests through the early 1980s. Describe the strategy and tactics, ideology, discourse, symbols, and practices of ACTION. Discuss the relationship between ACTION and leading African American organizations during this period. Describe and evaluate the different strategies and tactics utilized by the National Association for the Advancement of Colored People, the Congress for Racial Equality, and the Black United Front.

Notes

This chapter is a revision of an article, "Between Civil Rights and Black Power in the Gateway City: The Action Committee to Improve Opportunities for Negroes (ACTION), 1964–75," published in *Journal of Social History* 37 (Spring 2004): 725–54. The author thanks Jim Barrett, Sundiata Keita Cha-Jua, Minkah Makalani, Jennifer Hamer, Dave Roediger, Katharine Douglass, Juliet E. K. Walker, Dina Young, Doris A. Wesley, Peter Stearns, Carol Sturz, Helen A. Neville, Ted Koditschek, and Vernon Burton.

1. Begun in the 1930s, and completed in the late 1960s, the Jefferson National Expansion Memorial was envisioned as a sprawling park on St. Louis's central waterfront area. The monument commemorated President Thomas Jefferson's Louisiana Purchase from France in 1803 (which brought the future territories of Louisiana, Arkansas, Missouri,

Iowa, Minnesota, Nebraska, and Kansas into the fledgling United States), and the Lewis and Clark expedition west of the Mississippi. Urban planners adopted architect Eero Saarinen's design for the stainless-steel Gateway Arch in 1948.

2. I capitalize the term *Civil Rights* when alluding to the mass direct action, nonviolent protest tactics, and liberal ideology that dominated African American social movement activity roughly from the 1950s to the mid-1960s. This is meant to distinguish the concept from more general usages of "civil rights."

3. I use the term *Black* to denote a racial-national and political identity. I use it interchangeably with the designation *African American*.

4. Robert J. Moore Jr., "Showdown under the Arch: The Construction Trades and the First 'Pattern or Practice' Equal Employment Opportunity Suit, 1966," *Gateway Heritage* 15 (1994–1995): 30–43; Negro Scrapbook, vol. 2, compiled by the Missouri Historical Society Library and Research Center, hereafter cited as MHS. See also George Lipsitz, *A Life in the Struggle: Ivory Perry and the Culture of Opposition* (Philadelphia: Temple University Press, 1988), 84–85; and Thomas J. Sugrue, "Affirmative Action from Below: Civil Rights, the Building Trades, and the Politics of Racial Equality in the Urban North, 1945–1969," *Journal of American History* 91 (2004): 145–73.

5. Armstead L. Robinson and Patricia Sullivan, eds., *New Directions in Civil Rights* (Charlottesville: University Press of Virginia, 1991); Charles M. Payne, *I've Got the Light of Freedom: The Organizing Tradition and the Mississippi Freedom Struggle* (Berkeley and Los Angeles: University of California Press, 1995); Timothy B. Tyson, "Robert F. Williams, 'Black Power,' and the Roots of the African American Freedom Struggle," *Journal of American History* 85 (1998): 540–71; Tyson, *Radio Free Dixie: Robert F. Williams and the Roots of Black Power* (Chapel Hill: University of North Carolina Press, 1999); Thomas M. Spencer, *The St. Louis Veiled Prophet Celebration: Power on Parade, 1877–1995* (Columbia: University of Missouri Press, 2000), 114–39; Peniel E. Joseph, "Waiting till the Midnight Hour: Reconceptualizing the Heroic Period of the Civil Rights Movement, 1954–1965," *Souls* 2 (2000): 6–17. See also Jeanne F. Theoharis and Komozi Woodard, eds., *Freedom North: Black Freedom Struggles Outside the South, 1940–1980* (New York: Palgrave Macmillan, 2003).

6. Clayborne Carson, "Civil Rights Reform and the Black Freedom Struggle," in *The Civil Rights Movement in America,* edited by Charles W. Eagles (Jackson: University Press of Mississippi, 1986), 19–32.

7. William Barnaby Faherty, *St. Louis: A Concise History,* 3d ed. (St. Louis: Masonry Institute of St. Louis, 1999); Joe William Trotter Jr., *The African American Experience* (Boston: Houghton Mifflin, 2001), 181; Jon C. Teaford, *Cities of the Heartland: The Rise and Fall of the Industrial Midwest* (Bloomington: Indiana University Press, 1993).

8. Afro-Americans in St. Louis, Collection 36, Folders 2–20, Western Historical Manuscript Collection, University of Missouri at St. Louis, hereafter cited as WHMC; James Neal Primm, *Lion of the Valley: St. Louis, Missouri, 1764–1980,* 3d ed. (St. Louis: Missouri Historical Society Press, 1998); Lana Stein, *St. Louis Politics: The Triumph of Tradition* (St. Louis: Missouri Historical Society Press, 2002), 13–26; Katharine T. Corbett and Mary E. Seematter, "'No Crystal Stair': Black St. Louis, 1920–1940," *Gateway Heritage* 16 (1995): 82–88.

9. Segregation Scrapbook, MHS; The Ville, Collection 5, Folders 1–2, WHMC; Paul Dennis Brunn, "Black Workers and Social Movements of the 1930s in St. Louis" (Ph.D. diss., Washington University, 1975), 91–101.

10. Mary Kimbrough and Margaret W. Dagen, *Victory without Violence: The First Ten Years of the St. Louis Committee of Racial Equality (CORE), 1947–1957* (Columbia: University of Missouri Press, 2000); August Meier and Elliott Rudwick, *CORE: A Study in the Civil Rights Movement, 1942–1968* (New York: Oxford University Press, 1973); Aldon D. Morris, *The Origins of the Civil Rights Movement: Black Communities Organizing for Change* (New York: Free Press, 1984), 128–38.

11. Naomi W. Lede, *A Statistical Profile of the Negro in St. Louis: Research Report of the Urban League of St. Louis* (St. Louis: Urban League, 1965), 16; "'A Strong Seed Planted': The Civil Rights Movement in St. Louis, 1954–1968," Oral History Collection, Box 1, MHS.

12. Negro Scrapbook, vol. 2, MHS; "'Strong Seed Planted,'" Box 1, MHS.

13. "'Strong Seed Planted,'" Box 1, MHS; Lipsitz, *Life in the Struggle*, 76–80; Meier and Rudwick, *CORE*, 237; Clayborne Carson, *In Struggle: SNCC and the Black Awakening of the 1960s* (Cambridge: Harvard University Press, 1981).

14. Stein, *St. Louis Politics*; Primm, *Lion of the Valley*, 496–97; St. Louis City Plan Commission, *History: Physical Growth of the City of St. Louis* (St. Louis: St. Louis City Plan Commission, 1969), 34–35.

15. Ernest Calloway Papers, Collection 11, Box 3, Folder 23, WHMC; "'Strong Seed Planted,'" Box 1, MHS; Negro Scrapbook, vol. 2, MHS.

16. Lede, *Statistical Profile*, 20–22; David M. Streifford, "Racial Economic Dualism in St. Louis," *Review of Black Political Economy* 4 (1974): 63–83; Deborah Jane Henry, "Structures of Exclusion: Black Labor and the Building Trades in St. Louis, 1917–1966" (Ph.D. diss., University of Minnesota, 2002), 229.

17. ACTION circular, April 20, 1965, in author's possession.

18. Percy Green, taped interview with author, August 20, 1997; Percy Green Papers, WHMC.

19. "Local Civil Rights Groups Feud over Negro Job Progress at Phone Co.," *Argus*, April 30, 1965, A1; "Dispute Runs on Phone Co.'s Hiring Policy," *Argus*, May 7, 1965, A1; "ACTION Leaders Here Jailed in Telephone Co. Demonstration," *Argus*, June 11, 1965, A1; "ACTION Hits 'Mac' with Bias Charge," *Argus*, July 9, 1965, A1.

20. David R. Calhoun, president of the St. Louis Union Trust Company, was one example of the interconnectedness between the city's economic and civic elite. One of the three most powerful local decision makers in the early 1960s, he served simultaneously on the boards of directors of Union Electric Company, Emerson Electric, Anheuser-Busch, Monsanto Chemical, and the Stix, Baer, and Fuller department store. Similarly, J. Wesley McAfee, president of Union Electric, and W. R. Persons of Emerson Electric both served on the board of directors of St. Louis Union Trust—as did August A. Busch Jr., head of Anheuser-Busch. Like Busch, Calhoun, and Persons, aircraft manufacturer James S. McDonnell also sat on the board of First National Bank (of which Calhoun's company was the principal shareholder). See *Poor's Register of Corporations, Directors, and Executives, 1964* (New York: Standard and Poor's Corporation, 1964).

21. Spencer, *St. Louis Veiled Prophet Celebration,* 130.

22. Frantz Fanon, *The Wretched of the Earth* (New York: Grove Press, 1966).

23. Negro Scrapbook, vol. 2, MHS; Matthew J. Countryman, "Civil Rights and Black Power in Philadelphia, 1940–1971" (Ph.D. diss., Duke University, 1998), 311.

24. "ACTION Group Obstructs Veiled Prophet Spectacle," *Argus,* October 8, 1965, A1; Negro Scrapbook, vol. 2, MHS.

25. Primm, *Lion of the Valley,* 503; St. Louis City Plan Commission, *History,* 33–34; Negro Scrapbook, vol. 3, MHS; Ernest Calloway Papers Addenda, Collection 540, Box 5, Folder 128; Lipsitz, *Life in the Struggle,* 173–74.

26. "'Strong Seed Planted,'" Box 1, MHS; William L. Van Deburg, *New Day in Babylon: The Black Power Movement and American Culture, 1965–1975* (Chicago: University of Chicago Press, 1992), 230–34.

27. Green Papers, WHMC; Negro Scrapbook, vol. 3, MHS; Paula Giddings, *When and Where I Enter: The Impact of Black Women on Race and Sex in America* (New York: Bantam Books, 1984), 312–14.

28. Negro Scrapbook, vol. 3, MHS; "Strong Seed Planted," Box 1, MHS; Green, taped interview with the author.

29. "'Strong Seed Planted,'" Box 1, MHS.

30. Robert S. Lecky and H. Elliott Wright, eds., *Black Manifesto: Religion, Racism, and Reparations* (New York: Sheed and Ward, 1969).

31. Negro Scrapbook, vol. 3, MHS; Robin D. G. Kelley, *Freedom Dreams: The Black Radical Imagination* (Boston: Beacon Press, 2002), 123.

32. *Hearing before the United States Commission on Civil Rights, St. Louis, Missouri, January 14–17, 1970* (Washington, D.C.: U.S. Government Printing Office, 1970), 106.

33. Green Papers, WHMC.

34. Sugrue, "Affirmative Action from Below," 170; Rudolph Alexander Jr., "A Mountain Too High: African Americans and Employment Discrimination," *African American Research Perspectives* 9 (2003): 33–37; Henry, "Structures of Exclusion," 256, 264.

35. Negro Scrapbook, vol. 3, MHS.

36. *Counterintelligence Program (Black Nationalist Hate Groups),* microfilm reel 3 (Wilmington, Del.: Scholarly Resources, 1978); Green Papers, WHMC.

37. Joshua B. Freeman, "Hardhats: Construction Workers, Manliness, and the 1970 Pro-war Demonstrations," *Journal of Social History* 26 (Summer 1993): 725–44; Jefferson Cowie, "Nixon's Class Struggle: Romancing the New Right Worker, 1969–1973," *Labor History* 43 (2002): 257–83.

38. Manning Marable, *Race, Reform, and Rebellion: The Second Reconstruction in Black America, 1945–1990,* 2d ed. (Jackson: University Press of Mississippi, 1991), 199.

39. Henry, "Structures of Exclusion," 271; Robert L. Joiner, "St. Louis Ranked 2nd Most Depressed City in New Study," *St. Louis Post-Dispatch,* July 8, 1980, A4.

40. Joe Holleman, "Colorful Rights Activist to Work for City," *St. Louis Post-Dispatch,* November 10, 1993, A14; Henry, "Structures of Exclusion," 278–79; Theodore D. McNeal Jr., "Where Are the Construction Jobs for African-Americans?" *St. Louis Post-Dispatch,* January 21, 2002, B7.

41. Frances Fox Piven and Richard A. Cloward, *Poor People's Movements: Why They Succeed, How They Fail* (New York: Pantheon Books, 1977).

42. Charles Payne, "Debating the Civil Rights Movement: The View from the Trenches," in *Debating the Civil Rights Movement, 1945–1968,* edited by Steven F. Lawson and Charles Payne (New York: Rowman and Littlefield, 1998); Carson, "Civil Rights Reform," 23–27; Peniel E. Joseph, "Black Liberation without Apology: Reconceptualizing the Black Power Movement," *Black Scholar* 31 (2001): 2–19.

43. Dean E. Robinson, *Black Nationalism in American Politics and Thought* (Cambridge: Cambridge University Press, 2001); Michael C. Dawson, *Black Visions: The Roots of Contemporary African-American Political Ideologies* (Chicago: University of Chicago Press, 2001).

44. Vernon Burton, "Stranger in a Strange Land: Crossing Boundaries," in *Shapers of Southern History: Autobiographical Reflections,* ed. John B. Boles (Athens: University of Georgia Press, 2004), 281.

45. Theoharis and Woodard, *Freedom North,* xii.

46. Carl N. Degler, *Place over Time: The Continuity of Southern Distinctiveness* (Baton Rouge: Louisiana State University Press, 1977).

47. V. O. Key Jr., *Southern Politics in State and Nation* (New York: Alfred A. Knopf, 1949); C. Vann Woodward, *The Strange Career of Jim Crow,* 3d ed. (Oxford: Oxford University Press, 1974); Earl Black and Merle Black, *Politics and Society in the South* (Cambridge: Harvard University Press, 1987); Leon F. Litwack, *Trouble in Mind: Black Southerners in the Age of Jim Crow* (New York: Alfred A. Knopf, 1998); Charles Eagles, ed., *Is There a Southern Political Tradition?* (Jackson: University Press of Mississippi, 1996).

48. Robin D. G. Kelley, "Stormy Weather: Reconstructing Black (Inter)Nationalism in the Cold War Era," in *Is It Nation Time? Contemporary Essays on Black Power and Black Nationalism,* edited by Eddie S. Glaude Jr. (Chicago: University of Chicago Press, 2002), 67–90.

49. Ken Leiser and Paul Hampel, "Group Demands That 35 Pct. of Jobs on Project Go to Minorities," *St. Louis Post-Dispatch,* July 13, 1999, 1; Alvin A. Reid, "Protesters Turning on to Highway 40," *American,* July 15–21, 1999, 1.

11

Common Legacies, Similar Futures
African American and Latino Studies

PEDRO CABÁN

Black, Puerto Rican, and Chicano studies programs are the legacy of the militant student movements of the 1960s. In large measure the civil rights and anti–Vietnam War movements created the conditions for students to challenge the university and call for its transformation. However, the nationalist movements, in particular the Black Power movement, Young Lords, and Chicanismo were the more proximate political precipitants of the nationwide campus protests that established programs to study the oppressed racialized communities in the United States. During the 1960s, African Americans and Latinos forged multiracial and cross-class alliances and confronted the racist practices of public institutions and corporate capital. The Black, Chicano, and Puerto Rican student movements of the 1960s were important dimensions of this history of protest. During this period of social ferment, the American university became a pivotal site of political struggle for Black, Chicano, and Puerto Rican students because of its undeniable role in legitimating racial inequality and obscuring the history of racial oppression in the United States. They were keenly aware that the university was a repository of political authority and intellectual power, and had enduring connections with the U.S. state and corporate capital. Although students understood that the university was a commanding symbol of privilege and power, they believed it was more susceptible to political pressures for reform than other public and private institutions. The idea that the university was a public good, rather than the exclusive possession of the White middle and upper classes, and that it was capable of rendering service to a multiracial society, was revolutionary for its time.

For more than a century the public university, particularly the land-grant universities, went about its business often in splendid ignorance of the array of enervating forces that daily pummeled the majority of African American,

Mexican American, and Puerto Rican people. The establishment of university-based academic programs in the 1960s and 1970s that presented an alternative historical narrative of the experiences of these racialized communities was a momentous political achievement, and is one of the more enduring legacies of that decade of social upheaval and popular insurrection. The advent of Black, Chicano, and Puerto Rican studies programs inaugurated a sustained period of innovative intellectual production that documented how racial victimization was endemic to the process of nation building and capitalist development of the United States. Moreover, through their scholarship, faculty in race and ethnic studies programs documented the myriad mechanisms through which racism is perpetuated in this society and have provided the evidentiary and intellectual basis for progressive social policy.

Beyond these contributions to the research profile of academe, the Black, Chicano, and Puerto Rican studies posed four challenges to the university. First, scholars wanted to deploy the university's resources and generate new knowledge that could benefit embattled racialized communities. These scholars soon produced scholarship and critical pedagogies that ripped off the veil of self-proclaimed value neutrality and dispassionate pursuit of knowledge the university invoked to cloak it from public accountability. Second, scholars of color revealed how the university reproduced the racial hierarchies extant in society and privileged knowledge that sustained these inequities. The scholarship chastised academe for evolving into a highly insulated site of knowledge production that failed to employ its arsenal of research tools to study the history and causes of political exclusion, economic exploitation, and social marginalization of racialized communities. Third, Black, Chicano, and Puerto Rican studies programs were committed to doing research that was socially and politically relevant. This new scholarship would dismantle the racial barriers between the universities and communities and affirm the belief that particular forms of knowledge were emancipatory and not the property of the university. Finally, Black, Chicano, and Puerto Rican studies programs demonstrated that collective and collaborative interdisciplinary research was necessary to generate a new scholarship capable of radically reformulating the negative histories of racialized communities sanctioned by academe. The coalescence of these challenges or goals into a plan to transform the university, the will and capacity to put these ideas into action, and the realization that African Americans, Chicanos, and Puerto Ricans had discovered their shared history of racial victimization in the service of building empire and capitalist development were notable achievements that continue to influence the scholarship on the African American and Latino experience. These four challenges—the production of alternative scholarship and critical pedagogy, elimination of racialized hierarchies in the university, use of knowledge for community empowerment, and cross-racial and

-ethnic collaboration and collective intellectual production—were elements of a campaign to transform the university, or failing this to create autonomous academic spheres in which Black and Latino scholars could pursue innovative research without the strictures of the traditional disciplines.

Initially, the quest to transform the university met with the determined opposition of administrators and faculty. However, the university did gradually heed the criticism that it had become the preserve of White men, and in response established hundreds of academic units in race and ethnic studies and hired thousands of scholars of color. Despite these changes, the American university remains fundamentally unaltered from the institution students targeted for change more than three decades ago. It is evident now that the transformative goals of the heady era of the 1960s have not been realized. Although Black and Latino student movements of the 1960s did not radically transform higher education, their demands became the basis for a normative framework that guided the scholarship of African American and Latino studies.

African Americans and Latinos identified three areas for research and theory building that were derivative of the transformative goals advocated by the student movements. The three areas of intellectual engagement that have proved to be remarkably durable are: the subject of historical and political inquiry and the construction of identity, citizenship and the role of racialized communities in the building of empire, and cultural nationalism and class identity. These three areas can form the basis for a comparative research agenda in contemporary African American and Latino studies. It is clear that race and ethnic studies programs have been the site of significant research and writing that have transformed our understandings not only of the African American and Latino experiences but also of the larger history and politics of the United States. But in the context of the ongoing assault on African American and Latino studies programs it is also necessary to reaffirm the need for collaborative comparative research undertaken by autonomous programs of study on racialized communities.

Student Movements to Democratize the University

Although they emerged in different regions of the country and in different types of institutions, the Black, Chicano, and Puerto Rican student movements advanced similar academic objectives and shared transformative visions. Students faulted the university for failing to study the history and intellectual production of African American and Latino contributions, while it cavalierly dismissed the rich field of African American scholarship and literature as unworthy of a place in the college curriculum.

Throughout the 1960s American higher education underwent rapid expansion, and deepened its involvement in the corporate sector and government affairs. However, rampant discrimination largely excluded Black and Latino students and educators from the university. The curriculum was notable for its exclusion of "the totality of the black experience"—and, I should add, the experience of all oppressed racialized communities.[1] A report commissioned by the Ford Foundation explained that one goal of the rapid expansion of higher education was to increase the numbers of Blacks and Latinos attending the nation's colleges and universities. This new student population, which has historically been excluded from higher education, generated demands for Black, Chicano, and Puerto Rican studies programs. Some of these demands resonated with liberal faculty and administrators who believed in the integrationist ideals of the civil rights movement and believed the university had an obligation to promote social justice and improve conditions of "disadvantaged groups."[2]

The Black student movement did not promote the integrationist goals of the civil rights era. It was heavily influenced by the militancy and nationalism of the Black Power struggle for social and economic justice. According to Robert Allen, "The demand for Black studies cannot be separated from the rise of the militant black student movement of the 1960s." Indeed, in 1966, before the militant student movements galvanized the nation's campuses, the Black Panther Party had demanded an "education for our people that expose[s] the true nature of this decadent American society. We want education that teaches us our true history and our role in the present day society."[3]

The Black Power movement erupted as a militant alternative to the integrationist and reformist aspirations of the civil rights campaign and resonated deeply with educated and alienated Black youth, who viewed the university as an embodiment and defender of White privilege. Indeed, the student movement was "an institutional representation of the contemporary African American struggle for collective survival and human rights." Manning Marable observes that one of the central educational objectives of Black Studies was to advance an understanding of the "collective experience of the African diaspora" that would be the basis for a "corrective of the dominant myths, stereotypes and misinterpretations of the Black experience that prevailed." Black Studies was also proscriptive because of "its efforts to suggest paths for the constructive resolution of problems which confronted African American people." A radical critique revealed that university-sanctioned scholarship obscured the role of the state in oppressing and persecuting this segment of the American people, and facilitating the exploitation of the Black labor force by capital. According to Floyd Hayes, Black Studies "undertook to unmask the power/knowledge configuration of Eurocentrism and White cultural domination characteristic of the American academy."[4]

The Black student movement exposed the hegemony of a White supremacist mind-set—the presumption of a superior western European intellectual culture that was progressive, scientific, and neutral—in the U.S. academy. Before the advent of the Black student movement, African American history was interpreted through a "race relations paradigm" that privileged the White experience and was the basis for portrayals of African Americans as "passive victims rather than active agents." The Black student movement forced the university to cede a space for research and theorizing that "accentuated the self activity of African American people. In the new scholarship African Americans were subjects rather than objects."[5]

Many of these same concerns motivated the activism of the Puerto Rican Student Union of the City University of New York during the late 1960s. The Puerto Rican Student Union wanted to "bring the services of the university to the community which is denied the knowledge behind those 'ivy walls' because of jive requirements, that are made to keep the majority of the people ignorant."[6] The students insisted "on applying university resources to struggles and issues in the community as university-based, intellectual workers" and to empower the "non-academic community as a central subject and agent in the production" of policy-relevant knowledge.[7] The transformation of the institutions of higher education, its "content, practice and focus as it related to disenfranchised sectors of society," was an explicit goal of the Puerto Rican studies movement.[8]

Puerto Rican studies research would ideally be conducted as a collective enterprise intended to produce practical solutions for the societal ills that afflicted the community. This collaboration would displace isolated individual scholarship and ensure that public resources would be used for socially relevant policy rather than for the pursuit of personal professional advancement. The Puerto Rican activists called for an end to U.S. colonial rule and exposed the role of university-supported social science research in legitimizing colonialism. Puerto Rico studies would generate knowledge to promote the self-realization of an independent Puerto Rican political subject in the United States who would work to effect the decolonization of Puerto Rico. According to Frank Bonilla, one of the preeminent scholars in the field, Puerto Rican studies must "set out to contest effectively those visions of the world that assume or take for granted the inevitability and indefinite duration of the class and colonial oppression that has marked Puerto Rico's history."[9]

Chicano studies was the product of the Chicano movement and represented an extension of *el movimiento* into the academy.[10] The Chicano movement began as a civil rights movement that was inspired by the United Farm Workers and quickly developed a strong community and student base that waged multiple social justice campaigns in California and the Southwest. Chicano community activists fought to improve the working conditions of farmworkers, worked to end police repression and Jim Crow segregation, organized anti–Vietnam War protests, campaigned for access to quality education, and lobbied for political representation and participation.[11] In 1969 the Chicano Coordinating Council on Higher Education developed a comprehensive plan of action for Chicano community empowerment. The "Plan de Santa Bárbara" was a profoundly influential foundational document that guided the strategy of the Chicano student movement. The plan criticized the colleges and universities because "they have existed in an aura of omnipotence and infallibility," and should "be made responsible and responsive to the communities in which they are located or whose members they serve." The university was not perceived as a neutral site, but instead "has contributed mightily to the oppression of our people by its massive one-sided involvement in agri-business, urban dislocation and war, as well as by its racist admissions and employment policies."[12] The Black, Puerto Rican, and Chicano student movements developed an analysis of exploitation and marginalization of racialized communities in the United States. But their immediate task was to create a liberated zone from which to launch sustained initiatives to democratize the university and make the ivory tower accessible and responsible to people it had historically excluded. The success of these movements is measured by the willingness of the university to establish novel academic programs in Black, Chicano, and Puerto Rican studies. The scholarship developed in these programs helped rewrite a university-sanctioned historical narrative of the United States that privileged male Whiteness to the exclusion of racialized communities. However, as these programs became institutionalized in some universities, they increasingly produced academically focused scholarship and relinquished the idea of the academy as a center for revolutionary activism. I will turn now to consider the three areas of intellectual engagement that helped define Chicano, Puerto Rican, and Black Studies.

Racialized Communities and the Construction of Identities

White supremacy relies on myriad practices to justify the subjugation and exclusion of racialized communities. Denying the humanity of the oppressed by using denigrating signifiers is a powerful device to sustain the racist social order. For this reason self-identification and identity formation are important areas of inquiry and theorizing in African American and Latino studies. African Americans and Latinos share a history of creating independent self-identities to counteract racist labels that are meant to demean and degrade their humanity. They have challenged racially denigrating signifiers by creating their own racial or ethnic designations or reaffirming the integrity of a historically situated national identity. African Americans, more so than Latinos, have a history of periodically assessing the power of the prevailing self-designations to build solidarity and political consciousness. When these are found lacking, African Americans tend to define a new positive identity. Domestic political and social transformations, cultural and intellectual production, economic readjustments, and global dynamics that reverberate domestically prompt African Americans and Latinos to interrogate the utility of the prevailing identity labels. Each shift in the nomenclature is an attempt by the leadership of these communities to re-create a positive collective racial identity in a hostile environment.[13]

African Americans share a collective legacy of enslavement, political disenfranchisement, and economic exploitation. In order to deny them agency, the ideology and practice of racism methodically sought to deprive African slaves of an identity as a distinctive people, "leaving them with a sense that they were lacking a fundamental wholeness as human beings."[14] Puerto Ricans and Mexican Americans have also been positioned as subordinate racialized groups within the U.S. social and economic order. Puerto Rico was annexed in 1898, and its people remain colonial subjects of the United States. During the immediate post–World War II era, hundreds of thousands of displaced Puerto Rican agricultural workers migrated to the industrial centers of the Northeast and Chicago. Mexicans were victims of Manifest Destiny, their lands and properties were expropriated, and they were converted into foreigners within their former nation. The national and territorial governments supported efforts by Whites to eradicate Mexicans as viable political and economic forces in Texas, California, and New Mexico. Mexicans have served as an expendable, low-paid wage-labor force in the U.S. economy.

Puerto Ricans and Mexicans, both victimized by the practice of Anglo-Saxon racial superiority, were, like African Americans, constructed in the popular imagination as a people without a viable culture and lacking historical significance. Although Puerto Ricans and Mexican Americans have not typically been identified as a race of people, they are a racialized community in the United States by virtue of their presumed distinctive cultural, linguistic, or physical traits that differentiate them from the norms of Whiteness.[15] Through most of their history in the United States, Mexican Americans and Puerto Ricans have been portrayed and treated as inferior to White ethnics. As a racialized and economically oppressed people, they have been victimized by a panoply of discriminatory practices.

Unlike African Americans, Mexicans and Puerto Ricans were not an enslaved people, and formed a cultural and political consciousness that was partially shaped by their recent experiences in their native lands. The term *Chicano* was a politically constructed ethnic label of the late 1960s, the product of a search for a new identity forged by militant community activists and students as an alternative to the one created by the Mexican American Generation. The Mexican American Generation was composed of U.S.-born Mexicans and led by the middle sectors (professionals and small business), and by members of the working class who led labor unions and community organizations.[16] The goals of this generation were criticized by nationalist Chicanos as assimilationist and steeped in middle-class values. By contrast, Chicano activists created a new political identity by differentiating their militant oppositional movement from the Mexican American civil rights movement that favored assimilation.[17] Assimilation was rejected because it meant the eradication of a unique culture and the appropriation of norms and values of the dominant, and ultimately antagonistic, "Anglo" society. The goal was the unification of working-class Mexican Americans on the "basis of a nonwhite identity and culture."[18]

To do this, however, the Chicano movement sought to bifurcate the Mexican American population into a nationalist and progressive sector and an assimilationist and conservative sector. The historical record, however, amply documents Mexican American oppositional campaigns and political mobilization well before, and during, the Chicano movement. In his study of the Mexican American Generation, Mario T. García writes that this generation represents a transition to the Chicano era of the 1960s, but it is more than a transition. It possesses a character of its own, a richness of political struggle, and a deep search for identity.[19] Although criticized for accepting the legitimacy of the prevailing social order and promoting access rather than transformation, Mexican American organizations did struggle to improve the condition of Mexican Americans who "are losers in an unfairly constituted social or political system."[20]

Mexican Americans are the largest Latino population in the United States, and are concentrated primarily in California, Texas, and the Southwest. Economic, cultural, political, and linguistic differences among Mexican Americans living in these states partially explain the difficulty they have encountered in developing a universally accepted signifier. Some Mexican Americans identify as Chicano/as, while others eschew this label in favor of *tejano* (a Texan of Mexican descent) and *New Mexico hispano,* whereas others adhere to the traditional hyphenated "Mexican-American" label. The newer arrivals, including permanent immigrants, prefer to self-identify as *Mejicanos.*

The ideologically and geographically based political identities of the 1960s era of social protest are unsuited to capture the exceeding complexity of the changing Mexican American and Mexican immigrant population of today. Differences in culture, language usage, class, political attitude, and ethnic self-identification mark the growing Mexican immigrant population from the native-born Mexican Americans. The Chicana/o label still evokes an imagery of collective opposition to a racist social order, a resolve to achieve progressive social change, and a rejection of denigrating portrayals of their community. In large measure this explains the appeal of the Chicana/o label among Mexican American activists, intellectuals, educators, and artists. The once vibrant debate at the national level over the use of Hispanic or Latino signifiers has gradually subsided.

The labels *Hispanic* and *Latino* vie for prominence and are imbued with distinct ideological meanings. Since 1980, the federal government has employed "Hispanic" as a census category for individuals who indicate their origin as

"Mexican, Puerto Rican, Cuban, Central or South American or some other Hispanic origin." However, in 1997, in part as a consequence of widespread criticism of the "Hispanic" label, the Census Bureau accepted "Latino" as interchangeable with "Hispanic." Hispanic, with its implied connection to Spain and the White European lineage of privileged sectors of Latin America, stood in opposition to the image that Chicano nationalists and Puerto Ricans created of an indigenous and racially mixed people. Chicano/a and Puerto Ricans were particularly opposed to the creation and imposition by a federal government agency of a concocted label that eradicated identities formed during struggles for social justice. The term *Latino* was born of resistance to the Eurocentric demarcation of a Hispanic-origin peoples, and is the preferred term of activists, intellectuals, and college and university students. In her study on ethnic labels, Suzanne Oboler observes that the term *Hispanic* serves "to blur the distinctions between the newly affirmed national and cultural identities emphasizing indigenous and third world legacies and the concomitant respective demands made by Mexican Americans/Chicanos and Puerto Ricans." According to Frances Aparicio, *Latino* carries within it "a diverse array of competing authenticities or paradigms of identity that, together, and in conflict with each other, constitute heterogeneous experiences of various Latino national groups."[21]

Despite substantial internal difference in a community that numbers about thirty-seven million, Latinos are periodically portrayed as a distinctive racial minority that refuses to assimilate and harbors intense loyalties to their countries of origin. A provocative article by Harvard political scientist Samuel P. Huntington recently warned, "The persistent inflow of Hispanic immigrants threatens to divide the United States into two peoples, two cultures, and two languages. Unlike past immigrant groups, Mexicans and other Latinos have not assimilated into mainstream U.S. culture, forming instead their own political and linguistic enclaves—from Los Angeles to Miami—and rejecting the Anglo-Protestant values that built the American dream. The United States ignores this challenge at its peril." According to Huntington and others, the Latinos' resistance to assimilation threatens national unity and justifies restricting Latin American and Caribbean immigration. The concept of Latino/Hispanic has been reified through negation and simplification. The essence of *Latinidad* is purportedly excessive reliance on the Spanish language and a fervid adherence to cultural and religious norms and values that are antithetical to the principles on which the United States was founded. Opponents of immigration have reconstituted the Latino as a threatening racial category by virtue of these distinctive traits that they claim permanently mark Latinos as antagonistic to the dominant culture. Marable's observation that race and ethnicity are usually used interchangeably because of the centrality of Whiteness within the dominant national identity has created a "closed dialectic of race" is remarkably applicable here.[22]

In contrast to Puerto Ricans and Chicanos, African American indigenous identities were violently stripped away through enslavement. Their individual ethnicities as African peoples, with distinct cultures and languages and dialects, were essentially erased by the early to mid-1830s. By then the number of U.S.-born slaves exceeded those born in Africa, and this demographic change "delineates the demise of a preponderant African sociocultural matrix and rise of an African American one in its place."[23] Through the systematic application of repression, Blacks were denied the capacity to develop an autonomous collective self-identity. Whites formulated an identity of African Americans as an undifferentiated, culturally barren mass of inferior beings. One of the central problems of racism was the practice of Whites to define people of "African descent singularly in racial and color terms, ignoring their ethnic characteristics, which they recognized in White Americans."[24] As a consequence, African Americans "lacked a common indigenous term that corresponded to their social definition in America. . . . [T]hey had to forge a new identity and adopted a term to describe themselves rather to retain and adapt a well-established, preexisting identity and name."[25]

Michael Gomez observes that the formation of an African American collective identity emphasized race rather than ethnicity as the criterion for inclusion. For more than a half century after the abolition of slavery African Americans employed a variety of designations, but eventually the term *Negro* became accepted as the prevailing self-formed racial identity. Between 1930 to the mid-1960s, *Negro* was the primary designator when it was challenged by the rise of the Black Power movement. Black Power proponents repudiated *Negro* as a racist term imposed by Whites that denoted Black complacency and subservience. The appropriation of *Black* as the collective signifier signaled an ideological shift that rejected the assimilationist underpinnings of the Negro integrationist civil rights movement and was an explicit negation of Whiteness. Ultimately, "freedom could not be achieved without a healthy racial consciousness underscored by a strong belief in the collective Black will to change the conditions of oppression."[26]

Black Power advocates condemned racial assimilation and integration as a form of cultural suicide. In the words of Stokely Carmichael, "integration is a subterfuge for the maintenance of White supremacy." By emphasizing racial unity, Black Power sought to collapse the class differences within the black community. Black Power's "political strategy aimed then at developing a power base for a relatively autonomous black community rather than achieving civil rights for individuals or encouraging interracial contacts."[27] By the mid-1970s, *Black* had emerged as the dominant designation, but it also began to gradually lose its radical connotations and separatist rhetoric. Black Power was evolving into a strategy of accommodation to the extent that it promoted economic self-sufficiency within the prevailing political economy rather than the transformation of the racist capitalist system.

During the late 1980s, a group of prominent Black leaders initiated a campaign to create a new nomenclature that emphasized historically derived cultural attributes. The aim was to replace *Black* with *African American*. One of the main goals of the proposed name change was to give Blacks a cultural identification with their heritage and ancestral homeland. The hyphenated nomenclature evokes the history of slavery, as well as acculturation into the dominant values of White America. By advancing an image of African Americans as a culturally distinctive people with historical ties to Africa, the term emphasizes the global scale of the African Diaspora, while minimizing the idea of Blacks as an American minority whose history commenced when they landed in shackles on the shores of what was to be the United States. The "African American" nomenclature implicitly advances an integrationist discourse that positions the African American experience as one of a number of American ethnic-group experiences.

The established African American leadership moved to replace a racial label that was closely associated with an earlier period of Black nationalism, separatism, and radical politics. The new hyphenated nomenclature that linked *African* with *American* was introduced during a decidedly right-wing moment in national politics. During eight years of neoconservative rule, Reagan had orchestrated a sustained assault on social welfare, affirmative action, and civil rights protections. These regressive policies had disproportionately injured the African American community. Linking *African* with *American* was a linguistic device that simultaneously dissociated the Black American of the late 1980s from the militancy and radicalism of the 1960s Black Power movement. *African American* also implicitly disavowed the separatism as a path for racial liberation.

The history and dynamics of constructing gender-neutral self-identities that engender racial pride, a sense of collective political consciousness, and solidarity are important areas of scholarly work in African American and Latino studies. Identity formation of racialized communities is not static but contingent and variable. The self-identifiers African Americans and Latinos adopted are historically evolving and strategically formulated to mark their presence in this society. While the racial and ethnic labels are transmutable, they are always powerful assertions by a people fighting to eradicate disparaging and dehumanizing monikers that White society has imposed.

Building Empire and Restricting Citizenship

The process of state building and capitalist development in the eighteenth and nineteenth century was undertaken on the backs of enslaved, vanquished, and displaced subject peoples that formed a powerless pool of cheap, expendable labor. They were routinely denied those citizenship rights granted to Whites. African Americans, Mexicans, and Puerto Ricans had distinctive roles in the building of the American empire. By the end of the nineteenth century the U.S. nation-state had established a global economic and military presence. The century-long U.S. imperial project (from the late eighteenth to late nineteenth centuries) entailed the appropriation of continental territories through military force and by purchase and the acquisition of overseas territories through war. The genocide of indigenous Native American populations, enslavement of Africans, territorial conquest and displacement of Mexicans, and overseas expansion and colonization of Puerto Rico and the Philippines were constitutive elements of modern state building and capitalist development. The unrelenting growth of the U.S. economy during the eighteenth and nineteenth centuries required an inexhaustible supply of wage labor and millions of slaves to exploit the country's seemingly inexhaustible natural resources and supply for its burgeoning industries.

In 1846, as it was steadily building its industrial and technological capability, military capacity, and financial prowess, the United States waged war on a politically unstable and economically troubled Mexico. Mexico was defeated and under the terms of the Treaty of Guadalupe de Hidalgo ceded approximately one million acres of its national territory to the United States. The United States annexed expansive agricultural lands and valuable natural resources, acquired ports in the Pacific, and with the discovery of gold in California notably increased the nation's capital stock.[28] The treaty granted the United States authority "for the removal of the Indians from any portion of the said territories, or its being settled by citizens of the United States." The status of Indians, who were referred to "as a savage tribe," was dramatically altered, for under the Mexican political system Indians were citizens. Under U.S. law Indians enjoyed no such privilege.

The War of 1898 was a new phase in the evolution of the U.S. empire building. The U.S. decision to embark on this imperialistic war reflected the nation's role as an ascendant global power in need of overseas naval bases and markets. The U.S. victory against a decaying Spanish power in 1898 significantly expanded the reach of the U.S. empire. The vanquished Spanish were forced to cede Puerto Rico and the Philippines and to grant Cuba its formal independence, although the nation became a de facto colony of the United States until 1933. The United States acquired not only sovereignty over strategically significant territories but also jurisdiction over the lives of the eleven million inhabitants on that island. Although as colonial subjects Puerto Ricans legally became U.S. "nationals," the U.S. Constitution was not extended to Puerto Rico, and its people were not granted citizenship. The Puerto Rican experience was one of colonization, and not one of extermination, enslavement, or territorial displacement. Rather, with its population of nearly one million impoverished people, Puerto Rico became an important sugar-producing territory for the U.S. economy and a source of extraordinary profits for an oligopoly of vertically integrated sugar corporations.

The racial politics of empire had consequences for African Americans. After the U.S. Supreme Court upheld Congress's right to deny subject peoples in the territories the protections accorded by the Constitution, authorities routinely sanctioned separation of Blacks from White society in education, transportation, political disfranchisement and exclusion from juries, and involuntary servitude.[29] In turn, a legacy of treating Native Americans and Blacks inferior to Whites influenced U.S. policy toward the colonial peoples of the Philippines and Puerto Rico.

By the time the Supreme Court ruled that Congress had the constitutional authority to deny citizenship and the franchise to the people of Puerto Rico, the doctrine of denying Blacks these constitutional protections had been established for seven decades. Citizenship and Whiteness were indelibly linked, and in fact the former was one of the privileges bestowed to the latter. In 1842 in the nonslaveholding state of Michigan, a senate committee asserted, "Our government is formed by, for the benefit of, and to be controlled by the descendants of European nations." Consequently, granting Blacks suffrage would be "inexpedient and impolitic."[30] The Supreme Court ruled in the 1856 *Dred Scott* case that Blacks as individuals who had "no rights which white men were bound to respect" could not be citizens under the U.S. Constitution.

Mexican subjects in the conquered territories were also denied equal citizenship under the Treaty of Guadalupe de Hidalgo. Mexicans who chose to remain in the ceded territories after one year, "without having declared their intention to retain the character of Mexicans, shall be considered to have elected to become citizens of the United States." This, however, did not mean automatic U.S. citizenship. Mexicans would be admitted "at the proper time (to be judged by the Congress of the United States) to the enjoyment of the rights of citizens of the United States." The treaty was notable for the U.S. government's abject failure to enforce the provisions for equal citizenship and protection of the civil and property rights of the Mexicans and their descendants. Richard Delgado observes that the treaty was modeled on those drawn between Indian tribes and the U.S. government, and treated with comparable disregard. The Mexicans' "land and property were stolen, rights were denied, language and culture suppressed, opportunities for employment, education, and political representation were thwarted."[31]

The imperialist crusade of the 1890s and Manifest Destiny were thoroughly imbued with a racial ideology that extolled the superiority of the Anglo-Saxon people. Puerto Ricans, Blacks, Mexicans, and Native Americans were collectively portrayed as inferior races, and as lacking the moral attributes, intellectual capacities, and industry of the Anglo-Saxon master race. This racial logic was deployed to deprive these "subject peoples" the first-class citizenship rights reserved for White men. In the 1848 Senate debates on the grant of U.S.

citizenship to Mexicans, South Carolina senator John Calhoun declared, "No race but the Caucasian race should be incorporated into the Union." After Congress enacted limitations on the grant of citizenship, the *New Orleans Picayune* reported that the United States would not be exposed to the dangers of admitting a "race of men, differing from us in language, religion, descent . . . to equal participation."[32]

The identical rationale was employed in 1898 to deny Puerto Ricans citizenship. Lawrence Lowell, president of Harvard University, believed that political equality should be applied "rigorously only to our own race, and to those whom we can assimilate rapidly."[33] The Treaty of Paris of 1898 did not obligate the United States to grant citizenship to the inhabitants of Puerto Rico and the Philippines. The treaty simply noted that Congress would determine the "civil rights and political status of the native inhabitants of the territories." Not until 1917 did Congress grant Puerto Ricans citizenship. However, it was a second-class citizenship that denied Puerto Ricans residing on the island representation in Washington, as well as the presidential vote. The United States employed an unmistakable colonial logic to justify granting Puerto Ricans U.S. citizenship in 1917. On the eve of U.S. entry into World War I, the head of the Bureau of Insular Affairs, the agency with jurisdiction over Puerto Rico and the counterpart of the Bureau of Indian Affairs, counseled the Congress that "the people of Puerto Rico should be made citizens of the United States to make clear that Puerto Rico is to remain permanently connected to the United States."[34]

Booker T. Washington became involved in the imperial project of Americanizing the colonial subjects. He believed that the United States had the "responsibility of educating and elevating" about eight hundred thousand blacks in Cuba and Puerto Rican, this in "addition to the problem of educating eight million negroes in our Southern States and ingrafting them into American citizenship." According to Washington, "The experience acquired in the education of my own race . . . will prove most valuable in elevating the blacks of the West Indian islands." He reported that a "few of the most promising men and women" from Puerto Rico and Cuba were brought to the Tuskegee Institute "with the idea of getting the methods of industrial education pursued . . . at Tuskegee permanently and rightly started" in the islands.[35] Puerto Ricans were also sent to the Carlisle Industrial Training School that had been established to facilitate the assimilation of the Native Americans. The United States attempted to convert Puerto Ricans into bilingual and bicultural colonial subjects through compulsory universal public education that stressed U.S. history and English-language instruction. The Americanization project in Puerto Rico was a process of state-led acculturation designed to eradicate the indigenous culture.

Imperialism and Manifest Destiny entailed the subjugation of the indigenous people of the conquered territories. Conquest was fueled by a racist ideology that extolled the civilizing mission of the "superior" Anglo-Saxon people and portrayed Mexicans, Native Americans, and Puerto Ricans as racially inferior and dependent but potentially redeemable. The parallels between a suprema-cist racial ideology that was employed to subordinate African Americans and an Anglo-Saxon racialist ideology used to legitimate colonization and Mani-fest Destiny are compelling. U.S. elites believed in their inherent capability to educate these "dependent peoples" to be good workers and subjects imbued with Protestant virtues of industry, thrift, and discipline. However, even the most ardent proponents of civic education and training accepted the idea that Blacks, Puerto Ricans, and Mexicans were incapable of ever equaling the su-perior Anglo-Saxon values. Although these racialized groups were potentially redeemable as functioning members of the American polity, the acquisition of full citizenship rights and equal treatment before the law would be a slow and deliberate process, much slower and more deliberate than for White, non-Anglo-Saxon immigrants.

Cultural and Economic Nationalism

Black nationalism had a pronounced effect on the formation of Chicano "eth-nic militancy."[36] The Black, Chicano, and Puerto Rican movements developed a militant cultural nationalism that emphasized their shared attributes as poor and oppressed racialized communities. These communities were concentrated in highly segregated regions of the country and were economically exploited and politically marginalized. The urban ghettos, *colonias*, rural "Black Belts," were, and remain, racially defined and culturally distinct enclaves. Cultural national-ists claimed direct ties to an imagined moral and cultural homeland. African Americans, Chicanos, and Puerto Ricans sought to draw on a rich legacy that evoked a historical continuity that transcended their shameful experience as oppressed people in this country.

Afrocentrism is a conceptual framework for analyzing the trajectory and global dimensions of the African American experience in the United States. It advances a historically grounded analytical perspective that counters the hege-monic paradigm of Eurocentrism. The impact of Afrocentrism in framing the academic focus of Black Studies is much more pronounced than cultural nation-alism has been for Chicano and Puerto Rican studies. Afrocentrism introduced a necessary critique of Western scholarship, particularly its role in creating a distorted and damaging portrayal of the African American. Afrocentricity ex-posed Eurocentrism as an ideological project to socialize African Americans into accepting the legitimacy of White supremacist racial order and their own racially determined inferiority. According to Molefi Kete Asante, Eurocentric thought asserts that "the particular reality of Europeans is the sum total of the human experience. It imposes Eurocentric realities as *universal*."[37] Afrocentric scholars consider that "the curriculum is the major vehicle for the transmission and legitimation of White Supremacy."[38] Afrocentricity's critique of European (and by extension U.S.) thought as essentially a White supremacist discourse to justify and enforce a racial hierarchy is relevant for understanding the U.S. imperial project in the Caribbean, Philippines, and areas of Mexico appropriated by the United States.

The Afrocentric critique of Eurocentrism resembles the Mexican American and Latino challenges to Americanization. For Mexican Americans and Puerto Ricans, Americanization was an ideology that diminished them as a people as it proclaimed the biological superiority of the Anglo-Saxon race. In the 1960s Mexican Americans and Puerto Ricans constructed national narratives that reaffirmed the centrality of their culture and history as an antidote to the disparaging images promulgated by White supremacist thought. The early Chicano movement adopted a cultural nationalist perspective that emphasized the history of the Mexican American as a displaced, racialized, and economically exploited minority. The Chicano movement articulated a cultural nationalism based on an idealized, mythical construct of the indigenous cultures of Mexico. El Plan Espiritual de Aztlán was imbued with profound cultural significance and ethnic pride. "We declare the independence of our Meztizo nation. We are a Bronze People with a Bronze Culture. . . . We are a Nation, We are a Union of Free Pueblos, We are Aztlán-Por la Raza Todo, Fuera de la Raza Nada."[39]

The plan was an important ideological tool aimed at building solidarity and ethnic pride to counteract the reality of life for the Mexican American: "Segregated, maligned, despised, subjugated, destroyed for what he is, and barred from becoming what he would be, the Mexican American turns toward a new path." With this resurrected Chicano identity, "he can face the onslaught of cultural racism perpetuated by the Anglo." The new ethnic myth sought to link Mexican Americans to their indigenous, non-European heritage. One scholar notes that "with its emphasis on indigenism, self-determination . . . the Plan inspired a romantic return to the indigenous roots of 'Mexicanidad' and a firm rejection of both the Spanish and Anglo 'colonizing' influences."[40] Cultural nationalists constructed a racially bifurcated portrayal of society that ignored differentiation within the racialized communities. They created a conflict model of ethnic relations in which beleaguered Chicanos were pitted against a hostile Anglo population.

The socially imagined Chicanocentric and Afrocentric identities, that is, an essentialist racialized subject with a monolithic cultural heritage and homogeneous class identity, did generate criticism as a simplistic representation and an ideologically motivated distortion of the complexity of African American and Mexican American life. Chicano nationalists were criticized for ignoring differences in social-class position, political ideology, and cultural backgrounds of the Mexican American population. The Chicano movement's construction of a homogeneous ethnoracial community was criticized as based on a myth of a collectively shared experience. Many opposed "a regnant Chicano nationalism [that] sought to establish Chicanos as a . . . monolithic group."[41] Mexican culture "is a multidimensional phenomenon," and proponents of Chicano nationalism should not "lose sight of the heterogeneous origins of Mexican American culture."[42] Similar challenges were directed at Afrocentricity, for being "an organic, elitist, often male-centered conception of black identity that obscures differences within the black population."[43]

Feminists attacked Chicano cultural nationalism for its male-centric and homophobic construction of idealized nationhood. Feminists exposed the numerous ways that the Chicano construction of *Aztlán* perpetuated sexual and racial oppression.[44] Sosa Ridell's stinging critique of *el movimiento*'s sexism and her elucidation of the Chicanas' double oppression (racism and sexism) had a major impact on the debates of Chicano/a subjectivities.[45] Afrocentricity has similarly been criticized for advancing a Black nationalist perspective steeped in "masculinist, heterosexist rhetoric," and for its portrayal of homosexuals as "deviant, degenerate and unmanly."[46] The Afrocentric perspective that privileges a male-centric interpretative framework has been challenged by an incisive and academically rich feminist scholarship.

During the 1960s Black and Chicano nationalists employed the concept of internal colonialism to elucidate the relationship between racialization and domestic (U.S.) capitalist development, noting in the process the similar properties of European colonialism and the consequences for third world peoples. Internal colonialism imparted a material logic to racialization, and emphasized that racially grounded exploitative economic practices were constitutive of the capitalist order in the United States.[47]

Internal colonialism was adopted by the Chicano movement as the dominant paradigm to explain exploitation and helped crystallize a Chicano nationalist ideology that projected class homogeneity. The internal-colony model resonated deeply with a generation of militant Chicano students who identified with its emphasis on economic exploitation, Marxism, and rampant racism against Mexican Americans. Tomás Almaguer was among the first Chicano scholars to apply internal colonialism to the Chicano condition. He defined "internal colonialism . . . as the colonization of a group of people by the common process of social oppression that developed out of the imperialist era of classic colonialism." The barrios and *colonias* served a similar function as the ghettos and rural Black Belts. These highly segregated areas in the Southwest "were once the sites of migrant labor camps and living facilities for section gangs of the railroads."[48]

The racial oppression and economic exploitation of African Americans were analyzed in the context of capitalist development, in its domestic and international dimensions. The internal-colonialism concept was also integral to the early Afrocentrists, including Maylana Karenga and black revolutionary nationalists, including Kwame Ture/Stokely Carmichael. Proponents of internal colonialism envisioned a landscape in which Blacks were forced to live in segregated, poverty-ridden ghettos. Ghettos and rural "Black Belts" functioned as domestic colonies that provided the White-controlled political economy a vast pool of cheap labor and functioned as markets. Stokely Carmichael referred to African Americans as "a colony within the United States. . . . [T]he black communities in America are victims of white imperialism and colonial exploitation." African American and Chicano nationalists appropriated the internal colonialism as a heuristic analytical device that imparted an imagined economic uniformity to their racialized communities. Ben L. Martin observed that the Black elite portrayed Blacks "as uniformly disadvantaged in socio-economic status, contributing to stereotyping as poor, uneducated, unemployed, and dependent, despite a large majority living above the poverty line."[49] Internal colonialism was an element in a strategy to create a political consciousness that portrayed exclusion and impoverishment as structural properties of a racialized capitalist order, and not the failings of these vulnerable and exploited communities.

Despite its contributions to early revolutionary thought, internal colonialism's weakness lay in theorizing class conflict as an antagonistic racial binary (people of color versus Whites). It reduced the complexity of political struggle to an "us versus them" mentality. This is the deficiency that Marable also observes in Afrocentrists who "frequently retreat to a bipolar model of race relations, which delineates the contours of the black experience from a photographic negative of whiteness."[50] The deficiencies of the internal-colony paradigm for progressive research and political action are also apparent. Internal colonialism subsumed class, and the multiplicity of differences that emerge from class distinctions, into a hypothesized common ethnicity that "marked the Chicano as the other." By setting up a conflict model that positioned Anglos against Chicanos, internal colonialism seemed to create an imperative for researchers to study Mexican American working-class exploitation and political organization to the exclusion of other features of the Mexican American experience.[51] In 1973, with the founding of the National Association of Chicano studies, internal colonialism was subjected to further withering critiques for its essentialist, sexist tendencies and rejected by some for being "incorrect, ineffective, and ultimately a counter revolutionary theory" that failed to "correspond to the objective situation of minorities in the United States."[52]

Puerto Rican activists and scholars did not see the theoretical or ideological utility of internal colonialism. Puerto Rico was a "classic colony" that exported almost a third of its population to the United States during the post–World War II era to labor in the burgeoning factories of the Northeast and Chicago. Nonetheless, Puerto Rican settlement patterns and their relationship to the economy closely paralleled those of African Americans and Chicanos. Puerto Ricans settled in highly segregated urban areas near the factories and experienced the same poverty, neglect, and exploitation as other racialized communities. Puerto Rican scholars and activists did not develop a cultural nationalist paradigm to apprehend the Puerto Rican experience in the United States because Puerto Rico was a nation under colonial rule. Their political nationalism was heavily shaped by decades of anticolonial struggle. Political organizations, including the Young Lords Party, Puerto Rican Socialist Party, Puerto Rican Student Union, and Movement for National Liberation, were all committed to achieving Puerto Rican independence. They also agreed that the deplorable economic and social conditions of Puerto Ricans in the metropolis were the direct consequence of colonialism and capitalism, and shared the belief that independence was a necessary condition for social justice. However, they were divided on the "national question." Were Puerto Ricans on the island and in the metropolis members of one nation, or were there two separate Puerto Rican nationalities? Should Puerto Ricans organize around a "national" identity or a class identity?[53]

Nationalists (the One Nation view) believed in pursuing a militant anti-imperialist strategy that subordinated the struggle for social justice in the United States to the struggle for independence in Puerto Rico. They argued that the defining characteristic of Puerto Ricans was their nationality, their status as an identifiable racial and ethnic community with a common language, history, and culture and unwavering loyalty to Boriquen. This identity is not dependent on whether Puerto Ricans reside in the United States or Puerto Rico; residence was not determinative of nationality. Puerto Rican independence was a necessary condition to achieve social and economic justice for the Puerto Rican "nation," and the anticolonial struggle had to be waged in the colony as well as the metropolis. Advocates of class analysis (Two Nation view) called for class solidarity and revolutionary activity in the metropolis to overthrow or reform the capitalist order as a necessary condition to achieve independence on the island.[54] They argued that Puerto Ricans in the United States constituted a racialized oppressed community that retained its cultural distinctiveness but suffered economic exploitation and social exclusion. Consequently, the struggles for economic and social justice had to be waged in the metropolis by these "exiled" Puerto Ricans. This campaign for equality could not be subordinated to the struggle for national emancipation but was to be waged simultaneously. The debate was never resolved. However, the declining urgency of the independence struggle and gradual realization that Puerto Ricans in the United States are a permanent racialized community have essentially made the debate on the national question moot.

The debate over the Puerto Rican nation was a consequence of the Puerto Rican diaspora in the aftermath of World War II. The hundreds of thousands of Puerto Ricans who migrated to the United States were primarily poor, overwhelmingly rural, and ethnoracially similar. They formed a relatively homogeneous group and joined a low-paid working class in the manufacturing sector. The Puerto Rican student movement noted this characteristic of the diaspora and appreciated the implications for praxis. "Unlike the great forced migrations from Africa during the slave trade, the Puerto Rican migration was one of an entire people. We brought not only our families intact . . . but our leaders, our culture. We brought our culture with no intention of forgetting it for some jive gringo culture."[55]

Unfortunately, the Puerto Rican independence movement incorrectly deduced that the class and cultural characteristics of the diaspora Puerto Rican were representative of the population that remained in the colony. However, in the context of a complex interplay of class, racial, gender, and ideological crosscurrents on the island of Puerto Rico, any attempt to construct an essentialist version of a distinctly Puerto Rican worldview that fused the experiences of U.S. resident Puerto Ricans and those living on the island was doomed. The accumulated weight of the internal contradictions of life in the colony clashed with the reality of racialized Puerto Ricans in the United States who functioned as a proletariat in exile. The complicated racial history of the small nation, which was based on a fluid mixture of indigenous Taino, African, and European lineages, made a Puerto Rican variant of Afrocentricity unlikely, and impeded efforts at constructing an essentialized racialized subject.

Conclusion

Although African American, Chicano, and Puerto Rican studies developed independently as distinct academic fields, during their formative period they shared similar analytical and political concerns. Programs of study on racialized communities were closely associated with the militant social movements of the 1960s. While Black, Chicano, and Puerto Rican communities challenged a racist political order, students and professors called for transforming a comparably racist university system. This synergy between community-based social movements and working-class students who came from these communities helps to partially explain similar analytical perspectives and research objectives among nascent academic programs. Identity, citizenship, and economic exploitation formed the corpus of scholarship of these programs. These were also themes central to the civil rights and Black Power movements, the Young Lords and the Puerto Rican independence movement, and the United Farm Workers, Crusade for Justice, and Chicano Youth Movement.

A new scholarship written from the perspective of racialized communities on identity formation in a hostile environment, racialized hierarchies and citizenship, capitalism, and racially defined labor exploitation helped forge a new understanding of race in the United States. Exploration of these themes also contributed to the elaboration of a more nuanced and complex appreciation for political dynamics within these racialized communities in their campaigns to reform a racist social order. African Americans, Chicanos or Mexican Americans, and Puerto Ricans occupied comparable positions as subject populations that were trapped in a web of exploitative relations. They were also victims of racist policies and practices that denied them first-class citizenship and deprived them of the full panoply of constitutional protections. Moreover, these racialized communities shared a common history as exploited labor in the service of the U.S. empire. Each of these racialized communities also sought to write a new history. This history drew on a real or imagined cultural legacy and helped fashion racial and ethnic pride and a new political consciousness. The cultural nationalism of African Americans, Chicanos, and Puerto Ricans equated identity with objective class position. Activists and scholars drew on the work of Marx and Lenin to explain the construction of racially segregated poor economic enclaves as intrinsic to capitalist development in the United States.

All of these approaches helped create the intellectual foundations for modern programs of study on racialized communities. Each contributed new ways of knowing and of reinterpreting a skewed history of this nation's formation that privileged its Anglo-Saxon roots. The scholarship was provocative, highly controversial, but theoretically underdeveloped. For these reasons it forced a debate within African American, Chicano, and Puerto Rican studies that ultimately strengthened the scholarship on racialized communities. Some have rejected the formative scholarship as celebrations of victimization. But more serious observers contextualized their critique by noting that the scholarship was partially flawed because of the urgency to develop alternative conceptualizations to biased university-sanctioned scholarship. Some of the scholarship generated in African American and Latino studies replicated the ills of society. The male-centric, fiercely antifeminist, and obsessively homophobic orientations of these academic fields during their formative periods reflected the biases of militant young activists who lived in a political culture that celebrated masculinity and the legitimacy of a gendered hierarchy. The sexism and absence of gender equality set the context for profoundly important feminist critiques. As feminists interrogated gendered dynamics within racialized communities, they launched a critique that exposed White privilege within the national feminist movement.

Despite its theoretical limitations, internal colonialism was a heuristic conceptual device that exposed the linkages between imperialism and a racialized working class in the United States. Racialized communities were constructed, for ideological reasons, as culturally homogeneous and uniformly poor. By portraying society as a racial binary (African American versus Whites, Chicanos versus Anglos, colonizer versus colonized), the scholarship created a context for others to undertake sophisticated explorations of internal differentiation within racialized communities. Chicano cultural nationalism and Afrocentricity, internal colonialism, and undifferentiated racial and ethnic identity constructs are no longer the defining concerns of African American and Latino studies. Yet the contribution of these concepts to building a knowledge base for the emerging academic fields of race and ethnic studies should be recognized. The controversial scholarship provoked theoretical debates and empirical inquiries that would not otherwise have taken place in academe.

In this chapter I have tried to make the case that comparative studies on racialized communities stand to make significant contributions to the understanding of this society and can produce research that helps to shape viable policies for community development and advance a reinterpretation of American society from the perspective of racialized groups that have historically been powerless and marginalized. The revolutionary fervor for transforming the university has waned, if not disappeared, in the years since the first battle cries for ethnic studies at San Francisco State. A new generation of scholars has discarded static notions of ethnic and racial group identity in favor of more fluid, nuanced, and multidimensional identities that are continually negotiated in a dynamic multicultural environment. Yet the three general areas of inquiry that were central during the formative stage of these programs of study continue to orient research, although the scope of these concerns has been considerably expanded.

The existence of hundreds of academic units in African American, Chicano, and Latino studies, as well as the nominal inclusion in the curriculum of traditional departments' courses on racialized communities, suggests for some that significant institutional transformation has been attained. Conversely, it may suggest that a professionalized academic body of Black and Latino scholars, with limited commitment to activism and community empowerment, has gained ascendancy. Carlos Muñoz has commented on the decline of activist scholarship and notes that "enduring social relations reproduced by the structure of the university" compelled most scholars interested in professional advancement "to comply with the dictates of the traditional disciplines" and eschew training scholar-activists, which was one of the priorities of the Chicano student movement. One prominent African American scholar notes that "today the 'studies,' having been institutionalized, struggle mostly for their maintenance and expansion, and to some degree for recognition from endowed parental authorities."[56]

This incisive observation does capture the reality of the situation for many programs. Programs of study on racialized communities tend to operate in relative isolation; their "radicalism" is often confined to institutional survival or mere acquisition of resources. Yet this situation is not the result of programs of study having been institutionalized as equal academic participants. Rather, it is quite the opposite. Academic legitimacy of African American and Latino studies is withheld, and they are rarely seen as first-class citizens in the university community. Their contributions to the academic mission of the university are seldom acknowledged. The function of these units is portrayed primarily as enhancing diversity or as evidence of the university's unwavering commitment to affirmative action.

University administrators have exhibited demonstrably greater enthusiasm for the study of comparative racial formations through American studies programs, Centers for the Study of Race or Ethnicity, or ethnic studies programs than they have in fortifying Latino and African American studies as autonomous sites of knowledge production and instruction. Such comprehensive programs of study are supposed to create an environment for much needed comparative studies of racialized communities. In reality, however, these centers "are conceived as interdisciplinary teaching and research units that do not have the normative commitment to activist scholarship, transformative politics and community development that were the central tenets" of the student movements.[57]

What is at risk is the autonomy of African American and Latino studies to independently develop research agendas that advance our understanding of how race in America functions. In the absence of academic autonomy, scholarship that does not address discipline-based concerns and meet the idiosyncratic standards of academic excellence will seldom be validated. It is nonetheless indispensable to promote the comparative study of racial formations. I am convinced that comparative work across racialized communities will enhance the intellectual and political weight that university administrators and faculty are willing to accord African American and Latino studies. The most intellectually promising avenue for generating such scholarship is through formal administrative arrangements that create an environment conducive to intellectual cross-fertilization, collaborative research, and joint conceptual exploration of the history of racialized communities in the United States. The intellectual production generated in autonomous academic units feeds into this collaborative research endeavor. In this essay I have sought to demonstrate that given their similar developmental trajectory, African American and Latino studies are positioned to embark on a program of rigorous comparative social inquiry and theorizing.

CHAPTER 11 READING QUESTIONS

1. Why does Cabán argue that the university became a "pivotal site" for Black, Chicano/a, and Puerto Rican struggles for social justice and self-determination? Do you find his argument convincing? Why or why not?

2. According to Cabán, what are the three areas of scholarship and teaching that formed the crux of Black and Latino/a studies intervention? How can the three thematic areas identified by Cabán form the basis of a project in comparative domestic racial studies?

3. Cabán argues that Black and Latino/a student movements failed to "radically transform" U.S. higher education; in his view, in what ways did they succeed? What are the legacies of the Black and Latino/a student movements of the 1960s and '70s that contemporary student activists can build on?

4. Analyze Cabán's argument that the creation of the nomenclature *African American* was a move to dissociate Black America from the militant and radical sixties and to return an integrationist project to strategic hegemony in that community.

5. Explicate the theory of internal colonialism. Why did it become the dominant paradigm by which both Blacks and Chicano scholar activists interpreted the conditions of their respective people during the 1960s and '70s?

6. Why did nationalism and self-determination supersede integration as the dominant paradigm for militant and radical Black, Chicano/a, and Puerto Rican scholar-activists?

Notes

1. Robert L. Allen, "Politics of the Attack on Black Studies," *Black Scholar* 6 (1974): 3.

2. Nathan I. Huggins, *Afro-American Studies: A Report to the Ford Foundation* (New York: Ford Foundation, 1985), 21.

3. Allen, "Politics of the Attack," 2; William L. Van DeBurg, ed., *Modern Black Nationalism* (New York: New York University Press, 1997), 249.

4. Floyd W. Hayes, "Taking Stock: African American Studies," *Western Journal of Black Studies* 18, no. 3 (1994): 154; Manning Marable, *Beyond Black and White* (London: Verso, 1995), 109; Hayes, "Taking Stock," 155.

5. Helen A. Neville and Sundiata K. Cha-Jua, "Kufundisha: Toward a Pedagogy for Black Studies," *Journal of Black Studies* 28, no. 4 (1998): 448.

6. Puerto Rican Student Union, "Somos Puertorriquenos y Estamos Despertando" (New York: Puerto Rican Student Union, 1969), 17.

7. Frances Aparicio, "Reading the 'Latino' in Latino Studies: Toward Re-imagining Our Academic Location," *Discourse: Latina/o Discourse in Academe* 21, no. 3 (1999): 14; Josephine Nieves, "Puerto Rican Studies: Roots and Challenges," in *Toward a Renaissance of Puerto Rican Studies: Ethnic and Area Studies in University Education,* edited by Maria E. Sanchez (Highland Lakes, N.J.: Atlantic and Research Publications, 1987), 6.

8. Jesse M. Vazquéz, "Puerto Rican Studies in the 1990s: Taking the Next Turn in the Road," *Centro: Journal of the Centro de Estudios Puertorriqueños* 2, no. 6 (1989): 10.

9. Frank Bonilla, "Puerto Rican Studies and the Interdisciplinary Approach," in *Toward a Renaissance,* edited by Sanchez, 17.

10. José Cuello, "Introduction: Chicana/o History as a Social Movement," in *Voices of a New Chicana/o History,* edited by Dennis Valdéz and Refugio I. Rochín (East Lansing: Michigan State University Press, 2000), 7.

11. Robert Rodríguez, "The Origins and History of the Chicano Movement," in ibid., 296.

12. Chicano Coordinating Council on Higher Education, *El Plan de Santa Barbara* (Santa Barbara: La Causa Publications, 1970), 69, 23.

13. Ruth W. Grant and Marion Orr, "Language, Race, and Politics: From 'Black' to 'African-American,'" *Politics and Society* 24, no. 2 (1996): 143.

14. Bettye Collier-Thomas and James Turner, "Race, Class, and Color: The African American Discourse on Identity," *Journal of American Ethnic History* 14, no. 1 (1994): 8.

15. Eduardo Bonilla-Silva, "Rethinking Racism: Toward a Structural Interpretation," *American Sociological Review* 62 (1996): 469.

16. Mario T. García, *Mexican Americans: Leadership, Ideology, and Identity, 1930–1960* (New Haven: Yale University Press, 1989), 19.

17. Cuello, "Introduction," 7.

18. Carlos Muñoz, *Youth, Identity, and Power* (London: Verso, 1989), 13.

19. García, *Mexican Americans.*

20. Benjamin Marquez, *Constructing Identities in Mexican American Political Organizations* (Austin: University of Texas Press, 2003), 144.

21. Suzanne Oboler, *Ethnic Labels, Latino Lives* (Minneapolis: University of Minnesota Press, 1995), 82; Aparicio, "Reading the 'Latino' in Latino Studies," 10.

22. Samuel P. Huntington, "The Hispanic Challenge," *Foreign Policy*, no. 141 (2004): 1; Marable, *Beyond Black and White*, 186.

23. Michael A. Gomez, *Exchanging Our Country Marks* (Chapel Hill: University of North Carolina Press, 1998), 5.

24. Collier-Thomas and Turner, "Race, Class, and Color," 11.

25. Tom W. Smith, "Changing Racial Labels from 'Colored' to 'Negro' to 'Black' to 'African American,'" *Public Opinion Quarterly* 56, no. 4 (1992): 512.

26. Gomez, *Exchanging Our Country Marks*, 11; Geneva Smitherman, "'What Is Africa to Me?': Language, Ideology, and African American," *American Speech* 66, no. 2 (1991): 121.

27. Stokely Carmichael, "Black Power," *New York Review of Books* 7 (1966): 6; Ben L. Martin, "From Negro to Black to African American: The Power of Names and Naming," *Political Science Quarterly* 106, no. 1 (1991): 85.

28. Rodolfo Acuña, *Occupied America*, 3d ed. (New York: Harper Collins, 1988), 18–20, 112–18.

29. Rogers Smith, *Civic Ideals: Conflicting Visions of U.S. Citizenship in U.S. History* (New Haven: Yale University Press, 1997), 448, 49–53.

30. Matthew Frye Jacobson, *Whiteness of a Different Color* (Cambridge: Harvard University Press, 1998), 27.

31. Richard Delgado, "Derrick Bell and the Ideology of Racial Reform: Will We Ever Be Saved?" *Yale Law Journal* 97 (1988): 940.

32. Juan P. Pera, "Fulfilling Manifest Destiny: Conquest, Race, and the Insular Cases," in *Foreign in a Domestic Sense: Puerto Rico, American Expansion, and the Constitution*, edited by Christina Duffy Burnett and Burke Marshall (Durham: Duke University Press, 2001), 148.

33. Pedro Cabán, "Subjects and Immigrants during the Progressive Era," *Discourse: Journal for Theoretical Studies in Media and Culture* 23, no. 3 (2001): 33.

34. Pedro Cabán, *Constructing a Colonial People: Puerto Rico and the United States, 1898–1932* (Boulder: Westview Press, 1999), 200.

35. Booker T. Washington, "Signs of Progress among the Negroes," *Century Magazine* (1900).

36. Ramon A. Gutierrez, "Community, Patriarchy, and Individualism: The Politics of Chicano History and the Dream of Equality," *American Quarterly* 45, no. 1 (1993): 45.

37. Quoted in Van DeBurg, *Modern Black Nationalism,* 290–91.

38. Neville and Cha-Jua, "Kufundisha," 48.

39. Ernesto B. Vigil, *The Crusade for Justice: Chicano Militancy and the Government's War on Dissent* (Madison: University of Wisconsin Press, 1999), 98.

40. Armando B. Rendon, *Chicano Manifesto: The History and Aspirations of the Second Largest Minority in America* (New York: Collier Books, 1971), 13; Vigil, *Crusade for Justice,* 98.

41. Eric R. Avila, "Decolonizing the Territory: Introduction," in *The Chicano Studies Reader: An Anthology of Aztlán,* edited by C. A. Noriega et al. (Los Angeles: Chicano Studies Research Center, 2001), 5.

42. Fernando Peñalosa, "Toward a Perspective on Chicano History," in ibid., 17.

43. Dean Robinson, *Black Nationalism in American Politics and Thought* (Cambridge: Cambridge University Press, 2001), 133.

44. Ramon A. Gutierrez, *Chicano History: Paradigm Shifts and Shifting Boundaries* (East Lansing: Michigan State University, Julian Samora Research Institute, 1997), 11.

45. Adaljiza Sosa Riddel, "Chicanas and el Movimiento," *Aztlán* 5, nos. 1–2 (1974).

46. Johnnetta Betsch Cole and Beverly Guy-Sheftall, *Gender Talk* (New York: Ballantine Books, 2003), 158–59.

47. See Robert Blauner, *Racial Oppression in America* (New York: Harper and Row, 1972), 12.

48. Tomás Almaguer, "Ideological Distortions in Recent Chicano Historiography," *Aztlán* 18 (1989): 10, 18.

49. Carmichael, "Black Power," 6; Martin, "From Negro to Black to African American," 94.

50. Manning Marable, ed., *Dispatches from the Ebony Tower: Intellectuals Confront the African American Experience* (New York: Columbia University Press, 2000), 122.

51. María Montoya, "Beyond Internal Colonialism: Class, Gender, and Culture as Challenges to Chicano Identity," in *Voices of a New Chicana/o History,* ed. Valdéz and Rochín, 186.

52. Gilbert G. Gonzalez, "A Critique of the Internal Colony Model," *Latin American Perspectives* 1, no. 1 (1974): 161.

53. Andres Torres and Jose E. Velazquez, *The Puerto Rican Movement: Voices from the Diaspora* (Philadelphia: Temple University Press, 1998), 112–16.

54. Ibid., 14.

55. Puerto Rican Student Union, "Somos Puertorriquenos y Estamos Despertando," 7.

56. Muñoz, *Youth, Identity, and Power,* 154–55; Joy James, "The Future of Black Studies," in *Dispatches from the Ebony Tower,* ed. Marable, 154.

57. Pedro Cabán, "Moving from the Margins: Three Decades of Latina/o Studies," *Latino Studies* 1, no. 1 (March 2003): 30.

12

"Livin' Just Enough for the City"

An Essay on the Politics of Acquiring Food, Shelter, and Health in Urban America

DAVID CROCKETT

This essay investigates the impact of racial inequality on primarily the experiences of African American consumers in markets for basic goods and services in an urban setting. However, rather than documenting price disparities, I explore in greater depth the experience of acquiring food, health care, and housing in Milwaukee, a medium-sized city in the midwestern United States. I begin with a general description of the city and the conditions under which consumers living in "Black Milwaukee," the city's predominantly Black residential area, as well as Black consumers living in other areas of the city, acquire necessary goods and services. I conclude with a discussion and analysis of these conditions and consumer strategies designed to navigate various forms of disadvantage.

The insights in this essay emerge from observations and interviews collected in Milwaukee County during 1998 and 1999. Twenty-eight informants (seventeen African Americans and ten Whites) recorded interviews regarding their experiences in markets for housing, general health care, and food. (The demographic composition of the sample is included in Table 12.1.) I supplemented interviews with direct observation of informants on trips to grocery stores to acquire food, by living and working in the city and participating in its civic and cultural life. This approach has been widely employed in similar studies in consumer research.[1] In addition to interviews with consumers, I maintained contact with members of important local institutions (for example, churches, local businesses, and civic organizations). Individuals in these organizations were helpful in providing access to other community-based organizations, serving as a source for cross-checking what I learned from interviews, and most important in helping deepen my understanding of race, class, gender, and neighborhood dynamics in the city.

Milwaukee: A Great City on a Great Lake

Milwaukee, Wisconsin, is a metropolitan area of roughly 1.5 million people that sits on the shores of Lake Michigan.[2] Compared to other larger cities in the Rust Belt, Milwaukee experienced a rather late, and rather small, migration of Blacks, who constitute about 15 percent of the metropolitan area.[3] It is a city of infamous winters, a decidedly blue-collar aesthetic, and friendly people. One informant, Mr. Chandler, the owner of a barbershop in the heart of Black Milwaukee, compares it favorably to a southern town due to what he describes as its slow pace and family orientation. In an interview he alludes to social and economic decay originating in the recession of the 1980s, which belies his overall favorable attitude about the city. Nevertheless, he unreservedly extols the city's virtues.

> *Researcher:* Why do you think Milwaukee's such a family oriented city?
> *Mr. Chandler:* Not a lot of the action here. It's not a fast place, first of all. It's not a fast-paced place like New York, Chicago, or L.A., places like that where things are happening so rapid every day. It's a slow-paced place. You know, the people—you can raise—you can have your kid out in the community going places and stuff. There's not a lot of danger at hand.
> *Researcher:* And you're saying that that's still the case even after some of the [aforementioned] changes in the '80s?

Table 12.1. Sampling composition (N = 28)

	Race			
	Black		White	
Social Class	Black Neighborhood	White Neighborhood	Black Neighborhood	White Neighborhood
Upper-middle class	Ellis Liz	Craig Eric Anne	**No Informants**	Katrina
Middle class	Mr. Chandler Florine	Pat	**No Informants**	Maggie
Working class	Lester Gary Alonzo Ms. Bernice Dianne Denise	Mary Lisa Josie	Candy Donna	Kevin Kim Shirley Martha Kris Cindy Dorothy

> *Mr. Chandler:* Yes, still the case. [This] has always been "ol' Milwau-
> kee." When they say "ol' Milwaukee," that connotation—[is] old
> values, old family values, old southern values.

Despite its reputation for lower overall rates of crime and poverty compared
to other Rust Belt cities, few metropolitan areas in the U.S. experienced ghettoization as rapidly as Milwaukee between 1970 and 1990. "Ghettoization" refers
to the concentration of social and economic decline in Black neighborhoods
and its subsequent expansion into adjacent Black neighborhoods. I employ the
term *ghetto* to reference predominantly Black neighborhoods (approximated
by census tract) that are at least 40 percent poor. To illustrate, in 1970 only 8.4
percent of Milwaukee's Black population and 16 percent of its poor Blacks lived
in the dozen or so tracts forming Milwaukee's ghetto. By 1990 nearly half of
the city's Black population and nearly two-thirds of the Black poor lived in the
more than fifty tracts that form the ghetto.[4]

This rapid expansion of ghetto neighborhoods took place against a backdrop
of high residential segregation between Blacks and Whites in the city. Those
neighborhoods with the largest percentage of Black residents are clustered together, surrounded by progressively "Whiter" (and on average higher-income)
neighborhoods. Milwaukee displays the "chocolate city–vanilla suburbs" pattern of Black population dispersion characteristic to highly segregated cities.
Milwaukee has been referred to at times as the most segregated city in the
nation.[5] Typically, sociologists consider any metropolitan area with a segregation index above 0.60 to be highly segregated. (A value of 1.0 is theoretically
apartheid, *absolute* segregation.) At the time of data collection, Milwaukee had
a Black-White residential segregation index of 0.826. Sociological literature on
residential segregation is clear. High levels of segregation restrict opportunity.
"Compared with whites of similar social status, blacks are more likely to live in
systematically disadvantaged neighborhoods, even in suburbs."[6]

At the level of lived experience, many residents of Milwaukee, Black and
White, have a sense of the city's segregated history, articulated through jokes
and cautionary tales. The following oft-repeated joke was first uttered to me by
a White professional and longtime resident of the city. As part of a historical
primer on segregation in the city, he said, "I really shouldn't be saying this, but
there's an old joke in this town about segregation. It goes, What's the longest
bridge in the world? It's the Sixteenth Street viaduct. You know why? It's the only
bridge in the world long enough to connect Poland to Africa." This is indeed an
old joke, as a rather sizable influx of Spanish-speaking immigrants from Central
and South America, as well as the Caribbean, has changed the racial and ethnic
makeup of Milwaukee's near south side. However the joke's staying power lies
in its description of racialized metropolitan space. Perhaps the clearest articu-

Table 12.2. Measures of evenness in select midwestern cities, 1990

Metropolitan area	Total population (000)	Percent Black	Index of dissimilarity
Milwaukee	1,432	13.8	.826
Chicago	6,067	22.0	.855
Cleveland	1,831	19.4	.850
Detroit	4,382	21.5	.876

lation of racialized metropolitan space and its impact on consumers came in a conversation with a Black male that occurred soon after entering the setting. This was a chance meeting with a man who appeared to be in his mid- to late fifties at a gas station in Black Milwaukee in 1998.

> *Researcher:* Boy, gas sure is expensive up here. In St. Louis it's not even a dollar per gallon.
> *Black Male:* I was just down in Racine [Wisconsin] the other day. They only payin' a dollar-eight *for premium!* We payin' more than that for regular! Man, I'm tellin' you. We are under attack! We're being targeted. Wherever our people are concentrated, they get targeted for higher prices.

Of course, now such prices might seem quite low. Generally, city-to-city differences in gasoline prices are explained by differences in municipal tax structures and other factors. So this gentleman's claim that Black consumers are purposely "targeted" for higher prices is not empirically verifiable in this context. His comments are nonetheless telling and insightful in a different way. He expresses a sentiment that appears to be commonly held by Black consumers in Milwaukee. That is, the spatial concentration and arrangement of Black households constitutes a basis for disadvantage, particularly in markets for basic goods and services, among them food, housing, and health care.

War on the Poor in the Stores: The Uneven Distribution of Emergency and Retail Food

THE UNEVEN DISTRIBUTION OF EMERGENCY FOOD

In the United States, food security is a persistent and growing social problem for those living near or below the poverty line. Food security is defined by one researcher as "access . . . at all times to enough food for an active, healthy life. Food security includes at a minimum, (a) the ready availability of nutritionally adequate and safe foods, and (b) an assured ability to acquire acceptable foods in socially acceptable ways."[7] Food security is not difficult to grasp conceptually, but measures of it vary widely. On the whole, at the time this study was conducted, food security problems were clearly trending upward. In 1995, well over one-quarter (26.2 percent) of all U.S. households between 50 and 130 percent of the poverty line experienced food security problems. By 1999 the percentage had risen to 27.7.[8]

The Uneven Distribution of Retail Food

Most Americans acquire the vast majority of their food from traditional markets, primarily grocery stores.[9] Thus, local retailers most directly structure access to nutritionally adequate food. That is, access to food—price, quality, and availability—is not merely a function of consumers' desire and ability to pay. It is also subject to retailers' desire to locate in a given area and ability to turn a profit.

Some research indicates that attenuated access to food in Milwaukee's largely Black and Hispanic neighborhoods is an ongoing social problem. For instance, the Center for Urban Initiatives at the University of Wisconsin at Milwaukee published the *Comparative Study of Food Pricing and Availability in Milwaukee.*[10] The major findings indicate that consumers who shopped in the predominantly Black and Hispanic sections of Milwaukee County at that time faced higher average prices and a smaller selection of products than did a person shopping outside the area. Not surprisingly, the research highlighted the absence of large food retail outlets (between 100–249 employees) and the proliferation of small (5–19 employees) and microsized (4 or fewer employees) in the target areas. Out of twenty-two large stores located in Milwaukee County overall, only a single large retail food store could be found in the combined Black and Hispanic target areas. By contrast, small and microsized stores constituted 92 percent of the food retail outlets in the target area. An indication of the importance of large stores came when plans to build a new large grocery store in the heart of Black Milwaukee made the front page of the *Milwaukee Journal-Sentinel,* the city's largest daily.[11] The impact of this spatial arrangement of retail on price and selection is unambiguous. When arrayed by store size, identical baskets of food purchased from large retail food stores in Milwaukee County cost 24 percent less than in the smallest stores. Small and microsized stores typically offer fewer products, few if any unbranded (generic) products, and fewer items available at discount than large and medium-sized food retail outlets.[12]

Shopping in Black Milwaukee's stores is likely to result in paying higher prices for a more limited selection of goods available elsewhere in the metro area. However, the costs continue to escalate for those with limited social and spatial mobility. Ms. Bernice, a working-class Black woman, works in the cafeteria at a local public elementary school. In her late fifties, she is a longtime resident of Black Milwaukee. She lives in a house with three adult children and a grandchild.

She usually does the food shopping for the household at Michelle's, a Black-owned medium-sized grocery chain, roughly three miles from her home. This particular Michelle's is a busy food store, being one of only two medium-sized grocery stores in that area of the city. Ms. Bernice most frequently takes the bus to the store. On the return trip she often uses one of the unlicensed taxis that offer store-to-door service for a flat fee. She makes two to three trips weekly to multiple stores. She claims to prefer shopping at a single large store, but that is virtually impossible without reliable personal transportation. In lieu of this, Ms. Bernice, as is the case with many shoppers in Black Milwaukee, must simply make do. She uses a relatively complex calculus to settle on a store. She factors distance, mode, and cost of transportation to and from the store and the relative prices of the goods her family demands into her determination of where and when to shop. First, she determines household needs. For example, for "general stuff" like dry goods she will typically shop at Michelle's. However, she hesitates to purchase fresh produce and canned goods from Michelle's. The fresh produce is frequently not fresh, and she says canned goods at Michelle's are quite expensive. She then factors mode and cost of transportation into her decision. Michelle's sits on a bus line, and offers the flat-rate taxi service for the return trip. The taxi allows her to purchase more, because she will not need to carry heavy bags on a bus. For fresh produce she prefers to purchase from another store, Karl's. This grocery chain is widely perceived as having quality merchandise but high prices. It too sits on a bus line, roughly the same distance from her home as Michelle's. However, it features no flat-rate taxi service, which limits the amount she can purchase and reasonably expect to carry home. When she needs to purchase canned goods for the house, she prefers yet another store, Apples, that features by far the best prices on canned goods, offering deep discounts for purchasing in large quantities. Accessing this store unfortunately requires taking the bus, and also offers no flat-rate taxi for the return trip. So Ms. Bernice can take advantage of bulk-purchase discounts only if she can physically carry her purchases home on public transportation.

Ms. Bernice attempts to optimize store choice subject to budget, transportation, and carrying-capacity constraints. But even though she excels at this optimization exercise, she is well aware that she is often making do with less than "them folks that shop in the White neighborhoods." While Milwaukee's predominantly White neighborhoods feature shoppers who face similar transportation-cost and carrying-capacity constraints, the absence of large stores in Black Milwaukee makes it much more likely that its shoppers will travel to multiple smaller stores to acquire food.

In sum, Black Milwaukee is akin to a social watershed. Residential segregation and ghettoization combine to shape the terrain such that disadvantage concentrates and settles, pooling its ill effects there. For working-class women like Ms.

Bernice, shopping in Black Milwaukee virtually ensures that they will negotiate higher food prices, diminished brand choice, and quality. They will also navigate a retail environment plagued by the highest levels of violent crime in the metro area. It is within this context that consumers make store and product choices that are as much social and political as they are economic. Consumers inside Black Milwaukee, with sufficient social and economic status and mobility, are able to resolve their attenuated access to food only by leaving Black Milwaukee. Although status and mobility may facilitate improved store and product choice, the consequent social and political impact of migrating outside the Black neighborhoods to acquire food must also be negotiated. For some, this is a dilemma without clear or immediate resolution.

Trying Not to Get Sick: Acquiring Health Care in Black Milwaukee

WORKING-CLASS INSTABILITY

The working-class informants in this sample are almost all employed in the service economy without employer-subsidized health benefits. In this sector of the economy even steady employment is not a guarantee of access to health insurance. Candy is a White former Aid to Families with Dependent Children recipient who lives in Black Milwaukee. She has worked steadily since her youngest son, age eleven, has been old enough to attend school. At the time of this interview she was working in retail cosmetics at a local pharmacy.

> *Candy:* When was the last time I went to see a doctor? About two and
> a half weeks ago. Cost me $350.
> *Researcher:* Out of pocket?
> *Candy:* Yep. I have no insurance.

For Candy, her first complete physical examination in the past seven years is a capitulation to concerns about her health based on her physical condition and a history of diabetes in her immediate family. The unexpected expense, however, tore into her meager savings, illustrating the instability of her financial situation.

> *Candy:* I didn't plan for it. But I had the money in the bank. I paid the
> bill, and totally to tell you the truth, I just told God, you take care of
> the rest. You either—because I do many things. I don't only just work
> at Walgreens. I mean and I don't have to receive cash. I can do trade
> easily and obtain the things that [other] people bought. And that's
> how I make it. And I keep my rent current and no more than two
> months behind on electric and phone because it's usually that I'm
> switching off one of the two, but most of the time they're current too.

Candy engages in budget juggling, a strategy common among the working class and poor women to remain current with their most pressing debts.[13] In this instance she is choosing between telephone service and electricity. She also alludes to barter and "off-the-books" labor to compensate for the shortfall in cash caused by the unexpected physical. Interestingly, Candy is suspicious of insurance coverage through a private health maintenance organization (HMO). She is convinced that coverage is subject to market-driven restrictions.

> *Candy:* Okay. If you were on an HMO and you were working, you get what I would call standard quality.
> *Researcher:* Meaning what?
> *Candy:* As long as your insurance is going to pay for it, it's okay. But if your HMO and that says no— [pause]
> *Researcher:* They won't do any procedures?
> *Candy:* Well, they just say the procedure is not necessary when the procedure is necessary. Well, because if you pay for it in cash, it costs less than if your HMO pays for it.

Candy has spent a significant portion of her work life uninsured. However, she has recently been able to secure white-collar employment in the service sector, eventually taking a position that brought with it full-time status, a corresponding rise in pay, and health benefits. However, for many other members of the working class, particularly those without higher education, the prospects of joining the white-collar ranks of the service economy are quite dim. For them, a pattern of part-time employment with frequent periods of unemployment is more common. Dianne is a working-class Black woman who lives in Black Milwaukee. She is working on obtaining a general equivalency diploma. According to her husband, Lester, she is currently working in child care. Dianne is typical of working-class women confined to the pink-collar segment of the service economy. She suffers from a variety of physical ailments with little hope of proper medical attention.

Employment instability often leads to at least brief dependence on public assistance. In 1997 Wisconsin replaced Aid to Families with Dependent Children with Wisconsin Works! (referred to as "W2"), a block-grant initiative that implements work requirements. The impact of the program on access to public health assistance is still a subject of considerable debate and little consensus. Candy, a community activist for welfare issues, is very critical of the inadequacy of the health care provisions in W2.

> *Candy:* If you're on what the W2 people are on and stuff like that, the quality's not there. You're just like a slaughterhouse. They tell you where you can go, what doctors you can see. They say they give

you a choice, they give you a couple of names, but those people are already been signed up with them. They've already been told what they can and cannot do. And that is to me—it's not adequate care. And to me, that's the one thing that [former governor] Tommy Thompson and I highly disagree upon. Highly disagree upon.

For Candy, coverage under W2 is not adequate because it is restrictive. Consistent with her critique of private coverage through HMOs, she believes that administrators have determined a priori which procedures are "unnecessary." A focus group conducted in Kenosha with eight women who are participants in W2 job training found them to be generally less critical of the program. They thought the medical coverage was adequate for them and their dependent children, but for those who were married it did not cover their husbands, many of whom worked in jobs without health insurance. They were all more critical of the system of private health insurance for failing to cover people with steady employment. For working-class men without dependent children in Wisconsin who are not eligible for Social Security or veterans benefits, access to public health care from the state comes in the form of the General Assistance Medical Plan (GAMP). This kind of coverage is designed to function as a safety net in emergency situations. Thus, it does not cover the kind of preventive care necessary to detect potential health problems at their earliest stages.

For working-class informants in this sample the world of work structures their access to and discourse about health care. As these informants all work in the service sector of the economy, most have experienced periods of unemployment and all currently work, or have worked, without health insurance. Adequate insurance is simply too expensive to purchase privately for many in the working class. They go without coverage or, if eligible, perhaps turn to public assistance. For women with dependent children this typically means participation in Wisconsin Works! For men this often means coverage by the state in an emergency. In general, notions of access and adequacy dominate working-class informants' comments about health care acquisition in Milwaukee. The economic instability inherent in service-sector work leads to unstable access to health care. Working-class informants also offer a critique of public and market-based systems of health care distribution. Some, like Candy and Lester, argue that the public system is often unable to meet people's basic health needs or that it reinforces dependency. Meanwhile, the private system distributes vital services away from those with great need but limited ability to pay, causing Candy to quite literally choose a physical examination over telephone service.

MIDDLE-CLASS NETWORKS

For middle-class informants in the sample, access to health care was practically a given. Health benefits are a feature of the kinds of employment that typically accompany middle-class status. Thus, it is not programmatic access to health care but distinguishing between health care alternatives that constitutes the major challenge in acquisition for these consumers. Understanding the distinctions between various types of employee health plans is far from a trivial task.

> *Maggie, a middle-class White woman living in a predominantly White neighborhood:* My husband just picked [a primary care physician] out of the [HMO] brochure—that's exactly what he did. He wouldn't let me help him. My daughter, I got referrals—my brother is a pediatrician, so, I had him go through the book and point out. . . . And my daughter sees the same pediatrician that my sister takes her son to. So it was a family referral, I guess, and another doctor referral—family doctor, or whatever, however you want to call it. . . . And my doctor . . . How did I pick him? Oh, oh, he's a friend of the family's.

Maggie's choice procedures represent a quintessential instance of a social network functioning to provide access to information that otherwise would be very difficult to get or completely unavailable. She has direct social ties to local expertise in the form of her brother, a pediatrician. He not only understands her and her family's needs, but which alternatives are most likely to meet them. Maggie's own physician is a friend of the family. Her strong ties to these experts provide valuable assistance with her initial selection of physicians, and later help her distinguish between health care plans after changing jobs. Her networks have endowed her with exceptional knowledge about available alternatives. Maggie's social network of physicians is not typical of middle-class informants. More common among middle-class informants are networks of other consumers and perhaps lower-level health care professionals.

Nonetheless, the kind of access to private systems of health care enabled by stable middle-class employment, and subsequently enhanced by personal and professional networks, invites a particular kind of critique from middle-class informants that is not surprisingly oriented around purely personal-choice criteria. For instance, Eric, a Black executive at a large local firm, offers a critique of local health care markets that is completely consistent with his personal values. For Eric, who migrated to a predominantly White Milwaukee from the Southwest, lack of emphasis on improvement and advancement is a consistent theme running through his critiques of health care, retail, education, local government, and the working-class culture in Milwaukee. He suggests that the health care distribution system in Milwaukee simply does not offer a set of alternatives whose quality is commensurate with his expectations.

> *Eric:* But I do know, just from some things I've learned at work as I sit on the [health care] Steering Committee, that there are some unique things about the HMOs here. [They] are not as competi-

tive, and, therefore, the consumer is at a disadvantage as opposed to other cities.

Well, just for whatever reasons the way health care has evolved here and the HMOs that evolved here, we just don't have the best HMOs here. There's different systems, but no one system is dominant, and it just seems to be more of a management issue with the HMOs that you have in this area. Those are general comments, but I do think that particular aspect is unique to Milwaukee, from what I understand.

Eric's is a purely consumer-oriented critique of the metro-area health care distribution system. The diminished skills of providers or the incompetence and poor organization of HMOs place consumers in the private system at a disadvantage in comparison to other cities.

A prevalent concern among Black middle-class informants is the notion that providers do not take their health concerns seriously. Liz, a Black woman who lives in Black Milwaukee, often feels that Blacks are particularly likely to have their concerns ignored or patronized. Blacks, she suggests, must "prove" the validity of their health claims. In an initial interview, Liz spoke about having to, in her words, "train" the family doctor to trust her concerns as a parent. In a follow-up interview she elaborated:

> *Researcher:* The last time we spoke you mentioned having to "train" your physician. What did you mean by that?
> *Liz:* Not so much "train" them, but people have to realize that parents know their children. [. . .] Sometimes with doctors, and sometimes I think with African Americans [patients], they don't really take us seriously. I really haven't had that problem with Dr. Jones, but there were occasions where he questioned whether or not [Liz's asthmatic son] Travis was as sick as he was. And it was like, well, we got there [to the hospital], and they [hospital staff] said he was sick, so it was the right call. Travis, like I said before, has taken offense when he would overhear the nurses or doctors making a statement about him and he would have to explain to them what all he was going through.

Making attributions about the source of dissatisfaction can be a trying proposition for consumers. But the clear issue for Liz is that her concerns, and those of her son, are presumed to be inaccurate, or exaggerated. She attributes this, at least in part, to the relatively low status of Blacks in that setting. Pat, a Black woman living in a predominantly White neighborhood, expresses similar concerns about being ignored by her physician, but her implicit attribution is to the gendered interaction with her male doctor. Some research suggests that customer service–provider relationships in health care are particularly complex and conflict ridden for many women.[14] Pat went on to employ a female doctor at the recommendation of a colleague. For Pat, employing a female doctor was salient:

> *Pat:* I had an infection once, and my other [male] doctor insisted that
> I must have been doing something I wasn't doing, and when I went
> to the other [female] doctor, she says, 'Oh, no, it's possible [to have
> the infection without being sexually active]—it's an infection, it's
> not the same one, but it is an infection, and it is possible to have—,'
> you know. And she said she'd have to give me medication. So I took
> the medication at one time, and now it's a year and a half later, and
> I never had a [recurrence]. Whereas with him it kept reoccurring,
> and that was because he wasn't treating the right thing. He just
> made the assumption [. . .] that I must be—and I'm like [look of
> bewilderment]—and that's the part that would really burn me up.
> But I didn't know where else to go. And I *didn't* want Sonia [daugh-
> ter, age fourteen at the time] to go [to him]. I didn't know where else
> to go. For now I like the doctor I have now.

In this instance, being cured is practically synonymous with being heard. Pat expresses this sentiment in the form of a morality tale in which the male doctor is cast as the villain by questioning her sexual integrity through his diagnosis. The female doctor, cast as hero, not only validates Pat's integrity but cures her by listening to her concerns. Pat also plays the maternal heroine in this drama, as she protects her teenage daughter's sexual integrity by ridding herself of the male doctor. A defining feature of morality tales, of course, is the ability of the protagonist's values to overcome in the face of adversity. For the narrator, the ending is happy—because her values have been restored through her exercise of choice. Unfortunately, even for informants enabled by middle-class status to have access to health care, there exist horror stories about the quality of care in which the storyteller's values are not restored in the face of adversity.

CONSUMER DISADVANTAGE IN HEALTH CARE ACQUISITION

In the context of health care acquisition, employment structures the flow of disadvantage. For consumers in Milwaukee, the kind of consumer disadvantage one is likely to experience in markets for health care is determined by access to health insurance. For informants who are uninsured, or whose access is through the public health care system, these data suggest potentially inadequate family care and prohibitive expense for preventive medical services. Working-class informants claim that the public health care system is frequently inadequate, because of either limitations in the quality of medical service or limitations in coverage. For instance, according to participants in the focus group, W2 coverage extends only to mothers and their children under the age of eighteen. Of course, for informants with no medical insurance who pay a fee for service, even a simple preventive procedure like an annual physical can be a prohibitive expense. Working-class informants generally frame disadvantage as a systemic feature of health care distribution itself. That is, they structure the discourse on disadvantage as a function of their employment status or as a feature of the market itself.

For middle- and upper-middle-class informants, access to the system of health care insurance is for the most part a given based on their employment status. Thus, although they shared similar concerns about quality of care with members of the working class, their insiders' perspective leads them to frame disadvantage differently. Whereas working-class informants framed disadvantage as a feature of the system of health care distribution, middle-class informants made more individual attributions about the nature of mistreatment. For middle-class consumers, disadvantage often occurs in the form of mistreatment. It is here that gender and race emerge most explicitly as structuring features of customer service–provider interactions. What emerges from these informants' critiques of service provision is that Black middle-class consumers, perhaps due in part to their own privileged position in the marketing system, take the distribution of health care services for granted. That is, they are active participants in the health care distribution system, with general acceptance of the system's basic precepts about to whom health care resources should flow. These resources flow toward them and away from others less able to pay without much explicit consideration by these informants. However, Black middle-class informants express a range of concerns about particular components of the health care distribution system. What underlies both their morality tales and their horror stories is a pervasive reliance on their own self-efficacy to navigate the market for health care.

Race, Class, and Housing

Home ownership is perhaps the centerpiece of the American Dream. For many, owning a home represents having "made it" in America. Melvin L. Oliver and Thomas Shapiro document the role of home ownership in accumulating wealth and the extraordinary disadvantages African Americans face in building wealth this way.[15] For most Americans, the largest single component of their wealth portfolio is their home. A home represents financial stability. It can at least partially shield families from economic distress. It can also provide access to credit that would otherwise be unavailable. And, of course, for many families, a home is an investment in the future of their children. But the likelihood of renting instead of owning a home increases in Black Milwaukee. Widespread discrimination in markets for home financing leaves Blacks with fewer loan options, paying higher interest rates on houses that often do not appreciate in value relative to those of comparable Whites.

The role of housing as a store of wealth has been well documented. But housing's role in race and class politics within the Black community itself has not been as extensively studied. In a city as segregated as Milwaukee, where the majority of Blacks live in close physical proximity regardless of income, people use home ownership to provide stability. Home ownership also serves the critical symbolic role of making distinctions between and among the working and middle classes.

Home ownership represents one of the few ways that working-class and middle-class people in Black Milwaukee can acquire stability in a setting often characterized by instability. At minimum, a house provides a measure of stability not afforded to those living in apartments by granting more control over who else inhabits the living space.

The distinction between those who own and those who rent, interestingly, is perhaps the key social-status marker employed by the middle classes to distinguish themselves from the working class in Black Milwaukee. It was most clearly expressed by Saulo, a middle-class Hispanic man living in a Hispanic neighborhood at the southern border of Black Milwaukee. He spoke about a recent conflict he had with neighbors. Saulo confronted the neighbors, asking them to direct their guests to on-street parking away from his driveway. According to Saulo, the neighbors relented, but gave him "attitude." Now they sneer at him and refuse to speak, behavior that he attributes to their status as renters. Saulo makes it very clear that he considers those who rent as lacking the same pride as home owners, and this sentiment seems to pervade interclass relations in Black Milwaukee. The "pride" to which Saulo refers is a social-status marker often invoked by the middle class to reinforce an otherwise invisible status distinction between themselves and members of the working class. Of course, this is rarely necessary for similarly situated middle-class Whites in metro Milwaukee. They rarely share neighborhood space with the people from whom they wish to dissociate. For Whites in Milwaukee, neighborhood is sufficient to distinguish the middle classes from lower-status groups. However, for Blacks and Milwaukee's growing Hispanic population, who are confined to a small, densely populated subsection of the metropolitan area, neighborhood distinctions are largely unsustainable. The "ghetto" in Milwaukee has followed Black middle-class migration from the center of the city and headed north and east.[16] Thus, in lieu of clear spatial separation, other factors, such as home ownership and longtime residence, serve to mark social status in Black and Brown Milwaukee.

Interestingly, negative markers of status also emerge to protect the constantly threatened status of the working class living in Black Milwaukee, few of whom own their own homes.

> *Candy:* In fact, the people that was in here before—and I probably didn't tell you—she was on rent assistance, and she let her boyfriend move in here, and he was a dealer. And he was not only dealing in drugs, he was dealing in everything else—prostitution. I highly suspect that even they were making porno films. [. . .] Talk about paranoid, yeah! I mean, I could no longer leave Sam [her youngest son]. I wouldn't leave Sam alone, period. Not even for an hour. It was, "Either you have to go by Danielle's, or you have to go here. You can't be alone," because I didn't know what was going to be in the hallway or, you know, whatever.
>
> From my understanding, because of rent assistance [. . .] the inner-city people [were] coming here, and they were used to being able to do certain things that I had moved away from Bender [Street] for, you know. And all of a sudden I'm facing it again. I'm talking the guns, the dope, and just blatant disrespect and everything.

Clearly, Candy is a beleaguered resident. She is a single working-class mother, trying to keep herself and her children out of harm's way. She identifies "rent assistance" as the bridge that spans the narrow chasm between life in the service sector and life in the underground economy. It also serves as a negative marker of social status. That is, Candy is primarily articulating who she is not. She is not dependent on public subsidy or engaged in criminal activity. Having entered the service sector, she identifies public subsidies like rent assistance as the bridge across the perceptual and economic gulf separating (or shielding) the morally virtuous working class from the immoral underclass. A similar negative status marker is "rent hopping," the practice of moving into a home and refusing to pay rent for the maximum amount of time allotted under state law and then vacating the property prior to eviction. Rent hopping illustrates the instability in housing so prevalent among the working class and poor in Milwaukee and many American cities.

> *Liz:* [In] Milwaukee, some of the [people], they may not have the money to stay in that particular house, or they just stay there for X amount of time, knowing that they are not going to stay. Then they just move on to skip out on the rent or whatever. They don't have the money for whatever reason, and they leave. Sometimes kids do this six or seven times a year.

Rent hopping also serves to distinguish residents of Black Milwaukee. Despite living in a neighborhood struggling against economic and social decline, Liz's middle-class family owns its home and has roots in the community. They are not people who "skip out on the rent."

Abolition of the Ghetto as a Transitional Program

What has been presented to this point is a brief description, from a consumer-behavior perspective, of people's lived experiences in a setting that is character-ized by race, gender, and class inequality. That is, I have provided an illustration of how macrolevel social processes (ghettoization and residential segregation) come to be codified and enacted in markets for basic goods and services (food, health care, and housing). The disadvantage engendered by Milwaukee's ghetto expansion and segregation is not simply codified in unemployment statistics or crime rates. It is also enacted in the most basic and routine activities, like going to the grocery store, responding to illness, and finding a home.

The remainder of this chapter will attend to one of the macrolevel social processes identified as key in this research, residential segregation. Whereas ghettoization has been much discussed among sociologist, policy planners, and public officials, residential segregation has faded almost completely from the national consciousness about race and racism. Douglas Massey and Nancy Denton argue persuasively that at least part of the reason for its disappearance is that otherwise competing interests in Black and White America have profited monetarily, electorally, and symbolically from it. In the aftermath of the civil rights movement and the passage of fair housing legislation, they argue, White liberals simply chose to declare victory in the "war" on discrimination in housing markets. White conservatives, in large part, understood the obvious failure of antidiscriminatory housing legislation as a validation of their critique of Black culture or a validation of their laissez-faire response to housing discrimination. Within Black America, Massey and Denton argue that the interest in ignoring residential segregation was largely similar. As William J. Wilson suggests, the civil rights movement and resulting fair housing legislation enabled a sizable segment of the Black middle class to flee traditional Black enclaves. Like the middle class in every ethnic group in the United States, the Black middle class has attempted to flee its working class and poor. It has simply been the least able to do so.[17] Black middle-class flight from predominantly Black enclaves has led to new rounds of White flight and consequent ghetto expansion.

Also, despite a reliance on corporate and government patronage that has reduced its concentration in primarily Black consumer markets, the Black busi-ness strata still have clear incentives to support self-imposed restrictions on

Black spatial mobility. Much as St. Claire Drake and Horace Cayton suggested in *Black Metropolis,* the success of the Black business and political strata has always been directly tied to a highly segregated Black working-class customer base, voting bloc, institutions, or, more recently, to self-identification as Black-owned. Even in this latter instance, as many direct minority set-aside programs have been washed away in political and legal sea-changes, "minority-owned" remains meaningful to the broader business community only when it serves as an entrée to a larger minority customer base. Arlene Dávila's ethnography of Hispanic-owned advertising agencies illustrates how the tenuous privilege of non-White business elites hinges on their (real or perceived) connection to "the masses" in non-White communities.[18] Their success is tied directly to how "authentic" they are perceived to be by White corporate executives. This authenticity is presumably a measure of their ability to deliver the rapidly expanding consumer dollars in the Hispanic segment. Dávila suggests that African American advertising agencies have followed a similar development process.

In short, many had direct and indirect incentives to ignore high levels of Black-White residential segregation even while decrying the rapid expansion of the ghetto in Milwaukee and many cities in the United States. Residential segregation and ghettoization, taken together, help maintain institutional racism in the United States. Residential segregation is at root a system of social control that allows for the distribution of resources toward the dominant racial group without requiring the symbolic deference and spatial intimacy necessary for the maintenance of Jim Crow segregation. Urban residential segregation, unlike Jim Crow, directs resources away from Black neighborhoods—but not explicitly away from Black people. In this way, urban residential segregation may, ironically, be the most thoroughly integrated form of institutional racism since slavery. The never verbalized, implicit collaboration among private sellers, public and private lenders, real estate agents, neighborhood associations, and municipal zoning boards necessary to maintain persistently high levels of Black-White residential segregation is astounding when considering the high demand for integrated housing among Blacks at all income levels.[19] And even when this elaborate system of race-based discrimination fails to maintain severe racial disparity, it may be quickly supplemented with racial harassment and violence.[20] Thus, residential segregation virtually ensures that any resource that flows across an urban landscape either will not flow or will flow less rapidly to the areas that Blacks inhabit.

Perhaps nowhere is America more invested in the maintenance of racial inequality than in its lived environment through residential segregation. Yet ending segregation is absolutely essential to the future of American cities, with their crumbling infrastructure, persistent capital flight, and rising costs for basic services. If segregation is to be toppled, no single set of policy initiatives or single act is likely to defeat it in isolation. Only people dedicated to abolishing it can accomplish this. Much more important than any singular set of policy prescriptions is the notion that the abolition of the ghetto and simultaneous reconstruction of the Black community is paramount to the nation's well-being. To that end, the policy prescriptions offered here are mere thumbnail sketches, meant to be brief and conceptual in nature.

FAIR HOUSING LEGISLATION AND POLICY

Current legislation regarding racial discrimination in housing markets is riddled with loopholes and problems of low-priority enforcement. In the short term the focus must be on lowering the costs of making formal complaints and bringing discrimination charges into the legal system. Intermediately, the focus must be on shifting the burden of proof solely from plaintiffs. Currently, plaintiffs must meet an almost impossibly high standard in proving discrimination. In the absence of information about prior sales or data from "testing," real victims of discrimination stand virtually no chance in court. Consequently, many legitimate complaints are never even pursued. In the long term, shifting the burden of proving nondiscrimination must become a condition for sellers to participate in real estate markets.

LENDING INSTITUTIONS

Discrimination against Black loan seekers is also widespread. Nonetheless, lending institutions are required to maintain records about demographic characteristics of qualifiers and nonqualifiers. The federal government must hold these institutions responsible for discriminatory actions against Black loan seekers. In addition, under the affirmative mandate of the Fair Housing Act, special consideration should be given Black and Hispanic loan applicants by federal lending agencies.

REPARATIONS

In recent years the call for reparations has gained considerable momentum in the United States. As the myriad proposals and plans continue to undergo modification and revision, the physical reconstruction of Black America must be a central feature.

BETTERING PRESENT CONDITIONS

Even if these initiatives are taken up by persons with committed progressive politics, it is unlikely that the degraded material conditions present in Black communities will change substantially in the short term. Central among these conditions is attenuated access to reasonably priced, healthy food. Entering progressive coalitions or public-private partnerships to bring vital business entities such as large grocery stores back to the inner cities can also be part of enacting a progressive politics, provided that measures are taken to ensure that businesses are meeting the needs of the community through both their offerings and their treatment of labor.

CHAPTER 12 READING QUESTIONS

1. According to Crockett, few U.S. cities experienced as rapid a second ghettoization as occurred in Milwaukee between 1970 and 1990. How do you account for the swift growth of Milwaukee's second ghetto in this period, and what effect did it have on African Americans' income, job opportunities, and consumption experiences in the food, health care, and housing markets?

2. In Milwaukee during this period, no militant social movement organization emerged, but individuals adopted a series of coping strategies to combat the disadvantages and discriminations they faced in food, health care, and housing markets. Why do you think no social movement developed? Can you describe some of the coping strategies and evaluate their effectiveness?

3. How did increasing class stratification and polarization within the Black community affect grassroots resistance to deindustrialization and the increasing concentration of working-class African Americans in segregated ghettoes?

Notes

1. Lisa Peñaloza, "Immigrant Consumers: Marketing and Public Policy Considerations in the Global Economy," *Journal of Public Policy and Marketing* 15 (1995): 83–94; Elizabeth M. Liew Siew Chin, *Purchasing Power: Black Kids and American Consumer Culture* (Minneapolis: University of Minnesota Press, 2001).

2. U.S. Census Bureau, "Ranking Tables for Population of Metropolitan Statistical Areas, Micropolitan Statistical Areas, Combined Statistical Areas, New England City and Town Areas, and Combined New England City and Town Areas, 1990 and 2000 (Areas Defined by the Office of Management and Budget as of June 6, 2003), (PHC-T-29)" (2003), http://www.census.gov/population/www/cen2000/phc-t29.html.

3. Joe William Trotter, *Black Milwaukee: The Making of an Industrial Proletariat, 1915–45* (Urbana: University of Illinois Press, 1985); U.S. Census Bureau, "Table DP-1, Profile of General Demographic Characteristics, 2000, Geographic Area: Milwaukee—Racine, WI, CMSA" (2000), http://censtats.census.gov/data/WI/390555082.pdf.

4. Paul Jargowsky, *Poverty and Place: Ghettos, Barrios, and the American City* (New York: Russell Sage Foundation, 1997).

5. Jonathan Coleman, *Long Way to Go: Black and White in America* (New York: Atlantic Monthly Press, 1997).

6. Douglas S. Massey, "The Residential Segregation of Blacks, Hispanics, and Asians, 1970–1990," in *Immigration and Race: New Challenges for an American Democracy,* edited by Gerald D. Jaynes (New Haven: Yale University Press, 2000), 2; Joe R. Feagin and Melvin P. Sikes, *Living with Racism: The Black Middle Class Experience* (Boston: Beacon Press, 1994).

7. Janet Poppendeick, *Sweet Charity? Emergency Food and the End of Entitlement* (New York: Viking, 1998), 79.

8. Ellen Vollinger, "New Data Show Persistent Hunger and Food Insecurity among American Families: Effects of Strong Economy Subverted by Decline in Food Stamp Participation," in *Current News and Analysis* (2000), http://www.frac.org/html/news/foodsecurity99.html.

9. Phil Kaufman and Steven M. Lutz, "Competing Forces Affect Food Prices for Low-Income Households," *Food Review* (1997): 8–12.

10. Karl Johnson, Stephen Percy, and Edward Wagner, *Comparative Study of Food Pricing and Availability in Milwaukee,* report for the Food System Assessment Project, the Center for Urban Initiatives and Research, University of Wisconsin at Milwaukee, 1996.

11. Tom Daykin, "$10 Million Jewel-Osco Coming to Central City," *Milwaukee Journal-Sentinel,* April 29, 1999, 1, 8.

12. Linda F. Alwitt and Thomas D. Donley, "Retail Stores in Poor, Urban Neighborhoods," *Journal of Consumer Affairs* 31, no. 1 (1997): 139–64; Kaufman and Lutz, "Competing Forces Affect Food Prices," 8–12; Judith Bell and Bonnie Maria Burlin, "In Urban Areas Many Poor Still Pay More for Food," *Journal of Public Policy and Marketing* 14, no. 1 (1993): 48–59.

13. Kathryn Edin and Laura Lein, "Work, Welfare, and Single Mothers' Economic Survival Strategies," *American Sociological Review* 62, no. 2 (1997): 253–66.

14. Renee Gravois Lee, Julie L. Ozanne, and Ronald Paul Hill, "Improving Service Encounters through Resource Sensitivity: The Case of Health Care Delivery in an Appalachian Community," *Journal of Public Policy and Marketing* 18, no. 2 (1999): 230–48.

15. Melvin L. Oliver and Thomas Shapiro, *Black Wealth/White Wealth: A New Perspective on Racial Inequality* (New York: Routledge, 1995); Thomas Shapiro, *The Cost of Being African American: How Wealth Perpetuates Inequality* (New York: Oxford University Press, 2004).

16. Jargowsky, *Poverty and Place.*

17. Douglas S. Massey and Nancy A. Denton, *American Apartheid: Segregation and the Making of the Underclass* (Cambridge: Harvard University Press, 1993); William J. Wilson, *The Truly Disadvantaged: The Inner City, the Underclass, and Urban Policy* (Chicago: University of Chicago Press, 1987); Richard D. Alba and John R. Logan, "Minority Proximity to Whites in Suburbs: An Individual-Level Analysis of Segregation," *American Journal of Sociology* 98 (1993): 1388–1427.

18. St. Claire Drake and Horace Cayton, *Black Metropolis: A Study of Negro Life in a Northern City* (New York: Harcourt Brace, 1945); Arlene Dávila, *Hispanics* (2001).

19. Reynolds Farley et al., "Stereotypes and Segregation: Neighborhoods in the Detroit Area," *American Journal of Sociology* 100 (1994): 750–80.

20. Joe R. Feagin and Hernan Vera, *White Racism: The Basics* (New York: Routledge, 1995).

Conclusion

The past few decades have been a time of great ferment in race relations. Recent events such as the Katrina disaster have blown the covers off the myth of a color-blind society and have revealed the saliency of race in contemporary American life. The media have struggled for a language with which to understand this catastrophe, yet they have found it impossible to speak honestly and coherently about the phenomenon of race. On the face of it this is somewhat surprising, since this subject has not been neglected by the academic world. Over the past generation, flurries of books, articles, and ideas have issued in ever increasing volume from both university and popular presses. Disciplines that once had little or nothing to say on the subject are now bubbling with fresh perspectives and insights. Yet as the volume of new material has accumulated, it has been less readily synthesized and absorbed. The academics, who have been so successful in proliferating specialized knowledge, have been less effective in providing analytical frameworks for understanding either the general structures of racial oppression or the struggles of race resistance that these structures have evoked. This sense of disorientation amid an embarrassment of scholarly riches is strongly compounded by today's mood of conservative nominalism, on the one side, and postmodern eclecticism, on the other, neither of which are particularly conducive toward intellectual synthesis. The authors of the essays in this volume are all convinced that such a synthesis is necessary.

Although our book is not a finished synthesis, we do offer a broad view of an alternative framework that points us toward the development of a new materialist analysis of the race problematic. The authors in this volume refuse to reduce race to ethnicity, nationality, or any other phenomena. We also refuse to treat race as merely ethereal or epiphenomenal. Our starting point is the construction of the first racial formation, which took shape during the eighteenth and nineteenth centuries. We then trace the development of subsequent racial formation theories, ideologies, and movements for social change into the twenty-first century. Several features make our book unique. It is one of the few works that is genuinely interdisciplinary, goes beyond the Black-white binary of race, and transcends the nation-state. We hope that our study questions, as well as our introductions and conclusion, help the reader to set our separate studies in fruitful dialogue with one another. Taken together, they add up to a conversation about disparate subjects connected by convergent themes. Three core themes have been particularly highlighted in the volume: the saliency of race over time and across space, the intertwining and correspondence of racial structures and ideologies, and the organization of groups and the agency of individuals to perpetuate or contest the prevailing racial formation.

Our organization of this book, especially its division into three parts, on racial structures, racial ideologies, and racial struggles, respectively, reflects our desire to lay the foundations for some future synthesis that, at the moment, may be still premature. Our transit from structures through ideologies and onto the battle-ground of struggle might, indeed, be taken as shorthand for a rather orthodox Marxism, had we chosen to negotiate it in a reductive or crudely mechanical way. Although Marxism and neo-Marxism informs many of the chapters in our volume, the work has been tempered by a host of considerations that disrupt any notion of a unilinear process, governed by the predetermined telos of di-rectional change. Our opening part on racial structure registers this complexity and contingency of social structural transformation, which sets constraints on ideology and agency, but not in a rigidly deterministic fashion.

This can be seen in Sundiata Keita Cha-Jua's opening chapter, "The Chang-ing Same." This piece endorses, but also problematizes, the more convention-ally Marxist Black Racial Formation Theory proposed by Harold Baron in 1985. Though accepting Baron's basic periodization of U.S. racial structures (slavery, plantation economy, and proletarianization), Cha-Jua shows that they must be re-fined to make full sense of the African American experience, and supplemented, to understand how and why one structure gave way to the next. Most important, Cha-Jua's examination of the post-1980 period reveals the emergence of a fourth racial formation or period—what he calls the "New Nadir"—which could not have been predicted from Baron's essentially unidirectional view. For Baron, the superexploitation of Black people was the product of their segregation from the main body of the U.S. proletariat. As these explicitly color-coded restrictions and discriminations were gradually lifted during the 1960s, his theory might lead us to anticipate the emergence of a more classically Marxist scenario of class conflict, in which race would gradually diminish as a determinative factor in social con-sciousness and life. Cha-Jua, by contrast, shows how and why this development has not occurred. Deindustrialization, deproletarianization, superexploitation, and white backlash have all ensured that, in our era, structurally grounded racism has reemerged in a new and ostensibly "color-blind" form.

In Chapter 2, "Capitalism, Race, and Evolution in Imperial Britain," Theodore Koditschek transports us back—both chronologically and geographically—to the origins of the older color-coded racial formation as it emerged not in the United States but within the nineteenth-century British Empire. Unlike Cha-Jua, Koditschek writes within the context of a non-Marxist historiography in which this shift is conventionally explained in idealist, intellectual, or cultural terms. The first portion of Koditschek's chapter is therefore devoted to shifting the locus of explanation from malevolent theories of "scientific racism" to the material transformations in British and global capitalism that were simultaneously taking place during the second half of the nineteenth century. For the first time, colored peoples on the colonial periphery were being integrated into Britain's fledgling industrial (and increasingly globalized) economy. To mask their own dependence on colonial trade and colonial labor, white metropolitans adopted a new language of racial control and classification that enabled them to bring (or hope to bring) order to the global imperial world. It was here that the new scientific theories of biological and cultural evolution were important, for they provided the indispensable language through which this racial reordering could take shape.

Just how powerful and tenacious was this racial reordering of the British Empire, is revealed in our third chapter, "Globalization and the Cycle of Violence in Africa." Here, Tola Olu Pearce demonstrates, in a manner comparable to Cha-Jua, that the ostensibly color-blind terrain of twenty-first-century Africa is in fact riddled with hidden disparities of race and region that betray the legacy of the explicitly color-coded imperialism that 1960s decolonization was supposed to have overthrown. Conventionally blamed on tribalism, disease, war, ignorance, and corruption, the dysfunctions of today's Africa must be viewed within the structural context of rapidly globalizing capitalism. As Pearce shows, today's ostensibly independent African states remain in thrall to transnational corporations and the International Monetary Fund, in a manner that differs little from the explicitly racist subjugation of the older European-run empires. It is the fiscal policies imposed by these new transnational institutions that produce the above-mentioned evils for which the Africans themselves are often unfairly blamed. Although these transnational institutions profess an attitude of racial blindness, African peoples are routinely forced to accept harsh regimes of economic austerity that would never be tolerated in the West. Forced to sacrifice their desires for programs of social security, public health, and education that the first world takes for granted, Africans are expected to hand over huge annual payments of interest to the bankers and wealthy investors of the West. Pearce shows how a combination of local grassroots organizations, nongovernmental organizations, and international social-justice movements can put pressure on transnational agencies and catalyze internal social change. Such remedies will become effective, however, only when Western elites are forced to take responsibility for the racist legacy of imperialism that has created the African dysfunctions that are manifested today.

The task of promoting white self-awareness about the operation of oppressive racial structures has long been the focus of David Roediger's work. In Chapter 4, "White without End?" he alerts us to the dangers of trying to reconceptualize whiteness as a positive cultural identity that would be somehow divorced from the harsh legacy of racist structural oppression in which it has been historically embedded. Roediger's skepticism about the positive potential of "whiteness" seems particularly warranted in the context of a society that is rapidly shifting from the older color-coded racism to the newer—in some ways even more intractable—form of color-blind racism that Chapters 1 and 3 have diagnosed. In an ostensibly color-blind world, nothing looks easier than to strip "whiteness" of its formerly sinister connotations and to celebrate it as one more strand in an anodyne multiculturalism that equally valorizes the heritage and identity of every racial and ethnic group. Such a move, our authors warn, runs the risk of ignoring the continued operation of ideologically invisible racial structures that are working to perpetuate the privileges of racial domination, amid the happy celebrations of postracial flux and diversity.

Nevertheless, Roediger's call for a renewed commitment to the abolition of whiteness does raise the question of how both dominant and subordinate races historically have handled (and in the future will handle) the shift from diagnosing racial structures to participating in the lived experience of racial culture and racial identity. This is the focus of Part 2 of our volume, which begins with Helen A. Neville's "Rationalizing the Racial Order." On one level, Neville's analysis fits very neatly into Cha-Jua's typology of racial formations, inasmuch as her focus on the contemporary era highlights the transformation from color-coded to color-blind racism, which Cha-Jua analyzes on a more macro, systemic scale. As a psychologist, however, Neville is concerned with the microlevel of the individual personality, within which the shift actually occurs. It is a key feature of Neville's chapter—and those that follow in this part—that forms of personal consciousness, which are conventionally regarded as matters of individual *identity,* are here treated as manifestations of *ideologies* that have structural sources and structural consequences for society as a whole. In other words, the shift from a color-coded to a color-blind ideology is not an innocent personal choice. It is also an ideological move that legitimates the currently emerging system of racial oppression in much the same manner as the casual segregationist of the early twentieth century reinforced the racial structures of his or her own day. Such a conclusion may offend postmodern postracial liberals who believe that we have gotten over all that old unpleasantness. Neville's point is that, in a society where massive racial inequalities are still structurally present, the decision to repudiate race as a factor in one's own identity formation can only lead to delusory evasions, which actually work to reinforce and legitimize the unacknowledged inequalities that still remain.

As a psychologist, Neville has extensively documented this conclusion by showing the consequences of the new Color-Blind Racial Ideology for both Blacks and whites. Her data reveal that for white college students, the embracement of CBRI becomes an all too convenient way of complacently avoiding the unhappy subject of race and of refusing to recognize the racial privileges that they actually enjoy. By contrast, for racial minority students, CBRI sometimes becomes a disabling emotional burden, as it obliges them to take personal responsibility for the impediments and obstacles that (as Cha-Jua demonstrated in Chapter 1) a racist society has set in their path.

Minkah Makalani's "Race, Theory, and Scholarship in the Biracial Project" elaborates on the problem of racial identity posed in Neville's chapter. One of the consequences of the breakdown of rigid walls of racial segregation has been the rise in biracial marriages, in which one partner is white, and the other Black. How are the progeny of these unions to be characterized in racial terms? Much recent discussion has focused on the call for a new "biracial" category that would more accurately reflect the realities of our postmodern world. Such a category, according to its advocates, would complicate the palette of racial shadings, and have the effect of depolarizing racism, thereby hastening its disappearance from social life. Taking issue with this body of literature, Makalani draws on Cha-Jua's model to show that, historically speaking, the identification of a distinctly biracial identity has tended to reinforce racism and to weaken the unity and strength of African Americans as a group. This was manifestly the case during the nineteenth-century epoch of slavery and American apartheid, when the mulatto classification created a new colored elite of quasi privilege, driving a wedge within the African American community. In our current era of transition from color-coded to color-blind racial ideology, Makalani sees the demand for a new biracial identity as operating politically and psychologically in much the same way. In a world where color-blind racism works to deny the very racial categories that it simultaneously reconstitutes, the introduction of a new biracial category will merely create a new intermediate race (perhaps on the model of the nineteenth-century British Empire of Chapter 2). This is likely to leave unambiguously Black-identified African Americans even more isolated and marginalized than they were before.

Monica M. White's "Sociopsychological Process in Racial Formation" shows, from a different direction, that periods of great societal transformation are moments of opportunity—and of danger—when established racial ideologies are destabilized and conventional racial identities begin to come unglued. Where Makalani examines those who want to dilute the "Blackness" of their identity, White examines the autobiographies of former Black Panther Party members to understand why they traveled in the opposite direction. Coming of age during the turbulent 1960s, these men and women chose not to retreat from their Blackness. On the contrary, they forged positive, counterhegemonic racial identities based on the assertion of Black pride and the aspiration to Black Power. White emphasizes the importance of both structural and psychological factors in this achievement. What is most revealing about her essay, however, in relation to the other chapters in this volume, is its illustration of the positive power of racial identity in propelling popular movements for transforming society as a whole. All of the activists that White has studied received powerful messages from both their kin and their environment as to when resistance to racial oppression might become possible, and as to how this racial oppression might be otherwise endured. The sociopolitical context of the 1960s suddenly enabled these individuals to translate these cautious messages into a new, transcendent revolutionary agenda in which the advocacy of race could be made into a vehicle for its own eventual abolition.

On the other hand, the subsequent fate of many of these former Black Panthers since the 1980s (the period that Cha-Jua labels the New Nadir) suggests that this ideology and identity of color-coded racial transcendence could no longer resonate under changed conditions, when the harsh realities of the new color-blind racism began to emerge. This conclusion is reinforced by our final chapter in this part, Jeffrey Williams's "Benjamin Brawley: Black Victorian in the New Negro Movement." This chapter shows just how profoundly racial identity and ideology were dependent on the racial structures in which they were enmeshed during the original Nadir of the early twentieth century. As a product of fin de siècle southern apartheid, Brawley had little choice but to channel his hopes for racial improvement into the uplift ideology of "black Victorianism." Williams's analysis of the educational and literary work of this long-forgotten figure helps us to rescue him from the condescension of his more fashionable successors of the Harlem Renaissance. At the same time, Williams shows us how and why Brawley's servile and derivative hankering after Black respectability would begin to seem gratuitous and degrading to hip, young urbanites during the 1920s and '30s, when Black apartheid was challenged and Harlem came into vogue.

What general conclusions can we draw from the second part of our book? All the chapters focus in different ways on critical moments of structural fluidity, when one racial formation was giving way to the next. As each author shows, such transitions are moments of potential opportunity, when old stereotypes and ideologies are suddenly questioned, and the possibility for more fluid racial identities opens up. Unfortunately, as the chapters also demonstrate, the consolidation of a new racial formation can all too easily lead to the emergence of new stereotypes and new ideologies that reassert racial privilege and prejudice in some altered form. The possibility of creating fundamentally transformative and emancipating racial ideologies and identities depends very largely on the outcome of race struggles, to which we have devoted the final part of our book.

Scott Kurashige's "Organizing from the Margins" begins soberly enough by tracing the remarkable story of a small, dedicated band of Japanese American Communists who tried to build a multiracial labor movement in Los Angeles during the early 1930s. At a time when American capitalism was in a state of acute crisis, these labor leaders drew on the intellectual resources of Marxism and their own courage and commitment to attempt the impossible. On the one hand, they began to organize Japanese workers in the California produce and restaurant industries, where small-scale production, cutthroat competition, and ethnic discrimination made it extremely difficult to create and sustain a *class* solidarity. On the other hand, they sought to make common cause with Black labor groups and organizers in the region so as to combat employer strategies of divide and rule. Yet, as Kurashige shows, the very success of this movement summoned up powerful forces of repression, which led to the deportation of key leaders, followed by the internment of many activists during the war. The result was the complete extirpation of this promising insurgent interracial movement, which might have been completely forgotten but for Kurashige's work of historical reclamation.

In "Between Civil Rights, Black Power, and the Mason-Dixon Line," Clarence Lang turns his attention to St. Louis during the 1960s. Where Kurashige shows the difficulties of organizing in an economic sector undergoing belated industrialization, under highly volatile and rapidly deteriorating political conditions, Lang's chapter takes us into the era of corporate capitalism, in a political climate where fresh opportunities for large-scale popular mobilization were rapidly opening up. As Lang shows, the St. Louis Action Committee to Improve Conditions for Negroes fought for expanded job opportunities for African Americans in the city's utility companies and construction and aircraft industries while also focusing on other areas of discrimination, such as housing and police brutality. Transcending the divide between mainstream civil rights and militant Black nationalism, ACTION's tactics combined elements of both. At the same time, in contrast with Kurashige's Communist organizers of the 1930s, ACTION's leaders lacked a clear theoretical road map for charting where their movement was going and for understanding how they might connect up with other movements on a larger national or global frame. During the peak period of the Black freedom struggle (1965–1975), ACTION's expediency and eclecticism may actually have been an advantage, but it served the movement ill in the period after 1975, when mass mobilization began to falter and only a long-term, theoretically informed strategy could have enabled it to reconstitute itself and thrive in the harsher conditions of the New Nadir.

To some extent, this more detached, analytically focused long-term strategy has been provided—on a different level of struggle—by the academic programs in Black and ethnic studies that were established in many U.S. universities during the early 1970s and have survived—in many cases thrived—ever since. Pedro Cabán's "Common Legacies, Similar Futures," examines the way in which these programs offered a new site for Black and Latino freedom struggles, when those movements were at their peak. Even more important, however, they have continued to provide a relatively safe haven for activist intellectuals, even after the mass mobilizations of the 1960s and '70s collapsed. As Cabán shows, this development would have been inconceivable without the striking democratization of American higher education that also occurred during this period. Over three decades, such programs have provided vehicles for educating minorities (as well as sympathetic white students) in their own history of struggle and oppression. No less important, they have emerged as sites of intellectual production for reclaiming lost histories and generating new knowledge on which future struggles might someday be based. As such, these programs offer the promise of bringing emancipatory struggles to a new level of sophistication and self-consciousness, in which further advancement would be grounded in reflexive examination of the history of past struggles.

Nevertheless, several factors have so far prevented this promise of Black and Latino studies from being fully realized. The spread of narrow, inward-looking petty-bourgeois nationalist consciousness in many racial and ethnic communities and the concomitant decline in transracial movements of class have sapped the vitality of some of these programs. Others, which have remained intellectually vital, have tended toward an increasingly esoteric, depoliticized academicism, as the community support and mass mobilization that originally nurtured them has receded. In Latino Studies, a division has arisen between those scholars (like Cabán himself) who wish to reaffirm the linkages of a common trajectory with Black Studies and those who would emphasize the prospects for Hispanic assimilation into the white mainstream. Finally, it remains to be seen how these programs will fare in the new postmodern university that is currently taking shape. Formed in an era of corporate capitalism, when the state was willing to invest in public education and the public good, such programs must now function in a cutthroat environment of public defunding in which universities (and their constituent units) must become profit-making enterprises while simultaneously defending themselves against the fury of right-wing ideological attack.

The urgent necessity of overcoming these obstacles is perhaps nowhere more evident than in David Crockett's final chapter of our book, "Livin' Just Enough for the City." In a striking refutation of the assumptions of color-blind racism, Crockett shows that Milwaukee has steadily grown ever more segregated over the past thirty-five years. What this means, in practice, is that residents of predominantly Black neighborhoods have access to lower-quality food at higher retail prices, to substandard or nonexistent health care, to poor-quality rental housing, to higher crime rates, and to fewer and poorer-paying jobs. Absent the collective movements detailed in previous chapters, the "race struggles" chronicled in Crockett's Milwaukee have now become bleak, atomistic individual struggles to get by.

What, then, may we conclude about our final part, and about this volume as a whole? First, racial formations are structured by capitalism and are transformed as the development of that system proceeds. So far from exhibiting a clear trajectory of progress, these structural transformations have abolished certain forms of racial oppression, only by creating new ones to take their place. Second, we have learned that the racial identities exhibited by individuals—internalized into their sense of self—are also collective ideologies, engendered by external social structures. By thus harnessing the inner personality of every individual, either to reproduce or to challenge the racial hierarchies of the day, these racial ideologies can be an enormous force either for evil or for good. Finally, we have seen how engagement in racial struggle can profoundly affect the way in which racial structures and ideologies are transformed. Yet these struggles are themselves profoundly molded by the structural and ideological contexts in which they are waged. Beginning initially in local communities with limited horizons, they require the interjection of more global perspectives if they are to succeed beyond a certain point. The episodic character of the struggles outlined in our pages is perhaps more characteristic of the social history of race resistance than the myth of a unified, ever expanding insurgency, which orthodox Marxism (or nationalism) prescribed. In a given era, with its distinctive structures and ideologies, only certain types of movements and struggle are possible. Moreover, when the repression of earlier movements renders their experience and history unavailable to successors, it requires the work of historically minded scholars and activist-intellectuals to recover the legacy that has been lost.

If Lang's St. Louis ACTION had been able to benefit from the lessons that Kurashige's 1930s Japanese Communists might have taught, it would probably have been less rudderless after the mass mobilizations of the 1960s and '70s collapsed. On the other hand, if the official U.S. Communist Party leadership had ever gained control of either movement, it might have nipped all spontaneity and initiative in the bud. Had either group been able to situate itself more reflexively, in Cha-Jua's general model of capitalist racial formations, it might have been better able to understand the limits and possibilities of its situation, and to formulate its goals and strategies in a more measured, effective way. If nothing else, we hope that our collection will help activists and intellectuals of the future to avoid the wasteful effort of reinventing the wheel.

Perhaps the lesson of these movements—and the others we have examined—is that every struggle is a partial achievement, which is no more liable to absolute failure than it is capable of unconditional success. To be sure, this is a soberer, more provisional, and less self-confident conclusion than the great organized parties, programs, theories, and movements of earlier eras were wont to assert in their day. Nevertheless, it suggests that there will be the need for many further circumscribed interrogations and investigations like the present volume that will cover different ground, and recast the structure-ideology-struggle interface in a different way. Only then, after much scholarship, and much activism, will we be able to contemplate a future from which race has been expunged.

This volume is an initial step to the creation of such a coherent materialist analysis of race, racial oppression, and resistance. We have structured the collection to assist the reader in developing a deeper analysis of the theories and research and in synthesizing the themes that cut across the chapters by providing a synthesis of each of the three core sections and by posing study questions. Although there are a number of ways in which this collection contributes to the literature, it also reveals several areas of inquiry needing further attention. Of particular relevance is the apparent chasm between scholarly work and practice. As a way to further link scholarship and activism, we suggest the partnering of activists with scholars in the production of knowledge and new technologies of resistance. Although this volume incorporates voices from a range of disciplines, we have concluded that it is premature to create a coherent narrative reflecting an interdisciplinary paradigm. In particular, we are conscious that the interface between race and gender has been insufficiently addressed in our collection. We encourage the creation of interdisciplinary research teams to further interrogate key questions concerning the problematic of race.

Glossary: Race Struggles

AFDC (AID TO FAMILIES WITH DEPENDENT CHILDREN): was a federal program that was started in 1935 as part of the New Deal, and became the linchpin of federal support for state welfare systems throughout the United States. AFDC remained in place until it was repealed by the Clinton administration in 1996. Under the new system, a five-year lifetime limit was set on welfare benefits. Critics have argued that the real aims of this welfare reform were to lower the birthrate among poor people and minorities and to force such individuals into the labor market, where they would be obliged to take low-paid and otherwise unattractive jobs.

BLACK POWER: was a social movement for African American self-determination during the mid-1960s and mid-1970s. Coined by Stokely Carmichael/ Kwame Ture and the Student Nonviolent Coordinating Committee, it denoted a wave of the Black Liberation movement that emerged from the disappointments of the Civil Rights movement and the aspirations of a reemerging Black nationalism. The movement included four political tendencies that, despite pronounced differences, overlapped in many practices and tactics. On the left was a highly visible, though minority radical or revolutionary, tendency that included divergent Marxist, socialist, and nationalist organizations, journals and presses, and individuals. The Black Panther Party, the League of Revolutionary Black Workers, and the Third World Women's Alliance, journals the *Black Scholar* and *Soulbook,* and individuals such as Huey P. Newton, Maulana Karenga, and Assata Shakur represented this tendency. Left of the middle was a large but diffuse popular autonomic tendency for independent institution building and cultural transvaluation. Representative of the organizations, journals, and individuals in this tendency were the Institute for Positive Education (IPE), Third World Press, their founder, Haki

Madhubuti (Chicago), and the East, led by Jitu Weusi (New York). The Hoyt E. Fuller edited *Black World* and the IPE's *Black Books Bulletin* were premier journals of this tendency. At the center, the dominant liberal incorporativist tendency emphasized the traditional pluralist strategy of ethnic bloc voting. Charles V. Hamilton was perhaps this tendency's principal architect. The Congressional Black Caucus was and remains its primary organization. On the right, a minority conservative tendency stressed capitalist business formation. The movement's legacy concerns the formation of autonomous institutions, the building of new organizations and businesses, the construction of an African-oriented culture, the transformation of African Americans' political consciousness, and the election of unprecedented numbers of black public officials.

BLACK VICTORIANS: refers to middle-class Blacks who adopted the strategy of racial uplift and the politics of respectability. They adopted white middle-class culture and advocated the values of industry, order, cleanliness, punctuality, and frugality as essential for individual and collective success and, perhaps more important, to convince whites of Blacks' humanity.

CLASS FRACTION: is a subgroup within a larger class (for example, proletariat, or bourgeoisie) that is the product of the particular social relations prevailing in any given time and place. Thus, the commercial bourgeoisie, the industrial proletariat, and the global subproletariat are all class fractions that fit into Cha-Jua's structuralist account of the U.S. social formation.

COINTELPRO: was the counterintelligence program mounted by the FBI between 1956 and 1971 to disrupt dissident political movements and organizations throughout the United States. FBI agents were instructed to "expose, disrupt, misdirect, discredit, or otherwise neutralize" a variety of organizations, starting with the Communist Party and the Ku Klux Klan, but eventually encompassing the New Left, the anti–Vietnam War movement, and Martin Luther King's Southern Christian Leadership Conference.

COUNTERHEGEMONIC: refers to oppositional projects that seek to create alternative ideologies, organizations, institutions, values, lifestyles, and movements to challenge the hegemonic group.

CRISIS: is the official organ of the NAACP. Founding editor W. E. B. Du Bois launched the journal in November 1910; its inaugural name, *Crisis: A Record of the Darker of Races,* reflected the journal's Pan-African and global perspective. At its peak, in 1919, it had a monthly circulation of one hundred thousand.

HARLEM RENAISSANCE: was a Black cultural reawakening anchored in the New York City neighborhood of Harlem. The movement for cultural revitalization was an integral part of a more comprehensive African American social movement, the *New Negro movement.* The movement and its cultural component began with Blacks' response to the "bloody summer of 1919" and ended in the midst of the Great Depression, with the Harlem Race Riot of 1935. Notable artists associated with this cultural movement included writer Langston Hughes, author Zora Neale Hurston, painter Aaron Douglas, jazz composer Duke Ellington, and blues singer Bessie Smith.

HEGEMONY: As conceptualized by Antonio Gramsci, this word refers to the domination of a (racial) class or fraction by means other than force alone. Hegemony entails the construction of a ruling coalition of disparate social forces under the leadership of the dominant group. Through control over social institutions and its capacity to generate ideas and shape social relations, this group is able to legitimate a coherent and systematic worldview through which it manufactures consent for the social order.

IDEOLOGY: is considered a systematic theory of society composed of a relatively coherent set of interdependent concepts and values that adherents construct into historical narratives and contemporary discourses to articulate their interpretation of a social group's economic, political, and social interests and cultural beliefs to rationalize particular public policies. Ideology can help *legitimate* the status quo through the creation and dissemination of a dominant set of beliefs or narrative that serves to rationalize inequalities and justify unequal distribution of resources. Ideology can also disrupt the dominant narrative through the formation of *counterhegemonic* discourses.

INTERNAL COLONIALISM: During the 1960s and '70s a group of radical social theorists (most notably Andre Gunder Frank and Immanuel Wallerstein) argued that the essence of colonialism lay in the economic dependency and underdevelopment of a "peripheral" (colonized) region to the metropolitan (colonizing) "core" region. "Internal colonialism" was an effort to apply these concepts within large states (for example, the United States or Britain) that contained several unevenly developed internal regions (for instance, African American urban ghettos and Latino/a barrios or Ireland and Scotland). With the publication of *Black Power* by Stokely Carmichael/Kwame Ture and Charles V. Hamilton and *Black Awakening in Capitalist America* by Robert L. Allen, internal colonialism, or "domestic neo-Colonialism," became the dominant theory explaining the African American experience. Though this analysis provided some useful and important insights, it has been less frequently applied during the past twenty years.

MANIFEST DESTINY: a slogan coined during the 1845–1855 period by Jacksonian Democrats to articulate the belief that the United States was destined to expand from the Atlantic to the Pacific, across the entire North American continent. The phrase was revived again during the 1890s to justify the U.S. imperialism of that era.

MERCANTILISM: the system of economic development, criticized by Adam Smith in *The Wealth of Nations* (1776), that prevailed in Euro-America throughout the early modern era and promoted and regulated economic activity through the power of the state. As an economic system, mercantilism was preoccupied with achieving a positive balance of trade, which might necessitate tariffs to protect domestic industry, government monopolies in production or foreign trade, and the establishment of plantation enterprises in overseas colonies to produce raw materials that could be imported to the mother country for manufacturing, finishing, or reexporting elsewhere. Koditschek's essay seeks to link these elements by pointing out the element of coercion that they all share: state-controlled trade, state-sponsored monopolies, and state-supported slavery in the plantation sector. With the abolition of mercantilism (including slavery) and the advent of "free trade," he argues, new and more informal (that is, racial) methods of control had to be devised.

NGO (NONGOVERNMENTAL ORGANIZATION): a very broad (and often vague) term used to encompass citizen movements in developing countries that aim to benefit the poor and to protect human rights in the developing world; grassroots organizations in the developing world that campaign for democracy, civic rights, social benefits, and economic improvement; and international institutions, such as the International Labor Organization, the World Trade Organization, or even the UN, that play an important role in global development and human rights issues.

ONE-DROP RULE: is a practice dating back to U.S. slavery in which any person with a trace of sub-Saharan ancestry, whether visible or not, is classified as Black. This historical usage remains a commonly accepted practice of racial classification. Interestingly, this "rule" applies only to Black Americans, and no society outside of the United States has adopted the practice.

OVERDETERMINATION: the notion—originally derived from psychoanalysis—that so many causes contribute to a given effect that it is nearly impossible to disentangle them, or to calculate their relative weight.

POSTMODERNISM: a theoretical perspective that reflects disillusionment with big theories and grand narratives of progress, whether these are liberal-capitalist, Marxist, or other. The word *postmodern* implies that the whole notion of modernity, as a special period of human advancement and improvement, was an illusion that we have now given up. By abandoning this illusion, according to the postmodernists, we are now better able to appreciate the sheer contingency (accidental character) and indeterminacy of social life, in all its variety and diversity. Although postmodernism offers many useful critical insights into the limitations of classical theories of social and historical development, it brings these benefits at a huge cost. Because it eschews the very goal of explaining large-scale social transformations, it can offer only local insights and particular stories in their place.

RACIAL IDENTITY THEORIES: are a set of frameworks primarily developed by psychologists to describe the process in which individuals come to understand themselves as members of a racial group in a racially oppressive society. Theorists such as William Cross, Janet Helms, and Robert Sellers articulate stages or statuses to account for the varying ways in which people understand race and racism and the degree to which they identify with racial groups similar to and different from themselves. Racial identity is expressed in attitudes, cognitive frameworks, and behaviors (personal, social, political). Racial identity theory has more recently been expanded to explain the racial dynamics of groups and systems.

RACIAL UPLIFT: refers to a middle-class strategy for advancing the position and prospects of African Americans. It emerged during the Nadir (1877–1917), as the small Black middle class devised responses to the comprehensive nullification of African Americans' civil rights and the terror of lynching. As a class-specific strategy, racial uplift offered different discourses to white elites and to both the Black middle class and the Black working-class majority. To the aspiring Black middle class, it preached "the politics of respectability." Its message to the Black working class was to adopt Victorian values and behavior and support Black middle-class social and business initiatives (See *Black Victorians*). For the white governing class, it argued that respectable Blacks shared their values and sought to facilitate their capacity to differentiate the "good Negro" from the "bad."

RECONSTRUCTION: the post–Civil War program for transforming the U.S. South that played out between 1865 and 1877. The legal basis of Reconstruction was the Thirteenth Amendment to the U.S. Constitution (abolishing slavery), the Fourteenth Amendment (guaranteeing Black civil rights), and the Fifteenth Amendment (protecting voting rights for freedmen). After a period of being imposed on the White South, Reconstruction was reversed in the mid-1870s, when white supremacists gained control of most southern state legislatures.

REDEMPTION: the process by which white supremacists regained control of state legislatures in the former Confederate states during the mid-1870s, bringing the era of Reconstruction to an end and laying the foundations for the segregationist system of Jim Crow.

SOCIAL CONSTRUCTIONISM: the notion that a given category (such as race) is not biologically determined but rather is created by the attitudes and behavior prevailing in a given group at a specific moment in history. Cha-Jua distinguishes between those constructionists who regard the contradictions of race as merely the result of prejudice or ideology and those (like himself) who believe them to be embedded more deeply in the social relations of capitalism. The latter believe that racial relations, though ideologically constructed, cannot be fundamentally transformed without some transformation of the capitalist system as a whole.

SOCIAL FORMATION: In Marxist terminology, a social formation is something more specific than a "mode of production." Whereas the latter is a general theoretical construct, the former is the way in which one (or two coexisting) modes of production manifests itself in a given time and place.

STRUCTURAL ADJUSTMENT PROGRAMS: policies to end or drastically reduce deficit spending that are forced on the governments of developing countries by the World Bank and the International Monetary Fund as conditions for obtaining loans from these institutions. If such policies were applied to the United States, they would probably require the abolition of one or more major federal social program(s), such as Medicare, Social Security, or block grants to the states.

SUBPROLETARIAT: Marx and Engels define the proletariat as the class within capitalism whose members must sell their labor power in order to survive—in other words, the revolutionary class, which has "nothing to lose but its chains." But what of those who cannot even sell their labor power, or who—because of racial, ethnic, or gender discrimination—are forced to sell it below its average market value? This group is generally termed the *subproletariat,* and Marxists have argued about its likely political orientation. Marx himself spoke of a desperate "lumpen-proletariat" that might provide likely recruits for demagogues or reactionaries. Those who study the interface of class and race, however, are more likely to identity the subproletariat with racial minorities, who represent the most oppressed (and therefore most potentially radical) sector of the working class.

SUPEREXPLOITATION: According to Marxist theory, "exploitation" is the extraction of "surplus value" from laborers under capitalism. "Surplus value" refers to the product of labor above and beyond that which is necessary to support the worker and reproduce the next generation. "Superexploitation" thus involves the notion that a particular group of workers suffers a heavier burden of exploitation than others, based on discrimination of gender or race.

THIRD PERIOD: the period 1928 to 1935 in Communist history, when Stalin was consolidating his control in the Soviet Union and Western Communist Parties were expected to take their marching orders from Moscow. They were told to attack their liberal and social democratic counterparts, and to make alliances only on the radical Left. From a European perspective this was a disaster, since it turned moderate and Far Left parties against one another and opened a clear road for the rise of fascism and reaction. This policy was abandoned in 1935, and was replaced by the "Popular Front," a united Left initiative to combat fascism and the triumph of the Right. Kurashige suggests that, in the context of U.S. racial struggles, the Third Period opened the way for new transracial alliances, inasmuch as the Communists were looking for allies outside the ranks of organized labor and found them primarily among racial minorities.

TREATY OF GUADALUPE HIDALGO: the peace treaty that ended the Mexican American War in 1848. Largely dictated by the United States, the treaty provided for the transfer of more than a half-million square miles, encompassing the present-day states of Colorado, Arizona, California, New Mexico, Nevada, and Utah.

WHITENESS: a term introduced during the 1990s, by Roediger and others, to recognize the fact that race is a system of oppression in which both oppressed and oppressor are involved. As a result, it is a mistake to think that race is an attribute of people of color alone. White people also have race, and benefit from racial privilege. Part of that privilege is the power to make their race appear to be invisible. According to Roediger, to attack racial oppression, it is first necessary to make whiteness visible as a prelude to getting rid of it (along with racial oppression) once and for all.

Contributors

PEDRO CABÁN is the vice provost for diversity and educational equity at the State University of New York. From 1990 through 2002 he was at Rutgers University with a joint appointment in Political Science and the Department of Puerto Rican and Hispanic Caribbean Studies, where he was chairperson from 1990 through 1998. He is the author of *Constructing a Colonial People: Puerto Rico and the United States, 1898–1932*. Dr. Cabán was associate editor of *Latino Studies* (2001–2002) and is senior editor of the *Oxford Encyclopedia of Latinos and Latinas in the United States*.

SUNDIATA KEITA CHA-JUA teaches in the Department of African American Studies and the Department of History at the University of Illinois at Urbana-Champaign. Cha-Jua is the author of *America's First Black Town: Brooklyn, Illinois, 1830–1915*, which received an Award of Superior Achievement from the Illinois State Historical Society in 2001. His article "'Long Movement' as Vampire: Temporal and Spatial Fallacies in Recent Black Freedom Studies," coauthored with Clarence Lang, was the co-winner of the Organization of American Historians' 2009 EBSCOhost America: History and Life Award. He serves on the editorial boards of several journals, including the *Black Scholar* and the *Journal of Black Studies*, and his articles have appeared in numerous Black Studies, U.S. history, and radical scholarly journals. He is the vice president of the National Council for Black Studies. Cha-Jua has worked in many local and national organizations in the Black liberation movement, including Peoples College, the St. Louis–based Organization for Black Struggle, and the Black Radical Congress.

DAVID CROCKETT is an associate professor in the Moore School of Business at the University of South Carolina. He held a post-doctoral research fellow at the Harvard Business School. His research interests are in sociological aspects of consumer behavior, particularly the impact of race, class, and gender inequality. He has published articles in several journals, including the *Journal of Marketing and Public Policy, Journal of Macromarketing,* and *Journal of Consumer Research.* His December 2004 *JCR* article, "The Role of Normative Political Ideology in Consumer Behavior," was selected as an honorable mention finalist for the 2005 Robert Ferber Award.

THEODORE KODITSCHEK is an associate professor in history at the University of Missouri at Columbia. His publications include *Class Formation and Urban Industrial Society,* "The Gendering of the British Working Class," and "The Making of British Nationality." Koditschek is the recipient of R. L. Schuyler and H. B. Adams prizes from the American Historical Association.

SCOTT KURASHIGE is an associate professor of history, American culture, and Asian/Pacific Islander American studies at the University of Michigan. His research interests include Asian/Pacific American history, U.S. urban history, Los Angeles and Detroit, and comparative race-ethnicity. He is the author of *The Shifting Grounds of Race: Black and Japanese Americans in the Making of Multiethnic Los Angeles.* He has published in the *Amerasia Journal, Journal of American History,* and *Journal of Asian American Studies.* He is the recipient of the Alexander Saxton Award from *Amerasia Journal* in 2000 and the Albert J. Beveridge Award from the American Historical Association in 2008.

CLARENCE LANG is an assistant professor in history and African American studies at the University of Illinois at Urbana-Champaign. His primary research interests are Black social movements in the twentieth century and U.S. working-class history. His article "'Long Movement' as Vampire: Temporal and Spatial Fallacies in Recent Black Freedom Studies," coauthored with Sundiata Keita Cha-Jua, was the co-winner of the Organization of American Historians' 2009 EBSCOhost America: History and Life Award. He has published in the *Black Scholar, New Politics, Race and Society,* and *Against the Current.*

MINKAH MAKALANI is an assistant professor in history at Rutgers University. His research interests include African American (New Negro movement, social movements, nationalism), African Diaspora (theory, identity in the Dominican Republic), racial formation, and modern U.S. history. He is the guest editor of a special issue of *Social Text: Racial Difference in the African Diaspora.* He is the author of "A Biracial Identity or a New Race? The Historical Limitations and Political Implications of a Biracial Identity," *Souls: A Critical Journal of Black Politics, Culture, and Society,* and "Rejecting Blackness, Claiming Whiteness: Anti-Black

Whiteness and the Creation of a Biracial Race," in *Whiteout: The Continuing Significance of Racism,* edited by Woody Doane and Eduardo Bonilla-Silva.

HELEN A. NEVILLE is a professor in educational psychology and African American studies at the University of Illinois at Urbana-Champaign. Her research focusing on general and cultural factors influencing the stress and coping process and race, racism, mental health, and color-blindness has appeared in a wide range of psychology and Black Studies journals. She was an associate editor of the *Counseling Psychologist* (2004–2007) and serves on the editorial boards of numerous journals. She is the recipient of the American Psychological Association's Kenneth and Mamie Clark Award for outstanding mentoring of ethnic minority students.

TOLA OLU PEARCE is a professor in the Department of Sociology at the University of Missouri at Columbia. Her areas of specialization include medical sociology; race, ethnic, and minority relations; and development, particularly in Africa. She has published widely in journals such as *Social Problems* and the *Journal of Comparative Family Studies* and has served on a number of editorial boards, including *West Africa Review.*

DAVID ROEDIGER teaches history at the University of Illinois at Urbana-Champaign. His books include *Working toward Whiteness: How America's Immigrants Become White; The Strange Journey from Ellis Island to the Suburbs; Our Own Time* (with Philip S. Foner); *The Wages of Whiteness; Black on White;* and *Towards the Abolition of Whiteness.* Roediger has won the Merle Curti Prize, and awards from the Gustavus Myers Center, the Immigration and Ethnic History Society, and CHOICE.

MONICA M. WHITE is an assistant professor in the Department of Sociology at Wayne State University. Her research interests include social psychology, social movements, and the interaction and intersection of race, class, and gender in social movement participation.

JEFFREY WILLIAMS is an adjunct assistant professor and the director of access and urban outreach in the Office of Enrollment Management at the University of Missouri at Columbia. His research interests include questions of race, representation, and identity in late-nineteenth- and early-twentieth-century American literature. His article "Reassuring Sounds: Minstrelsy and the Hidden Hand" appeared in *ATQ: A Journal of American 19th Century Literature and Culture.*

Index

Note: Page numbers in *italics* refer to illustrative material; *t* indicates a table.

The University of Illinois Press
is a founding member of the
Association of American University Presses.

Composed in 10.5/13 Minion Pro
with Meta display
by Jim Proefrock
at the University of Illinois Press
Manufactured by Sheridan Books, Inc.

University of Illinois Press
1325 South Oak Street
Champaign, IL 61820-6903
www.press.uillinois.edu